Library of
Davidson College

GIVING DESERT ITS DUE

LAW AND PHILOSOPHY LIBRARY

Managing Editors

ALAN MABE, *Department of Philosophy, Florida State University, Tallahassee, Florida 32306, U.S.A.*

MICHAEL D. BAYLES, *Department of Philosophy, University of Florida, Gainesville, Florida 32611, U.S.A.*

Editorial Advisory Board

GEORGE FLETCHER, *School of Law, Columbia University*

HYMAN GROSS, *Corpus Christi College, Cambridge University*

WERNER KRAWIETZ, *Lehrstuhl für Rechtssoziologie, Rechts- und Sozialphilosophie, Westfälische Wilhelms-Universität, Münster*

ROBERT SUMMERS, *School of Law, Cornell University*

ALICE ERH-SOON TAY, *Faculty of Law, University of Sydney*

GEORG HENRIK VON WRIGHT, *Department of Philosophy, University of Helsinki*

WOJCIECH SADURSKI

Department of Jurisprudence, University of Sydney

GIVING DESERT ITS DUE

Social Justice and Legal Theory

D. REIDEL PUBLISHING COMPANY

A MEMBER OF THE KLUWER ACADEMIC PUBLISHERS GROUP

DORDRECHT / BOSTON / LANCASTER

Library of Congress Cataloging in Publication Data

Sadurski, Wojciech, 1950–
  Giving desert its due.

  (Law and philosophy library)
  Bibliography: p.
  Includes index.
  1. Social justice. 2. Law—Philosophy. 3. Distributive
justice. I. Title. II. Series.
K370.S23   1985   340'.11   85-14620
ISBN 90-277-1941-1

Published by D. Reidel Publishing Company,
P.O. Box 17, 3300 AA Dordrecht, Holland.

Sold and distributed in the U.S.A. and Canada
by Kluwer Academic Publishers,
190 Old Derby Street, Hingham, MA 02043, U.S.A.

In all other countries, sold and distributed
by Kluwer Academic Publishers Group,
P.O. Box 322, 3300 AH Dordrecht, Holland.

All Rights Reserved
© 1985 by D. Reidel Publishing Company, Dordrecht, Holland
No part of the material protected by this copyright notice may be reproduced or
utilized in any form or by any means, electronic or mechanical
including photocopying, recording or by any information storage and
retrieval system, without written permission from the copyright owner

Printed in The Netherlands

For my parents

TABLE OF CONTENTS

EDITORIAL PREFACE ix

ACKNOWLEDGMENTS xi

INTRODUCTION 1

PART ONE: JUSTICE – LEGAL JUSTICE – SOCIAL JUSTICE

CHAPTER 1: THE CONCEPT OF JUSTICE 9
1. Justice: Global or Particular? 11
2. Commutative and Distributive Justice 25
3. Social Justice and Legal Justice 36
4. Procedural and Substantive Justice 49

CHAPTER 2: PROBLEMS OF JUSTIFICATION: SOCIAL CONTRACT AND INTUITION 57
1. Why is Social Contract Relevant? 58
2. Contract and Reflective Equilibrium 64
3. Intuition and Intuitionism 72

CHAPTER 3: SUBSTANTIVE JUSTICE AND EQUALITY BEFORE THE LAW 77
1. Equality Before the Law and Equality in Law 78
2. Non-Discriminatory Classifications 83
3. Differentiation and Exclusion 93

PART TWO: JUSTICE AS EQUILIBRIUM

CHAPTER 4: THE PRINCIPLE OF EQUILIBRIUM 101
1. Equilibrium of Benefits and Burdens 101
2. Equilibrium and the Difference Principle 108

CHAPTER 5: DISTRIBUTION ACCORDING TO DESERT 116
1. The Notion of Desert 116
2. Natural Abilities and Desert 122

TABLE OF CONTENTS

3. Free Will and Desert — 131
4. Effort or Contribution? — 134
5. Arbitrariness of the Principle of Desert? — 138
6. Impracticability? — 141
7. Compensatory Justice and 'Status Inconsistency' — 144
8. Desert and the Principle of Competence — 153
9. The Role of Desert — 156

CHAPTER 6: NEEDS AND JUSTICE — 158

1. Basic Needs — 159
2. Basic Needs and Desert — 167
3. Needs and Rights — 170

CHAPTER 7: PREFERENTIAL TREATMENT — 184

1. The Problem — 185
2. Utilitarian Arguments — 189
3. Equal Opportunity and Preferential Treatment — 198
4. Groups and Individuals — 204
5. 'Victims' of Preferential Treatment — 213

CHAPTER 8: PUNISHMENT AND THE THEORY OF JUSTICE — 221

1. Distribution and Retribution — 221
2. Punishment and Equilibrium — 225
3. Retributivism — 233
4. Retributivist Fallacies — 243
5. Utility and Punishment — 250
6. Retributivism and Utilitarianism Reconciled? — 255

POSTSCRIPT

CHAPTER 9: BEYOND SOCIAL JUSTICE — 261

1. Justice and Liberty — 261
2. Utility and Justice — 267
3. The Importance of Justice — 275

NOTES — 285

SELECTED BIBLIOGRAPHY — 309

INDEX — 319

EDITORIAL PREFACE

During the last half of the twentieth century, legal philosophy (or legal theory or jurisprudence) has grown significantly. It is no longer the domain of a few isolated scholars in law and philosophy. Hundreds of scholars from diverse fields attend international meetings on the subject. In some universities, large lecture courses of five hundred students or more study it.

The primary aim of the Law and Philosophy Library is to present some of the best original work on legal philosophy from both the Anglo-American and European traditions. Not only does it help make some of the best work available to an international audience, but it also encourages increased awareness of, and interaction between, the two major traditions. The primary focus is on full-length scholarly monographs, although some edited volumes of original papers are also included. The Library editors are assisted by an Editorial Advisory Board of internationally renowed scholars.

Legal philosophy should not be considered a narrowly circumscribed field. Insights into law and legal institutions can come from diverse disciplines on a wide range of topics. Among the relevant disciplines or perspectives contributing to legal philosophy, besides law and philosophy, are anthropology, economics, political science, and sociology. Among the topics included in legal philosophy are theories of law; the concepts of law and legal institutions; legal reasoning and adjudication; epistemological issues of evidence and procedure; law and justice, economics, politics, or morality; legal ethics; and theories of legal fields such as criminal law, contracts, and property.

ALAN MABE
MICHAEL BAYLES

ACKNOWLEDGMENTS

Much of the first draft of this book was written when I was lecturing at the Department of Jurisprudence, University of Sydney. Work on the book was continued at the Research School of Social Sciences in the Australian National University in Canberra (with the benefit of a research fellowship which I gratefully acknowledge) and completed at the University of Melbourne Law School. I am grateful to my colleagues, friends and students at these three Australian universities, as well as those at the Faculty of Law, Warsaw University, where I first studied and worked. In addition, I have also benefited from discussions of my papers (which formed part of the book) at the University of New South Wales, Monash University, University of California at Berkeley, University of California at Los Angeles, University of Leiden and Centre Interuniversitaire de Philosophie du Droit in Brussels.

My greatest debt is to Neil MacCormick who encouraged me to write this book and who read the entire manuscript with painstaking care and provided many valuable comments and suggestions. Other friends and colleagues have also read various parts of the manuscript, larger and smaller, and contributed with helpful comments. My thanks go to Martin Krygier, Michael D. Bayles, Robert Goodin, Pat Leehy, Gabriël Moens, Garrie Moloney, Roma Sadurska, Peter Singer, Robert Stein, Julius Stone, Alice Tay and Roger Wilkins. Without their help, this book would be even worse.

I am especially indebted to those friends who, besides making comments on the substance, undertook to polish my English (no pun intended!). I also wish to thank Maria Luzza and her team of assistants at the University of Melbourne Law School for their efficient production of the manuscript.

Some parts of the book develop themes first advanced in articles published in *Archiv für Rechts- und Sozialphilosophie* **69** (1983) 504–514, *Australasian Journal of Philosophy* **61** (1983) 231–247, *Law and Philosophy* **3** (1984) 329–354, *Melbourne University Law Review* **14** (1984) 572–600 and *Oxford Journal of Legal Studies* **5** (1985) 47–59. I gratefully acknowledge the permission given to me by the editors and publishers of these journals to publish the revised versions of the papers.

The citations from *A Theory of Justice* by John Rawls are reprinted here by kind permission of the publishers, Harvard University Press and Oxford University Press, and are copyright © 1971 by the President and Fellows of Harvard College.

INTRODUCTION

In the second volume of *Law, Legislation and Liberty*, F. A. Hayek states:

> I may, as a result of long endeavours to trace the destructive effect which the invocation of 'social justice' has had on our moral sensitivity, and of again and again finding even eminent thinkers thoughtlessly using the phrase, have become unduly allergic to it, but I have come to feel strongly that the greatest service I can still render to my fellow men would be that I could make the speakers and writers among them thoroughly ashamed ever again to employ the term 'social justice'.[1]

Candid though this confession is, its aim is certainly far from being attained. Most obviously, it has not become a general conviction that social justice is, as Hayek suggests, "intellectually disreputable, the mark of demagogy or cheap journalism".[2] On the contrary, in our time we are witnessing the growing importance of the concept of social justice, in public consciousness, in political discourse and in philosophical discussions. With growing economic affluence, people realize more clearly the inequities of the social distribution of material goods, educational opportunities and life chances. They question established patterns of distribution of social goods more impatiently than ever as they see the extent to which the human condition is permeated with unjust schemes. When a society is viewed not as an impersonal and incomprehensible force which imposes at random burdens and benefits upon its members, but rather as a realm of conscious and rational action, injustices which were previously taken as 'natural' lose their traditional justification and call for social remedies.

The growing social awareness of the importance of social justice is accompanied by the increased interest of philosophers and social scientists in the problems of just distribution. In the 1960s and 1970s there was a real explosion of philosophical writings about distributive justice and it firmly established social justice as one of the major issues in political and moral philosophy. However, legal theory remained largely unaffected by this current. This is not to say that legal philosophers have not contributed to the philosophical discussions on social justice; on the contrary, some of the best essays in this field have been written by scholars who happen to be legal philosophers. The point is, rather, that there was surprisingly little attempt to incorporate the discussion of social justice into legal theory as an integral part. The very notion is often taken to be alien to jurisprudential considerations. This *désintéressement* is perhaps based partly on the belief that the operation of law has little to do with social (as opposed to individual) justice, and partly on the view that any attempt to use law as a tool to bring about some deliberately chosen ideas of distributive justice will result necessarily in the degeneration of law itself. Despite growing interest, on the part of legal theorists, in particular matters directly related to social justice, the mainstream of modern legal theory still reacts with scepticism to attempts to introduce social justice as a legitimate part of legal theory.

This book is intended to narrow the gap between legal theory and considerations of social justice. It attempts to demonstrate that both have much in common; the substantive principle of social justice postulated here ('equilibrium of benefits and burdens') is grounded in the operation of some legal rules and, in turn, is advanced as a standard of judging the legal system as a whole. It will be shown that this substantive principle gives special weight to the notion of desert. This is the central theme of the book. Discussion of it is further related to other issues of legal theory such as the concept of economic rights, preferential treatment and retributive justice. To pursue this argument, a precise notion of justice must be adopted. I will argue, in the first chapter, that to adopt too broad a notion of justice, identifying justice with all positive states of affairs, leads to conceptual confusion and limits the usefulness of the concept. Justice should be viewed as *one* of the standards of social evaluation; an extremely important standard, to be sure, but not the only one and certainly not an all-encompassing one. The strict notion of justice is employed in the first chapter to evaluate critically the usefulness of the various classifications of the concepts of justice, such as commutative *versus* distributive justice, social *versus* legal justice, procedural *versus* substantive justice. The aim of the first chapter is, therefore, to clear the path for our further discussions of justice as well as to suggest the relevance of social justice to the consideration of legal justice.

To explore the notion of justice is one thing; to propose a substantive conception of justice is another. On what basis can we legitimately defend substantive principles of social justice? What are the proper grounds for deriving principles of just distribution of benefits and burdens? In the second chapter, I will seek to show that currently the most influential method of deriving the principles of social justice, the contractual method, is either untenable (if 'social contract' is conceived as an independent, autonomous source of this derivation), or redundant (if, as in the case of Rawls, some assumptions prior to the 'contract' must be made). A moderate version of intuitionism is suggested as the more defensible standpoint.

The last important preliminary issue concerns the relations between substantive justice and equality before the law. In the third chapter it will be argued that no formal, 'objective' or neutral standard of legal equality can be maintained, since no law can do without any classifications and the point at which 'classification' becomes 'discrimination' depends upon substantive moral views which are irreducible to formal principles of equality. Consequently, our views about which legal systems respect the principle of equality before the law are derived from our more general views about which legal systems are 'just', not *vice versa*. The issue of social justice is, therefore, conceptually prior to the issue of equality before the law; thus the latter cannot serve as a standard of criticism of law which attempts to enforce the former.

It is against this general background that a substantive principle of social justice is proposed and its possible applications explored. The reasoning leading to the elaboration of this principle has the form of 'reflective equilibrium': a principle is deduced from a particular practice perceived as just, and then generalized and applied to other spheres of social justice. I argue in Chapter 4, on the basis of the intuitive moral plausibility of compensatory practices, that a general principle of social justice demands restoration of the balance of benefits and burdens. This general principle is further applied to three main spheres of social justice: distribution according to desert, satisfaction of basic human needs, and retributive punishment. It is argued that in these three cases, the upsetting of the moral balance requires compensatory measures which bring about an overall equilibrium of benefits and burdens.

'Desert' is discussed in Chapter 5 as the principal measure of justice as equilibrium. Its paramount role, among the principles of justice, lies in the fact that it makes a person's share in the social distribution dependent only upon circumstances and features which are under this person's control. It will be argued that factors which are totally beyond a person's control (such as natural endowments or the social position into which a person is born) are irrelevant to desert and that their influence upon a person's share in a social distribution should be minimized. The same principle of balance of benefits and burdens, which is used to analyse the concept of desert, demands also the satisfaction of basic human needs because certain needs, when unmet, constitute such a powerful burden in a person's life that the overall equilibrium of benefits and burdens in a society is upset. The relevance of needs to 'justice as equilibrium' is discussed in the sixth chapter. The concept of 'basic' needs is discussed, and the arguments which assess those needs in an extremely relativist way are found wanting. It is also argued that the satisfaction of basic needs is a prerequisite for the proper operation of the principle of desert, and the notion of rights to the satisfaction of basic needs is defended against those who attack it in terms of a classical theory of rights.

The conception of compensatory justice based upon the principle of balance of benefits and burdens, demands that those who bear burdens or handicaps resulting from factors beyond their control should be treated more favourably in the distribution of social benefits and that they should be given preference when their unearned burdens adversely affect their share in the social distribution. This principle provides a guidance to the issue of so-called 'reverse discrimination' which is discussed in Chapter 7. The problem is illustrated by the case of preferential admissions to universities for members of socially handicapped minority groups. I will propose that the decisive arguments are those which appeal to the concept of compensation for undeserved social disadvantages, and that this should be viewed in the context of the ideal of genuine equal opportunity. In Chapter 8, it will be argued that the principle of equilibrium of benefits and burdens is also useful in the case of just punishment. Crime may be seen as the illegitimate upsetting of an important social balance: that between the benefits of negative liberties and the burdens of self-constraint. After a criminal act is committed and the benefit of non-self-constraint is enjoyed by the criminal, the balance may be restored by the imposition of special burdens; that is, by punishment. Finally, in the last chapter, I will discuss some of the problems arising out of the conflicts and trade-offs between justice and liberty, and also between justice and utility.

A large proportion of the argument is polemical but it should be emphasized that discussion, and criticism, of other writers' opinions is not an end in itself but serves as a means of exposition of my own views. In particular, my recognition of the great importance of the ideas developed by John Rawls in *A Theory of Justice* will become clear to a reader who will soon realize how many pages are devoted to the discussion of those ideas. It is, indeed, only a little exaggeration to say that, after his book was published, "political philosophers ... must either work within Rawls's theory or explain why not."[3]

Overall, this book is concerned with demonstrating the relevance of social justice to legal theory and *vice versa*. It has two main aims. The first aim is to clarify the concept of social justice in such a way that it might provide a useful framework for discussion of the role of law in maximizing social justice. I wish to demonstrate that social justice and legal justice are not alien, and mutually incompatible, ideals. This is the aim of Part 1. The second aim is to advocate a substantive conception of social justice which provides a proper standard for assessing the justness of laws. To this aim, the second Part of the book is devoted.

The reader who wants to omit the introductory deliberations which constitute a background to, and a preparation for, the substantive conception of social justice, can go directly to Part 2. Most of the essentials of this conception are comprised in Chapter 4.1, Chapter 5 Sections 2, 4, 7, 8 and 9, Chapter 8.2 and Chapter 9.3.

PART ONE

JUSTICE – LEGAL JUSTICE – SOCIAL JUSTICE

CHAPTER 1

THE CONCEPT OF JUSTICE

What is the use of defining justice? One could argue that a definition of justice should be the *product* of reflections about justice, rather than a starting point. In the case of evaluative concepts such as liberty, democracy and justice, the distinction between defining and advocating is extremely hard to make. Any such definition presupposes certain values and those values should be defended rather than contained in an inevitably arbitrary definition.

This argument, however, blurs the distinction between a conception and a concept. The *concept* of justice merely informs us what justice is about, it delimits the scope of discourse about justice. The *conception* is a product of moral inquiry, but this must be made on the basis of clearly defined concepts. The question: "What is justice?" might be understood as a question about a concept or a conception, a word or an ideal, a definition or an ethical principle. In the first case, where the question concerns a concept, a definition or a word, an example of a possible answer could be: "Justice is a criterion by which good laws of a society are evaluated". In the second case, when we ask about a conception, ideal, or principle, a conceivable answer could be: "Justice is treating equals equally and unequals unequally in proportion to their inequality" or "Justice is rendering *suum cuique*". A concept of justice provides a framework within which a conception of justice is formulated; a conception provides a standard whereby a man, a rule, an act or a society is judged as just or unjust.[1] To be sure, this distinction between concepts and conceptions does not suggest that developing moral concepts is a morally neutral enterprise. This would be a misunderstanding for when we advance a particular concept of justice, for instance that which refers to the distribution of benefits and burdens, we are at least presupposing that the manner in which benefits and burdens are distributed is a significant moral issue. Such an ascription of moral weight certainly is not value-neutral. So, although alleged absence of value judgments cannot serve as a proper criterion for distinguishing concepts from conceptions, the very distinction is plausible and useful in the present context. It is the distinction between identifying the field of moral inquiry and filling it out with substantive principles; or, as Dworkin puts it, the distinction between posing a moral issue and trying to answer it.[2] However problematic this distinction may be philosophically, it reflects the two steps we take in our actual moral reasoning, and it introduces some clarity to disputes about moral matters.

Definitions are necessary in order to make the argument intelligible and to facilitate communication between people. Although necessary, defining ethical concepts is a risky venture and the least one can do is to recognize the dangers it involves. A social thinker proposing the meaning of an ethical concept as a starting point for his argument about the favoured conception, should make his way carefully between the Scylla of eclecticism and Charybdis of arbitrariness. What I call here 'eclecticism' of definition, consists of the belief that the best way to capture the meaning of moral concepts is to record what people (the general public or enlightened writers on the subject) mean when they make statements about those concepts. Justice is whatever people mean by 'justice'. Such an approach, although it defends itself against the charge of arbitrariness, is totally useless; even the most cursory glance at the literature on the subject, not to mention the general public's uses of the word, proves that there is a great variety of meanings of justice and that the search for their common denominator is doomed to failure, unless this common denominator is at so high a level of generality that discourse about justice is reduced to a few banalities. Besides, if a social thinker were at the mercy of actual usages of ethical concepts, it would make no sense to claim that one of his functions is to try to make them more precise, let alone to shape those concepts.

The opposite extreme would be a case of arbitrariness in definitions. To be sure, all definitions of moral concepts are to some extent arbitrary; this is the inevitable fate of all projecting, as distinguished from reporting, definitions. However, this arbitrariness should not go so far as to lead to the usage of an old word in a completely new and eccentric way. Current ways of understanding those concepts, although not binding, nevertheless impose some constraints upon the liberty of making definitions, in particular where high emotions are attached to traditional uses of those concepts. If those boundaries are ignored, and the meaning of an ethical concept strays too far from its usual meaning, a moral conception built upon such a definition loses its persuasive power. Moral issues cannot be resolved by a definitional *fiat*. Stipulation of moral principle disguised in the form of definition blurs the line between a concept and a conception; it resembles the attitude of Humpty Dumpty who believes that words mean whatever he chooses that they should mean. In moral discourse it leads to the effective end of any discussion about values; parties to the discussion at least should have a common subject-matter of dispute.

In the case of concepts with strong evaluative overtones, such as justice and democracy, the definition of a concept is inevitably linked to advocacy. In practice it is very difficult to distinguish between the question of what it is to have a just society and postulating such a society. A person formulating statements about justice rarely stands at a distance from his pronouncements to be able to say: "it is just, yet I do not like it". However, it does not always have to be so; if, as I will argue, justice is understood as a specific, and not an all-encompassing social ideal, then a just arrangement, although *prima facie* right, does not have to be the optimal arrangement, all things considered. The effort to distinguish between defining and advocacy is, therefore, not totally hopeless.

1. JUSTICE: GLOBAL OR PARTICULAR?

One of the fundamental demands of conceptual economy is that concepts should be as specific as possible. The basic use of concepts is that they help us to draw a line between different aspects of reality; we use different concepts because we think that their subjects can be distinguished from one another. All-encompassing or overlapping concepts render communication between people more difficult because different aspects of reality, including different parts of our moral landscape, are less clearly delimited. Applying this principle to discourse about justice suggests that justice should be defined as a specific virtue, rather than as an equivalent to overall moral goodness. Only then may a conception of justice obtain the status of a substantive moral ideal; otherwise a demand for justice is reducible to a general statement that a society should be good rather than bad. Of course, the more specific a social ideal is, the more controversial it becomes.

The distinction between global and particular concepts of justice is very old. It is, nevertheless, worth reiterating because, as I will show, the temptation to use justice as an overall judgment of moral appraisal, as the equivalent of a complete social ideal, is ever present in modern writings on justice. The idea that justice may be used at different levels of generality, either as a global sum of moral virtues, or as a specific virtue, was put forth by Aristotle in his *Nicomachean Ethics*. He distinguished there justice as "complete virtue with the addition that it is displayed towards others" and justice "in that sense in which it is a part of virtue". The opposite of justice in a 'complete' sense is "injustice which is coextensive with vice"; the opposite of 'partial justice' is "injustice which is a particular kind of vice". This specific kind of justice (and, correspondingly, of injustice) is a matter of distribution or redress.³ Now, one may of course decide to use the concept of 'justice' in both senses: a broader and a narrower one. But such usage creates a risk of confusion. Moreover, this broader sense of justice (as a 'complete' virtue) is so all-encompassing that it serves no useful function at all. If all good acts, rules or societies are 'just' in this sense, but some are also 'just' in the narrower sense, we might as well restrict the term to its latter meaning and so have the advantage of comparing and contrasting some virtues of those acts, rules or societies with other virtues.

Most modern moral theorists try to limit the concept of justice to the second one of those described by Aristotle (although they do not necessarily agree with his criteria of 'particular' justice) and in that they follow the warning of John Stuart Mill against conceptions which "merge all morality in justice".⁴ It seems to be consistent with general moral intuitions that there are certain actions which are evil without being unjust, in the same way as there are morally commendable actions to which the adjective 'just' is not relevant. It seems, for instance, that deceit cannot be qualified as an act of injustice although it is a moral wrong. Cruelty to animals, obscene language, treason — all these are examples of acts which in various moral systems are condemned, although condemnation in terms of 'injustice' hardly comes to one's mind on these occasions.

Just as a man can be cruel, dishonest or cowardly without being unjust, so social systems can display various deficiencies which do not necessarily entail injustice. Justice is a very important, perhaps even the most important, virtue displayed by a society, but certainly not the only one. There is nothing nonsensical in saying: "this is a just society, although very chaotically organized" and there is no inconsistency in saying: "there are a lot of injustices here although individual freedoms are generally well protected in this country". The concept of justice which I propose here is an important, but limited, social virtue. It is not an all-inclusive vision of an ideal social order. It does not do the job of a complete ideal of a good society although it is certainly a very important element of a good society.

This general point was well expressed by John Rawls:

A conception of social justice, then, is to be regarded as providing in the first instance a standard whereby the distributive aspects of the basic structure of society are to be assessed. This standard, however, is not to be confused with the principles defining the other virtues, for the basic structure, and social arrangements generally, may be efficient or inefficient, liberal or illiberal, and many other things, as well as just or unjust. A complete conception defining principles for all the virtues of the basic structure, together with their respective weights when they conflict, is more than a conception of justice; it is a social ideal. The principles of justice are but a part, although perhaps the most important part, of such a conception.[5]

I do not suggest that Rawls's view of the place of justice in a global set of moral values is without problems and that he consistently follows the general declaration quoted above. I will argue that, in a sense, the notion of efficiency is built into Rawls's Second Principle of Justice, and more specifically, in that element of the Second Principle which is named by Rawls the Difference Principle.[6] I also believe that there is a conflict between the general declaration quoted above and the idea that the Principle of Liberty is a part of a theory of justice. I will return to this point later.[7]

A good example of explicit adoption of a global concept of justice, indistinguishable from an all-encompassing ideal of the good society, is provided by an essay of Iredell Jenkins. For Jenkins, justice in a substantive sense, as distinguished from formal or procedural,

is a depiction of the good society, the ideal state of affairs, the consummation of man's hopes and dreams, the heaven on earth that we should seek to achieve . . . . In more homely terms, the just society is one that secures to men such familiar but elusive values as freedom, equality, security and opportunity: it gives them the public support and protection that they need to make good their inadequacies, and it also allows them the room to exercise initiative and direct their private lives.[8]

But identification of a just society with a good society *tout court* is troublesome: the questions about conflicts between justice and other social values cannot sensibly be asked. The usefulness of such a notion is therefore limited. On the other hand, the adoption of narrower notions of justice (and, consequently, of social justice) makes such questions legitimate. Since an important part of actual moral deliberations concerns not so much identification of absolute values but rather reconciliation of conflicting, often mutually irreducible values, there is an immediate appeal in considering social justice as one of those restricted values. The inevitable consequence of such an approach is that we agree that in some situations justice may give way to other considerations, that it is not always an overriding social value. This certainly helps to make our moral language more precise and capable of capturing our actual moral dilemmas.

What is specific about the concept of justice (and, in particular, of social justice) which distinguishes it from other social values? As a starting point, I propose to restrict the concept of justice to the distributive standards. As opposed to aggregative standards, which demand maximization of goods that are objects of human desire and reduction of burdens which are disliked, justice has to do with the way goods and burdens are divided among people. The concept of social justice which is used here is a distributive one; it applies to standards of distribution of benefits and burdens within a community. In Sidgwick's words, "the laws in which Justice is or ought to be realised, are laws which distribute and allot to individuals either objects of desire, liberties and privileges, or burdens and restraints, or even pains".[9] Conceptions of justice provide us with standards for deciding between competing claims on resources which are defined as anything that people have or may have an interest in obtaining, for instance: socio-economic gains, liberty, educational opportunity, etc. The mirror image of distributive justice, governing the distribution of desired goods, is retributive justice which applies to the distribution of punishment. In Chapter 8, I will defend the idea that distributive and retributive justice indeed may be regarded as symmetrical moral conceptions governed by the same general principle.

Justice, as a distributive value, is thus a concept governing the division of other values; in this sense justice is a second-order value, a meta-value. Before its application in practice, information about what goods are desired or valued by people, what they count as burdens and benefits, is required. It is a comparative concept because it implies a comparison of what particular persons obtain. Therefore, once we establish a general standard of justice, an assessment whether a particular act is just requires information about at least two persons' shares in benefits or burdens.

Now, the previous observation is not accepted universally. Some writers argue that justice is a distributive, but not necessarily a comparative, standard. They argue, for instance, that a principle of justice may require that "nobody in the reference group should fall below a certain fixed minimum level" which is allegedly an absolute, or a non-comparative, principle.[10] The case for a concept of justice that covers both comparative and non-comparative principles was put forcefully by Joel Feinberg.[11] His arguments deserve close attention because critical analysis of them may throw an additional light on the way justice is understood in this book. The critique of Feinberg's assertion that justice may be understood also in a non-distributive and non-comparative sense, helps us to grasp the present conception of justice.

Feinberg distinguishes between comparative justice, which "involves comparisons between various persons" and therefore where "a person's due is determinable *only* by reference to his relations to other persons" and non-comparative justice where "one's due is determined independently of that of other people" (266). In the case of non-comparative justice, Feinberg says, everyone is considered "on his merits" which means that everyone is compared with objective standards and not with other people; equality of treatment is not relevant for non-comparative justice because "[i]f we treat *everybody* unfairly, but equally and impartially so, we have done each an injustice" (268). Just treatment of an individual is, in the case of non-comparative justice, independent of how other people are treated. The most typical examples of non-comparative justice are, for Feinberg, "unfair punishments and rewards, merit grading, and derogatory judgments" (268). Non-comparative justice, we are told, is *not* built upon a formal principle of similar treatment of relevantly similar cases and dissimilar treatment of relevantly dissimilar cases. As another author has put it, non-comparative cases of justice are those "in which it is possible to determine whether someone has been treated justly with no knowledge whatever of the treatment given to others".[12]

Now offhand it might seem that those who write about 'non-comparative justice' simply assume a broader definition of justice than the one adopted here, and that they include in this concept some principles that the partisans of purely comparative notions of justice would not consider to be principles of justice. But this is a misconception. Most of the examples of what is considered to be non-comparative justice are actually cases of comparative justice, while the rest of the examples of alleged 'non-comparative justice' do not concern justice at all.

Let me deal first with the latter category. It is claimed that the principle that no one should fall below a certain level, for example, below the poverty line, is a principle of justice.[13] Apparently, in such cases we do not have to compare a person with other persons but only with a standard of poverty; it might seem that no information about the absolute well-being of other members of the community is needed to make such an assessment. However, is there such a principle of *justice*? Imagine that the available amount of resources in a given group is 100 units. The poverty line is at the level of 10 and there are twenty individuals. Now one reaction would be to say that it is unimaginable to have a poverty line in a community determined at a level which is unattainable for the average person. Much as I disagree with such an approach,[14] its necessary consequence obviously would be that the principle of not allowing anyone to fall below a poverty line is a comparative one, because comparisons of people are involved already in the standard of poverty. To say whether or not there is an injustice in a particular situation we would need not only information about one particular individual, but also about other people in the same group so that we could calculate the poverty line as a function of a generally achieved well-being. If, however, we disregard the argument that minimal standards are necessarily relative and agree that they can be objectively measured, then we cannot call unjust a distribution which fails to guarantee everyone a share above the minimum standard when the total amount of goods is too limited to permit the desired result. It seems to me counter-intuitive to say that, in our example, a distribution of 5 units for each of twenty individuals is unjust *merely* because 10 is considered to be a minimum poverty line. If a society is too poor to satisfy the basic human needs of its members, it is not a matter of injustice that they starve. It will be a matter of injustice only if that society allows a few wealthy people to indulge in luxury goods to the detriment of the suffering rest of the population. But if an entire society is suffering hunger, there is no injustice in it. It is still very tragic, but not unjust.

The above argument leaves aside, of course, the important question of what is the 'justice constituency'. This argument presupposed that 'society' is a self-contained unit within which justice is done, and that any information about other societies is morally irrelevant. But, obviously, this simplifying assumption can be, and should be, challenged.[15] The judgment of injustice may be made about the above-mentioned case of a starving society when one compares this society with other, more affluent, communities which could offer transfers of well-being in order to diminish starvation in this society. But then, of course, it *is* a comparative standard of justice, with this qualification that the comparative group of reference is broader than just one society. We cannot discuss this problem now. My argument was only intended to show that the principle of not falling beyond a set standard is either a comparative one or is not a principle of justice at all.

Incidentally, let us note that from the assumption that justice is distributive it does not necessarily follow that justice is comparative. These are two slightly different matters and my argument against the idea of non-comparative justice does not rely solely on the adoption of the distributive concept of justice. The case for non-comparative justice is sometimes believed to prove also the non-distributive character of certain forms of justice. For some writers (in particular for Feinberg), the distinction: comparative/non-comparative justice is identical with the distinction: distributive/non-distributive; non-comparative justice is understood as non-distributive (266–267). For others, in particular for Brian Barry, justice is always distributive but within the distributive notion of justice he identifies comparative and absolute types of justice.[16] My argument rejects both of these opinions. While agreeing with Barry that justice is always distributive (and thus disagreeing with Feinberg), I wish to claim that justice is also necessarily comparative, that it always involves comparisons between persons or groups. The essence of the argument which I attack here is that there are certain just distributions (or allocations, assignments, ascriptions) where everyone should obtain his due irrespective of what others get. Non-comparative justice allegedly consists in 'comparing' a person only with a standard and not with other persons. Now the coherence of the argument about the non-comparativeness of some forms of justice requires that the standard itself not be a product of comparison. If, as we are told, the difference between comparative and non-comparative justice lies in that in the first case, to reach a judgment of justice we must make an interpersonal comparison, and in the second case, the judgment is based solely on what is a person's due, then the difference is legitimate only if what is a person's due is not based on an interpersonal comparison.

Consider the following example. While marking students' essays I use, as an examiner, a scale of marks: fail, pass, credit, distinction, high distinction. Now the argument about non-comparativeness might run in the following way: independently of the quality of all other papers, an essay deserves a high distinction if I think that it is excellent. The essay is compared only with the 'objective' standard of excellence, not with the relative quality of the other essays. The only information required so that we could say whether justice was done concerns the quality of this one particular essay while information about other essays (our hypothetical argument would say) is allegedly irrelevant. But this is an illusion because a comparison is already involved in the standard itself. It would be absurd to reserve the high distinction only to those students' essays whose quality equals, say, the quality of academic achievements of Nobel Prize winners. In such a case, high distinction would be a superfluous mark and the real scale would start below this mark. The standard itself is tailored to the possible range of foreseeable quality of student essays. High distinction, therefore, reflects not an absolute standard, but the highest standard that could be reasonably expected from students. This standard is moulded by a comparison with other imaginable authors of essays, for instance, secondary school students and, on the other hand, scholars of great academic achievement. Consequently, a judgment that a particular student was *justly* awarded a high distinction, informs us not only about the student himself, but also locates him in relation to other members of his group and to other groups of reference, because the standard itself was moulded by reasonable expectations towards those groups. This is precisely the case in Feinberg's 'merit grading' (268, 274–275). According to Feinberg, "[w]hen the object of a grading system is simply to assess as accurately as possible the degree to which a person has some talent, knowledge, or other estimable quality, then the fairness or unfairness of a given grade assessment is of the non-comparative sort" (274). But, if what I have just said is correct, then it follows that 'merit grading' *is* comparative because it assigns certain benefits or burdens to people according to their place in the scale of merits.

Feinberg's second typical case of 'non-comparative justice' (along with merit grading) involves 'unfair punishment and rewards.' Indeed, the problem of unjust punishment seems to be the strongest argument of believers in non-comparative justice. Punishing the innocent is always unjust, they say, irrespective of whether all people who are punished in a certain country are innocent or whether the person in question is the only innocent person to be punished. In consequence, it would seem that in order to state the injustice of an act of punishment we need to know only of the innocence of one person. It appears that we do not have to make comparisons with other people. This is an important point: is punishing the innocent unjust irrespective of how other people are treated or is it unjust only in so far as it is arbitrary, that is, when some innocent people are punished and others are not? I agree with Feinberg that punishing the innocent is unjust irrespective of how others are treated. But is this statement of injustice really non-comparative?

At this stage it is necessary to recall the distinction between injustice with regard to the application of the rule and injustice with regard to the rule itself. When one and the same rule is applied inconsistently, that is, when equals (in a relevant sense) are treated in an unequal way, then it is injustice in the application of the rule and it is obviously a comparative injustice in the sense understood by Feinberg. This formal principle of justice requires merely that the rules be applied as enacted. If, for instance, a general rule proclaims that subjective guilt (in the form of intention or negligence) is a necessary condition for criminal punishment, and despite this rule an innocent person is punished, then it is unjust because this person is treated unequally as compared to other innocent persons who were, so far, acquitted. This injustice is, therefore, a violation of the principle 'treat equals equally': the statement about injustice belongs thus to a comparative type of consideration. An accused is equal, in a relevant sense, to previously acquitted persons (because both they and he were innocent), yet he is treated differently.

The notion that an unequal application of one and the same rule to different people is a comparative injustice is not questioned by Feinberg. However, 'punishing the innocent' constitutes for him a case of non-comparativeness of justice (and, consequently, of injustice) in those contexts where it cannot be qualified as an unequal application of a rule. In order to examine that view, consider a situation in which the punished person is not the only innocent person who is punished in the society. On the contrary, let us follow the path suggested by Feinberg and imagine that the practice of punishing the innocent is institutionalized in this legal system. For instance, there is a rule which stipulates that persons who are the relatives of someone who committed an act of high treason are to be punished by the criminal law. The courts in this country work with an impressive efficiency and discipline so that each and every relative of a traitor always was and is punished. The principle 'treat equals equally' seems, therefore, to be respected fully but still we tend, quite rightly, to treat this whole practice as unjust. In consequence, each individual punishment of the innocent relatives of a traitor should be considered as injustice, irrespective of the fact that other innocent people are also punished.

But why do we believe that this practice is unjust? Certainly, not because of the arbitrary *application* of the rule; the injustice here is in the rule itself. When a rule is unjust, its application will always produce unjust results irrespective of whether all the addressees of this rule are affected or whether only some of them are selected arbitrarily. But what does the *injustice* of a rule (as distinguished from the injustice of its application) really mean? Presumably, it means that we disagree with the way this rule distributes certain benefits or burdens amongst members of the community. If, therefore, in our hypothetical example of innocent relatives of traitors being punished, we believe that the rule is unjust, this suggests that we disagree with the way this group is treated as compared with other groups in the society. We believe that innocent people should not be punished; this means that if a general rule demands punishment of *some* innocent people, then it treats them unequally compared with other innocent people. Innocent relatives of traitors are, in a morally relevant sense, equal to other innocent people yet they are being selected by a rule of criminal law. They are, therefore, being treated unequally because they are punished while other innocent people are not.

The upshot of this observation is that what distinguishes the case of punishing the innocent from other cases of injustice is *not* its allegedly non-comparative character but the fact that it is the rule itself (rather than its application) which is the object of our negative assessment. This assessment is, nevertheless, of a comparative nature. The comparison is shifted from the sphere of application of a general rule to the sphere of the formulation of the rule. However, the injustice of a rule consists precisely in the fact that people who are, according to our moral convictions, relevantly equal, are treated by this rule in an unequal way. Now, these two dimensions of comparative injustice (injustice of the rule and injustice of its application) do not necessarily coincide. There are situations where an unjust rule is applied in a non-arbitrary manner, where an unjust rule is applied in an arbitrary manner (that is, when people considered as equals by this rule are not treated equally), or where a just rule is applied in an arbitrary manner. To return to our example, imagine a situation where only *some* relatives of traitors are punished while some others are acquitted. Is it less or more evil than the case where *all* of these unfortunate people are treated equally (which, here, means equally cruelly)? One might argue that it adds insult to injury when the unjust rule is applied without consistency; others might argue that it is a partial rectification of the unjust consequences produced by the application of a rule. I do not intend to provide an answer to this question but I wish only to remark that, contrary to Feinberg's suggestions, it is not a case of relations between comparative and non-comparative considerations, but rather of relations of comparisons made on two different levels: on the level of a rule and of its application.

If what I have said above is correct, then *a fortiori* this is true about other cases of retributive injustice. These are cases not of the innocent being punished but rather of the guilty being punished too severely. This category of injustice is also considered as non-comparative by Feinberg: "If beheading and disembowelment became the standard punishment for overtime parking, as the result of duly enacted statutes, the penalty as applied in a given case would be unjust (because too severe) even though it were applied uniformly and without discrimination to all offenders" (279). But, if punishing the innocent is a comparative injustice, then all the more this is true when we consider excessive punishment. Beheading is an unjust penalty for a parking offence because it is a *disproportionately* severe reaction to this particular offence. The rule that prescribes such a penalty certainly distorts proportions between this particular guilt and innocence. The moral difference between a parking offender and an innocent person is not *so great* as to warrant the difference between beheading and acquittal. The comparison which the rule makes between a parking offence and lawful behaviour does not correspond to prevailing moral judgments about the gravity of parking offences *as compared* with lawful behaviour. Therefore, the condemnation of the above rule as unjust follows from a comparison of treatment accorded to a group of people with treatment accorded to all other people.

In response one might say: cruel punishment is always unjust, irrespective of the gravity of the crime. It is not only unjust to punish parking offenders cruelly (in which case we can argue a comparative injustice, as we have just seen) but it is also unjust to punish murderers or rapists cruelly. The cruel punishment is unjust even when applied to the most invidious criminal. Now this argument is certainly *not* a comparative one but an absolute one; to make this argument no comparison of this criminal with other criminals is necessary. But I think this is not an argument about justice at all. It condemns cruel punishment because cruelty *as such* is evil; it is always wrong to inflict suffering beyond certain limits. But a prohibition of cruelty is not a principle of justice, not any more than moral prohibitions of deceit or of obscenity are principles of justice. As suggested earlier, there are moral principles which cannot be properly called principles of justice and the argument against cruel punishment belongs to these. To say that it is inhuman to inflict suffering is not identical with saying that it is unjust. This point is additionally confirmed by social psychologists who note that "[i]f the agent of harm is perceived as having legitimate authority *and* if consistency of treatment is evident (i.e., all cases of *A* are given treatment of *X*), it is unlikely that the sense of injustice will be aroused, irrespective of the treatment".[17]

We may, I hope, dispense with the discussion of the third case which Feinberg cites to demonstrate non-comparative justice or injustice, that is, judgmental injustice which consists "in the falsity of the derogatory allegation" (270). To the extent to which judgments and statements *do* fall under the rubric of justice at all (and, as I have argued elsewhere, that is a contentious matter)[18] they share the features of 'merit grading' and of retributive justice. If false and derogatory statements constitute, say, a wrongful destruction of one's reputation, or an unfair assessment of a particular person, the resulting 'judgmental injustice' is equally comparative as merit grading or punishments. So much for derogatory judgments. This whole discussion shows, I hope, what is distinctive about justice in the general landscape of our moral views. It is a concept which relates a person's treatment to that of another person or group in a society. Each type of justice is, therefore, comparative because it is an embodiment of a formal principle of treating equals equally and unequals unequally in proportion to their relevant inequality. However, as I have tried to demonstrate, a standard of justice may be directed towards two different levels: either the level of the application of a general distributive rule (and then the role of standards of justice is to make sure that equal people are treated equally) or the level of the content of the rule itself (and then the standard of justice assesses whether unequal treatment provided by the rule corresponds with inequalities relevant from the moral point of view). A state of affairs may be considered unjust either because a rule is unjustly applied or the rule itself is unjust; however, a comparison between people (or groups) is necessarily involved in every type of judgment of justice. Justice is comparative in the sense that, say, liberty or maximization of welfare are not. The statement that X is free to do Y does not contain any information about other individuals; the statement that X is treated justly by a judge (or that the law which this judge is expected to apply with regard to X is just) contains information about the position accorded to X as compared with the position accorded to other people, whom we consider as a relevant comparative group.

The two levels of reasoning about justice correspond to the well-known distinction between justice as a substantive principle and justice as a formal principle, regulating the application of substantive rules of distribution. The formal principle is, as it were, a rule of rules; it demands that a standard of just distribution be applied equally to equals assuming that, on the basis of the substantive rule, we know who are to be considered as equals. For Eugène Dupréel it is a distinction between 'static' and 'dynamic' justice; static justice requires strict application of existing rules while dynamic justice constitutes a standard of assessment of rules themselves. It is dynamic because it serves as a tool of criticism of valid rules from the point of view of their moral value.[19] Formal justice does not contain any design of a just society except for the postulate that social relations be based on general rules rather than on *ad hoc* decisions.

A frequent charge against a distributive concept of justice is that it presupposes that a social structure is a product of deliberate, conscious action; this notion of justice, the argument goes, may be applied only to a situation in which there is a human agency which 'distributes', in a literal sense, goods among people. Now, since there are ideals of social systems in which an allocation of goods is brought about by allegedly impersonal forces of the market, we are told that this notion of justice is simply not applicable to them. Hence, the very use of this standard presupposes a particular conception of society; the market society cannot be assessed in terms of distributive justice because no one distributes goods. This view is asserted with force by Friedrich Hayek: "Strictly speaking, only human conduct can be called just or unjust. If we apply the terms to a state of affairs, they have a meaning only in so far as we hold someone responsible for bringing it about or allowing it to come about".[20]

This proposition raises two problems which only partially overlap. One of them concerns the proper subject of justice: who (or what) is it which sensibly may be called just or unjust? Is justice (or injustice) a property of human conduct, of persons, of rules, or of states of affairs? Hayek emphasizes the applicability of justice to human conduct somewhat arbitrarily; for my part, I see nothing improper in saying that a particular standard of distribution is just or unjust, or that a state of affairs is just or unjust. There are various forms of conduct, rules or states of affairs to which the notion of justice is *not* applicable, but there is no manifest reason why justice should be applicable primarily to human conduct, and can only apply derivatively to states of affairs.

There are situations in which conduct corresponding to procedural principles of justice does not produce a state of affairs which might be called just. But this is a matter of relations between procedural justice and justice of outcome, and we will discuss it under a separate heading in this Chapter. The real reason why Hayek emphasizes the notion of justice as an attribute of human conduct is that then the stigma of injustice would not be applicable to a society which, according to him, embodies best the ideal of freedom: to a market society. The allocation of goods in such a society is, we are told, an unpredictable result of innumerable individual transactions, luck and accident, where no one can be "held responsible for bringing it about"; thus the concept of justice is irrelevant. But this conceptual restriction is not at all value-free but, rather, it is a stipulation that the criteria of justice should be applicable only to individual human conduct. Those who do not share Hayek's values do not have to endorse this stipulation.

The first question raised by the passage from Hayek quoted above concerns the notion of justice as the property of human conduct. The second question is the following: if we assume that the standards of distributive justice can be applied sensibly to states of affairs (basic structures, allocations of goods, institutions, etc.), does it make sense only when there is a clearly identifiable person or a group of persons who actually operate the whole business of distribution? Is it true that, as Hayek says elsewhere: "There can be no distributive justice where no one distributes"?[21]

The following simple-minded observation may serve as a starting point for reflection upon this sentence. The concept of distributive justice obviously would be irrelevant if applied to purely natural facts, even though in everyday language we talk about 'natural distributions'. A 'distribution' of physical beauty amongst members of a society, or a 'distribution' of rainfall amongst the regions of a country is not a subject of distributive justice because these things are not 'distributed' in any social sense: they are natural facts. But social or economic benefits and burdens resulting from natural facts are not 'natural' any longer. Between a natural fact and a distribution of benefits and burdens there is a mediation of the values which society attaches to those facts, and this mediation makes justice-talk possible. I must admit that the very distinction between 'natural' and 'social' is controversial and begs important questions. But in the case of allocation of goods in a society we may argue without any risk that it is 'social' rather than 'natural'. To return to the above-mentioned examples: differences of physical strength or beauty are neither just nor unjust, but an arrangement that the strongest becomes the chief of the tribe may be assessed in terms of justice because it has to do with social distribution of power. That rain falls in one region of a country more often than in another cannot be held unjust, but that the agricultural products are not transferred from a more fortunate area to one plagued by drought may be properly discussed in terms of injustice.

Leaving aside the question of factual truth of Hayek's observation that in a market society "no one distributes", I wish to challenge the inference from "no one distributes" to "criteria of distributive justice are inapplicable". The weakness of Hayek's thesis comes out if we make an analogy with a sphere of morality which lies outside the considerations of distributive justice. If someone burns to death in a bushfire, no moral judgment about this fact is legitimate. The event may be described as tragic or unfortunate but not as morally wrong because no moral responsibility can be attributed to anyone (unless, of course, someone deliberately started the fire). However, if a child drowns and X, who is a strong, healthy man (and a good swimmer) fails to render aid, he is morally (and in some legal systems, also legally) guilty. The principles of Good Samaritanism stipulate that we should do our best to prevent evil consequences to others. In weaker formulations, it depends on an assessment of costs: we should prevent something very bad from occurring to someone else if a good that we sacrifice is substantially lower. X cannot claim a moral excuse by saying that he had not helped to save the life of a child because he feared catching a cold.

Yet X of course did not *cause* the child's drowning in the 'strong sense' of causation, that is to say, X's behaviour was not *the* cause of an accident in the sense of initiating the peril. However, it can be referred to as one of the causal conditions of the child's death because it allowed an already operative peril to continue.[22] To use counterfactual reasoning again, were X's behaviour different, the harm would not have occurred. His guilt stems from the fact that he could have prevented the tragedy and yet he did not. We may consider this case in moral terms because the tragedy was avoidable, and it was within human power to alleviate the situation. It is not necessary for moral condemnation to state that someone is responsible in a strong sense (by committing an act leading to a child's death, in our example); moral liability is based here on failure to act, on failure to avoid the tragedy when it was within a person's power to prevent it. As John Stuart Mill said: "A person may cause evil to others not only by his actions but by his inaction, and in either case he is justly accountable to them for the injury".[23] Note that the ascription of responsibility in Mill's statement follows not from the causal link in a strong sense between the reprehensible behaviour and the harmful effect (that is, when the behaviour in question initiates the harmful process, or actively contributes to it) but from causation in a weaker sense, whereby as a result of an inaction, another person is put in a worse position.

An analogous argument may be made about distributive justice (unless, of course, one denies the validity of the duties of Good Samaritanism, such as are illustrated by the drowning-child example). In order to be able to assess a particular distribution as just or unjust, we do not need to believe that it was caused by a particular person or a group of persons. This is not a prerequisite of justice-talk. The prerequisite is that it is within human power to alter the distribution of which we disapprove. Returning to our natural/social distinction: it was not within human power to influence the location of rainfalls but is within human power to transfer food from more fertile areas to rainless regions. The hunger in these latter regions was avoidable if there was a surplus (over the basic minimum) of food in other places and if it was technically possible to transport it to those regions. We may, therefore, talk about distributive injustice although no individual did distribute the food between those different areas. It is unjust that we should tolerate such undeserved differences (and the suffering resulting from them) while it is within our power to do something about it.

2. COMMUTATIVE AND DISTRIBUTIVE JUSTICE

My previous remarks restricting the concept of justice to distributive matters might arouse the suspicion that commutative justice, or justice in exchange, has not received the place which it deserves in the theory of justice. If justice is defined as merely a distributive notion, what is the role of its commutative counterpart?

Distributive justice, according to Aristotle, governs "things that are divided among the members of the body politic": honour, wealth, etc. It follows from the principle of proportional equality in that it divides those goods amongst people in proportion to their merit. Commutative justice is a matter of "redress in private transactions" and requires equivalent exchange; it follows, therefore, from the principle of arithmetical equality.[24] However, the distinction is not as clear in actual social life as it is in theory; in reality the processes of allocation and of exchange are closely interconnected and may be viewed as two aspects of the same process. For instance, the payment of a wage by an employer to an employee may be viewed as the exchange of money for services rendered (commutative justice) or as a process of distribution of material gain among members of an organization in proportion to their merit as assessed by the allocator (distributive justice). In this case, the process is perceived as an exchange (equal for equal) only if isolated from the entire context in which it occurs. I wish to claim, therefore, that the considerations of 'commutative' justice either have distributive criteria built into them (and then the commutative/distributive dichotomy is groundless because commutative justice derives from distributive considerations) or do not belong to the realm of justice because they represent the idea of keeping promises irrespective of whether they are just or not.

To take the first point first, the example of employee/employer relations illustrates the idea that commutative justice standards are derivative, not primary. What is an 'equal exchange' between employee and employer cannot be determined without making a judgment about the hierarchy of merits within the structure. The principle of commutative justice demands equivalent exchange but whether an exchange is equivalent cannot be ascertained without seeing what is the relevant contribution of this particular worker (as compared with other workers) to the production of the total output of the enterprise. What amount of money is commensurate with my work may be determined only in the light of my share in the making of the total product; there is no absolute and objective equivalent where the exchanged goods (here: labour and salaries) are not of the same nature. Therefore, the just wage is determined, of necessity, by distributive considerations; there is no escape from a consideration of distributional context when discussing justice in exchange.

The primacy of distributive considerations is brought out even more clearly in another case of equivalent exchange, cited by Aristotle: justice in punishment. I will argue later that justice in punishment is based on the pattern of distributive justice[25] but the intuitive appeal of this idea seems evident. Unless we accept some sort of '*lex talionis*' approach, or unless we postulate purely utilitarian criteria of penalty-fixing (such as deterrence, prevention and reform), the principle of just punishment is inevitably based on the idea of punishment proportionate to crime. The idea of proportionality belongs to the realm of distributive justice. Clearly, in the case of punishments, we 'distribute' burdens of different gravity to people who harm others, just as in the distribution of rewards and prizes we distribute goods to people in proportion to what we regard as their desert. Punishment 'fits' the crime not in the sense that it is equal to it but only in the sense that it remains in an adequate proportion to other punishments for other offences.

A useful way of looking at Aristotelian commutative justice is to identify it with the principle that no one should gain by another's loss. It aims at restoring the *status quo ante*, that is, before the exchange has begun; in contemporary language, it says that "the party who has lost resources to another has a claim for the amount necessary to restore his original position".[26] But only very rarely may this restitution be taken literally. If you damage my fence, it is just (in a commutative sense) that you restore it to its prior shape. But in the case of exchanges between people the issue is usually more complicated than in the case of simple restitution: we have to compare goods of different types. No one should gain by another's loss, but what is a loss for particular people often depends upon their relative power. Andrew exchanges five oranges for two pineapples of Bert's but Charles, who is very rich and hasn't had any oranges for a long time, will gladly exchange his two pineapples for one orange of Bert's. Has he lost anything? Well, this depends on the relative value which he attaches to oranges and pineapples. Having a great surplus of pineapples, he will value each individual pineapple much less than Bert, who is much poorer. Therefore, Bert will be happy to trade his two pineapples for five oranges, while Charles doesn't mind giving up his two pineapples for one orange only. But the fact that the exchange of two pineapples for one orange is viewed as equitable relies upon a prior distribution of oranges and pineapples between Andrew, Bert, and Charles.

As another example, one might consider this. I know that if I drive on Sunday twenty kilometres out of town to a farmer's market, I will buy meat much more cheaply than at my local butcher's shop. However, being a rich man, I value more highly the pleasure of going bushwalking on Sunday than the economies which I may make by buying meat at the farmer's market. Should I say that the exchange between my expensive local butcher and me is inequitable; should I say that his gain is to my detriment? No, because what I gain (leisure time) is more important for me than my loss: there is, therefore, no overall loss. But my neighbour, who is much poorer than I am, would feel that the transaction at our neighbourhood butcher's is inequitable since he can buy the same quality meat much more cheaply at a farmer's market. Hence, he would feel a sense of injustice in this exchange. The judgment of commutative justice here depends on a feeling of loss and, hence, on the structure of preferences, which in itself is a result of a prior distribution of resources.

In this sense distributive considerations constitute the basis for commutative ones: the justice of the exchange cannot be separated totally from the justice of (prior) distribution. However, there is a sense in which 'commutative' justice is independent of distributive considerations: if Andrew and Bert freely agree to exchange five oranges for two pineapples, it is 'just' that Bert gives his pineapples to Andrew against Andrew's oranges *solely* because he promised to do so. This demand belongs to the group of principles such as keeping promises or obeying rules: rules and promises give birth to persons' entitlements and other persons' correlated obligations. But this does not warrant the justness of the outcome. Promises should be kept but relations produced by their fulfilment are sometimes unjust; rules should be obeyed but they, again, may happen to be unjust. Your entitlement may be consistent with social justice but, again, it may be contrary to it. To say that it is just that you get whatever you are entitled to, relies on the notion that the rules which confer the entitlement are just. Thus, 'commutative justice' reducible to the duty to fulfil promises is not really a matter of justice because promises themselves (or rather, the structure of distribution produced by their fulfilment) may be assessed by standards of justice. There may be a conflict between the 'justice' of keeping promises (or of following rules) and social justice since there may be a conflict between justice in the application of the rule and the justice of the rule itself.

That free consent is not a sufficient criterion for a just agreement is recognized by the law of contract in so far as it departs from strict and rigid juridical individualism (labelled properly by Georges Burdeau 'imperialism of independent wills').[27] A brief and by no means exhaustive review of different laws of contract will demonstrate that relief from contractual obligations is in fact widely and traditionally given in various countries on the grounds of unfairness, and not merely on the grounds of fraud or 'undue influence'. A few illustrations will show how the English, Australian and American laws of contract confront the situations of unfairness and of inequality in bargaining power between the parties. In English law, one of the important purposes of equity is to protect one of the parties to the contract even when, apparently, the principles of freedom to contract are satisfied. Courts of equity have acted to protect persons in case of inequitable and unconscionable bargains, that is in cases of bargains that "no man in his senses" would make and "no honest and fair man" would accept.[28] It was stated in 1818 that "[a] Court of Equity will inquire whether the parties really did meet on equal terms; and if it be found that the vendor was in distressed circumstances, and that advantage was taken of that distress, it will avoid the contract".[29] And, similarly, 70 years later, it was affirmed that "where a purchase is made from a poor and ignorant man at a considerable undervalue, the vendor having no independent advice, a Court of Equity will set aside the transaction".[30] The equity jurisdiction, therefore, recognizes in practice that there are standards of just contract independent of the will of the parties and that, in certain situations, legal intervention is warranted not only for the public interest but also by the protection of a contracting party. This view was expressed in a dictum by Lord Cozens-Hardy M. R., in 1916: "it is no answer to say that an adult man, as to whom undue pressure is not shown to have been exercised, ought to be allowed to enter into any contract he thinks fit affecting his own liberty of action".[31] In this case, the Court declared void the terms of an agreement which reduced one of the parties to a position of strong subjection to the will of another (almost to an *adscriptus glebae*').

A good illustration of the statutory use of the concept of a 'harsh and unconscionable' transaction (the function of which concept is to introduce distributive considerations into the realm of commutative justice) may be found in the English Moneylenders Act of 1900.[32] The Act conferred extensive powers upon the courts to reopen transactions when the interest charged, in respect of the sum actually lent, is excessive and the transaction is 'harsh and unconscionable'. Similar provisions, but applying to a greater variety of unfair contracts, have been included in recent statutes such as the Unfair Contract Terms Act, 1977 (U.K.) and the Contracts Review Act, 1980 (N.S.W.). These statutes were, no doubt, influenced by the growth of consumerism and the growing general awareness about the lack of bargaining power of the consumers in the market-place. The Contracts Review Act provides that "[w]here the Court finds a contract or a provision of a contract to have been unjust in the circumstances relating to the contract at the time it was made", the Court may grant relief by making a declaration that a contract is void, or by refusing to enforce the contract, or by varying its terms.[33]

Yet another example of applying standards of just agreement, independent of free consent given by contracting parties (without any fraud, undue influence, etc.) may be provided by cases relating to the unreasonable restraint of trade. In 1960, the Supreme Court of New South Wales declared void part of an agreement because under the provisions of this agreement it was possible for the plaintiff (an owner of a dry-cleaning enterprise) unilaterally to determine the net amount of the commission payable to the defendant (its agent to conduct the business) at a figure which might not yield to the defendant a return which would reasonably compensate her for the loss of her right to engage in other trade.[34] More recently in England, on similar grounds, the House of Lords struck down the agreement between a young song-writer and a music publishing company as involving unreasonable restraint of trade.[35] The agreement combined a virtual lack of obligation on the part of the publisher (who was not required to publish any of the song-writer's compositions) with a total commitment on the part of the composer who assigned to the publisher the full copyright in each composition created by him for a period of five years. Lord Diplock stated:

the question to be answered as respects a contract in restraint of trade of the kind with which this appeal is concerned is: was the bargain fair? The test of fairness is, no doubt, whether the restrictions are both reasonably necessary for the protection of the legitimate interests of the promisee and commensurate with the benefits secured to the promisor under the contract.[36]

Implicit in these decisions is the premise that the reasonableness of the agreement may be assessed independently of the party's consent. After all, the consent of a party may be the result of urgent need, ignorance or lack of experience,[37] and even though no force or fraud is applied, independent criteria of substantive justice may override the 'commutative' justice based merely on free consent.

In his dissenting opinion, Justice Frankfurter of the United States Supreme Court in *United States v. Bethlehem Steel Corp.* considered it to be "the fundamental principle of law" that "the courts will not enforce a bargain where one party has unconscionably taken advantage of the necessities and distress of the other" and quoted with approval the words of Lord Chancellor Northington in 1761: "And there is great reason and justice in this rule, for necessitous men are not, truly speaking, free men, but, to answer a present exigency, will submit to any terms that the crafty may impose upon them".[38] In this case, the United States Government claimed that the shipbuilders' profits under wartime government contracts were excessive and that they were due to the exploitation of a wartime emergency. Although the majority of the court rejected Justice Frankfurter's approach, his dissent remains a powerful argument for the thesis that the sphere of contract is not immune from distributive considerations.[39] Based upon this general proposition, the doctrine of 'unconscionability' is perhaps the most characteristic and direct technique in American law (and, as already noted, in English law too) of policing the fairness of contracts. In the United States, although the doctrine was established in the 19th Century,[40] it entered in 1950's into a new period of growth when section 2-302 of the Uniform Commercial Code permitted courts to refuse to enforce an entire contract, or its particular clause, if it found that the contract or its clause were unconscionable. Courts may also limit the application of any unconscionable clause so as to avoid any unconscionable result.

The cases in which the courts in the United States struck down unconscionable contracts (both in the application of the Code and in non-Code cases) show that, among other things, two considerations of a clearly distributive character have to be taken into account. First, gross inequality of bargaining positions of the parties may indicate that the aggrieved party had no meaningful choice, was in a 'take-it-or-leave-it' situation and had very little ability to protect himself. In the *Frostifresh* case [41] the Court found unconscionable the contract signed by a non-English speaking buyer (the contract was printed in English and contained complex instalment provisions) after he negotiated, with a salesman, in Spanish for the purchase of a refrigerator. Secondly, gross disparity in the values exchanged indicates the unconscionability of the contract; the contract is unfair when, for instance, the amount paid for goods is radically in excess of their market value. In the *Campbell Soup* case, the Court struck down a contract in which the farmer had agreed to supply carrots at a price three times lower than the market price at the time of delivery. The Court came to a conclusion that the contract protected only the manufacturer's interests and not the farmer's: "We think it too hard a bargain and too one-sided an agreement to entitle the plaintiff to relief in a court of conscience".[42] These two types of arguments about unconscionability correspond to two different types of arguments about unequal contracts: the former suggests that gross inequality of bargaining power implies that the weaker party had no real choice; the latter, that the contract is so unfair that it should be struck down even though it was freely made. In actual legal practice, the first type of argument carries more weight since the deficiencies in free will enable a court to strike down a contract without undermining the classical liberal theory of freedom of contract. That is why the argument about unconscionable contracts has been so often made in terms of the lack of genuine choice, hence, lack of genuine freedom.[43] However, we do not need to go as far as inferring lack of freedom from inequality of bargaining positions. The construction of 'free but unfair' contracts is relevant to the commutative/distributive distinction because it illustrates the thesis that the application of distributive considerations to exchange transactions is an entrenched current that runs through our legal tradition. Obviously, as in any other moral problem, this is not unanimously accepted and important criticisms of 'substantive unconscionability' have been launched.[44] This is natural, and yet, the fact that a 'free-but-unfair' argument has found its way into accepted legal doctrine may constitute support for those who argue for the primacy of distributive, over commutative, concerns.

Also the Civil Law systems of contract permit the courts to take into account considerations which transcend the expressed will of contracting parties. For example, the French *Code Civil*, article 1674, confers upon the seller the right to rescission of the sale (even if he expressly renounced in the contract the right to demand rescission) if the seller has been harmed by more than 7/12 in the price of an immovable. This doctrine of *lésion* was expanded by 20th Century legislation to other objects of contract; for example, to literary and artistic works. This particular technique of approaching the problem of gross unfairness of exchange originates in the mediaeval doctrine of *laesio enormis* developed on the basis of a late Roman Law principle which allowed sellers of the land to obtain rescission if the contract price was less than half of the 'just price'. These are only a few illustrations of the proposition that justice of fulfilling contracts transcends a purely formal principle of keeping promises and incorporates (in various ways in different legal systems) ideas of what is just independently of the expressed will of the parties.

Significant doubts about the commutative/distributive distinction in theorizing about justice were expressed by Thomas Hobbes:

And therefore this distinction, in the sense wherein it useth to be expounded, is not right. To speak properly, Commutative Justice is the Justice of a Contractor; that is, a Performance of Covenant, in Buying, and Selling; Hiring, and Letting to Hire; Lending, and Borrowing; Exchanging, Bartering, and other acts of Contract. And Distributive Justice, the Justice of an Arbitrator; that is to say, the act of defining what is Just.[45]

The upshot of Hobbes's argument is that the distinction between commutative and distributive justice is not a proper dichotomy. They do not apply to two parallel types of situation but rather involve standards located on different levels: distributive justice is a matter of "defining what is just" while commutative justice is a matter of "a performance of covenant". Principles of distributive justice answer the question about what rules are just rather than about an obligation to obey the existing rules or to keep promises. As we are concerned with the standard of just law (and not merely with the justice of obeying valid law, irrespective of its moral value), we are also concerned with what makes a distribution produced by an agreement just, and not merely with the justice of fulfilling an agreement. In other words, the Aristotelian idea that distributive and commutative justice operate independently, applying to two distinct spheres of life (public distributions and private transactions), obscures the fact that in reality both concepts of justice apply at the same time though in a different way. 'Commutative' justice, in the interpretation suggested above, is identical with a vindication of legal rules; distributive justice is a matter of moral demands.

This is nicely brought out by the Biblical parable:

The kingdom of Heaven is like this. There was once a landowner who went out early one morning to hire labourers for his vineyard; and after agreeing to pay them the usual day's wage he sent them off to work. Going out three hours later he saw some more men standing idle in the market-place. 'Go and join the others in the vineyard,' he said, 'and I will pay you a fair wage'; so off they went. At noon he went out again, and at three in the afternoon, and made the same arrangement as before. An hour before sunset he went out and found another group standing there; so he said to them, 'Why are you standing about like this all day with nothing to do?' 'Because no one has hired us', they replied; so he told them, 'Go and join the others in the vineyard.' When evening fell, the owner of the vineyard said to his steward, 'Call the labourers and give them their pay, beginning with those who came last and ending with the first.' Those who had started work an hour before sunset came forward, and were paid the full day's wage. When it was the turn of the men who had come first, they expected something extra, but were paid the same amount as the others. As they took it, they grumbled at their employer: 'These late-comers have done only one hour's work, yet you have put them on a level with us, who have sweated the whole day long in the blazing sun!' The owner turned to one of them and said, 'My friend, I am not being unfair to you. You agreed on the usual wage for the day, did you not? Take your pay and go home. I choose to pay the last man the same as you. Surely I am free to do what I like with my own money. Why be jealous because I am kind?' Thus will the last be first, and the first last.[46]

Now this is an obvious case of a conflict between the principles of distributive justice and 'commutative justice' reducible to the fulfilment of an agreement. Let us call, for brevity, those workers who worked the whole day, Blacks, and those who worked merely one hour, Whites. On the basis of distributive justice the allocation of their wages should be proportionate to their merit; since the only relevant information that we have about their merit is the length of their work (that is, there is no reason to suppose that their productivity, or quality of their products, was different to such an extent that it could explain the differences in wages), the just distribution should operate proportionately to the length of their work. But the second principle, invoked as an argument for equal pay, is contained in the words: "You agreed on the usual wage for the day, did you not?" The owner does not break the agreement: he gives the Blacks what he promised. The agreement became a source of their mutual legal obligation; since they exchanged their services and money in accordance with the agreement, law was respected. But the action may be both lawful and unjust. The Blacks' complaint is not of a legal but of a moral nature. They have got their due in the legal sense, and yet they feel morally wronged because, as compared with the Whites, their contribution was not reflected in their share of the total benefit distributed. If they hadn't known the Whites' wages, they would not be in a position to make any judgment of justice; they would simply have to acknowledge that the wages obtained conformed to their legal entitlements.

These are, therefore, considerations of different types; the Blacks argue about social justice, the owner about his legal duty. Here the conflict between two orders of reasoning is not very dramatic because the Blacks received what they expected (before having learnt about the Whites' wages) while the Whites have got *more* than distributive justice dictated. Injustice which consists in allocating more than one deserves is not a tragedy but still it is an injustice because the proportion of benefits (or burdens) is not respected. The analogy would be to a parent who punishes one of his children and forgives another one for the same misbehaviour. No one has *lost* anything but injustice was committed because the proportion of guilt and punishment was not respected. A parent could do it because he has power over his children, but still it is not just. Similarly in the vineyard parable: the owner was entitled to distribute wages in such a way, but it was not just. The true source of his power is disclosed in his words: "Surely I am free to do what I like with my own money". Surely he is. Money gives him power over the allocation of wages, including power to be unjust. Being free to do what he likes, he is free to be unjust as long as he keeps his promises. But this freedom does not make his unjust acts just, it only renders them lawful on the grounds of existing legal rules.

It is possible to conceive of objections to that way of tackling the problem. Suppose someone says that what the parable really exemplifies is not the conflict between social and legal justice but between justice and generosity. The owner asks: "Why be jealous because I am kind?" In this question he focuses on the moral character of his action: kindness. He has decided to be generous although in an arbitrary way; he did not deprive anyone of his entitlement but he gave some workers *more* than they deserved. Suppose, for the sake of this hypothetical argument, that the Blacks were paid as much as they would be anywhere else, so that in terms of comparison with other workers in a community (with the exception of the Whites in this particular day) there was no distributive injustice done. Suppose also that the Whites were not otherwise treated preferentially and that this particular remuneration was a windfall rather than a part of the general pattern of privileges. We might then say that the vineyard owner was generous yet unjust, kind yet arbitrary.

If, however, we accept this hypothetical argument and view the main issue of the parable not as legal *versus* social justice (as I have suggested earlier) but as justice *versus* generosity, then we inevitably reach the limits of the moral argument within the conception of justice. The latter is unable to decide the conflicts between justice and other values. What it can do, is to declare incompatibility of justice with some other values. Justice excludes arbitrariness; generosity (in the form manifested by the vineyard owner) *is* arbitrary. Justice requires good moral reasons for a proposed distribution; generosity does without them; actually, part of the nature of a charitable act is that it does not have to be just. That was, in any event, the case of the vineyard owner who explicitly declined to give any reasons for his distribution other than 'being kind'.

And yet it should be noted that even if the parable is interpreted in terms of supererogatory action rather than justice, still the legal justice constitutes the basis of the charitable act. The owner *can* be generous only because he has legal entitlements over his resources; therefore, he has legal power to allocate wages. In this sense, these two phrases are inherently linked: "Why be jealous because I am kind?" and "I am free to do what I like with my own money". The supererogatory action suggested by the first sentence is made possible by the legal entitlement described by the second. In this way, charity derives from legal justice. But this only means that a legal set of entitlements makes it possible for some people to distribute goods arbitrarily, even if generously. These legal entitlements may, as in our example, provide some people with power over other people's labour and rewards.

In the case, already quoted, of *United States v. Bethlehem Steel Corporation* it was argued that "[i]t always is for the interest of a party under duress to choose the lesser of two evils. But the fact that a choice was made according to interest does not exclude duress".[47] Equal legal status of parties may lead to unjust agreements when economic disparities give one of the parties (in the Biblical parable, the vineyard owner) power to dictate the conditions of contract. "[I]f one party has the power of saying to the other:

'That which you require shall not be done except upon the conditions which I choose to impose' no person can contend that they stand upon anything like an equal footing."[48] This is illustrated by the vineyard parable and that explains the incongruity between legal correctness and the substantive injustice of the distribution of salaries among vineyard workers. We may say that the Blacks legally had no cause for complaint over their shares but still we may believe that injustice was done: what appears offhand to be a commutative/distributive distinction, is actually the distinction between legal obligation and social justice.

3. SOCIAL JUSTICE AND LEGAL JUSTICE

The above-cited examples, and in particular the vineyard parable, suggest the main scheme of distinction between social justice and legal justice. Legal justice is about conforming to the rules *whatever they may be*, social justice is about the distributive qualities of those rules. The principle that we should treat people according to their rights belongs to the sphere of formal justice (or legal justice, if the rights in question are legal rights) because, in itself, it does not determine any requirements or conditions of the moral quality of those rights. This distinction corresponds (just as comparative/non-comparative or distributive/commutative justice) to a general distinction which underlies all thinking about justice: justice in following rules and justice in the rules themselves.

Judgments about legal justice have, as their object, consistency of an act with legal rules; they confirm that a general rule is properly applied to a particular case. Judgments about social justice have, as their object, the content of those rules; they confirm that the rule distributes burdens and benefits justly among the members of a community. This distinction is, therefore, a particular case of a more general distinction between formal and substantive justice, where formal justice corresponds to the consistent administration of existing rules and substantive justice is the standard of assessment of those rules. Social and legal justice are neither mutually exclusive nor necessarily correlated; they apply to different phases of the social process. Social justice applies to work done by a legislator, legal justice to work done by a judge (or any other person acting authoritatively in applying rules).

Now, this last statement contains, of course, a serious simplification: it assumes a particular theory of sources of law, namely the theory which makes a clear distinction between the legislative and the judicial roles. This has certainly a justification in the Civil Law countries where, in the generally recognized conception of legal sources, the function of law-making is carefully distinguished from the application of general laws. In the Common Law this distinction is much more questionable and the clear borderline between law-making and judicial decision-making does not exist. But it does not invalidate the distinction 'social justice/legal justice'. The latter concerns the question whether a judge correctly 'discovers' (or, upon a different theory, 'makes') law within the valid conception of sources of law, that is, whether he properly takes notice of judicial precedent, statutory provisions, legal customs, and so on. This evaluation happens to be sometimes controversial giving rise to 'hard cases', that is to say, cases where informed people can reasonably disagree about the bearing of the law on the facts of the case. Two theoretical approaches to 'hard cases' are possible. We might conclude that a judge 'makes' law in hard cases, that is, he acts as if he were a legislator. His decision is then a proper subject of evaluation by the criteria of social justice. Alternatively, we might agree with Ronald Dworkin that even in the hard cases there is always one right answer to the issues raised by the case and that the judge has a duty to discover it by resort to the legal standards other than the rules.[49] On this theory, his decision may be considered as *legally* just or unjust depending on whether he correctly discovers rights existing under the principles of the legal system, but these principles themselves may still be considered *socially* just or unjust. I will return to this problem at the end of this Section.

To say that the law may be just or unjust seems to be such a truism that reviving old discussions of "no law can be unjust" *versus* "unjust law is no law" is probably superfluous. Let us note, however, that the acceptance of any of these propositions would make, ultimately, an assessment of law in terms of justice impossible. "No law can be unjust", for Hobbes, expressed a certain quasi-empirical truth: since people tacitly consent to any of the Sovereign's acts, they cannot complain that those acts are unjust. "The Law is made by Sovereign Power, and all that is done by such Power, is warranted, and owned by every one of the people; and that which every man will have so, no man can say is unjust".[50] The internal logic and coherence of this reasoning is unquestionable, but the argument is based on the dubious assumption that people actually do consent to a Sovereign's acts and that they give to the authorities a cheque *in blanco* to make laws as they like. In so far as this is not the case, the Hobbesian formula "No law can be unjust" is a fiction. For John Austin, Hobbes's proposition was "indisputably true" because it meant that "no *positive* law is *legally* unjust".[51] But, in this interpretation, it becomes a mere tautology; if 'legally unjust' means 'unlawful' then the Austinian phrase turns out to mean that no law can be unlawful. What we need to know, however, is whether we are allowed to say that law is unjust *tout court*, not "legally unjust". The Hobbesian formula was meant, I suppose, to express certain important truths about man, society, and law. To suggest that what he had in mind was a self-evident truism is simply selling him too short. Finally, for Kelsen "No law can be unjust" is a question of methodology; the application of principles of justice to law is beyond the scientific theory of law. If, strictly speaking, 'just' is only another word for 'legal' or 'legitimate'[52] then any evaluative judgments about unjust laws are necessarily unscientific. Only positive law, asserts Kelsen, is revealed to reason; the assessment whether this law is just belongs to the realm of irrational ideals. But, leaving aside the complex problem of emotivism in ethics, what we are interested in, when analysing the status of justice-judgments, is not whether they are 'scientific' in the strict sense of the word. What we want to know is whether statements like "this law is unjust" are internally contradictory or not; whether they contain conceptual nonsense or not.

The opposite proposition, which would also make this distinction suspect: "*lex iniusta non est lex*", was rarely expressed in a categorical form. As John Finnis has shown recently, the attribution of this formula to all natural law theories is a gross over-simplification.[53] A discussion with the unqualified principle "*lex iniusta non est lex*" is, therefore, a fight with a man of straw. More serious is the theory that law which does not satisfy certain formal requirements related to its content is not law properly speaking. I have in mind, of course, Lon L. Fuller's theory of the inner morality of law. In his well-known and entertaining parable about King Rex II, Fuller describes "eight ways to fail to make law". They are: a failure to make rules at all, a failure to publicize them, retrospective legislation, a failure to make intelligible rules, the enactment of contradictory rules, the enactment of rules requiring conduct beyond the powers of the affected party, introducing too frequent changes and the lack of congruence between general rules as announced and their administration.[54]

Now there are two slightly distinct ideas in Fuller's conception that are relevant to our present discussion. The first one is definitional: whether rules that do not satisfy one (or more) of the principles of 'internal morality of law' lose the attribute of being law, even if enacted by a sovereign in a procedure provided for the enactment of law (in this legal system). The second problem is empirical: whether the internal morality of law constitutes a guarantee of 'external' morality, that is of substantive justice. These two questions should be considered separately because a positive answer to one of them does not exclude a negative answer to the other.

To take the second issue first, it is worth noting that nowhere does Fuller affirm that the internal morality of law constitutes a strong and sufficient guarantee of a substantively just law. However, there is the assumption that formal justice and substantive justice are very closely interrelated and that substantive injustice can hardly arise from a system of legality. This thought is expressed nicely in Fuller's argument that to oppose anti-homosexual laws one does not have to resort to arguments about substantive morality because "any such law simply cannot be enforced and its existence on the books would constitute an open invitation to blackmail, so that there would be a gaping discrepancy between the law as written and its enforcement in practice". Fuller further suggests that "many related issues can be resolved in similar terms without our having to reach agreement on the substantive moral issues involved".[55] But the belief that laws prohibiting private homosexual acts between consenting adults are incompatible with the principles of formal legality simply does not withstand empirical and historical evidence. It is not true that anti-homosexual laws "cannot be enforced". It may be true that their enforcement encounters serious obstacles and, hence, that they are not as effective as many other laws. But this does not substantiate Fuller's conclusion about the connection between the form and content of law. The same applies to the general idea that "many related issues" can be resolved without appeal to substantive moral issues. Evidence shows that 'internally moral' laws, i.e. laws consistent with Fuller's eight principles, may be iniquitous and immoral. There is no reason to believe that there is an affinity of legality and justice; neither history nor theoretical speculation confirm it. If one considers, for instance, the principle of publicity of law, it is true that one will find many examples confirming the general assumption that evil cannot stand the light of day; immoral state actions are usually committed behind the veil of secrecy. But also one would find equally disturbing acts committed in an ostentatious and public manner: tortures, summary trials and executions made in enforcement of laws publicly known. Actually, authoritarian and totalitarian governments usually propagate their legal rules actively: it is part of the process of terrorizing and of indoctrinating people.

A similar argument may be made about all of Fuller's other principles, including consistent administration of general rules. One can speculate, with Rawls, that it is better to have unjust laws administered impartially than unjust laws administered arbitrarily and without regularity: "even where laws

and institutions are unjust, it is often better that they should be consistently applied".[56] I do not think, however, that this is true: sometimes the only good thing about an inhuman legal system is that its apparatus for enforcement is inefficient or corrupt. Certainly, regularity is important *per se* because, as Rawls notes, it helps people to plan their actions rationally; they know what to expect from law enforcement institutions. However, the good of regularity may well be overridden by the good of exploiting the irregularity of a corrupt system by its prospective victims. A Jew, in a Nazi legal system, would probably prefer the judges to be inconsistent and arbitrary in applying oppressive anti-Jewish laws than to see them enforcing the laws with rigorous accuracy.[57] But even if regularity is considered valuable, this does not suggest that regularity (or any other formal principle) tends to inject any substantive moral values into the legal system. This thought, expressed by Fuller elsewhere in a more general way, that "coherence and goodness have more affinity than coherence and evil",[58] belongs, I suspect, to the realm of wishful thinking and cannot be substantiated as a strong, empirically verifiable, rule.

The other question about Fuller's conception is a definitional one: whether 'law' which fails to satisfy any of eight principles of internal morality of law is a 'law' properly speaking. For Fuller such failure "does not simply result in a bad system of law; it results in something that is not properly called a legal system at all".[59] The reason is the following:

Certainly there can be no rational ground for asserting that a man can have a moral obligation to obey a legal rule that does not exist, or is kept secret from him, or that came into existence only after he had acted, or was unintelligible, or was contradicted by another rule of the same system, or commanded the impossible, or changed every minute. It may not be impossible for a man to obey a rule that is disregarded by those charged with its administration, but at some point obedience becomes futile – as futile, in fact, as casting a vote that will never be counted.[60]

But Fuller does not provide any argument that it is a logical impossibility to have a law which imposes duties retrospectively, secretly or incoherently. He says that it is not reasonable: either because it is immoral or futile. That may be true, yet it does not answer the question why such rules do not constitute a legal system properly so-called. To say that a law does not attain some ideal function does not amount to saying that it is not law; it is simply a bad or an ineffective law. Fuller's principles of internal morality of law constitute rules of good legal craftsmanship (that are likely to make law fulfil its functions) and not the criteria of what it means to have law.

This conclusion is supported by a reflection upon Fuller's analogy between rules of internal morality of law and "laws of carpentry". He says about his principles of inner morality of law that "[t]hey are like the natural laws of carpentry, or at least those laws respected by a carpenter who wants the house he builds to remain standing and serve the purpose of those who live in it".[61] This is a nice metaphor because it helps to grasp the essence of the definitional problem that is discussed. Is an improperly built house a deficient house or something that is not a house at all? Is it a bad house or is it too bad a structure to be called a house? One might ask whether it makes any difference. After all, it may be simply a problem of definitional fiat: we agree not to call a bad house a house, just as we agree not to call a bad law a law. But there is more to it than merely an arbitrary definition. By refusing to call a badly constructed building a house, we attach some positive value to the word 'house', we suggest that it carries with it some honorific significance. "It is undeserving of the title of house" — by saying this, we suggest that 'a house' is not *any* construction but a construction of certain value.

Similarly in the case of law. By refusing the name 'law' to those rules of sovereign authority which do not satisfy the principles of good legal craftsmanship, we attach some honorific significance to law as such. By refusing the title of law to 'internally immoral' law, we imply some *prima facie* moral value of 'law' properly speaking. This is, indeed, the crucial point about Fuller's conception of law: it rests on the fundamental assumption that law is morally good.[62] Notwithstanding particular legal regulations which are morally iniquitous, and the existence of which is not denied by Fuller, the legal system as such makes possible the implementation of moral rules. In this sense, law is the foundation of morality. 'Law', for Fuller, is therefore an honorific term. One may argue about the usefulness of such an understanding of law, as compared with the positivistic interpretations which do not rely upon the assumption that law as such is good. It seems to me, following H. L. A. Hart's remarks, that to adopt a value-neutral conception of law is more conducive to the strengthening of critical and reflective attitudes towards law and our moral duties. To say that something is law does not necessarily imply that it must be obeyed: we perhaps still have to weigh our moral principles against the *prima facie* duty to obey the law. But such weighing makes sense only if law is not *ex definitione* good, if we conceptually allow law to be law even if it is too evil to be obeyed. As Hart says:

What surely is most needed in order to make men clearsighted in confronting the official abuse of power, is that they should preserve the sense that the codification of something as legally valid is not conclusive of the question of obedience, and that, however great the aura of majesty or authority which the official system may have, its demands must in the end be submitted to a moral scrutiny.[63]

Fuller admittedly does not conclude that 'internally' immoral law must be obeyed; on the contrary, as it is a 'no-law', the question of the duty to obey it as law does not arise at all. However, Hart's positivistic notion of law grasps the possibility of conflict between law and morality better. The dilemmas of conflict of loyalty towards rules issued by authority and rules of morality, *are* viewed and perceived by people as conflicts of law and morality; to conceptualize these dilemmas we need a value-neutral notion of law.

The upshot of these considerations is rather banal and yet it is important for our discussion of social and legal justice. Both maxims: *"lex iniusta non est lex"* and "law cannot be unjust" are unwarranted; *'lex iniusta'* is often *'lex'* and that is why assessment of law from the point of view of morality has such an important place in our attitudes towards positive law. To accept any of these maxims is to deny the importance of our dilemma when we face conflicts between law and morality, between legal justice and social justice. Statements about legal justice inform us about entitlements conferred upon people by valid legal rules or by acts which, on the basis of those rules, have the legal significance of creating entitlements. The general maxim of legal justice may be formulated as: "To each according to his legal entitlements". Legal justice is therefore a species of "justice of conformity to rules".[64] Social justice is, then, the ideal standard of assessment of law, legal justice is the standard of assessment of law enforcement within the structural values of a given legal system. That is why the distinction between legal justice and social justice (and, more generally, justice of conformity to rules and substantive justice) was often described as the distinction between 'static' or 'conservative' justice on the one hand and 'dynamic', 'reformative', 'ideal' or 'prosthetic' justice on the other hand.[65]

We may see, in consequence, that the distinction between social and legal justice is parallel to the distinctions discussed above: non-comparative/ comparative, commutative/distributive. These are different formulations of the most fundamental distinction in justice-talk: justice of rules and of their enforcement. Now, this suggests that legal and social justice do not apply to two different spheres of social life. It is not the case that they regulate the distribution of goods of different kinds: legal justice dealing with legal entitlements while social justice with socio-economic goods. After all, legal entitlements are *over* socio-economic goods, opportunities, liberties, and so on. This distinction reflects two different stages in reasoning about justice but in social reality these justice-judgments apply to the same things; in the final analysis, what people seek are actual goods, opportunities and so on, and legal rights are important in so far as they protect our holdings over these goods.

The distinction between social justice and legal justice is conceptually sharp. In practice, however, various legal systems have worked out mechanisms for injecting considerations of social justice into law enforcement. Impartial and strict implementation of legal rules may lead to injustice in individual cases, not necessarily because these rules are unjust but because the magnitude and diversity of social situations cannot be grasped by legal rules in such a way that their application will always lead to socially just solutions. The rigidity of law must sometimes give way to consideration of individual cases by direct appeal to moral judgment in order to prevent the situation in which *'summum ius − summa iniuria'*. In those cases strict adherence to rules, or keeping to precedent, clashes with moral precepts of justice. As Justice Frankfurter said: "Courts need not be the agents of a wrong that offends their conscience if they heed the commands of law" and then added: "is there any principle which is more familiar or more firmly embedded in the history of Anglo-American law than the basic doctrine that the courts will not permit themselves to be used as instruments of inequity and injustice?"[66] Avoiding injustice requires sometimes departure from rigid rules: to prevent a situation where social justice demands legal injustice, various legal systems 'open themselves' towards moral considerations and include direct appeals to moral judgments into the legitimate operation of the application of legal rules.

Historically, this was one of the main functions of Equity in English law. The Lord Chancellor, in developing the law of Equity separately from the Common Law was acting for the sake of substantive justice that could have been frustrated by a rigid application of Common Law. The language of legal rules often includes so-called 'categories of indeterminate reference': for instance, standards of 'fairness', 'reasonableness', 'conscionableness', 'just cause', 'due care', 'adequacy'.[67] In decisions which apply those standards, courts cannot limit themselves merely to deduction from legal rules, or to keeping to precedent. They must make *moral* decisions about what justice requires in the instant case. This is, of course, by no means restricted to Anglo-American law. In Roman law, the *iudex* was instructed to decide according to *'bonum et aequum'*, *'aequitas'*, *'humanitas'*, *'bona fides'*, etc. These standards, in one way or another, are taken up by all legal systems arising out of Roman law. In socialist law, invocations of 'socialist morality' or so-called 'principles of community life' are equivalent to equity in Western law. Legal rules containing references to 'principles of community life' (as in

Polish law) are, as it were, blank forms: the substance of jural relations must be decided upon by a judge on the basis of 'socialist morality'. Like equity, these standards serve mainly to temper legal rigidity.

A student of the specific applications of 'principles of community life' cites several examples of how the appeal to principles serves as a justification for by-passing strict legal rules which, in some individual cases, would lead to clearly unjust results.[68] They were used, for instance, to suspend the eviction of a tenant, to declare void a settlement in a personal injury case which provided for a disproportionately low amount of damages, to mitigate the liability of a person who caused an automobile accident resulting in personal injuries on the ground of his financial situation, to annul (in exceptional cases) a termination of employment even though formally the employer had the right to dismiss an employee. The common element in all these usages of a 'general clause' is that they prevent legal justice going astray from social justice. This was put by the Polish Supreme Court in the following words:

The role of the principles of community life consists in synchronizing the legal rules with the directives of morals and customs, in making the law more elastic and preventing situations to which the well-known dictum *summum ius-summa iniuria* is applicable.... They are objective rules of behavior which serve as a criterion for an evaluation of what merits and what does not merit approval from the viewpoint of the ideas of the society.[69]

It is interesting to note how these phrases correspond with the words of a judge belonging to a completely different legal and political system. Justice Frankfurter warned against the courts becoming "instruments of injustice in disregard of moral and equitable principles which have been part of the law for centuries".[70] By different legal techniques various legal systems explicitly validate the use (in the process of application of law) of considerations drawn from outside positive legal sources.

But all this does not undermine the validity of the "social justice/legal justice" distinction. It shows only that in practice the distinction is not so sharp because various legal systems 'inject' considerations of social justice into the application of legal rules. To take a useful formulation by Hans Kelsen, when the positive law expressly refers to moral norms, "the delegated morality becomes law".[71] The nature of this delegation is, however, a complicated matter and depends largely on the binding conception of sources of law adopted in a given legal system. We must be careful not to create a false impression that, in the conceptual scheme outlined above, we assume a restricted view about the judicial function which does not hold good in all legal systems. In particular, the following objection might be made. The 'social justice/legal justice' distinction suggested above assumes a very simple model of judicial decision where rules determine uncontroversially what is law in every particular case brought before a judge. When there are no rules about the case, then, in this simple model, a judge is free to exercise a discretion (that is, to legislate about the novel case) or he is prevented from making any decision whatsoever. His moral sense comes into play when the legislation expressly permits him to exercise his moral judgment as is the case in the legislative use of open-ended standards and general clauses.

However, it might be further said, this simple model seriously distorts the nature of the judicial function. Moral considerations (including considerations of social justice) are resorted to not only when the legislator openly embeds moral tests in legal rules but also always whenever a judge confronts a controversial case and when it is unclear what the law requires. Considerations of social justice are, in such an approach, an inherent part of the judicial reasoning in hard cases, not merely an exercise of legislative delegation. Such an argument (although not with reference to 'social justice' but to moral principles of legal systems in general) was emphatically made by Ronald Dworkin [72] and we should consider carefully its consequences for our distinction between social justice and legal justice.

In 'hard cases', Dworkin suggests, the ideal judge must determine whether the asserted right exists in the legal system or not. In doing so, he cannot rely solely on existing legal rules; after all, the case would not be 'hard' if the judge did not run short of rules. But the absence of clear rules, Dworkin says, does not warrant the thesis that there is no right answer within this legal system and, therefore, that the judge is free to rely upon his own preferences in constructing his theory of fundamental values upon which to base his decision. Since the duty of the judge is to identify the rights of the parties, he has to appeal to arguments about principles which neither have the form of legal rules nor express the subjective preferences of the judge. The discovery of those principles is a matter of "what background morality requires" [73] and of trying "to find the best *justification* [judges] can find, in principles of political morality, for the structure as a whole". [74] The judge must reconstruct the principles by reflecting upon the nature of law in his community in order to find out whether the proposed principle "figures in the soundest theory of law that can be provided as a justification for the explicit substantive and institutional rules of the jurisdiction in question". [75] If it does, then the principle *is* a principle of law and the answer dictated by this principle is the right one. But a consequence of this description of judicial reasoning is that the appeal to background morality is an inherent part of the judicial function in hard cases. Principles of morality are unavoidable in identifying the law "not only when legal principles embodying moral concepts are concededly decisive of legal arguments, but also when the question in play is just the question of what principles are to be taken as decisive".[76]

Dworkin's theory of rights and of the judicial function is sufficiently well-known so that it need not be further summarized. For our present purposes it is important to note that his thesis might be thought to affect our 'social justice/legal justice' distinction in at least two ways. First, by suggesting that the considerations of social justice are an integral *part* of judicial decisions in hard cases and, if that be the case, they cannot constitute the test of evaluation of law (being a part thereof). If some of the principles that the judge must discover have the shape of principles of social justice, then they become a part of the administration of legal justice and not a meta-value in relation to the value of legal rules. Secondly, Dworkin's thesis might be thought to deny that social justice is an expression of the moral views of a person who pronounces the statements about social justice. At least for judges, some principles of social justice might be found as the right answers contained within the valid legal system (in the 'soundest theory of law' underlying this sytem) and not outside, or above, valid legal standards.

I wish to show that the 'rights thesis' (with these two implications) is far from obvious and, even if it were correct, it does not entail consequences that are fatal to the validity or the usefulness of our distinction. Imagine that you are a judge and you have to hand down a judgment about a 'hard case'. Suppose you are a judge of the United States Supreme Court and you have to decide whether the affirmative action in university admissions is consistent with the 14th Amendment (containing, *inter alia*, Equal Protection Clause) or whether capital punishment is in conformity with the 8th Amendment (prohibition of 'cruel and unusual punishments'). Each of these two constitutional clauses can give rise to controversies in particular cases, not necessarily foreseen by the draftsmen of the Constitution. There are *prima facie* reasonable arguments put forward in defence of diametrically opposed interpretations of 'equal protection' or of 'cruel and unusual punishment'. But, according to Dworkin, there is only one right answer about each of the controversial issues like these and therefore you, as a judge, have to discover the principles which will dictate this one right answer. In doing so, Dworkin says, a judge must act similarly to a referee in a chess game who has to decide in a novel case, unforeseen by the authors of rules and regulations of chess: whether, for instance, a player who continually smiles at his opponent in such a way as to unnerve him, annoys him 'unreasonably' and, hence, is liable to disqualification.[77] Dworkin believes that the chess referee will be able to find the right answer by reflecting upon the nature and the function of the game. Once he realizes that chess is an intellectual game, he "must apply the forfeiture rule in such a way as to protect, rather than jeopardize, the role of intellect in the contest".[78]

But is it true that the realization of this fact brings the referee anywhere closer to the detection of *the* right answer? To say that chess is an intellectual game does not provide us with any definite answer about the problem that the referee confronts unless we make some additional value judgments about what are the particular implications of this 'intellectualism' of chess. These judgments are by no means uncontroversial. From the statement that chess is an intellectual game we may reasonably draw the opposite conclusions about the example given by Dworkin. We might say that no player has a right to smile continuously at his partner because it distorts the intellectual character of the game by introducing factors external to the 'pure' intellect. But we might as well argue that modes of behaviour such as smiling are so external to the actual rules of the game that they are clearly irrelevant to the game itself; to prohibit them would be excessively oppressive towards a player who, say, cannot restrain his smile because he predicts his own victory, or because his opponent has a funny tie or for any other reason. The referee has to weigh the arguments in favour and against the proposed rule and it may well happen that he will not find ultimately any guidance in the letter or spirit of the rules and regulations about whether this particular behaviour constitutes unreasonable annoyance. He will then have to exercise discretion in judging what is 'unreasonable'.

The judge deciding about the legality of affirmative action, or of capital punishment, will have to rely, in the absence of unambiguous statutory provisions, on his conception of what really constitutes 'equal protection' or 'cruel and unusual punishment'. In deciding about this, the judge cannot, of course, ignore the basic values and aims of the legal system: he must take into account what Dworkin calls the 'background morality' and what was traditionally labelled '*ratio legis*'. But, at the end of the day, his decision will express *his* understanding of what are the practical implications of a general demand of 'equal protection' or of the prohibition against 'cruel and unusual punishment'. The previous sentence may be taken to suggest that it is merely trivial to say that a judge must fall back on his own consciousness if all that it is meant to convey is that the judge's moral judgments must be *his* own. There is certainly no prize for this discovery. And yet, it is not as trivial as it at first blush seems if we realize that concepts such as 'equal treatment' or 'cruel and unusual punishment' can warrant a number of *prima facie* plausible interpretations. Each of them is based upon a different substantive moral conception, and so the choice of a particular conception will ultimately affect the verdict. In interpreting these general constitutional clauses in one way rather than the other, the judge will make the moral decision about the relative weight of certain moral principles as compared with others. The judge does not merely 'discover' a principle of law: he must also ascribe to it a relative weight and introduce a priority order among the competing principles so that in the particular circumstances the final decision may be made. After all, Dworkin himself admits that "the great bulk of the principles and policies judges cite are controversial, at least as to weight".[79] But law does not provide any clear guidance about this relative weight of rival claims. The only guidance comes from the moral consciousness of the judge about how the morally controversial concepts should be understood in the hard cases.

Now, if this type of criticism of Dworkin's theory is correct,[80] then the judge's decision in a 'hard case' has a status similar to that of the legislator's decision and we can assess it from the point of view of substantive moral criteria. But suppose that this 'positivistic' criticism of Dworkin is for some reason invalid and that there is indeed one 'right answer' about every hard case. Accordingly, judges have no actual power to make law or exercise discretion in the sense suggested above. It would follow that the judges make no actual choice about which principle to select or about its relative weight because the decision about the principle and its weight is unambiguously predetermined by the legal system itself. But even if this is true, still it does not follow that the moral principles of the given legal system are above criticism from the point of view of the *other* moral principles. The judge has a professional duty to regard as binding "the political morality presupposed by the laws and institutions of the community"[81] but *this* political morality is merely one of possible moralities shared by informed, reasonable and morally aware people. The judicial solution to 'hard cases' may well lie in the correct discovery of moral principles that dictate the distribution of rights but these are still moral *principles of the law*, and they may turn out to be unjust from the point of view which is external to the values of this law. In this sense the statements of social justice express the values of those who pronounce them and not the institutionally accepted values that are binding on the officials of the system.

In consequence, even if the 'one right answer' thesis is correct, the views about social justice as expressed by the judges in the process of the exercise of legal justice may be subject to external criticism from the point of view of the other conceptions of social justice which are not necessarily embodied in this legal system. That is why statements of 'social justice' always reflect value-judgments of the person who pronounces them; they do not have to be identical with the judges' moral values expressed in their understanding of equity, fairness, or principles of community life. While a judge is bound by the internal values of a legal system, a person making judgments about social justice is not. Ultimately, social justice is in the eye of the beholder. The formulae of social justice may serve, therefore, as a standard of criticism of legal justice, even if in the process of legal justice some other views about social justice were already expressed by a judge to whom was delegated the power of interpreting moral principles.

4. PROCEDURAL AND SUBSTANTIVE JUSTICE

It is often maintained that substantive justice is the justice of *outcome* while procedural justice is the justice of *process* which brings about this outcome. Procedural justice, it is claimed, imposes restraints on processes by which a distribution comes about, and, in so far as these restraints are respected, the action is 'procedurally just'.[82] I will argue that this distinction is misleading: so-called 'procedural' justice is either a derivation from and reducible to 'substantive' justice or is not a category of justice (in the strict sense of the word) at all.

Let us start with the latter type of so-called 'procedural' justice: one which cannot be shown to maximize the probability of a just outcome. Gambling is a good example: there are no criteria of a 'just outcome' in roulette or poker; whenever the procedural rules are kept, the action is said to be 'procedurally' just. Gambling is the example John Rawls gives to illustrate his concept of 'pure procedural justice': there is no independent criterion of a just result but only criteria of "fair procedure such that the outcome is likewise correct or fair, whatever it is, provided that the procedure has been properly followed".[83] It is significant that Rawls avoids using the adjective 'just' in this context and talks about 'fairness' of the procedure. Also in the phrases following this definition of 'pure procedural justice' he talks about *'fair* bets', *'fair* conditions', and *'fair* distributions' arising out of these procedures. Now, the fact that he is reluctant to talk straightforwardly about *'just* bets', *'just* conditions' of gambling, and *'just* distributions' arising out of gambling where particular procedures were followed is an important symptom. Indeed, it would be odd to talk about 'just gambling' even with the explicit reservation that 'justice' is used merely in the procedural sense. We demand that procedures be kept, in gambling as well as in other social practices, but in the case of gambling we do not evoke 'justice' as an argument for keeping procedures. An appeal addressed to a croupier in a casino: 'Be more just!' sounds out of place; he is not in the business of being just, his duty is to see to it that the whole game is carried out according to the rules. Whatever is the outcome of a game properly carried out, it must be accepted as final and binding for participants. There is, as Rawls rightly observed, no criterion of just outcome and, we might add, there is no criterion of 'just procedure'. Procedures in games may be most arbitrary and bizarre, but once we agree to play the game, we must respect the outcome. It is not the alleged 'justice' of procedure that compels us to abide by its rules but our voluntary consent to participate in the game.

The example of gambling *qua* a paradigm of 'pure procedural justice' shows that 'procedural justice' is a matter of combination of these two principles: (1) abiding by the publicly announced rules (whatever the rules are, they must be followed) and (2) the liberty of adult individuals to engage in lawful practices, even if they are detrimental to them. Neither of these principles is a principle of justice properly so-called. The first principle excludes cheating in gambling, not because of injustice but rather because it is *improper* to cheat, just as it is improper to break any other rules. This is a purely formal principle: general rules (here, rules defining procedures) must be correctly adhered to. If, therefore, someone reduces procedural justice to the strict application of general rules of procedure, he speaks in fact about the principle of consistency in the enforcement of valid rules. The second principle is one of non-paternalism: people may voluntarily agree to participate in practices which might be detrimental to them. '*Volenti non fit iniuria*' is not a principle of *justice*. There is nothing inconsistent in saying that I engaged in an unjust practice voluntarily. I may be silly to do it or I may do it just for fun, knowing in advance that I have little chance to turn the practice to my benefit; in either case, my voluntary access does not automatically make the practice just. I may be entitled to the money I win at roulette but there is nothing just about the distribution after the game.[84] My entitlement is of a formal, not moral, nature: according to valid public rules, or promises given, I have entitlements over certain goods if I satisfy the conditions stated in the rules. Procedures which yield those entitlements cannot be called 'just' if the resulting distribution is not characterized properly in terms of justice.

'Pure procedural justice' is, then, no principle of justice at all. It is not the case that, as Rawls alleges, "[a] fair procedure translates its fairness to the outcome".[85] Rather, it is the other way round: a just outcome makes the procedure just if this procedure maximizes the probability of bringing about this outcome. Since in 'pure procedural justice' cases no outcome can be just (or, for that matter, unjust; there is simply no standard of justice of outcome), talk about 'just procedure' seems inappropriate there. It seems appropriate, however, where we *do* have a criterion of a just outcome. Those types of justice Rawls calls 'perfect procedural justice' and 'imperfect procedural justice'. The difference is that 'perfect procedural justice' fully guarantees the attainment of the just outcome when a proper procedure is followed (e.g., equal division of a cake by the person who is to get the last piece) while 'imperfect procedural justice' yields the just result in most cases, although not always (e.g., procedural justice in criminal trials).[86]

Let us leave aside the question whether 'perfect procedural justice' is possible at all: Rawls himself expresses doubts about it ("perfect procedural justice is rare, if not impossible, in cases of much practical interest").[87] His example about the division of the cake would cease to be one of 'perfect procedural justice' if we rejected his assumption that "the fair division is an equal one" and adopted a desert-based assumption; for instance, that the person who contributed most to baking the cake should have the biggest slice. But the main point is that in those cases of 'procedural justice' where the justice of procedure is derived from the justice of outcome, it would be an error to make a dichotomous distinction between 'procedural' and 'substantive' (or 'material') justice. 'Procedural' justice is derivative from substantive justice. We call certain procedures 'just' in so far as we believe that they tend to produce materially just outcomes.

A criminal trial is a good example of the latter point. We have certain criteria of substantive justice referring to the outcome of the procedure: we believe, for instance, that only the guilty should be punished, that punishment should be proportionate to guilt and we also accept codified measures of punishment as just. Procedures are just if they are designed in such a way as to maximize the probability of this outcome. The prerequisite of a just outcome is the discovery of the truth about the criminal. Guarantees of 'natural justice', as it is called in England, or of 'due process of law', in the American terminology, are meant to maximize the probability of such a result.[88] They deserve to be called 'just' only in so far as we believe that, better than any other procedure, they lead to a just result; they are not just *per se*. They are considered to be principles of justice because of their tendency to produce just outcomes; consequently, it may happen that their observance, in some particular cases, will not lead to a just result, or even that just outcomes may be reached while proper procedures of 'natural justice' are disregarded.

This last case is, of course, highly unlikely; however, if we consistently believe that there are independent criteria for a just outcome, we must at least theoretically envisage a situation in which justice is achieved after any procedure whatsoever; that, for example, an innocent defendant is acquitted after a procedurally incorrect trial. A connection between procedural safeguards and material justice is empirical, not conceptual; we are entitled to ask whether the outcome of a correct procedure in any particular case is itself just. Whilst we admit that there are independent criteria for assessing just outcome, there is no reason to believe that "any treatment that would have been just according to an independent criterion for assessing outcomes, is in fact unjust if performed without employing an appropriate judicial process".[89] I find this last statement internally contradictory; the existence of an "independent criterion for assessing outcomes" entails that any distribution consistent with this criterion *is* just (not: 'would be' just), no matter how it was brought about. If, in a particular case, a random procedure happens to lead to the punishment of a guilty person, the outcome is just even though we would not praise a person for using such a technique. A distribution may be just by accident; the superiority of the principles of 'natural justice' is that they design procedures which maximize the probability of just decisions, while random procedures do not. But this is a matter of empirical wisdom, not of the intrinsic character of 'procedural justice'. Therefore, it is not true that "[d]ue process is a necessary, but not sufficient condition for just treatments".[90] It is neither a sufficient, nor a necessary condition, although it is probably the most reliable safeguard for reaching substantive justice.

My proposition that procedural justice is derivative from justice of outcome may be subject to the following objection. There are certain principles of due process of law which cannot be shown directly as more helpful than other alternative procedures in the discovery of truth about a criminal. For example, torturing the accused might, in particular circumstances, be a more efficient way of obtaining evidence; however, in civilized legal systems it is considered impermissible. The entire issue of inadmissible evidence cannot be reduced (an opponent of my argument might continue) to the question of achieving a *just* verdict because in some situations certain types of evidence which are considered inadmissible might lead more effectively to a just verdict, yet it would remain 'unjust' to use them. Hence, the argument would run that the justice of procedure is not always derived from the justice of the outcome.

My reply to this hypothetical argument would be as follows. There may be several reasons for making some types of evidence impermissible and not all of these are reducible to arguments about justice. For one thing, some methods of obtaining evidence entail the commission of a crime: torturing a suspect in order to obtain a confession involves infliction of suffering which is unlawful. Legalizing its use in the process of extortion of confessions would lead to a situation of using one evil in order to discover the truth about another evil. Certain prohibitions on some types of evidence (such as involuntary confessions) should be viewed, therefore, not as a matter of procedural justice but as bans on committing particular crimes. Even if these methods increase the probability of the discovery of the truth about a crime in some cases, it will be done at the price of committing another crime: between the justice of punishing the criminal and avoiding cruel measures, criminal law chooses the latter for humanitarian reasons. To a similar (although not exactly the same) category belong procedural privileges against self-incrimination or incrimination of a spouse (in some legal systems). The principle that a wife is absolved from a duty to give evidence against her husband means that the law deliberately gives up the possibility of maximizing substantive justice for the sake of humanitarian ends. Cross in his textbook on evidence admits that "reliance on the privilege [of non-self-incrimination] will sometimes obstruct the course of justice in the case in which it is claimed, and may militate against the discovery of crimes which ought to be traced in the public interest"[91] but this consideration is overriden by the humanitarian principle that no one should be obliged to jeopardize his life or liberty by answering questions on oath. The rationale for these privileges is similar to the rationale for inadmissibility of the previous examples of evidence unlawfully obtained. The just outcome of the criminal trial is its most important aim but it cannot be achieved by any means whatsoever. In certain situations justice must be sacrificed for the sake of important humanitarian values which must be protected even more stringently than the principle of justice. In other situations, the centrality of substantive justice is overriden by other important values, such as candour in relations between patients and physicians, necessary for the proper exercise of the medical profession (hence, medical professional privileges in criminal trials); mutual trust required in the exercise of the legal profession (hence, privileged professional communications between a lawyer and his client); confidentiality of religious confessions (hence, privileges of clergymen); national security (hence, privileges protecting military and State secrets), and so on and so forth. In a word, many restraints are imposed upon a procedure not for the sake of justice but in order to protect other substantive values.

But the rules governing inadmissibility of certain types of evidence are not always justified by arguments relating to humanitarianism, confidentiality, security, etc., as opposed to arguments of justice. Two other main types of argument are related directly to justice of outcome: the first is about frustrating criminal justice *in the long run*, the second is about the unreliability of certain types of evidence. First, it may be said that although certain types of evidence (for example, that extracted by torture) might in individual cases be useful in discovery of the truth, they will lead to the degeneration of the entire apparatus of law enforcement if legally permitted and, therefore, in the long run they will frustrate the justice of outcome. The legal possibility of using such inhuman means as torture would necessarily lead to disrespect (by police officers) for important procedural guarantees, including those that *are* justified by maximization of a just outcome. Thus, the use of those measures would entail the sacrifice of substantive justice in the long run, for short-term gains in substantive justice. A second argument is that most of these measures are unreliable, *ergo* counter-productive in attaining justice of outcome. After all, one of the reasons why involuntary confessions are inadmissible is that they may well be untrue: history provides many examples of people confessing, under physical violence, to crimes which they did not commit. The argument about lie-detectors is similar: as long as scientists are not absolutely sure about their reliability, the mandatory use of lie-detectors in the criminal process could lead to false impressions about certain things being proved beyond reasonable doubt through the use of this device. To this category also belong arguments about the hearsay rule in those legal systems where hearsay is inadmissible as evidence. It is claimed that reported statements are untrustworthy evidence of the facts stated. The weakness of this type of evidence is supported by the fact that the accuracy of the person whose words are quoted by another witness cannot be tested under cross-examination.[92] By the same token, the rule mentioned earlier that husband and wife are incompetent as witnesses for or against each other, is defended not only on humanitarian grounds but also on the basis of "a general unwillingness to use testimony of witnesses tempted by strong self-interest to testify falsely".[93]

In a word, certain procedural prohibitions which, at first sight, seem to put obstacles in the way of obtaining substantive justice, in reality are dictated by the principle of justice of outcome. If not, they are dictated by principles other than justice and cannot be called principles of 'procedural justice' but rather of humanitarianism; the only type of 'justice' which might be attributed to them is a purely formal principle of consistent application of valid rules.

It should be noted that procedural conceptions of justice may be formulated in a way which suggests that a conception is substantive in character; what matters is whether on its basis we may reconstruct restraints imposed upon the process or upon the outcome. For instance, a principle that a just solution should correspond with the view of a majority of those concerned is procedural because it does not impose any restraint upon the end-state which might be considered as an independent standard of justice. It cannot serve as a criterion of social justice because it does not provide the individuals concerned with any criterion upon which to base their opinions about justice. If Andrew, Brian and Charles are to decide about the distribution of nine apples among them, it is of no help to say that whatever they decide (unanimously, or by a 2 : 1 majority) is just since such a standard cannot be applied by each of them separately before the vote is taken. Each of them asks himself a question: "What is a just division of these apples?" and the answer must appeal to a standard independent of the outcome of their future vote. In turn, this outcome may be evaluated by the standard of justice. It may happen that the majority is *more likely* to grasp a just solution than a minority, but again, this may be not the case. Whatever the virtues of democracy (majority rule being considered here as synonymous with democratic procedure), there is no intrinsic relation between democracy and substantive justice.

This point, although seemingly self-evident, is worth stressing because now and again arguments are advanced which identify justice with democracy. For C. J. Friedrich, a political action is just when "it involves a comparative evaluation of the persons affected by the action and when that comparison accords with the values and beliefs of the political community"; hence, the fundamental aspect of justice is "the comparative evaluation of persons according to the prevailing values of a political community".[94] For Clarence Morris, justice is a translation of the public's aspirations into programs of action and no reference is made to any objective, substantive content of justice: "Lawmakers ... serve the cause of justice only when they seek to realize, not their own, but the public's aspirations".[95] But how do we know that what the current majority aspires to, is just? We may, as Friedrich and Morris actually do, adopt this view by definition but then what is the use of defining one political ideal in a way identical to another? It would not correspond to our intuitive notions if we identified justice with the prevailing opinion of a community, *whatever this opinion happens to be*. After all, questions such as: "Is what most of the people in this country seek, just?" are not nonsense. Even if we believe that the majority view should always be implemented (and probably very few people would accept this proposition without any reservations), still we wish to be able to retain the power of moral evaluation of the majority view. The democratic procedure is, at best, an embodiment of 'imperfect procedural justice' (in Rawlsian terminology) since, more often than not, it leads effectively to just results. Therefore, whatever its other virtues are, the arguments about justice of democracy must refer to justice of results, not to the mere fact that the results accord with the majority's opinion.

A special qualification must be added to the previous paragraph. There is an exception to the rule that democratic procedure does not yield just results automatically. When influence upon a political decision is considered a social good in itself, then, with regard to this particular good, the democratic procedure is the one that comes closest to equal distribution of this good. Now if we adopt the view that political justice demands equal say about public matters, then democracy is inherently just in the sense of justice of outcome. But this applies only to that particular good, and although it is an important one, it does not entail just distribution of other goods: welfare, educational opportunities, and so on. Political justice (understood as just distribution of the means of political influence) is an important part of social justice but not the overriding one. There may be situations when political justice (requiring democratic procedure) conflicts with social justice in the distribution of other important goods; when, for instance, the majority of society wants to deprive a small minority of its deserved welfare. I do not claim that political justice typically conflicts with other demands of social justice but there is no reason to exclude such a possibility. If, as I have mentioned already, there is a strong link between political justice and the just distribution of other social goods, this link is of an empirical, not a conceptual, nature. Since political justice is discussed traditionally under the heading of democratic theory, for the most part of this book (unless otherwise stated) I will take social justice to mean the just distribution of goods other than political influence.

CHAPTER 2

PROBLEMS OF JUSTIFICATION: SOCIAL CONTRACT AND INTUITION

What is just, what is unjust? Sometimes a voice within us claims to know. Whether or not we are trained as lawyers, that voice likes to announce, at times even to cry out: this is just, this is unjust. Not always, it is true, will this inner voice speak so decidedly. Sometimes it will remain indifferent, or waver, or even hold contradictory answers in readiness. But in many cases it will respond clearly and distinctly to a fact. What voice is this? Is it God who speaks? Is it nature?[1]

One possible answer to the question asked by Arnold Brecht is that this 'inner voice' is nothing but an expression of irrational emotions and, hence, any attempts at justification of various judgments of justice are bound to fail. If, as Alf Ross says, "[t]o invoke justice is the same thing as banging on the table",[2] then nothing sensible can be said about justification or defence of the principles of justice.

Many philosophers, however, have tried to find more solid grounds for proposed principles of justice than mere emotions. They propose methods of deriving principles of justice which, in a case of moral disagreement, can serve as an impartial test to distinguish the more plausible conceptions of justice from the less plausible. Perhaps currently the most influential view consists in derivation of principles of justice from a hypothetical social contract among imaginary persons in a situation where temptations to further one's own specific interests are eliminated. In my following remarks, I will discuss the validity of this view and I will take John Rawls's social contract theory as its illustration. My own position about moral justification will be presented negatively, through the criticism of other people's views (mainly Rawls's) rather than by a positive exposition. The reason for this is that, as will become clear, I accept the concept of reflective equilibrium as a significant and useful device in moral argument, and in fact apply it in Chapter 4 to defend a substantive conception of social justice. Hence, it is rather important to show in what respects, and why, one can accept Rawlsian reflective equilibrium without endorsing his contractarianism which I consider indefensible. The aim of this Chapter, so stated, dictates therefore an essentially polemical style of argument.

1. WHY IS SOCIAL CONTRACT RELEVANT?

The essential question raised about social contract theories is, of course: why should *we* be bound by a contract that did not take place, that is merely a hypothetical speculation and that was 'made' by persons in circumstances that do not resemble at all any of the real life situations to which this contract is applicable? In other words: why should people *not* in the 'original position' (to use Rawls's term for the precontractual stage) take any notice of a contract made by people in the original position? Why should *we* be bound by a contract made by *them*?

Rawls's explicit answer is much less plausible than the one implied in the general spirit of his theory. His explicit answer, given in almost the same wording at the beginning and at the very end of his book, is that "the conditions embodied in the description of the original position are ones that we do in fact accept" or, if we do not accept them, "then perhaps we can be persuaded to do so by philosophical reflection" (21, see also 587).[3] But it is strikingly inadequate as an answer to the question about the reasons for the relevance of an hypothetical social contract to real people. For one thing, what matters is an acceptance of the *principles* reached in the contract, not of the *conditions* of the original position. The description of the original position, once we have decided that the whole contract is but an hypothesis, is a matter of speculation. We may agree to them or not, just as we may agree to some of them (e.g. the condition of rationality) and reject others (e.g. the veil of ignorance) without necessarily endorsing the principles agreed upon by the original contractors. The agreement about the conditions of the original position does not commit us to any substantive principles of justice.

Furthermore, Rawls qualifies his initial strong statement about our *de facto* agreement by a reservation that "we can be persuaded" to agree to his proposals. But that clearly undermines the whole construction of consent as a source of the importance of the principles of justice. A contract may be binding because of an *actual*, even if only tacit, consent; it cannot be made binding by hypothetical consent as a probable result of 'persuasion'. Ronald Dworkin correctly remarks that "an hypothetical contract is not simply a pale form of an actual contract; it is no contract at all".[4] It is not enough, nor indeed appropriate, to say that I am bound by certain principles on the basis of a contract to which I would have adhered (but have not) were I enlightened by someone wiser or more virtuous. Perhaps I would, perhaps I would not; that is irrelevant because in fact I did *not* adhere to it and therefore this contract has no relevance for me.

But to follow the path suggested by Rawls in his passages about the relevance of the hypothetical contract is to pay him lip service: it leads to a search for consent that did not take place and, in addition, consent about something else (the conditions of the original position) rather than what is in question (the principles of justice). The appropriate answer to the question: "why should we be bound by an imaginary social contract?" is that the source of the importance of the principles of justice in this theory lies not in the consent but in the rightness, in the moral quality of those principles. Principles of justice are 'binding' by the force of moral arguments that they have in their support. The relevance of the principles of justice to us, actual people, is therefore to be found in good moral reasons for their application. The justificatory force of the original position consists in the creation of circumstances in which only the power of reason moulds a contract. To ask: "why should *we* be interested in principles reached by *them*?" is to misunderstand the essence of a social contract argument; 'they' are 'ourselves' but projected into an imaginary, more rational and more moral world. The hypothetical-contract argument by its very nature rejects the distinction between: (1) an agreement between the parties to the original social contract, (2) an agreement between you and me about what is just. Therefore, in order to discern morally defensible principles of justice we should imagine ourselves as fully rational human beings *minus* all our bias stemming from our actual self-interest and then try to see if in such a situation we could reach an agreement acceptable to all. The fact that it *would* be acceptable is not an argument in favour of its validity but of its reasonableness. However, in the case of a theory of justice, that is all we need.

Although, as I have noted, Rawls himself partly contributes to the confusion between the morality of the principles and their obligatoriness (by suggesting that we actually accept the conditions of the original position), a careful reader of his book will realize that the real grounds of the obligatoriness of the principles of justice lie elsewhere, not in the contract argument. They are discussed by Rawls in the part of his book which deals with 'natural duties'. Here is the crucial phrase explaining the citizens' obligations stemming from the principles of justice: "[A] person is under an obligation to do his part as specified by the rules of an institution whenever he has voluntarily accepted the benefits of the scheme or has taken advantage of the opportunities it offers to advance his interests, provided that this institution is just or fair, that is, satisfies the two principles of justice" (342–43). Political obligation is derived therefore from *real* facts, not from an *hypothetical* contract. Those real facts are constituted by persons' adherence to a scheme of distribution, even if it is only a tacit adherence through actually benefiting from it. Hence, Rawls's theory regains a coherence: the reasonableness of the rules is derived from an hypothetical social contract, their obligatoriness — from the actual social facts referred to in the last quotation.

A good deal of the confusion of the reasonableness and obligatoriness of justice can be attributed, I believe, to the fact that traditionally various social contract theories either did not make a distinction between both (and served both aims at the same time) or were oriented toward the derivation of principles of obligation rather than of justice. The apparent similarity between traditional social contract theories (of Hobbes, Rousseau and in particular Locke) and the theory of Rawls, confused several critics[5] who took Rawls's theory to be a continuation and only a slight modification of the former, with a similar general aim. But there is an essential difference. For Locke, the social contract was fundamentally the source of the *legitimacy* of a government; for Rawls, the social contract is a device for demonstrating the *morality* of certain principles of justice. Locke's ideal of "government by consent" served to explain the grounds and principles of political obligation; there is a conceptual *iunctim* in his theory between arguments about the legitimacy of government and the principles of political morality. However, this parallel justification of both criteria can be served by a contractarian theory only under a certain condition that is met by Locke's theory but not Rawls's: that in a real society we can find actual traces or proofs (for example, in the form of consent) of the original social contract. To substantiate this view, this original social 'compact' must be thought to have been made between people as they are (or: as they were in a pre-contractual state), not as they are 'created' by the writer for the purposes of his theory. To be sure, Locke's social contract is not really 'hypothetical' in the same sense as the Rawlsian one; it is not a speculation about something purely fictitious yet useful for the purposes of social theory (as is the case with Rawls) but rather, it is an argument about the historical thesis that in all probability a contract took place about which for obvious reasons we have no record. In the 'Second Treatise' Locke advances several rational and historical arguments in order to prove "that Men are naturally free, ... that the *Governments* of the World, that were begun in Peace, had their beginning laid on that foundation and were *made by the Consent of the People*".[6] He also attempts to prove that people already born under a government voluntarily join the Commonwealth by tacit or express consent.[7] Thus Locke's social contract is purportedly an *actual* contract and it is entered into by *actual* consent.

It is therefore useful to distinguish those contractarian theories that derive the *obligatoriness*, and those that derive the *reasonableness* of certain principles from social contract. The first type, as exemplified by Locke or Hobbes, is constrained in its description of the conditions of a contract by the knowledge about actual human wants and aspirations and must trace the original contract to the consent to, or benefits derived from, civil society by real people. The second type of theory, as exemplified by Rawls, is not restricted by such conditions but, in turn, it has no claim as a justification of the obligatoriness of justice. Apart from this distinction, we can draw another classification of contractarian theories, along different lines. We can distinguish between those theories that conceive parties to a social contract as they actually are (or were) and those that construct imaginary people, deprived of certain actual characteristics and enriched with others, that actual people do not possess. This distinction only partly overlaps with the former. It is clear that a social contract which is a source of the *obligatoriness* of principles of justice must be made between people as they are (or are thought to be or have been); this guarantees some connection between the original social contract and the actual facts of social life that can be shown as traces of this contract. Characteristically, the very first phrase of Rousseau's *The Social Contract* reads: "I mean to inquire if, in the civil order, there can be any sure and legitimate rule of administration, men being taken *as they are* and laws as they might be".[8] But the second type of contract, that is, a social contract demonstrating *reasonableness* only, can be construed either as made between people 'as they are', or between imaginary people, 'created' especially for the occasion. The two distinctions described above cut across one another creating the following three main categories of social-contract arguments:

(1) a social contract among people as they are (or are thought to be, or to have been, in a precontractual state) grounding political obligation;
(2) a social contract among imaginary, ideal people, grounding the moral reasonableness of certain principles;
(3) a social contract among people as they are (or are thought to be ... etc.) grounding the moral reasonableness of certain principles.

The first and third social-contract arguments are compatible. Locke's social contract, for instance, justifies both political obligation and the morality of just principles. Hobbes, in turn, has only the first type of argument; from the original social contract "are derived all the *Rights*, and *Facultyes* of him, or them, on whom the Soveraigne Power is conferred by the consent of the

People assembled"[9] without implication that those arrangements can be described in terms of 'justice'. The example of a theory containing only the third type of social contract is provided by James Buchanan who constructs a complex contractarian process starting from the stage of 'natural distribution'. The major difference between his and Rawls's theory (which exemplifies the second type of contract theory) is that in Buchanan's contract "[t]here is nothing to suggest that men must enter the initial negotiating process as equals. Men enter *as they are* in some natural state . . . "[10] At the stage of this negotiating process, people are *already* in a situation of inequality and propose alternative solutions from their respective unequal positions. There is therefore no reason to predict that the postcontractual situation will be substantially different from the precontractual one. This is expressly admitted by Buchanan:

The specific distribution of rights that comes in the initial leap from anarchy is directly linked to the relative commands over goods and the relative freedom of behavior enjoyed by the separate persons in the previously existing natural state. . . . To the extent that such [precontractual] differences exist, postcontract inequality in property and in human rights must be predicted.[11]

But if the social contract is aimed at deriving just principles of distribution, how can this moral quality be obtained if the contract cannot but maintain and ratify the precontractual differences? And this is, Buchanan admits, the only reasonable expectation about the outcome of the contract. The contract is at the mercy of the 'natural distribution' and the latter cannot of course claim any moral legitimacy because, according to Buchanan's own assumption, at this precontractual stage quantities of scarce goods 'fall down' in fixed proportions onto several persons.[12] The way in which those goods 'fall down' cannot have any moral justification because it happens at the precontractual stage, and the contract is the necessary initial source of the morality of distribution. In short, if the *status quo ante* was not just, how can the outcome of a contract be just under the circumstances where the contract must replicate that prior state? The weight given to an initial allocation of goods is unjust; in consequence, the procedure devised by Buchanan amounts to sanctifying the *status quo*, and nothing else.

Buchanan's argument is subject to a further limitation. One could ask how unanimous agreement is conceivable *at all* in an hypothetical situation which does not exclude important differences (and the awareness of them) between the parties to the contract? What would be the motivation for the endorsement of, or adherence to, a contract ratifying prior inequalities on the part of the worse-off persons? One possible answer would be that those who are worse off have no choice anyway; they must agree to second-best options since the normalization of their situation under a contractual agreement is better than a state of uncertainty. The plausibility of this answer is questionable: one could argue, for instance, that in a situation of deprivation, uncertainty is to be preferred to certainty because at least there is some hope of improvement, and one could argue also that have-nots would choose revolutionary violence rather than ratification of their situation. Be that as it may, one thing seems clear: contract in the situation of inequality is *not* a proper ground for the derivation of principles for a just society. Consent under economic compulsion can hardly qualify as a source of the 'agreement among free men' postulated by Buchanan as a moral source of good social arrangements.[13] Those who are worse off under the conditions of 'natural distribution' do not choose the terms of the contract they enter; they adhere to it because they have no choice.

Buchanan maintains further that although wealth redistribution resulting from the hypothetical agreement is in principle inconceivable, both haves and have-nots will find the contract advantageous. Haves — because the contract safeguards their property rights, have-nots — because under contractual provisions richer people will "pay differentially higher shares in those goods and services provided jointly to the whole community".[14] But here again, serious doubts arise as to whether this sort of arrangement will indeed be found advantageous by all parties: it seems very likely that some contractors would prefer to use the contract to completely reorder the pattern of property relations. What is more important for the present argument, however, is that even if such an agreement were reached, it would be a *workable* arrangement but not necessarily a *just* one. The contractual sanction for non-moral distribution cannot make it just if, by force of the assumptions made, no alternative distribution would be consented to by those who are better off and who *know* they are better off.

In contrast, the Rawlsian idea of the 'veil of ignorance' and his assumption about the rationality and equality of people in the original position, offer significant advantages from the moral point of view as conditions for the derivation of principles of justice. It is an attempt to imagine a situation in which our views on justice are not clouded by our actual, real interests affected by our place in a distribution. In Rawls's words: "The veil of ignorance prevents us from shaping our moral view to accord with our own particular attachments and interests" (516). Intuitively, I see a good deal of sense in asking ourselves questions like this: "Assuming that I were not a taxpayer in this country, would I consider this taxation scheme just?" Even if, actually, I *am* a taxpayer in that particular country, this way of imagining an hypothetical situation is conducive to unbiased answers in which moral views are not affected by actual interests.

2. CONTRACT AND REFLECTIVE EQUILIBRIUM

At this point of my argument, I part company with Rawls. It is one thing to apply the test of the "veil of ignorance" to particular individual persons to detect their impartial views on justice. It is another thing to claim that the adoption of this perspective by all members of a society would lead to unanimous agreement about the principles of justice. In order to prove this second point, Rawls would have to defend two important propositions. He would have to demonstrate, first, that the conditions of the original position represent only the pure model of a rational choice situation and do not presuppose any substantive moral judgments (otherwise the argument would be circular). Second, he would have to prove that the same conditions of the original position cannot lead to the derivation of any other set of principles. Now, as a legion of critics of Rawls have shown, both these propositions are untenable; the common strategy for refuting them is to show that it is necessary to appeal to moral intuitions both in order to construct the original position and in order to derive the principles of justice, and that this appeal to intuitions conceptually precedes the derivation of the principles of justice.

Interestingly, Rawls does not deny this. With a striking frankness, he admits: "We want to define the original position so that we get the desired solution" (141). He also describes his aim as "to characterize this situation [that is, the original position] so that the principles that would be chosen, whatever they turn out to be, are acceptable from a moral point of view" (120) and he believes that his interpretation of the original position "best expresses the conditions that are widely thought reasonable to impose on the choice of principles" (121). But all this suggests that he has a view about a 'desired solution', about criteria of what is 'acceptable from a moral point of view' and a knowledge of 'conditions that are widely thought reasonable from a moral point of view' that are *prior* to the original position and the derivation of principles of justice. How is it possible to reconcile these *a priori* moral assumptions with the general purpose of his method which is "to derive satisfactory principles from the weakest possible assumptions" and with the methodological postulate that "[t]he premises of the theory should be simple and reasonable conditions that everyone or most everyone would grant" (520-21)?

If, as Rawls admits, the derivation of the principles of justice is tailored to suit some prior moral conceptions, the obvious question is: what are the justifying grounds of those *prior* moral judgments? It is certainly not the fact that they are 'widely' thought reasonable'. The justification of moral principles is not a matter of counting heads; Rawls obviously does not hold a theory that whatever people think just, is just. He expressly states that "[f] or the purposes of this book, the views of the reader and the author are the only ones that count" (50). But if, at the same time, the description of the original position and the derivation of the principles must fit some prior moral judgments (even if only those of the reader and the author), the only way to interpret the nature of these judgments is to take them as a product of moral intuitions. In that case the social contract has no independent justificatory force but is merely an expository or didactic device for describing principles already held.

Consider a simple example. Two young men meet to play tennis. It is a sunny morning and one of them has to play with the sun in his eyes, which is an obvious disadvantage. For the sake of this argument let us assume that there do not exist (or the players do not know about) the generally accepted rules to do with alternating ends. Those two players are therefore to advance just principles for the purpose of their match. After the first game, Albert who happened to play looking into the sun, proposes a change. Their dialogue:

Albert: All right, now it's time to change ends.
Bill: Why? We have not agreed to any rule about changing ends so let us continue playing as we did up to now.
A: It is true that we did not agree expressly but I took it for granted that we would change. After some time we will change again.
B: Why did you take for granted such a rule? *I* did not and therefore I have no duty to do something I haven't agreed to.
A: You have no duty but it is the only just solution available in a situation when one of us has to play looking into the sun.
B: What is just about it?
A: Well, imagine that before we started playing, we sat down to discuss a just solution to this problem (something that as I see, we should have done but it is not too late because we can try to imagine our possible discussion). Do you think that if we reached an agreement acceptable to both of us (in a situation where neither of us knew who would actually play first looking into the sun), such an agreement could be called just?
B: Certainly, under the condition that both of us would have good reasons to agree to it.

A: Fine. Now look: we *knew* in advance that one of us would have to play looking into the sun but we did not know who it would be. We would agree also that there would be nothing just in solving this problem by *faits accomplis*, that is, in taking the better end by surprise, force and so on. Right?

B: Right.

A: In this case we would intend to design a procedure which would evenly distribute the burden. No one would then be disadvantaged overall. Right?

B: No.

A: (surprised) Why not?

B: Because such guidelines for designing a procedure would be based on some *a priori* assumption to which we had not agreed in advance. It would be, in this case, the assumption that some of the burdens of playing should be equally distributed.

A: Yes, but it is of the essence that in sport all participants should face equal obstacles and burdens, so that the person who is physically or technically better, wins.

B: No, it is not of the essence. It is only *your* view about the nature of sport.

A: But what is the sense of a sporting contest where the contestants do not have an equal chance of winning?

B: That is another matter, subject independently to agreement. Besides, your views about equal chance are controversial. Imagine that before our discussion we knew that one of us was a better player. Even if we did not realize *who*, we had good reason to believe that in the ranking list of our club one of us had recently fared better than the other. We do not know who, but we can check it after reaching agreement in principle. In such a case, it is just that the one (whoever it is) who is lower on the ranking list, play at the better end of the court. In this case the one, presumably the less skilful, has an equal chance and only in this way can the equality of opportunity postulated by you, be implemented.

A: This is ridiculous. Such a principle, if generally adopted, would totally distort all sporting competitions. Do you suggest that slower athletes should run half the distance only, or that stronger boxers should be allowed to use only one hand? All participants to the competition should be bound by the same rules, should face similar challenges and difficulties; otherwise sport would cease to be sport!

B: No, it would only cease to be sport as *you* understand it. For me the real nature of sport lies in the sheer pleasure of the game: this aim is best served when actual opportunities are equalized, and that requires taking into account also differences in skill. Therefore, the rule I propose (and would have proposed if we had discussed it before the match) would be: whoever is more skilful, plays looking into the sun.

This dialogue illustrates, I hope, that one and the same contract situation (note that neither of the players questions the conditions of the hypothetical 'original position') can be a basis for two (or more!) completely different sets of principles as a function of different prior evaluative assumptions. In the theory of Rawls, those are prior moral assumptions that cannot have any other source than intuition. Consider his idea of the lexical priority of liberty, that is, a rule saying that no amount of socio-economic gain (to which his Second Principle of Justice applies) is a good reason for accepting less extensive or less than equal liberty (described by the First Principle). This priority rule is derivable from the original position only if some additional moral judgments are accepted, which are not inherent in the initial contract situation itself. It does not follow solely from a rational choice situation with its 'weakest possible assumptions'. Although Rawls several times (*inter alia*, at pp. 542–43) promises that he will demonstrate *why* at a certain stage of socio-economic development, after the most urgent material needs are satisfied, "it becomes and then remains irrational from the standpoint of the original position to acknowledge a lesser liberty for the sake of greater material means and amenities of office" (542), he actually does not honour this promise. Nowhere in the passages dealing with the priority of liberty does he explain *why* it would be *irrational* for the original contractors to design a scheme of trade-off between liberty and economic gain. Whenever he asks himself a question about the grounds of the priority of liberty, he answers by asserting that, after basic needs are satisfied, liberty is more important than material gains. He says, for instance, that "[i]ncreasingly it becomes more important to secure the free internal life of the various communities of interests" (543), and he stresses "the central place of the primary good of self-respect and the desire of human beings to express their nature in a free social union with others" (543). This is simply the assertion of the moral primacy of the value of freedom over other values, and in particular, an assertion of the principle that no amount of economic gain (however large) can compensate for any loss of liberty (however slight). Those assertions are no "justification" of the priority of liberty in non-tautological terms, that is, in terms other than the supreme value of liberty. But Rawls repeatedly suggests that this principle would be adopted by the original contractors as the most reasonable, and therefore, that it can be justified by appealing to a value other than those directly postulated by this principle (otherwise the argument would be circular).

The most likely candidate for this other value would be prudence. In a characteristic 'justification' of the two principles of justice, Rawls says that

> the two principles of justice have a definite advantage [over the principle of utility and other conceptions of justice]. Not only do the parties protect their basic rights but they insure themselves against the worst eventualities. They run no chance of having to

acquiesce in a loss of freedom over the course of their life for the sake of a greater good enjoyed by others (176).

It is, however, a restatement of his position rather than an argument. The last two phrases warrant an opinion about the superiority of Rawlsian principles only if we assume that parties to the original position will unconditionally prefer freedom to material gains in case of conflict between both. But perhaps they are less seduced by the vision of the most extensive possible freedom than by the possibility of some additional socio-economic gains; perhaps they prefer rather to "run no chance" of having to give up some of the economic benefits? In this case it would be reasonable for them to approve a loss of a portion of their freedom "for the sake of greater good enjoyed by others" if the scheme satisfies the Difference Principle, that is if greater good is enjoyed by the worst-off. The priority of liberty is therefore assumed by Rawls rather than justified; it is one of the evaluative assumptions of his theory that cannot be considered to be among "the weakest possible assumptions".

If these remarks are correct, then it seems that the original contractors would consider Rawls's view of the priority of liberty to be the most reasonable one only on the basis of some prior judgments. But in the Rawlsian social contract, such prior judgments have no moral force. Rawls stresses that "in their deliberations the parties [to the original contract] are not required to apply, nor are they bound by, any antecedently given principles of right and justice" and that "there exists no standpoint external to the parties' own perspective from which they are constrained by prior and independent principles in questions of justice".[15] If such prior moral constraints do not exist, the derivation of the principles of justice from the original position (as the most reasonable set of principles derivable from this position) is unwarranted. This conclusion cannot but be strengthened by Rawls's own account of the original position in terms of 'pure procedural justice' in which there exist no independent criteria of the just outcomes but only criteria of just procedures. With regard to the social contract in the original position "[t]his means that whatever principles the parties select from the list of alternative conceptions presented to them are just".[16] Now, if they are not bound by any constraints, there is no reason to believe that they will choose the priority of liberty or any other elements of his conception of justice. Everything of course depends on *who* presents to the contractors the list of alternatives and by what constraints *he* is bound. Now, if the original position is designed in such a way as to exclude the possibility of choice of some principles which are contrary to prior moral judgments, then the parties to the original contract are nothing more than puppets moved by the invisible hand of the author and are bound by *his* moral constraints. But that only shifts the matter of precontractual, substantive, moral intuitions from the position of the 'contractors' to the position of their creator.

To be sure, there is in Rawls a device for establishing a coherence between intuitive moral judgments and principles of justice, as agreed to in the original position. 'Reflective equilibrium' is a two-way deliberative movement between our considered convictions of justice and the principles derived from the original position. In order to achieve equilibrium, we may either change the circumstances of the original position (so that the principles derived from it match our intuitive judgments) or modify our convictions, especially when we are not confident about them. In the case of very strong moral convictions (such as, Rawls says, that religious intolerance or racial discrimination are unjust) we would rather alter the conditions of the original position in order to derive principles that are consistent with these judgments. In other cases (such as, Rawls suggests, distribution of wealth and authority), we will look into already established moral principles to find some guidance in these matters. Equilibrium is achieved when our principles finally match our judgments.

This view seems to recognize the role of intuition quite expressly. In its 'from judgments to principles' part, reflective equilibrium appeals directly to our strongly held judgments which cannot be derived from the original position because it is the latter that is scrutinized using those considered judgments: "[w]e can check an interpretation of the initial situation ... by the capacity of its principles to accommodate our firmest convictions and to provide guidance where guidance is needed" (20). So far so good; the problem arises over *where* the distinction between the judgments about which we are 'confident' (and which therefore serve as the test for the original position and principles derived from it) and those about which "we have much less assurance" (and which, in consequence, are modifiable to comply with the principles) is to be drawn. The distinction between more and less strongly held principles determines the direction of argument in the reflective equilibrium: in the first case it is 'from judgments to principles', in the second: 'from principles to judgments'. The appeal to intuition is evident only in the first type of reflective-equilibrium process; in the second type, the appeal to intuition is indirect, via the coherence argument (that is, the coherence of judgments about which we are uncertain with the principles that we have already firmly established). But the line between the first and the second type of judgment cannot be drawn otherwise than by an appeal to intuition. Rawls considers the condemnation of religious intolerance and racial discrimination as strongly held moral convictions ("fixed points of our considered judgments of justice") while, according to him, views about the correct distribution of wealth and authority give rise to moral doubts and are held without confidence (19–20, see also 206). But we can very well imagine a person having an opposite moral position; that is, confident about the morality of a certain type of political structure and wealth distribution, but hesitating about the justification and the scope of religious tolerance. To suggest therefore a moral system in which a line between those two types of judgment can be drawn is again to rely heavily on intuition which would determine the different levels of certainty of various judgments.

It is not, of course, my pretence that there is anything startlingly novel in showing that a conception of justice relies on moral intuitions. No philosopher is a magician who can derive substantive moral principles from neutral assumptions. Rawls himself admits that "any conception of justice will have to rely on intuition to some degree" (41). But if this 'degree' turns out to be very high, the justificatory power of the contract argument becomes questionable. Let us sum up: one half of moral reasoning (that is to say, of 'reflective equilibrium') appeals directly to intuitions, the other half – indirectly (in so far as the conditions of the original position are tailored to fit moral intuitions). It is hard to see any room for a contract argument as an independent source of moral opinions. Rawls, however, very clearly attributes such an independent justificatory role to the original contract: "certain principles of justice are justified because they would be agreed to in an initial situation of equality" (21). But this 'initial situation' itself is constructed so that it matches our convictions; it cannot therefore serve as an independent justificatory argument.

Now, 'reflective equilibrium' *does* have an important role in actual moral reasoning as a device for bringing about coherence of general moral principles and particular moral judgments. It is also a fair description of our usual reasoning about hard moral cases: we try to work out a general principle on the basis of our strongly held particular judgments (inductive reasoning) and then apply this moral principle to a difficult or controversial issue (deductive reasoning). In the situation of a clash between a general principle (established on the basis of some other particular convictions) and a particular judgment of justice, we may either modify the general principle or change the particular judgment. Aversion to changing the principle when it clashes with strong moral convictions is a symptom of moral dogmatism; incapacity to change judgments of justice when principles so dictate is a sign of an unprincipled, case-by-case approach to morality. Those two deviations should be avoided by a two-way approach to a 'reflective equilibrium', but a decision about which way should be chosen in any particular instance is to be made by the person who makes the moral decision or proposes the moral principle. Ultimately, it depends on the relative intensity of our convictions and principles. If, however, we decide to modify a principle under the influence of a very strong particular judgment of justice, we must remember that its change will lead to a change in some other particular judgment of justice on the basis of which we have established the very principle that is subject to a change now.

'Reflective equilibrium' is, thus, a useful and adequate description of the introduction of coherence into a moral system through a combination of inductive and deductive reasoning. This is a method I will invoke when advancing a substantive principle of social justice.[17] But if we want to avoid the error of circularity, the 'equilibrium' must have its 'external' source. It is not a satisfactory argument if we say, for instance: racial and religious discrimination are immoral therefore all discrimination on irrelevant grounds is immoral (induction); discrimination against women is based on irrelevant grounds therefore it is immoral (deduction). Although that is probably the way we actually often think, a moral theory tries to find some justificatory source for the whole argument. Such an 'external' source of reflective equilibrium in Rawls's theory is provided by an hypothetical social contract but, for reasons suggested above, I think it cannot be seen as an independent moral source because the conditions of the contract are already moulded by the convictions of justice that are believed to be a part of 'reflective equilibrium'. What is the source of those convictions that influence the conditions of the initial contractual situation? Answering this question Rawls, as I have indicated above, must appeal either directly or indirectly to intuition. Hence social contract is superfluous as a part of moral justification: it can be viewed as a useful didactic tool, but as a part of 'reflective equilibrium' it creates an illusion that it is an 'objective', non-intuitive factor in justification. In a recently published article Rawls declares that:

[t]he aim of political philosophy ... is to articulate and to make explicit those shared notions and principles thought to be already latent in common sense; or, as is often the case, if common sense is hesitant and uncertain, ... to propose to it certain conceptions and principles congenial to its most essential convictions.[18]

Hence it is clear that, for Rawls, common-sense precepts, 'essential convictions' and 'historical traditions' are *prior* to, not derived from, conditions for a social contract. They shape the structure of the original position, not the other way round.

3. INTUITION AND INTUITIONISM

The upshot of these considerations is that ultimately we appeal to our moral intuitions when proposing principles of justice and that the job done by an hypothetical social contract is derivative from prior moral intuitions. Now this view may seem very unsatisfactory to those who seek more reliable grounds for the principles of social justice than something so enigmatic and obscure as moral intuitions. Besides, this view may also be objectionable to those who are offended by the apparent absolutism of 'intuitionism' conceived as a theory postulating the discovery of self-evident moral truths by means of 'direct insight'. Ironically then, direct appeal to moral intuition is susceptible to quite opposite objections: that it is too weak and that it is too strong, that it does not help solve moral controversies and that it attempts to impose arbitrarily 'true' answers to difficult moral questions.

To take up the second point first, I should like to suggest that the ultimate appeal to moral intuitions in defending moral principles and judgments does not necessarily entail endorsement of a meta-ethical theory known as 'intuitionism', with all its traps and overstatements. In particular, it does not necessarily entail two views shared by meta-ethical intuitionists: firstly, that truth and falsity can be attributed to moral judgments and hence that morality is a matter of 'knowing' (although in a different sense than knowledge about natural facts), and secondly, that moral truths are self-evident, necessary and indubitable because they are propositions synthetic *a priori*.[19] Without entering into the debate on merits or demerits of such radical intuitionism, it seems to me that the view endorsing these two points has at least one practical setback: it clouds rather than illuminates the seriousness of moral disagreements about judgments and principles of justice. If the persistence and the inevitability of such disagreements is taken to be one of the most important facts about morality, and in particular about judgments of social justice, then meta-ethical intuitionism is hardly helpful in explaining the nature and the sources of such disagreements. The version of intuitionism which endorses the two propositions cited above, cannot avoid the conclusion that in cases of moral controversy some people know the truth, others are mistaken. In consequence the intuitionist will end up with a statement that "the fact that people disagree in moral matters, even concerning basic, ultimate moral issues, is evidence that they cannot all be right, not that the judgments involved are incapable of truth or falsity."[20] This view, although theoretically coherent, is of no help when actual moral disagreements arise. If, on the one hand, people's moral judgments are thought to be a matter of truth and falsity and, on the other hand, those judgments obviously differ among themselves, how are we to know whose intuition is capable of discerning the moral truth and whose intuition is deficient? Intuitionism claims that there is a moral truth and that it is discernible by intuition but it fails to help us to select the moral truth from among the variety of moral judgments. How can we distinguish a genuine moral intuition from a false one?

To be sure, an intuitionist does not have to answer this question. It is theoretically possible to hold the view that moral propositions are about the truth and at the same time that this truth is unverifiable in cases where disagreement arises. The very fact of the existence of moral disagreements is therefore too weak an argument against intuitionist meta-ethics, contrary to what some of its critics claim.[21] But it is a sufficient argument against the usefulness of this theory. After all, the most obvious question that arises about the intuitionist claim that moral truth is self-evident is: self-evident to whom? Actual moral disagreements suggest that this 'self-evidence' must be represented by some special inner faculties of persons whose intuitions are better than those of others — but this is a path that very few contemporary intuitionists would like to follow.

The other type of objection to intuitionism is put forward by Rawls. His main argument is that intuitionism is of no help in weighing moral principles against one another in case of conflicting values, because it contains no priority rules and "we are simply to strike a balance by intuition, by what seems to us most nearly right" (34). This 'no-priority-rules' argument is by far the most important objection that Rawls formulates in his criticism of intuitionism. We are told that "[t]he intuitionist believes ... that the complexity of the moral facts defies our efforts to give a full account of our judgments and necessitates a plurality of competing principles" (39). However, what Rawls is arguing against is but one possible version of intuitionism, rather unrepresentative and manifestly implausible. The view that he is refuting is that moral intuitions (which are sources of our judgments) cannot prescribe any priority rules in case of competing values or principles: no principle is ultimate, there is a plurality of second-to-ultimate principles and conflicts among them are practically solved only on a case-by-case basis. According to Rawls, "[i]ntuitionism holds that in our judgments of social justice we must eventually reach a plurality of first principles in regard to which we can only say that it seems to us more correct to balance them this way rather than that." (39) This is, however, to attack a man of straw. The version of intuitionism criticized by Rawls, although conceivable, contains an incomplete conception of justice. It states that there are several 'first principles' (in fact, by virtue of their plurality, they are only 'second principles') but by failing to prescribe priority rules it is useless for guiding our actions in hard cases. There is no reason to think that a meta-ethical theory of intuitionism must be linked to an incomplete conception of justice; intuitionism may, just as any other theory, postulate definite priority rules. If we can intuit several 'first principles', why can we not intuit *the* first principle? There is no reason for moral intuition to stop at an intermediate level in the hierarchy of moral principles. Actually, Rawls himself observes: "Perhaps it would be better if we were to speak of intuitionism in this broad sense as pluralism" (35). I suppose it would be better, indeed. But in this case his objections would hold against *any* form of moral pluralism that might just as well be a social-contract theory as an intuitionist one, and then it would become obvious that his arguments are not relevant as a criticism of intuition as a moral source. R. M. Hare rightly observes that "[t]here can also be another, non-pluralistic kind of intuitionist — one who intuits the validity of a single method, and erects his entire structure of moral thought on this".[22] Rawls's arguments about the weakness of intuition are therefore misdirected; they probably stem partly from a confusion of the meta-ethical theory of intuitionism with the normative intuitionist moral philosophy that is actually refuted (in one of its versions) by Rawls.[23]

Intuitionism's weakness lies elsewhere: not in the fact that it does not guide our actions by clear priority rules but that the scope of interpersonal arguments about them is so limited. People's values, including principles of justice, are not, as emotivists maintain, merely expressions of their emotions or recommendations of actions. They are not totally 'arbitrary' or 'irrational'. Principles of justice are often the result of rational considerations about the possible consequences of various rules, structures and actions; the consequences for human beings in terms of their life, dignity, prosperity, liberty. People value certain principles because they *know* (or think that they know) possible consequences of putting them into practice: this is a 'rational' part of the arguments about justice and this is a legitimate field for moral dialogue. If someone bases his moral position on a proposition of fact which is false, then we are justified in disqualifying this moral position on this ground alone. Moral judgments are not derived from facts but they correspond in a certain way to facts. People make their judgments not always arbitrarily and not always as emotional responses to challenges but also as considered convictions based upon expected consequences resulting from acting upon them. Yet, the ultimate evaluation of those consequences hangs upon subjective principles, upon standards of right and wrong underivable from empirical facts or from even higher standards. Those ultimate value judgments cannot be argued about in terms of empirical facts because the latter are assessed by the former. Reflection upon the facts and the facts *alone* does not entitle us to make value judgments about them. In this sense the appeal to intuition is subjectivist without being emotivist and without, on the other hand, necessitating any claim to discovery of self-evident 'moral truth'.

The suggestion that intuitions are not mere emotions implies that there is some room for debate about, and defence or criticism of, moral judgments. To begin with, we may properly ask about the reasons for having particular moral judgments: the inability to produce any reasons seems to disqualify the judgment in question. Further, we may see whether these reasons pass the test of universalization, that is, whether they can be regarded as grounds for moral *rules* controlling human behaviour in a regular fashion, rather than as mere *ad hoc* postulates of a particular action by a particular person. We may also inquire into whether the proposed moral judgment reflects something more than the self-interest of a person who holds this judgment. We tend, properly, to see some degree of impartiality as endemic to morality as a whole. Further, we may stipulate that it is not good enough, in defending moral judgments, merely to point to some external authority dictating these judgments: the acceptable reasons must rely on their substance rather than on their pedigree. Accordingly, the fact that this judgment is held by others does not amount to producing a good reason for it. We may also, as I have just mentioned, test the truth of assertions of facts referred to in conjunction with the moral reasons for holding particular judgments, for example, about the causal relation between observing a proposed moral rule and achieving some desired state of affairs. But having exhausted all these methods of testing reasons supporting value judgments, there is little we can do to 'disprove' them if they still conflict with our judgments which, we believe, also pass these tests. Ultimately, any moral disagreement is reducible to a statement of opposite values which are neither arbitrary expressions of emotion nor the opposition of truth and falsity. Appeal to intuition entails an admission of the limits, not the impossibility, of reason in moral matters.

The alternative: either our value judgments express 'moral truth' and therefore in case of disagreements at least one view is mistaken, or our judgments are totally arbitrary and irrational, does not exhaust the whole list of possible approaches to morality. The view that I would like to endorse is that moral judgments are neither arbitrary nor verifiable in interpersonal discourse. The fact that people cannot prove the truth of their principles of justice and that those principles cannot be attributed 'truth' from any human point of view, does not necessarily mean that those people hold their respective views without any rational justification. Those judgments cannot be 'proved' but they can be justified; they can be justified, but they cannot be agreed upon by all. Not because some of them are less strongly justified, and not because some people are less rational or more biased; the lack of moral consensus is not a contingent, but an inherent feature of human morality. Human disagreements about considered principles of justice and the impossibility of reaching any consensus in interpersonal discourse, express the very nature of morality. It would be, of course, convenient if we could demonstrate that the value judgments which play an important role in a proposed reflective equilibrium are shared by a significant number of people. This does not add any moral weight to the argument, since the moral rightness is not contingent upon the scope of public support. However, if one attempts to propose a theory of justice aspiring to be an ideal standard by which law is to be judged, then it is useful to show that this standard is not totally eccentric but, on the contrary, that it derives from some values shared by the people who are subject to the particular legal system. To facilitate argument, it is an advantage to show that a theory of justice which is to be a yardstick by which a legal system is judged, identifies, interprets, and elevates to the level of general principles some of the deeply entrenched moral judgments shared by the members of this community. Such a procedure is inevitably selective in that it deliberately appeals to some values rather than to others, and we should realize that to strive for a universal moral consensus on matters of moral judgments is to be doomed to failure.

CHAPTER 3

SUBSTANTIVE JUSTICE AND EQUALITY BEFORE THE LAW

Conformity to the principle of equality before the law is usually considered one of the principal virtues which legal systems can exhibit. The meaning of this principle is, however, more problematical than it may at first appear. What does it mean to say that all should be equal before the law or that law should be equal for all? Does it mean that all citizens subject to a given legal system should have the same rights and duties, that they should be, in other words, addressees of the same legal rules? Each legal system contains rules which are addressed to certain classes of citizens (for example, professional groups): do these rules inevitably violate the principle of equality before the law? This is the central question as far as equality before the law is concerned.

The rationale of discussing the question of legal equality before I turn to the principles of social justice is as follows: one of the typical arguments against reforms aimed at achieving 'social justice' is that the use of law as a tool for bringing about substantive justice undermines the generality and the universality of legal rules. The quest for social justice is said to corrupt legal generality; in consequence, 'equality before the law' and the legal enforcement of social justice are incompatible, we are told by the critics of the ideal of social justice. Social justice is a matter of redistribution of wealth, power and opportunities among social groups; equal and universal law does not recognize people as members of groups but as members of the entire community and treats all of them, irrespective of their group characteristics, in the same way. If law (the argument concludes) is conceived as a purposive tool of specific social arrangements, it will inevitably lose its universality: it will become biased, favouring some groups and disadvantaging others.[1]

It is necessary to consider this argument before the discussion of social justice itself. I take it that legal equality is something good rather than bad. Hence, even though social justice may be valued by some people more highly, if implementing it had a destructive impact on legal equality indeed, the argument about legal equality would weigh heavily against the ideals of social justice.

1. EQUALITY BEFORE THE LAW AND EQUALITY IN LAW

Equality as applied to law may have two distinct meanings: equality *before* the law (or, in other words, equality in the application of law) and equality *in* law (that is, equality in the content of legal rules).[2] The principle of legal equality may therefore mean either that valid legal rules should be applied to all in the same way, which means that features irrelevant to the purpose of a given legal rule should not be taken into account in its application ('equality before the law'); or that legal rules themselves should not contain any discriminating and privileging provisions ('equality in the law'). This distinction was very clearly recognized by John Stuart Mill:

> The justice of giving *equal protection to the rights of all*, is maintained by those who support the most outrageous *inequality in the rights themselves*. Even in slave countries it is theoretically admitted that the rights of the slave, such as they are, ought to be as sacred as those of the master; and that a tribunal which fails to enforce them with equal strictness is wanting in justice . . . .[3]

Let us consider first equality *before* the law or, in Mill's words, "giving equal protection to the rights of all". This principle is nothing but an extrapolation to the field of law of the principle of equal treatment of equal individuals (or, more precisely, individuals who are equal according to relevant criteria, as determined by a general rule). Equal persons should be treated equally; unequal, unequally. As several theorists have correctly noted, this is not so much a principle of equality as one of non-arbitrariness. The principle of equal treatment of equal persons is a necessary consequence of the *general* nature of any rule which calls for certain treatment of certain persons in certain situations. The generality of a rule consists in its application to *all* future cases governed by that rule. The very essence of a rule is that it brings specific situations under a general scheme; hence all equal persons (equal, that is, from the point of view of that rule's criteria of classification) must be treated in the same way. By their very nature, rules (as distinguished from *ad hoc* decisions, addressed to a concrete individual at a particular point in time) prescribe the same treatment for persons who have the same characteristics. Those persons are, therefore, treated by this rule as equals in a certain respect. The principle of equal treatment is a logical consequence of controlling social life by a body of general rules as opposed to case-by-case and is identical with the principle of coherent and consistent action: 'in similar situations behave in a similar way'.

Equal treatment of equal persons is therefore nothing else but the *correct* application of a general rule. R. E. Flathman rightly states: "'Equally' means 'according to one and the same rule'. Whenever we treat according to a rule, we will be treating equally in respect to that rule."[4] Obviously the important question which arises is: *which* rule should be chosen? But the answer to that question cannot be provided by the principle of equal treatment. This last principle is neutral as to which differences are relevant and thus justify differentiated treatment.

The same applies to law. Equality in the application of legal rules means nothing more than that only differences which are relevant (from the point of view of the legal rule) should be taken into account when this rule is applied or enforced. It is the legal rule (and not, say, a judge's whim) that determines which differences are relevant. Equality before the law means, therefore, *correct* application of law — and nothing more. It means congruence between the rules as announced and their actual administration. In Kelsen's words, the principle of equality before the law "is the principle of legality, of lawfulness, which is immanent in every order. It is presented sometimes as justice under the law. But, in truth, it has nothing to do with justice at all".[5] This reduction of 'equality before the law' to lawfulness is made possible by the general and abstract nature of legal rules. And, as Mill noted in the passage quoted above, this kind of 'equal protection of the rights of all' need not entail equality in the rights themselves.

Let us now turn to the second meaning of legal equality: equality *in* law. Offhand it might appear that the ideal of non-discriminatory and non-privileging law is best expressed in the directive that law should be one and the same for all; that it should not prescribe any differentiated treatment; that all legal rules should be equally applicable to all legal subjects. In one of the decisions of the United States Supreme Court, Mr. Justice Jackson stated that "there is no more effective practical guaranty against arbitrary and unreasonable government than to require that the principles of law which officials would impose upon a minority must be imposed generally".[6] Jackson's concern is mainly practical; the requirement of universality and generality of legal rules is seen as a check on arbitrariness and unfair privileges or discriminations. This ideal finds its more theoretical expression in Jean-Jacques Rousseau's concept of the general will as the source of law. When discussing both the attributes and limits of the sovereign power, Rousseau states that "the general will, to be really such, must be general in its object as well as its essence; . . . it must both come from all and apply to all". He concludes:

By whatever path we return to our principle we always arrive at the same conclusion, viz., that the social compact establishes among the citizens such an equality that they all pledge themselves under the same conditions and ought all to enjoy the same rights. Thus, by the nature of the compact, every act of sovereignty, that is, every authentic act of the general will, binds or favors equally all the citizens; so that the sovereign knows only the body of the nation, and distinguishes none of those that compose it .... Thus we see that the sovereign power, wholly absolute, wholly sacred, and wholly inviolable as it is, does not, and cannot, pass the limits of general conventions; ... so that the sovereign never has a right to burden one subject more than another, because then the matter becomes particular and his power is no longer competent.[7]

Rousseau's radical aversion to all 'particular matters' is, of course, connected with his distrust of all associations, 'factions', all *corps intermédiaires* between the sovereign and an individual. In Rousseau, the sovereign power communicates with society as a whole and not with particular groups; otherwise it exceeds 'the limits of general conventions' and ceases to express a general will. But the ideal that law "binds or favors equally all the citizens" and that the Sovereign "distinguishes none of those that compose [the nation]" is obviously unrealistic. It would mean, for example, the abolition of maternity leave for women or special compensation for workers working in harmful and difficult conditions, and so on, and so forth. Intuitively, it seems self-evident that prohibition of every form of different treatment would be unjust, and impossible anyway.

The main problem is that equal treatment 'as such', in a global sense and without any qualifications, does not exist. Equal legal treatment of certain individuals in certain respects (that is to say, from the point of view of certain properties of those individuals) is, at the same time, inevitably unequal treatment of the same individuals in different respects (that is, from the point of view of other properties of the same individuals). Equal treatment of individuals with respect to one criterion presupposes unequal treatment of these individuals with respect to another criterion. Everything depends on the criteria of classification (and, consequently, the particular differences among persons) that one regards as relevant to treatment in a particular field.[8] As it is impossible to treat people equally in one respect without at the same time treating them unequally in other respects, 'equality in the law' concerns the appropriateness of the criteria by which one chooses to classify people by legal norms. One's positive evaluation of a given legal system on the grounds of 'equality in law' means, therefore, that one accepts the criteria of classification used by that legal system as justified. This means that the observer making a judgment about equality in law accepts the lawmaker's views about what people are similarly situated for the purpose of the particular treatment in question. If, to take the example of sex classification in the law concerning military service,[9] one believes, as does Mr. Justice Rehnquist, that men and women are differently situated for the purposes of the draft because women as a group, unlike men, are not eligible for combat, and if one approves of this practice, then sex classification in this case is demanded by the principle of equal treatment or, more precisely, the corollary principle of unequal treatment of unequals.[10] If, however, one believes with Mr. Justice Marshall that female conscripts perform equally well as male conscripts in certain military positions, then this classification must be viewed by him as the unequal treatment of persons who are equal in a relevant sense.[11] Both these conflicting conclusions are directly derived from divergent moral views about what is the proper role of women in a community as well as some beliefs about the physiological and psychological properties of women that make them fit or not for military service. The view that women and men are unequally situated in relation to this legislative purpose (registration for the draft) is *a consequence, not a premise*, of the view that for some reason of morality or expediency it is wrong to require women to go in for military service.

Social and legal practice provide innumerable other examples of the fact that 'equal' treatment may be viewed always as unequal treatment from the point of view of some other properties of legal subjects. Take, for example, admission to universities. A system which selects candidates primarily on the basis of their competence (assume, for the sake of this example, that competence may be measured by some reliable tests), treats them equally from the point of view of that particular conception of competence but unequally from the point of view of their real social chance of acquiring that competence. A system of preferential admissions for socially deprived minorities tries to establish equality from the point of view of social chances of obtaining knowledge judged relevant to university admissions, but at the same time treats unequally from the point of view of the actual 'amount' of their competence understood as a sum of knowledge. Thus one and the same system can be considered by some people as satisfying the demands of 'equality in law' and by others as conflicting with that equality. This judgment depends on which properties are considered relevant in that area.

The conclusion which can be drawn from these examples seems clear: it is both unjust and impossible to abolish classifications of legal subjects by legal rules; it is, therefore, a mistake to see the standard of 'equality in law' as being that law does not prescribe differentiated treatment. This postulate is identical with a rejection of any legal classifications of persons, with a demand that once a legal rule confers certain rights or imposes duties upon a certain group it should confer those same rights and impose those same duties upon all the citizens who are subject to the legal system. This demand is usually accompanied by an argument that the particular classifications are based on human properties that are in fact irrelevant to the ascription of particular rights and duties and therefore that the differences between people based on those properties do not justify different treatment. Now, very often it is true and often old beliefs that regard some human characteristics as relevant to different sorts of treatment turn out to be false or immoral. A little over thirty years ago, it was written approvingly in a prestigious American law journal that occupational limitation laws which prohibited women from working in liquor establishments, or from frequenting them after certain hours, constituted "an attempt to avert the possibility of the danger to public morals which [the legislature] sees inherent in a blend of liquor and women".[12] This strikes us today as blatant male chauvinism: why should 'a blend of liquor and women' warrant more concern by a legislator than 'a blend of liquor and men'? But it does not follow from this that the fewer classifications there are, the more just or non-discriminatory a legal system is. Progress in law is not an approximation to an ideal in which there are no classifications. Old classifications are replaced by new ones, based upon principles or beliefs which were not generally recognized as valid or true before. The prohibition of child labour is a relatively new legal invention and it introduces a classification of people into children and adults with respect to the legal regulation of labour. But it is not a violation of the principle of equality because it is universally recognized that with respect to work children and adults are relevantly different.

The hypothetical situation in which all the legal rules are applicable to all citizens is hence not a proper test for 'equality in law'. What we actually mean when we speak of equality in a certain legal system is that we accept the choice of particular properties as relevant to differentiated treatment. It is, therefore, a choice of certain *equalities* (and in consequence, certain inequalities) as justified (because relevant) which makes us speak about *equality* in law. But what does it mean to say that criteria of classification are relevant? In his excellent essay 'Notes on the Rule of Equal Law' Geoffrey Marshall convincingly shows that no objective and non-controversial standard of 'relevance' can be found.[13] The formulae that distinctions among individuals should be 'intelligible' or 'rationally related to the object' may be verifiable but are unsatisfactory from the moral point of view. The formula that these distinctions should be 'just' is obviously satisfactory but applying this criterion presupposes substantive ethical considerations.

The reasonableness of the choice of certain criteria for classification of people by legal rules rests upon value judgments; for instance, that it is 'just' (or 'useful' or 'wise') to admit people to the universities on the basis of their merit only. Any other practical solution would be considered 'unequal' by the same observer because he would judge it unjust. This evaluation is based upon a hierarchy of values which cannot be reduced to the value of equality.[14] The statement that a certain classification of legal subjects is compatible with equality in law requires the prior recognition of a particular basis of classification as morally right, or good, or just.

2. NON-DISCRIMINATORY CLASSIFICATIONS

Much of the jurisprudential discussion has been concerned with determining the criteria of benign classification. I will examine some of the typical arguments of this kind and will try to see if the proposed criteria of benign classification can be construed without direct appeal to substantive ideas about social justice. I will discuss here three main models of such criteria. The first model was offered by Friedrich A. Hayek in his *Constitution of Liberty*. He recognizes that the problem of classifications is crucial for the ideal of legal equality:

> The requirement that the rules of true law be general does not mean that sometimes special rules may not apply to different classes of people if they refer to properties that only some people possess. There may be rules that can apply only to women or to the blind or to persons above a certain age.[15]

The test for distinguishing discriminatory from non-discriminatory classifications Hayek sees not in the nature of those "properties that only some people possess", nor even in their relevance to the object of classification. He proposes the following criterion:

> Such distinctions will not be arbitrary, will not subject one group to the will of others, if they are equally recognized as justified by those inside and those outside the group. ... So long as, for instance, the distinction is favored by the majority both inside and outside the group, there is a strong presumption that it serves the ends of both. When, however, only those inside the group favor the distinction, it is clearly privilege; while if only those outside favor it, it is discrimination. What is privilege to some is, of course, always discrimination to the rest.[16]

Hayek's double majority condition raises important difficulties. One of the problems is its evident impracticability. Imagine that a community wants to impose, on meat producers, a requirement of sanitary inspection of meat before it is offered for sale. This is a rule which is addressed only to a certain class of people, namely, to meat producers. Hayek's principle requires the approval of the regulation both by a majority of producers and a majority of the rest of society. It is very improbable that meat producers will favour a regulation which imposes some additional burden on them. In the same way, the bulk of regulations imposing constraints on certain professional groups would probably fail to obtain double majority approval. But impracticability is not the only problem. I cannot see what justification there would be for giving to professional (or any other) groups a power to veto a regulation imposing on them certain obligations closely related to their social functions. Such a solution, like every form of 'double' or 'reinforced' majority rule, leads to minority rule for it gives a minority power to veto the rule favoured by a majority. It is difficult to see how this can be made compatible with a democratic creed.

Be that as it may, the crucial difficulty with Hayek's criterion is that it does not solve the problem but simply shifts it onto the level of majority opinion. A social or legal thinker, when asked about the proper criteria of classification, should try to state some more substantive criteria rather than merely point to majority opinions. For it may well happen that it is the majotity itself that expects the thinker to propose some criteria for them. This is perfectly compatible with adherence to democratic principles: the majority view should prevail when it comes to making binding decisions, but social or legal philosophers should give some more substantive answers beforehand about what discrimination is, rather than say that discrimination is what is considered discrimination by the group concerned or by the rest of society. Hayek's answer simply amounts to shifting the burden of answering onto two majorities. But opinion polls do not anoint moral judgments with reasonableness. A political or legal philosopher, unlike a legislator in a democratic country, is not obliged to follow current majority opinions. He may (and should) propose some substantive solutions. But Hayek's conception certainly does not satisfy that expectation.

Of course, it is not unimportant whether people subjectively feel discriminated against or not, just as it is not unimportant whether they feel hurt, harmed, persecuted, coerced, humiliated and so on. Important as it is, it may at best serve only as a signal that closer investigation into the matter is required. The sense of injustice may be caused by various factors not necessarily related to actual discrimination: the level of consciousness, ideological distortions, indoctrination. This feeling may accompany or not the actual facts of discrimination. The fact that, for instance, women relatively recently started to perceive their situation in many societies as discriminatory does not mean that this discrimination began at the moment of this change in social awareness. One and the same practice may be perceived by some groups as discriminatory and by others as not discriminatory; it is not a majority that decides what treatment is just, although it is a majority that should in most cases decide what is to be done. There are situations when *any* action, practice or rule will be considered as discriminatory by a certain group that has its vested interests in that issue. For instance, preferential admissions to universities for deprived minorities will be perceived as discriminatory by the non-preferred majority but admissions based solely on the qualifications will be perceived as discriminatory by the minority that did not have access to or the opportunity for an equally good secondary education. Nevertheless, on the basis of a definite system of values only one of these practices is discriminatory. Moral judgment about discrimination is not a matter of counting heads but of having good moral reasons. It does not follow that there are some absolute moral standards independent of people's actual beliefs but it does imply that judgments about discrimination are based on the moral principles and values of observers who make those judgments.

The second model of discriminatory *versus* non-discriminatory classifications is directly concerned with the nature of the criteria of classification or, to use Hayek's words, with the nature of "properties that only some people possess". There are many theories of this sort; their common feature is that they concentrate their attention solely on the criteria of classification themselves, ignoring the purpose of classification and the link between the classification and the legislative purpose. These theories converge on one very important point: they are based on a belief that equality in law is incompatible with classifications founded on those human features which are 'immutable' and 'involuntary'.

I will mention briefly some recent propositions of this sort. The author of a book on equality published a few years ago in Poland, Jan Wawrzyniak, distinguishes three types of criteria of classification of citizens by legal rules: 'rigid', 'flexible' and 'mixed'. We may put aside this last category, as irrelevant for our discussion. By 'rigid', he understands criteria whereby a citizen cannot change his membership in a class distinguished by this criterion (for example, sex, colour of skin, national origin); by 'flexible' — such criteria whereby an addressee of a norm can change his group membership determined by the operation of that criterion (wealth, education, profession, and so on). Wawrzyniak's conclusion: equality in law is incompatible with the existence of 'rigid' criteria of classification but fully consistent with 'flexible' criteria. The test for equality in law is, therefore, not that each citizen *is actually* an addressee of every legal norm but that each citizen *may be* or *become* an addressee of each norm.[17]

J. C. Smith suggests the following condition for equality before the law:

No rule may differentiate between people in terms of properties the possession of which is immediately knowable and determinate at birth for every person, and which are never after subject to change for the persons possessing them.[18]

Other differentiating rules do not contradict equality before the law. The context of the above-quoted principle makes it clear that, just as for Wawrzyniak, the main test for Smith is a person's objective (as contrasted to actual) possibility of changing his or her group membership and thus of becoming (or ceasing to be) an addressee of a norm:

It is only a law limited solely in terms of a property determined at or by birth, such that a person can neither choose nor change it, which offends the principle of equality before the law by excluding a determined class from the domain of the rule ... Differentiations between persons must take place in terms of actions and events rather than the properties of personal and group identification.[19]

The conviction which the proponents of this model hold in common is that certain classifying features are discriminatory *per se*, no matter what the aim of this classification is and what the relation is between that aim and the classification itself. For example, some of the most ardent opponents of racial affirmative action programs maintain that "the basis of the classification at issue [i.e. race – W.S.] is *intrinsically* unrelated to *any* legitimate purpose of government".[20] There is, therefore, no need to study the purpose of legislation if certain grounds of classification are *a priori* considered as intrinsically unrelated to any legitimate purpose.

Curiously enough, none of the advocates of this theory give a sound moral justification for the principle that certain classifications are discriminatory merely by virtue of the criterion used. But it is not difficult to reconstruct such a justification. The authors, quoted above, refer to human properties which are 'immutable', 'rigid', 'determinate at birth', that is, involuntary and unchangeable. Most certainly, the idea at the backs of their minds is that an individual should have free opportunity to achieve any desired position in society. It is a protest against a caste society: legal norms should not determine our status in a society in such a way that we have no possibility of changing it. How we will use this opportunity is another matter, but we should at least 'objectively' have an open way of changing our status.

This problem of voluntary *versus* involuntary features is crucial, I believe, for an understanding of the second model of non-discriminatory classifications. But if this is the case and if the 'involuntary' nature of certain classifying features is the main rationale for rejecting them, we should consider the weight of this argument more closely. After all, it is not only race, national origin and sex which are 'involuntary'; what about one's intelligence or wealth? More often than not low degree of possession of those characteristics is 'involuntary' (probably few will find controversial the old saying: "it is better to be healthy and rich than sick and poor"). Who does seriously believe that, typically, poverty is a result of laziness and not of structural determination? The possibility of changing group membership in the case of the poor is often purely 'theoretical': there are no formal obstacles, but often also no real chances.[21] The liberty to improve one's legal status is purely abstract. For a beggar, his economic situation may seem as determinate, involuntary and immutable as colour of skin for a Black. Why then should legal rules based on wealth as the classifying criterion be considered better than rules based on colour?

Proponents of this model base their theory on the obvious fiction that the properties such as wealth or intelligence are 'voluntary'. What they do not admit, however, is that *any* criterion for classifying addressees of norms 'discriminates' against some of them; a criterion of high school results or intelligence tests at the point of access to universities 'discriminates' against the less able or less intelligent as far as their chances of admission are concerned. This is an inherent feature of any distribution of scarce goods; there must be certain criteria of distribution, but the use of *any* criterion necessarily determines which groups will have a lower chance to obtain an object of distribution. In relation to university admissions, Ronald Dworkin has correctly observed that "[a]ny standard will place certain candidates at a disadvantage as against others".[22] It is, therefore, inappropriate to discuss any criterion 'as such', without reference to the social purpose of legal regulation. Since social purposes may conflict with each other (for instance, the highest possible quality of education *versus* a diversity of student body or compensation for past discrimination against a minority group, or upgrading of deprived minorities), the choice of criteria of classification is impossible in abstraction from these purposes. These are very real moral and political dilemmas which demand moral decisions, but these decisions are not aided by the illusion that an abstract ideal of equality in law can be decisive for choosing one of the alternatives.

This view, if correct, leads not only to the conclusion that some 'flexible' or 'voluntary' criteria may be illegitimate in many cases (such as wealth as the basis of distribution of electoral rights) but also, conversely, that criteria which are 'rigid' and 'determinate' may be in some cases quite acceptable, not as an exception to a general rule, but in their own right. Consider sex classification (which is undoubtedly a classification based on immutable traits) in protective labour legislation, e.g. occupational limitation laws which prohibit the employment of women in work involving constant lifting of heavy weights.[23] Does the use of sexual criteria make these provisions discriminatory? I do not think so. This is not to say that every piece of protective labour legislation is benign and non-discriminatory. Various laws which prescribed the time women could work and the types of work women could perform have been criticized as aimed at preventing women from competing with men for jobs.[24] However, theoretically at least, there is nothing discriminatory about a regulation which prohibits an employer from assigning a particular heavy task to women employees. Or consider another example of sex classification which was recently subject to judicial scrutiny in the United States. In *Schlesinger v. Ballard*,[25] the Supreme Court upheld differential tenure rules for male and female naval officers; under these rules women are entitled to a longer period of service before a mandatory discharge for want of promotion. The Court ruled that this differential treatment does not discriminate against men because "male and female line officers in the Navy are *not* similarly situated with respect to opportunities for professional service".[26] Since women have less opportunity for promotion than their male counterparts in the Navy (because, among other things, they may not be assigned to certain combat missions), the Court concluded that a longer period of tenure for women officers is not unfair to men. Now, we can leave aside the issue of the substantive wisdom of this particular opinion; some critics suggested that the judgment fails to attack the combat-duty prohibition which in itself is discriminatory[27] and, hence, that it reviews in isolation "one small facet of a large and complex scheme".[28] Given, however, that this 'complex scheme' (that is, a scheme of differentiation between men and women in respect of combat duties) is already in operation and that it is not blatantly unreasonable or unjust, there is nothing unreasonable in a classification along sex lines with regard to promotion rules. The immutable nature of gender does not impress a discriminatory slant upon this classification. If, in turn, one believes that the combat-prohibition *is* discriminatory and that the above-mentioned promotion rule does not affect this aspect of discrimination, then this moral criticism is not necessarily based upon the 'immutability' of gender characteristics but rather on the lack of rational connection between these characteristics and the performance of combat duties.

By the same token, many other 'immutable' characteristics may well serve as proper bases for legal classifications. We do not condemn as violative of the principle of equality in law special compensatory programs for disabled persons if we approve of the aim served by these programs and see the relevance of this classification to this aim. Or, on the other hand, the selection criteria which involve classifications on the basis of intelligence [29] or physical deformities [30] may be clearly related to one's prospects of performance, at least in certain fields, and hence justified. This issue is particularly illuminated by the problem of race as a classifying factor — an issue which has been given immense legislative, jurisprudential and philosophical exposure in the United States. It is now widely accepted that racial classifications are not forbidden *per se*. The old opinion that the Constitution is 'color-blind' [31] and, consequently, that race is 'constitutionally irrelevant' [32] was rejected in the American jurisdiction and has given way to the view that a racial classification is valid if it is "necessary to the accomplishment of some permissible state objective".[33] This doctrine was particularly relevant to appraising compensatory benefits (including measures in such fields as education, public employment and housing) to racial groups whose members have suffered because of prior discrimination.[34] In the famous *Bakke* decision the Supreme Court affirmed (by a 5 to 4 majority) that colleges and universities could consider race as one factor in the admissions process.[35]

To be sure, the use of racial criteria does not enjoy the same status in the American law as the use of many other criteria of classification. Classifications that are based upon racial criteria are considered to be 'suspect' and the so-called 'strict scrutiny test' must be applied to them. This means that, in order to defend them, it is not enough to prove a rational relation between a classification and a state interest; the classification must be shown to be a *necessary* means to a *compelling* or *overriding* state end.[36] What is significant, however, is that not only race and some other 'determinate', 'rigid' and 'involuntary' characteristics such as national origin, alienage and, in a less rigoristic version, sex have been considered 'suspect categories',[37] but even such a typically 'flexible' and 'voluntary' feature (in the liberal interpretation of proponents of the second model) as wealth was once considered 'suspect'.[38] In 1969 the United States Supreme Court stated that "a careful examination on our part is especially warranted where lines are drawn on the basis of wealth or race, ... two factors which would independently render a classification highly suspect".[39]

It seems, therefore, that the category of 'suspect classifications' in the American law can be of no help to the partisans of the *per se* theory'. For one thing, this category was never used to prove the unconstitutional character of certain classifications *per se*, irrespective of their purpose: it only established a much more strict scrutiny test for evaluating relations between the classification and legislative purpose. Moreover, the notion of 'suspect classification' is not based on the concept of 'involuntary' or 'determinate' characteristics, as is shown by the treatment of wealth as 'suspect'.

Consider now two typical statements expressing the view that there are certain classifying features which are 'inherently irrelevant' and, therefore, there are classifications (in particular – based upon race) which are 'inherently unjust', irrespective of their purposes:

There will never be sex or racial peace until the idea of sex or racial discrimination is dead and buried. ... The only means of ridding the nation of invidious discrimination is to tear it out ... 'root and branch'. ... Affirmative action only perpetuates it.[40]

The lesson of the great decisions of the Supreme Court and the lesson of contemporary history have been the same for at least a generation: discrimination on the basis of race is illegal, immoral, unconstitutional, inherently wrong, and destructive of democratic society. Now this is to be unlearned and we are told that this is not a matter of fundamental principle but only a matter of whose ox is gored. Those for whom racial equality was demanded are to be more equal than others. Having found support in the Constitution for equality, they now claim support for inequality under the same Constitution.[41]

But how is it possible to deal with the issues in which race *is* an important factor without considering race? The postulate of colour-blindness in situations where colour is *actually* relevant amounts to a postulate of problem-blindness. If certain race-defined cultures have denied to some minorities access to important social positions, refusal to consider race factors in designing rectificatory policies is identical with a refusal to improve the situation in these fields. Alexander Bickel's propositions imply that certain features are once and for all morally irrelevant as a basis of legal classifications. But if they served in the past as the basis of invidious discrimination, then they become morally relevant as the basis of a classification in law that attempts to redress the consequences of past discrimination; their invidious use *before* makes them morally relevant to serve benign purposes *now*.[42] The same point can be expressed in another way. It is a different characteristic that serves as a criterion of classification in redress from the one that was employed in the invidious discrimination before, namely, it is now the characteristic of *having been discriminated against* because of being Black, or Jewish, or a woman, or poor etc.[43] Both these interpretations seem to me plausible: either that it is the same characteristic that served as a basis of discrimination before, and that it derives its moral validity from the benign anti-discriminatory purpose, or that it is a new characteristic of having been discriminated against. These two interpretations answer two different questions: the latter is about what characteristic is now morally relevant, the first one – why the previously immoral classification became morally relevant.

Whichever of these two interpretations we choose, the conclusion is the same: they show that no characteristic is irrelevant *per se* and thus serve to refute the view that the very use of certain characteristics as criteria of classification is a symptom of inequality in law. The use of racial characteristics in compensatory law has a different moral status than the use of the same characteristics in discriminatory law: the first is made morally relevant by prior operation of the second. The effort to find some 'suspect' classification which may be considered as 'inherently' or *'per se'* unjust irrespective of the goal of legislation, must therefore fail. No distinctions are inherently just or unjust; a test for the non-discriminatory nature of classifications is determined by the validity of the goal of regulation. Distinctions on the basis of wealth may be discriminatory in distribution of political rights and non-discriminatory in taxation; distinctions on the basis of sex may be discriminatory if applied to salary schemes and non-discriminatory in decisions about military service; age distinctions may be non-discriminatory when applied to voting rights and discriminatory when applied to legal protection against physical violence. It is the appraisal of the purpose of legislation (and consequently, the relevance of the classification to this purpose) which determines the discriminatory or non-discriminatory character of legal classifications. It does not follow that a benign legislative purpose justifies all means leading to it but rather that evaluation of this purpose is a *conditio sine qua non* of the evaluation of the classification as non-discriminatory. In designing differentiated treatment "[w]e attempt to decide how to treat people by looking at the consequences of different policies for them and evaluating those policies in the light of standards that we can defend."[44]

That brings us to the third theoretical model of non-discriminatory rules. It stresses the importance of the relationship between a classification and its purpose: the relevance of a classification to a benign purpose makes the classification non-discriminatory. This relevance of a distinction to its aim is often considered to be the supreme standard of the validity of a distinction. A general formula in the American jurisdiction and in the dominant American legal theory affirms that a classification is valid if it includes "all persons who are similarly situated with respect to the purpose of the law".[45] As is obvious, this definition in itself does not provide any substantive test for non-discrimination. It leaves to interpretation not only the question of legitimate purpose of legislation but also criteria of similarity in the situation of citizens with respect to that purpose. More precise formulations of the problem include statements that "the classification must be reasonable, not arbitrary, and must rest upon some ground of difference having a *fair and substantial relation* to the object of the legislation, so that all persons similarly circumstanced shall be treated alike."[46] Consider also this proposition:

[I]f a court is convinced that the purpose of a measure using a racial classification is truly benign, that is, that the measure represents an effort to use the classification as part of a program designed to achieve an equal position in society for all races, then it may be justified in permitting the state to choose the means for doing so, so long as the means chosen are *reasonably related* to achieving that end.[47]

The italicized words in both these quotations indicate the complexity of the problem. It is not *any* relation of classification to the aim of the law that matters, it is not even a relation of relevance: it is a fair, substantial and reasonable relation of legal means to benign ends that is required. I have no difficulty in accepting this principle but it seems to me obvious that we are unable to make such a judgment without substantive evaluations of the purpose of a particular legal rule itself.

Consider again the example of admissions to universities and two competing policies: admission on the basis of 'competence' (a meritocratic system) *versus* admission where criteria of membership in some deprived minorities are also taken into account (affirmative action system). Which of these criteria is related to university admission in a more 'fair', 'substantive' and 'reasonable' way? The answer depends on the general goal of educational policy (meritocratic values *versus* the value of compensation, or of attaining a diverse student body, or of upgrading the position of deprived minorities) but this answer cannot be given in terms of a 'fair' relation to an aim because it is precisely this answer which is supposed to determine that aim! It is the resolution of substantive moral and political dilemmas which opens the way to an answer to our question: for a partisan of a meritocratic social ideal,

SUBSTANTIVE JUSTICE AND EQUALITY 93

affirmative action discriminates against non-members of a minority which is treated in a preferential manner; for an advocate of affirmative action, the meritocratic system discriminates against members of socially deprived minorities.

3. DIFFERENTIATION AND EXCLUSION

Suppose someone argues against the propositions outlined so far in this Chapter by claiming that there are two completely different situations which should be carefully distinguished in the context of a discussion of equality in law. The first situation (let us call it 'differentiation *sensu stricto*'): certain rights and duties are distributed unequally among different groups and strata of society. The second situation (let us call it 'exclusion'): certain rules, by virtue of their content, can be applied only to a certain group in society for they specify a certain property that only some people may possess. University admissions or taxation schemes provide examples of 'differentiation *sensu stricto*'; clubs which limit their membership only to people of a particular national origin, or profession, or age, provide examples of 'exclusion'. Suppose it is argued that we cannot speak of discrimination in the case of exclusion because the addressees of the rule are determined by the content of the rule, and therefore it cannot be applicable to anyone else. It is a case of application of only one standard of treatment (even if only to a rather narrow group) and not of different standards to different groups. Accordingly, we do not confront the problem of inequality in law in the cases of 'exclusion', for a legal rule treats all those to whom it applies equally though it does not apply to everyone. Quite to the contrary, the argument runs, we may speak of inequality in law in the case of 'differentiation *sensu stricto*' when certain goods or duties are distributed unevenly among different social groups.

There is, however, a possible answer to this criticism. To start with, the boundaries between the two situations are more than problematic: we can describe the cases of 'exclusion' in terms of 'differentiation *sensu stricto*' and *vice versa*. The statement, for instance, that some members of a community are excluded from joining a prestigious club is identical with a statement that the rights to join this club are unequally distributed among the members of society: some people have them, others do not, some others perhaps have the right subject to special conditions. On the other hand, the example of 'differentiation *sensu stricto*' can also be described in terms of 'exclusion'. The set of rules that prescribe differentiated standards of admissions to universities is composed of two types of rules: those that are applied to minority candidates and those that are applied to all the others. Non-minority candidates are excluded from the advantages arising from the rules of preferential admission for minority members. Take the example of the Indian Reorganization Act of 1934 in the United States which accorded employment preference to qualified Indians in the Bureau of Indian Affairs (B.I.A.). The Supreme Court decided in 1974 that the Act was not repealed by the Equal Employment Opportunities Act of 1972 since one of the primary goals of governmental policy towards Indians was the fostering of self-government and one way to achieve it was to increase the participation of tribal Indians in B.I.A. operations.[48] Now, is this an example of a rule unequally distributing rights of employment in the B.I.A. ('differentiation *sensu stricto*') or a rule that applies only to a particular group of citizens, *viz.*, Indians ('exclusion')? Both answers are correct and the choice of one of them depends on the aspect of the problem that one wants to emphasize. If one emphasizes admistrative efficiency and meritocratic values, one will tend to treat it as a case of a differentiating rule. One will then try to argue that the classification employed here is based on criteria irrelevant to valid purposes and that a classification based on actual professional qualifications is the only one relevant here. If, however, one defends this regulation on the grounds of a principle of Indian self-government, one will be inclined to point out that the rule does not distribute rights between Indians and non-Indians but rather excludes non-Indians from certain preferences prescribed by the rule.

Both these interpretations describe two aspects of one and the same practice. The source of the illusion that 'differentiation *sensu stricto*' and 'exclusion' are two different legal phenomena lies partly in the ambiguity of the notion of 'application of a rule'. To say that a rule applies to a certain group of people may mean either that those people are subject to a legal system of which this rule is a part (a broad meaning of 'application of a rule') or that those people are specified by the rule as holders of some right or duty conferred by this rule ('application' in a narrow sense). Now, taking into account what has been said earlier about the impossibility of having a legal system without some classification of citizens and without rules that confer certain rights and duties on sub-groups of the community, it is obvious that there will be situations in which these two meanings of 'application of a rule' do not overlap. A legal rule about the preferential employment of Indians in the B.I.A. applies to *all* citizens in the first sense of 'application' but only to Indians in the second, narrow, sense.

The distinction between those two meanings of 'application' can be translated into the distinction between 'application' and 'applicability'. Take

SUBSTANTIVE JUSTICE AND EQUALITY 95

the following phrase: "A rule for instance of income tax law *applying* only to persons with an income of less than £500 would be *applicable* without exception to all such persons".[49] The last few words may be reformulated as: "would be *applied* to all persons under the condition that their income is under £500". 'Applicability' means a conditional application: application under the condition that the persons concerned have certain characteristics specified by the rule. The complaint about the *unequal* treatment of those whose income is under £500 as compared to those whose income is over £500 is as inappropriate as the complaint that those who receive more than £500 are *excluded* from certain privileges conferred by the tax law, as long as we believe that the limit of £500 annual income corresponds to whatever economic reality is relevant for determining tax contributions.

Someone might suggest that there is hardly any 'applicability' of the rule mentioned above to those with an income greater than £500, or of the B.I.A. employment rule to non-Indians; one could argue that the notion of application in the broad sense ('applicability'), when not accompanied by the actual application, is useless and, therefore, that the whole distinction is superficial. It would be, however, a mistaken objection. There is a whole world of difference between a rule that belongs to a foreign legal system (or an historical rule which is no longer valid) and a rule of a legal system to which I am subject although it is not my legal position that is directly regulated by that particular rule. A law of country X that exempts people with an income less than £500 from paying tax has a greater impact on the legal position of a citizen of country X whose income is over £500 (and who, therefore, does not benefit from the privilege conferred by that rule) than any legal rule of country Z (except in quite exceptional circumstances, for example where he commits a crime in country Z). Although not addressed directly to him, this rule in country X indirectly shapes his status, if only by specifying what kind of tax exemptions he is *not* entitled to. The rules addressed to my fellow citizens shape also my legal environment; I cannot ignore them as easily as I can ignore the legal rules of Ruritania or of ancient Rome. There is an obvious difference in their legal relevance; that is why the latter are not even *applicable* while the rules addressed to my fellow citizens are *applicable* to all citizens but *apply* only to some of them. In short, specific legal rules (that is to say, rules addressed directly to some specified groups of people and not to the whole population) are also relevant for non-members of this group and therefore the 'exclusion' from the scope of the application of the rule is never total. There can be, however, exclusion from the *advantages* stemming from this rule but the justifiability of this has to be decided on the merits of each such rule and cannot be settled on the basis of a general assertion about exclusion.

From whatever side we approach the problem, we see that there is no way in which we can make judgment that a particular legal system excludes certain groups of citizens (or discriminates against them in the distribution of rights) on the basis of purely formal features of legal rules. We must needs appeal to more substantive judgments about the value of the ends of those rules and the relevance of legal means to achieving those ends. We say that the law is equal because we believe that it is just and not the other way round. The illusion that equality before the law can be ascertained independently of the substantive justness of the law is well expressed in these words by Justice Jackson: "Courts can take no better measure to assure that laws will be just than to require that laws be equal in operation".[50] But we had better realize that our opinions about equality in law are unavoidably determined by our opinions about what law is *just* (in terms irreducible to standards of legal equality) and not by some objective properties of this law. Opinions about what law is just cannot be, in turn, substantiated without opinions about what are the benign purposes of law. The controversies about different purposes of law (and their different relative weight) should be openly formulated in terms of competing social philosophies and the substantive social ideals that they endorse, rather than apparelled in guise of the problem of 'equality in law'. To those substantive social ideals the second part of this book will be devoted.

Having said all this, I must concede that there is a certain conception of equality that belongs to the realm of those substantive social ideals and that, in this sense, equality (but not *legal* equality) is primary and fundamental, rather than secondary and derivative. Equality in this sense *does* help us distinguish between those legal rules that are consistent with the principle of equality in law and those that are not. It is the principle of equal respect for all human beings and equal concern for them, irrespective of their qualities and characteristics. This higher notion of equality belongs to the order of supreme values of an ethical system: it is this order of substantive values from which our judgments about equality in law are derived.[51] This notion of equality does not necessarily bring with it equal or unequal treatment: it can be served by the one or the other depending on circumstances. It demands that we treat people as worthy of equal attention and concern, that we accord equal respect to the human dignity of each. The principle of treatment as an equal is based on the fact that all people are equal in their humanness and this is a sufficient reason for equal respect.

Beyond this single common factor (and important biological consequences stemming from it, such as the similarity of basic needs relating to survival), people differ in ways justifying different treatment. Equal respect has its source not in those matters that are unequal about persons (and which call for, *inter alia*, unequal rewards, honours, status, responsibility or even liberty) but in what is common to them and what is not subject to gradation. This equal humanness of all human beings justifies the principle that no-one deserves less concern than anyone else: that, in a word, no-one deserves less respect although he (or she) may deserve less praise,[52] reward, liberty, privileges, responsibility or prestige. The crucial issue: how to distribute those goods and bads that are distributable (also through the law) in such a way that people's relevant differences and their right to equal respect are taken into account, will be the subject considered in the following chapters.

PART TWO

JUSTICE AS EQUILIBRIUM

CHAPTER 4

THE PRINCIPLE OF EQUILIBRIUM

The principle of social justice proposed in the following chapters is advocated here by relying on the type of moral reasoning which has been described by John Rawls as 'reflective equilibrium' and which has been discussed above.[1] The principle of justice is a generalization based on particular moral convictions (namely: about the justice of compensatory measures) and then applied to those cases that call for a just arrangement although they do not strike us as typical cases of compensatory justice. In other words, principles derived from strongly held convictions of justice are applied to more controversial cases.

1. EQUILIBRIUM OF BENEFITS AND BURDENS

The simplest way of formulating the general principle referred to above is that whenever an ideal, hypothetical balance of social benefits and burdens is upset, social justice calls for restoring it. The idea is one to which other writers have appealed before, but which has usually been formulated with reference to concrete applications of principles of distributive justice; much more rarely has it been advanced *in abstracto*. The best example of such a concrete application of justice as equilibrium is offered by Joel Feinberg in his discussion of the problems of compensatory benefits:

> The principle that unpleasant, onerous, and hazardous jobs deserve economic compensation, unlike the claim that superior ability deserves economic reward, is an equalitarian one, for it says only that deprivations for which there is no good reason should be compensated to the point where the deprived one is *again brought back* to a position of equality with his fellows. It is not that compensation gives him more than others (considering everything), but only that it allows him to catch up.[2]

Although Feinberg does not push his argument any further, his words about the deprived person being "again brought back" are very significant. Brought back to what? The answer: "To a position of equality with his fellows" is not appropriate for we have no reason to believe that previously he actually *was* in such a position. Moreover, the principle cited by Feinberg states that compensation is required in case of deprivations "for which there is no good reason". What does this mean? Deprivations caused by unpleasant jobs have a 'good reason' from a societal point of view: certain things simply have to be done by someone. But there is no good reason why it is this particular person who is expected to suffer an unpleasant job, especially if there is no compensation for suffering it. Even if there is no good reason for it in this sense, that is, from the point of view of the individual concerned, this gives no ground for thinking that what he is "again brought back" to (as a result of compensation) is a position of prior equality. It is more than likely that previously he was *not* in a position of equality with his fellows and often this is why he has now to take an unpleasant or onerous job instead of an interesting and pleasant one: perhaps his parents hadn't enough money to pay for his education, or perhaps he was in an unequal position because his abilities were much lower than those of most of his fellows. Whatever the reason may be, it is not 'equality' in any other than a metaphorical sense that economic compensation brings him back to.

But the metaphor of 'bringing someone back to a position of equality' raises other doubts, too. Not only has a beneficiary of compensation not been previously in a position of actual equality, but he is not brought back to a position of equality in any literal sense. A person who has a very onerous job and obtains compensation cannot be said to be in a position of equality with a person who has a pleasant job unless we make certain assumptions about comparability of money with units of 'unpleasantness' of job. However, those assumptions are very questionable. Is a miner's job plus economic compensation equal to a teacher's job without such compensation?

The view that the aim of compensation is to create a certain sort of 'equality' (and if not strictly 'equality', then at least 'equivalence') is deeply entrenched in our moral thinking. This view, with reference to a different type of compensation than one mentioned by Feinberg, was recently expressed by Bruce A. Ackerman: "A blind citizen has a right to insist that others make a *greater* sacrifice of their rights in non-genetic domains if overall equivalence is to be achieved".[3] Although Ackerman appeals to 'equivalence' rather than 'equality', both his and Feinberg's propositions about these two particular instances of compensatory justice rely upon the same conception. Now, the idea that compensatory practices bring about 'overall equivalence' or 'bring people back to a position of equality' is intelligible only when we presuppose a particular balance of benefits and burdens and look upon any deviations as contrary to social justice. It is only against the background of this idea that the difficulties inherent in Feinberg's 'bringing back to a position of equality' can be overcome. The hypothesis about this ideal equilibrium gives sense and meaning to statements such as Feinberg's and Ackerman's who, in turn, grasp well our pervasive moral intuitions. But, if these intuitions have a prominent place in our moral landscape (and I believe they do), they imply also the moral validity of the idea which is a prerequisite of their coherence. In other words: if we think that it is just to compensate people for some deprivations or burdens and at the same time feel that this compensation brings about an equilibrium of benefits and burdens, then this equilibrium must be taken as a principle of social justice.

At this stage it is important to clarify the nature of my reasoning about justice. I begin by identifying a particular judgment of justice in which great confidence can be placed; intuitively, I consider the judgment about the compensatory benefits (such as described by Feinberg and Ackerman) to be very sound. It is, therefore, a good candidate to become a 'fixed point' in further reasoning about justice. Obviously, those who strongly disagree with the moral validity of compensatory benefits, or with Feinberg's description of restoration of hypothetical equality, are unlikely to accept the rest of the argument. Still, it seems to me that the 'restorative' description of compensation well captures widespread moral attitudes. Having decided about the 'fixed point' of reflective equilibrium, my next step is to reveal its premise which, as I have just suggested, consists of the hypothetical balance of benefits and burdens. This general idea seems to be well suited to constitute a general principle on which we can defend more particular judgments of justice. In order to facilitate this argument, we may well try to describe this hypothetical balance in terms of situations which intuitively strike us as requiring just solutions; that is, situations in which we feel that a distribution of benefits and burdens should be based on moral grounds. By describing a hypothetical equilibrium of benefits and burdens in terms of justice-relevant situations, a transition from the general principle to particular judgments is greatly facilitated. Naturally, the description of this general principle of equilibrium of benefits and burdens is moulded by prior judgments which already have their place in reflective equilibrium, both judgments which are strongly held and which, hence, constitute the raw material of which this general principle has been constructed (such as a judgment about compensatory benefits) and also much more controversial judgments which require further support by deduction from the already accepted principle (such as judgments about just desert based on effort, or just punishment). The latter judgments play *some* role in the description of the principle of the balance of benefits and burdens, even if only that they indicate the general spheres of life to which the concept of justice applies. For example, we are uncertain about principles of just punishment and that is why we need the general principle(-s) of justice from which to draw guidelines about justice in punishment. So the movement here is, apparently, from the general to the particular. But in order to formulate the general principle in a way conducive to the derivation of proper guidelines about punishment, we must establish beforehand that the concept of justice is applicable to the practice of punishing people for their wrongs. So our views about the general principle were, to some extent, affected by our intuitions about these particular convictions of justice as to the substance of which we are still uncertain. It is only after such a complex and repetitious movement between the general and the particular, after 'going back and forth'[4] between 'considered judgments' and their 'regulative principles',[5] that we can reach the state of 'reflective equilibrium' in which our general principles of justice match our particular convictions.

It should be also kept in mind that much of this Chapter is preparation and that various aspects of 'balance of benefits and burdens' are only touched upon to indicate the themes to be discussed in the following Chapters. Those eager to criticize the description of restoration of the hypothetical balance are asked to hold their fire until the very laconic account in this Chapter has been developed in Chapters 5–8. With this caveat in mind, we can now ask ourselves the question: what is the nature of this initial, purely hypothetical, equilibrium which determines the general balance of the distribution of benefits and burdens in a society and to which all members of the society should be 'brought back'? I submit that it has the following three characteristics:

First, it is a social condition characterized by a state of mutual abstention from harm, that is to say, by a mutual respect for liberties. It is an equilibrium in the sense that, in the situation of full respect for each person's sphere of autonomy, all enjoy equally the benefits of autonomy and the burdens of self-restraint. This requires that there be a set of general rules by reference to which it can be determined whether an act by anyone constitutes illegitimate harm to anyone else; such a set of rules guarantees autonomy to everyone in the sphere of their behaviour which is non-harmful to others. A harm done to another person is nothing else than an invasion of that person's sphere of autonomy. It is an intrusion into the sphere of the right to do what one wishes as long as it does not harm anyone else. A hypothetical balance which sets up a standard for the principles of justice consists in the respect for other persons' rights and in non-interference with other persons' legitimate sphere of free action. Although the scope of this autonomy is not of absolute character but is determined by changing social and cultural values, the existence of such a sphere is an uncontroversial pillar of this conception of justice. It should be noted that legal, official, distribution of rights in a society may or may not be congruent with the principle of mutual non-harm. Only if it were so, would restoration of balance as here defined consist always in the restoration of infringed *legal* rights. It may well be that the legal distribution of rights in itself infringes the principle of mutual non-harm. So the first characteristic of equilibrium is far from being identical with a purely formal rule of non-violation of legal rights whatever they may be.

Secondly, equilibrium is characterized by equal satisfaction for all persons of basic material conditions of a meaningful life: no-one suffers burdens which make his subsistence, or participation in a community life, impossible. This naturally does not mean that everyone has equal conditions of life but rather that no-one is excluded from the possibility of having a meaningful and decent life as measured by the general standards of his or her society. The possible forms of denial of means of meaningful life (which constitute disequilibrium in this aspect) do not necessarily involve positive action by someone but include also the failure to provide some essential thing, for example food, shelter, basic education. So equilibrium in this sense may be presented as consisting in a proper balance of positive liberties: no-one is at this initial stage deprived of elementary conditions of self-realization. It is obvious that this initial balance of positive liberties is purely hypothetical. This can be illustrated by reference to the case of a handicapped person. The compensatory measures called for under the present conception of equilibrium seek to secure a balance of positive liberties (or, to use a previously quoted phrase of Ackerman's, help to achieve 'overall equivalence') but certainly it would make no sense to suggest that there existed in the case of handicapped people a *de facto* prior equilibrium which was upset and hence should be restored. The equilibrium to be 'restored' is a certain ideal, hypothetical, state in which no-one is *a priori* deprived of, or gravely disadvantaged in, the means of self-realization which are at his or her disposal.

Thirdly, social equilibrium means that everyone's work, effort, action and sacrifice yields a benefit equivalent to the contribution; in other words, that a person's 'outcomes' are equal to his 'inputs'. A paradigmatic example of this aspect of equilibrium is that of a peasant who actually consumes the entirety of what he produces. At this initial, hypothetical stage of social equilibrium there is no exchange and no exploitation: everyone does everything for himself. There is, of course, nothing particularly good about that, except in that no-one can complain about any imbalance of benefits and burdens. Naturally, in an actual society people do not consume everything that they produce; by 'giving' more than they 'take', they create a situation of disequilibrium in which they accumulate some 'credits'. Persons who do more for others than they take from them, should be rewarded for this difference; extra benefits restore equilibrium which has been upset by an extra effort. In a complex social exchange one can hardly talk about 'equality' of inputs and outcomes because they are usually incommensurate. Equilibrium is achieved when the overall level is equal for all people, that is, when the ratio of one person's outcomes to inputs is equal to other persons' outcome/input ratio. This is how modern social psychology defines a principle of equity; inputs in this 'calculus' are described as a person's contributions to social exchange and outcomes — as the person's 'receipts' from this exchange.[6]

To these three aspects of hypothetical equilibrium correspond three methods of restoring it and they will be discussed in the next chapters. The method of restoration of the first aspect of equilibrium, the balance of mutual non-harm, is through punishment (Chapter 8). When a person increases his or her own sphere of liberties illegitimately, by infringing others' autonomy, and in this way upsets the general balance of mutual non-harm, the limitation of the offender's rights (that is, the punishment) restores the overall equilibrium of benefits and burdens. Distribution aimed at the satisfaction of basic needs is a way of restoring social equilibrium in its second aspect (Chapter 6). When a balance of positive liberties is upset and certain fundamental needs are not met, compensatory measures bring about equilibrium in this respect. And finally, distribution according to desert is the proper method for restoring the overall balance of inputs and benefits, that is, the third aspect of equilibrium (Chapter 5). Rewarding for desert is equalizing benefits with efforts: someone who has done for others more than he has actually received from them, may legitimately expect to be rewarded for this difference.

Naturally, there may arise situations when achieving one aspect of equilibrium conflicts with another: when, for instance, equilibrium in the second sense is incompatible with outcome/input equilibrium. In my further considerations, in particular when discussing relations between the satisfaction of basic needs and justice 'according to desert', I will attempt to propose priority rules dealing with situations of conflict between those principles.

While at first sight it may appear that there is no single idea which underlies all three spheres of justice, and that 'equilibrium' is simply serving as an umbrella to shelter three disparate elements, it should be stressed that all three can be represented as the applications of a more general principle of restoring a balance of benefits and burdens (an idea, as we have seen, which is presupposed in some of our important judgments of justice). In all three cases, the equilibrium consists in the balance of benefits and burdens.[7] In the case of punishments, the harm done to another can be viewed as an illegitimate benefit taken by the offender, namely the benefit of using some of another person's sphere of liberty, the benefit of not constraining oneself. This increased benefit is compensated by an increased amount of burdens in the form of punishment. In the case of distribution according to basic needs, an inability to avail oneself of normal social or natural opportunities, or to satisfy a basic need, is an important burden in a person's life and calls for special assistance from society. And in the case of distribution according to desert, a bigger effort or sacrifice by a person represents a bigger burden; it should then also be balanced by a bigger portion of benefits. In general: this idea of equilibrium implies that the overall balance be the same, i.e. that the level of benefits minus burdens be equal for all members of the society. It does not call for equal distribution of burdens or for equal distribution of benefits but for a differentiated treatment which is a reaction to the different amount of benefits enjoyed and burdens borne by members of a society.

The concept of equilibrium employed here hasn't any descriptive physical meaning. The equilibrium which is relevant to social justice is a normative one. But I hesitate to call it a 'moral equilibrium' in the sense suggested by Kurt Baier. He distinguishes between primary moral rules which "define what it is, morally speaking, to mind one's own business, to preserve the moral equilibrium" and secondary moral rules which "indicate what is to be done by whom when the balance has been upset". Those secondary rules

state what a person deserves, that is, ought to get or have done to him, as a result of the upset of the moral balance. A person who has not upset the moral balance deserves nothing. He has neither positive nor negative moral merit.[8]

For Baier, every instance of restoring the moral equilibrium is identical with a case of moral desert, positive or negative. The concept of equilibrium endorsed in this book is broader: there are situations when one deserves nothing (in a strict sense of 'desert', which will be discussed later) but still the equilibrium is upset and something should be done about it in order to have equilibrium restored. This is the situation of compensatory justice according to needs. Baier rightly links moral equilibrium with positive or negative 'moral merit' but since compensatory justice does not always operate as a function of merits, the formula of equilibrium employed here is not identical with Baier's moral equilibrium. Often in the case of distributive justice there is neither desert nor guilt; we cannot attribute someone's handicap or disadvantages to anyone's good or bad action but still we feel it is unjust to leave it as it is. Often the imbalance is 'created' by nature (as in the case of natural handicaps) and thus it is morally neutral, in the sense that no-one can be held responsible for it, yet there is a moral duty to nullify the consequences of those handicaps.

I suggest that the concept of equilibrium proposed here is broad enough to constitute a theoretical framework for thinking about social justice in general, that is, justice in the distribution both of good and of bad things. It assumes a consistent set of moral beliefs referring to justice; it provides a common ground for the various principles of distributive and retributive justice. Higher wages for more risky jobs, punishments proportional to crimes, preferential admissions for members of minorities which were discriminated against in the past, free medical care or education for those who could not afford it otherwise and so on: all those distinct and, at first sight, disparate actions, programs and principles have a common core, for they are based on one and the same ultimate moral intuition. I believe it is both general enough to provide moral support for all those particular practices and yet concrete enough to decide controversial cases. The principle of balancing benefits and burdens tries to answer the question of what distribution of the good and bad things of life among members of society is just. However, it does not attempt to establish any absolute, easily quantifiable standards because the decisions about what are to be counted as benefits and burdens and what is their relative weight rely upon controversial moral judgments. Even though Christopher Ake is quite right in saying that "the idea of something's being a burden or benefit applies equally well to a vast range of features, situations, items and happenings in life",[9] nevertheless universal agreement about the standards of benefits and burdens is unlikely. One may, therefore, accept the general idea of justice as equilibrium without endorsing some of the equalitarian implications that I suggest later. Those implications are a function of one's judgments about *measures* of benefits and burdens. I hope these judgments are not totally arbitrary; I shall try to give some reasons why I find certain measures more appropriate than others. But if one rejects those reasons, that will not necessarily entail the rejection of the general idea of equilibrium.

2. EQUILIBRIUM AND THE DIFFERENCE PRINCIPLE

A few remarks about the main differences between the conception of justice proposed here and John Rawls's theory of distributive justice will probably help to clarify the main lines of my argument. I have already explained my general dissent from Rawlsian methodology in justifying principles of justice.[10] At this stage, I should like to indicate the main contrasts between 'justice as equilibrium' and the principle which constitutes Rawls's most original contribution to conceptions of distributive justice: the Difference Principle (henceforth referred to as DP) which demands that "[s]ocial and economic inequalities are to be arranged so that they are ... to the greatest benefit of the least advantaged" (83).[11] It should be also stressed that DP is introduced by Rawls as the 'democratic interpretation' of a more general precept that "social and economic inequalities are to be arranged so that they are ... reasonably expected to be to everyone's advantage" (60). Maximization of the expectations of the least favoured provides, in Rawls, the proper indication of an improvement for everyone. As far as the other two Rawlsian principles of justice are concerned, the principle of equal liberty is beyond the scope of distributive justice as it is understood here [12] and the principle of fair equality of opportunity (in the Rawlsian sense) is endorsed without reservation for reasons which will be explained later.[13]

There is certainly some affinity between the idea of equilibrium as a standard of justice and the Difference Principle. This can be clearly seen in that part of Rawls's theory where he considers the relations between DP and the principle of redress, in particular when he demands compensation for undeserved "inequalities of birth and natural endowment" (100). After all, bringing about the equilibrium after it was upset is also a form of redress. In the next chapter, I will show that if we consider the concept of 'desert' through the prism of balance of benefits and burdens, it inevitably leads us to the conclusion that effort constitutes the only acceptable measure of desert, and this implies nullification of the effects of natural contingencies and accidental social circumstances. However, it should be noted that as far as DP is concerned, there is still room for diverging interpretations of what constitutes an advantage for those who are worse off. It is a matter of the economic or social theory added to a theory of justice so that the precepts of justice could be translated into statements of policy. Recourse to particular economic or social theories may provide justifications of even very strongly inegalitarian policies satisfying at the same time conditions of the DP. All sorts of inequalities may be interpreted as working *in the long run* for the advantage of those worst-off through the increase of global well-being (although in the short run the worst-off will have to carry the greatest burden of growth). Rawls himself suggests, as a plausible interpretation of the DP, a theory about the role of economic inequalities as incentives which "raise the long-term prospects of laboring class" (78). To be sure, he immediately makes a reservation: "I shall not consider how far these things are true" (78), but certainly he does not rule out the possibility of approving the economic inequalities-as-incentives *in terms of justice*. In another place in his book Rawls openly endorses such an interpretation of the advantages for the worst-off: "The appropriate expectation in applying the difference principle is that of the long-term prospects of the least favored extending over future generations" (285).

This flexibility of the DP which may serve as a justification of even strong inequalities (let me repeat: in terms of justice), if only a credible economic theory provides a promise of higher global growth as a result of incentives resulting from those inequalities, was recognized by Richard A. Posner:

The optimum distribution [satisfying the conditions of the DP] may thus be highly unequal, if, for example, the negative impact of a more equal distribution on the incentive to work would be so substantial that the larger slice received by the worst off was smaller in absolute value than the relatively smaller slice that they received under the less equal distribution.[14]

Now, it is by no means universally acknowledged in modern economic theory that there is a positive correlation between economic inequalities and the rate of growth. Some economists claim the contrary: that the level of *per capita* development tends to be higher in societies with lower levels of inequality, although it is admitted that there is a threshold beyond which decreasing inequality does not correspond to increments in development.[15] Scandinavian countries are often cited as examples of relatively egalitarian societies with high rates of economic growth. However, the validity of one or another economic theory is not relevant here; this is a matter external to Rawls's theory of justice. What is important is that Rawls does not exclude the inegalitarian, incentives-related interpretation of DP; to the contrary, he expressly admits its plausibility as *an* interpretation of DP. Economic inequality is reconciled with the principle of justice through the promise of efficiency.

Not only economic considerations point at possible inegalitarian interpretations of the DP. Sociologists advocating the functionalist theory of stratification (which is neither rejected nor endorsed by Rawls) will not have great problems with finding justifications for most inequalities in terms of their societal function. This is again suggested by Rawls himself with respect to the problem of educational opportunities:

[T]he difference principle would allocate resources in education, say, so as to improve the long-term expectation of the least favored. If this end is attained by giving more attention to the better endowed, it is permissible; otherwise not. (101)

By the same token it could be shown with respect to other areas of social life that the "long-term expectations of the least favored" are best served by giving more attention to the better endowed. The extreme case of such an argument is Hayek's suggestion concerning provision of medical facilities, that "it is probably in the interest of all" that those "with full earning capacity" should be rapidly cured (even if their illness is not very serious) at the expense of "some neglect of the aged and mortally ill".[16] Although Rawls would probably reject this view, it is fully compatible with the DP. If the 'interest of all' or 'advantages to all' (which work as part of a scheme which improves the situation of the least advantaged members of society) may be shown as those related to rapid economic growth brought about mainly by investors or managers, then their good health is more important for the general advantage than that of others. In this case they should be given more attention, just as in Rawls's example those better endowed should be given more attention in education if it could be shown that, on balance, it will improve the situation of all.

Now, it *may* be true that maintaining income inequalities at a certain level is conducive to economic growth, that giving more attention in education to the better endowed results in globally higher quality of education and even that giving priority in the use of scarce medical resources for those directly involved in economic management helps to maintain economic growth. All this may be true (or false), but what has it to do with justice anyway? This is the most general contrast between 'justice as equilibrium' and the Rawlsian Difference Principle. If it may be shown that some disproportionate advantages for some people (having no relation to their burdens) or, on the contrary, some higher burdens conferred on others (unrelated to benefits enjoyed by them) serve some useful social purposes that could be described in terms of 'advantages for all', or even 'advantages for the worst-off', this does not *eo ipso* make them *just*.[17] In the present conception of justice, the principle of efficiency and the principles of justice are completely distinct and mutually irreducible.[18] It may well happen that a just solution is at the same time a useful one or *vice versa* but then it is a purely contingent coincidence, not an inherent one. 'Advantages to all' may justify a policy contrary to the principle of equilibrium of benefits and burdens but then it is a case of utility overriding the principle of justice and not of its becoming an element of justice. If differences in pay are socially useful because they serve as an incentive, so much the worse for justice; a society has to make a moral choice between economic efficiency and a just scheme of wages. Rawls, however, makes ultimately his criterion of just inequalities derivative from the principle of efficiency: "justice is defined so that it is consistent with the principles of efficiency" (79). To be sure, not from *any* principle of efficiency but only from the one compatible with the DP. He also acknowledges this congruence explicitly when he takes Pareto's principle of optimality as a starting point in constructing the principles of justice. This principle defines the optimal structure as one which exists when it is impossible to change it so as to make some people better off without making anyone else worse off. Although Rawls states that Pareto's principle "cannot serve alone as a conception of justice" (71), its *supplementing* by DP guarantees the conceptual consistency of justice and efficiency. In consequence, under the conditions of DP, "it is indeed impossible to make any one representative man better off without making another worse off, namely, the least advantaged representative man whose expectations we are to maximize" (79). The principle of efficiency is therefore conceptually built into the principle of justice. In this very important point Rawls departs from his general declaration that justice is a specific virtue of institutions, independent of other values, and that it should not be confused with efficiency, liberty and so on (9). I suggest that the conception of justice as equilibrium is more consistent with the postulate of separation of considerations of justice and of efficiency. This reflects the fundamental difference between this theory and Rawlsian principles. Although in many particular points the demands of both conceptions may be very similar (as will become clear with respect to, for example, considerations of the natural assets),[19] these conceptions involve different criteria of justice. Rawls's theory scrutinizes the *functions* of inequalities: if the inequalities serve certain functions (namely: improve the prospects of the worst-off), they are considered as just. Justice-as-equilibrium scrutinizes the *grounds* of inequalities: if they correspond to unequal burdens or benefits, they are just. Justice-as-equilibrium calls for restoring the balance when benefits are not related to relevant burdens; Rawls postulates the abolition of those inequalities that cannot be shown to be efficient (in terms of everyone's advantage and the DP). Rawls is not interested in moral desert; the theory endorsed here is not interested in efficiency.

Rawls views distributive justice as "contain[ing] a large element of procedural justice" (304) in which the outcome is just whenever the procedure is fair (84–8). The justness of outcome is not assessed by any independent criteria but is derived from a just procedure. Once "a fair social process" is in operation, within certain limits which are defined by the two principles of justice, "whatever distributive shares result are just".[20] As a consequence of the 'pure-procedural' approach to distributive shares, information about "desires and needs of known individuals" (88) or about their "preferences and claims" (304) is considered by Rawls as irrelevant to a just distribution. Rawls argues that "justice as fairness is not at the mercy, so to speak, of existing wants and interests" and that "[t]he long range aim of society is settled in its main lines irrespective of the particular desires and needs of its present members" (261). Now these descriptions may easily be deceptive. Obviously, they should not be taken to mean that no preferences, desires or interests of the members of a society are relevant to the conception of distributive justice. In some important respects, his theory takes into account human psychological predispositions. For one thing, they play an important role in the 'thin theory of the good' (595–99) which is in many ways related to Rawls's theory of distributive justice: for instance, it is instrumental in explaining the preference of individuals for primary goods (397) and in defining the least favoured members of society (396). He also appeals to "the broad features of human desires and needs" (424) while advancing the Aristotelian Principle about the increased enjoyment derived by people from exercise of their more complex capacities (424–33). To the extent that the theory of the good is related to, and imposes constraints on, the theory of justice, these psychological predispositions are within the scope of distributive justice. So when Rawls dismisses preferences, desires and interests as unrelated to justice, he emphasizes that the basic structure of society is the primary subject of the principles of justice, and that it should not be confused with the principles regulating a "distribution of a given stock of things to definite individuals with known desires and preferences" (88).

The problem is, whether or not we can establish a clear line dividing distributive justice in the Rawlsian sense, i.e. applying to the basic structure, from the 'allocative justice' which dictates the principles of particular allocations made to particular individuals. Rawls himself certainly attaches great importance to this distinction (54–55)[21] and some of his commentators share his conviction.[22] For my part, the hiatus between basic structure and justness of particular allocations is inherently suspect: if the principles of justice (as applied to basic structure of society) are to "define the appropriate distribution of the benefits and burdens of social cooperation" (4) or, in a more recent formulation, to "shape the division of advantages that arises through social cooperation",[23] then it is hard to see how we can separate the judgment about 'basic structure' from the judgment of justice of particular distributions among particular individuals in a given society. The differences between these judgments merely reflect their different level of generality. Be that as it may, it will become clear that the application of the theory of justice as 'equilibrium of benefits and burdens' has to take into account some of this information about persons that is discarded by Rawls. This conception must not ignore at least some 'interests, needs and desires': one of the principal aims of a conception of justice is to define the criteria of legitimate interests, needs and claims which should be taken into account in a societal distribution. They constitute a factual background of the operation of a just distribution; the question why certain needs, wants and interests have greater moral weight in claims for just shares is an essential problem with which a theory of social justice should be concerned. The conception of justice-as-equilibrium therefore *is* 'at the mercy' of needs and wants of actual members of a community. This is one of the reasons why social justice cannot be ever fully put into practice: the circumstances of human interests, needs, legitimate claims and so on, are much too complex and dynamic to be fully controlled and used in the distributive mechanism. The Rawlsian conception has a definite advantage in this respect for "it is no longer necessary in meeting the demands of justice to keep track of the endless variety of circumstances and the changing relative positions of particular persons" (87). But this convenience has a high cost: a reduction of the concept of justice to a procedural notion. In so far as Rawls acknowledges the need to transcend a purely procedural theory, and postulates the need for a structural ideal to specify constraints upon the institutional and procedural processes,[24] this "great practical advantage of pure procedural justice" (87) disappears.

To sum up all these differences: the conception of justice as equilibrium calls for compensation whenever there are good grounds in terms of relevant burdens while Rawls seems to postulate compensation for increased burdens when the resulting inequality does not work for everyone's advantage. These differences are also reflected in different approaches to equality in Rawls's theory and in the conception of justice as equilibrium. Rawls starts with a presumption in favour of equality: the burden of justification is on those who demand unequal distribution. That is explicitly put forward in Rawls's 'general conception of justice' which demands equal distribution of all social values unless an unequal distribution is to everyone's advantage (62). The conception of justice as equilibrium does not make any presumption either of equal or unequal distribution as *prima facie* just. Unequal distribution of benefits is dictated by unequal burdens, equal – by equal. The same principle applies to unequal distribution of burdens, namely of punishments. The onus of proof is not *a priori* conferred upon partisans of equal or unequal distribution: *any* just distribution requires justification in terms of morally relevant grounds of allocation of social benefits or burdens. There is no way to decide that equal distribution is *prima facie* more just, natural or rational and that only unequal division calls for explanation.

Although in its practical applications the idea of justice-as-equilibrium is egalitarian (in the sense that its application would result in a great deal more equality than it is the case in actual societies), this is a result of practical conclusions of the theory, not of its theoretical presumptions. Without making any theoretical presumption in favour of equality, this theory reaches egalitarian conclusions through an interpretation of criteria of its main categories: desert and need. In Rawls's theory the situation is very much the other way round. Starting from the egalitarian presumptions, he easily accommodates even very inegalitarian conclusions through the incentives-oriented interpretation of inequalities which contribute to the benefits of the least favoured.

CHAPTER 5

DISTRIBUTION ACCORDING TO DESERT

Under the general conception of justice as equilibrium, desert is relevant to justice in distribution only where it expresses an actual burden, that is, when it involves some effort, sacrifice, work, risk, responsibility, inconvenience and so forth, when it is linked with an expenditure of energy and time. It is only this sort of 'desert' which should be in justice compensated by social benefits. The general underlying aim of this conception of desert is to screen out all those factors that are 'unearned', that are beyond human control, that are dictated by dumb luck, and for which a person cannot claim any credit. Only this notion of desert is consistent with justice considered as an introduction of a conscious moral order into human affairs. Even though, for practical reasons, rewarding according to results, or social contribution, may be sometimes more productive, and certainly easier, from the point of view of justice in distribution it is only the bearing of burdens which calls for compensation aimed at bringing about the equilibrium of advantages and burdens.

Of course, not *every* burden is relevant here: after all, murdering people or, to take a less serious deviation, jogging every morning, may be very burdensome too. What counts, is a conscientious effort which has socially beneficial effects. However, these beneficial effects do not constitute a proper basis of desert; it will be argued that effort is the only legitimate basis and measure of desert.[1] Considerations of effects are important in so far as only socially valuable efforts (according to the hierarchy of values of particular time and place) count in considerations of desert. This 'social value' cannot be ascertained in isolation from effects. Socially valuable effect is, therefore, a *conditio sine qua non* of taking a particular effort into account in considerations of desert. But only effort constitutes its basis and measure since it is effort, and not effect, which can be meaningfully regarded as a burden imposed (or self-imposed) upon an individual.

1. THE NOTION OF DESERT

Before we turn to the arguments about the role of desert in distributive justice, we should note three characteristics of desert which require separate though brief treatment. First, desert considerations are always person-oriented. When we are pronouncing judgments of desert, we are inevitably making judgments about persons whom we hold responsible for their actions. It makes no sense to attribute desert, positive or negative, to persons for actions or facts over which they have no control. In particular, as people have no control over their natural assets (although they *do* have control over the *use* of those assets), it would be unjust to consider those assets *per se* as relevant to any considerations of desert. Furthermore, the grounds of desert must have something to do with *this* concrete person directly; Joel Feinberg is quite right in criticizing John Hospers for his idea that some criteria of desert may be influenced by a worker's environment, for example, by 'the open market' or 'public need'.[2] Those factors may be relevant to a final decision about the proper remuneration but not about the desert of the worker. That is why the opinions about 'just' salaries (which are not identical with decisions about 'proper' salaries) should disregard matters which are external to the actual desert, in particular so-called 'scarcity rents'. They are those segments of salaries which stem from the fact that someone's qualifications are very rare and important. But it is not a matter of *desert* that, for instance, a society very badly needs computer operators who can therefore, in effect, dictate conditions. This has something to do with their environment, not with those individuals themselves except in a very loose and indirect sense. One might argue, for instance, that their 'desert' is earned by them having made a deliberate decision to take up those studies that will prepare them for jobs which are most needed by society. This may well be true but it is irrelevant here because this decision (and its consequences) typically does not constitute a burden and hence cannot be treated as a legitimate basis of desert. Even if, all things considered, we conclude that it is worthwhile to pay them a higher salary, that is, to pay them 'a scarcity rent', it does not follow that it is just to do so, for less than doing so is required in the name of justice.

Secondly, desert considerations are always value-laden. It would be rather inconsistent to state someone's desert and at the same time to say that there is nothing good about it (or bad, in case of 'bad desert'). Statements of desert imply a moral evaluation while, for example, an appreciation of someone as having scarce qualifications does not necessarily entail any moral judgment. This is also a feature which helps to distinguish between desert and need-considerations. As David Miller puts it rightly, "except in special cases, a person could not deserve on the basis of his need, because we do not admire ... people for their needs".[3] This suggests that desert is always associated with a human evaluation of someone *by* someone. Desert may be, therefore, manifested only when some social practices exist, such as rewards, prizes, medals, salaries, expressions of praise, and so on. To say that X deserves P makes sense only when it is imaginable that P can be distributed or attributed. To say: "I was working very hard all year therefore I deserve good weather during my vacations" is erroneous except as a metaphor. Obvious though this view may seem, it has certainly not been accepted by all.[4] Yet it works equally well for the converse case, that is, in cases of bad consequences. To say: "I didn't deserve such a tragedy as has happened to me" would make sense only under the condition that someone can properly be held responsible for what actually happened.

Third, desert considerations are always past-oriented. When talking about desert, we are evaluating certain actions which have already happened. That is why it is a confusion to base desert upon utilitarian grounds; for example, to say: "He deserves this job because he is most likely to do it well". This phrase really means that the candidate will be useful but not necessarily that he 'deserves' it. Even if this utilitarian assessment is based upon past achievement of the person hired or promoted, this past achievement is taken as an indication of probable future usefulness, not as a 'desert' to be rewarded. In practice, those two types of assessment, utility and desert, will often coincide because the demands of the job dictate that those most likely to do it well will have displayed this in past effort of some kind or other. Hence, past achievement will often be taken as an indication of probable future utility. Conceptually, however, these are two distinct types of evaluation and there is no necessary link between them. Situations in which these two types of considerations yield opposite results could well arise. Imagine that there are two candidates for a recently vacated chair in a university: A is an old scholar with great academic achievements (gained through considerable personal sacrifices) and who has made a great contribution to the development of this particular branch of learning; B is young and a very talented lecturer who has not yet had an opportunity to fulfil his capabilities. A selection committee might well appoint B, arguing that it prefers someone with great energy and promise for the future rather than someone who is 'over the hill'. In this case, the appointment will be based clearly upon utilitarian criteria which conflict, in this particular situation, with those of desert.

The underestimation of those three features of desert, and in particular of the second and third ones, leads to the confusion of desert with other grounds of distribution or allocation, for example on the basis of utility or entitlement. Surely desert is not identical with entitlement. There may be situations when someone is entitled to something without deserving it (for example, when a bad son who hasn't paid any attention to his dying father is the sole heir at law to his father's wealth), or when someone deserves something without being entitled to it (in the same example: when a person, not a member of the family, took care of the deceased for years). Similarly, it makes sense to say, with reference to sporting events, that a loser 'deserved' to win but, due to bad luck, he did not and so he is not 'entitled' to a medal.[5] This meaning of 'desert' might appear to conflict with some common usages of the word. We like to be able to say: "He is entitled to it, *therefore* he deserves it" and it strikes us as inconsistent to say: "He is entitled to it, but he does not deserve it". This last phrase conflicts unpleasantly with our desire for order and coherence in our moral universe. But if we seriously accept the idea that there are numerous conflicting bases of just distribution and, in particular, that legal entitlements may conflict with social justice and *vice versa*,[6] the inescapable conclusion is that there is nothing inconsistent about the last statement. Assertions about entitlements may be value-neutral but this is not true of statements about desert; in consequence, they may or may not coincide with statements about entitlements.

Entitlement is always rooted in some legal or quasi-legal rules. In consequence, statements about entitlements are non-controversial: they are either correct or false, depending on whether or not they derive from a valid rule. A rule is either valid or not: a person is either entitled to something on the basis of this rule or not; *tertium non datur*. In contrast, statements about desert are rooted in value-judgments and moral principles; as any act of appraisal, they are inevitably controversial. Even if they are universally shared, they do not operate in an all-or-nothing fashion: X may deserve something but Y may deserve it even more. Desert is a matter of degree, entitlement is not.

An illustration of the confusion of desert with other considerations (stemming from the underestimation of its past-oriented characteristics) may be provided, I believe, by the following passage from an essay by J. A. Passmore:

> Justice has to decide between people as they are, not between people as they might have been. Had a person's past history been different, he might not have embarked upon a particular contract; had it been different, he might not have been as devoted as he now is to a particular form of activity. But all of this is irrelevant, from the standpoint of justice, to the question whether he deserves to win a case based on the contract or to win preferment for his devotion.[7]

When Passmore is writing about 'preferment for [a person's] devotion', it seems to me that he somewhat too hastily decides that this is not an example of judging a person on the basis of his past history. We find this person deserves preferment by reason of his having made certain choices in the past. Had it been different, he would not be 'devoted to a particular form of activity' and that is why he would not deserve our preferment now. This judgment is, therefore, based on an evaluation of a person's 'past history' unless the 'preferment' in question is based on utilitarian grounds in which case 'a person's past history' serves as an indication of his probable future achievements and then the whole matter becomes irrelevant from the point of view of a consideration of desert.

The second example mentioned in the same passage (and treated as identical) is that of a contract. However, to say that a person is entitled to some contractual benefits is not the same as to say that he deserves them. To use the notion of 'desert' in this context makes sense only as a metaphor. Deciding about who is to win a case based on the contract is to make a purely formal, legal, assertion without entering into the realm of moral judgments. It is reasoning about entitlement, not about desert. This is most obviously brought out by Robert Nozick's 'entitlement theory of distributive justice' where all justice considerations are reduced to those of entitlement. But there is no reason to expect (indeed, there are many reasons to think otherwise) that legitimate ways of coming to holdings always coincide with the desert of persons. Entitlement is merely one criterion of proper distribution, not necessarily the most important, and certainly not the only one. In an often quoted passage about a wealthy basketball player, Robert Nozick asks:

Let us suppose that in one season one million persons attend his home games, and Wilt Chamberlain winds up with $250,000, a much larger sum than the average income and larger even than anyone else has. Is he entitled to this income? Is this new distribution D2, unjust?[8]

Yes, of course he is entitled to this income. He is entitled to it as long as he satisfied certain formal, institutional, legal conditions. And yet this distribution may be considered unjust on the basis of a theory of justice which demands that the social distribution correspond to some other standards than purely formal, legal rules of acquisition and transfer. In the above passage Nozick asks two different questions and it is a misconception to think that they can be answered at the same time. There is no contradiction between my two answers because they evoke two distinct sorts of considerations: those of entitlement and those of just desert.

Feinberg remarks correctly that desert is a non-institutional notion which means that its conditions "are not requirements specified by some rule in the sense of authoritative public, sanctioned regulation".[9] It may well be that the principles of just desert are embodied in legal rules but often this is not the case. Hence, the considerations of entitlement and of desert do not coincide. Besides, desert is not the only criterion of just distribution; it will be submitted later that in certain cases justice requires satisfaction of human needs even if the beneficiaries do not 'deserve' their shares.

Often it may happen that the social costs of legal enforcement of justice based on desert are too high and then the attempt should be abandoned without, however, changing the criteria of what is desert. In many situations rewarding according to desert might be detrimental to personal freedom; then difficult decisions concerning the priority of values may have to be made. Nozick tries to discredit the standard of desert in the considerations of justice or fairness: "*Is* it unfair that a child be raised in a home with a swimming pool, using it daily even though he is no more *deserving* than another child whose home is without one?"[10] The irony is misdirected. Yes, it is unfair, but the social costs of providing everyone with conditions of life corresponding to his desert would be too high, particularly in terms of restrictions on personal freedom, and these costs may limit our willingness to enforce distributive justice. When, therefore, in the next phrase Nozick asks: "Should such a situation be prohibited?", common sense clearly suggests a negative answer but not because the situation is fair but rather because the unfairness of the situation does not justify the social costs involved in a rapid changing thereof. When we, however, extrapolate the same problem to less trivial situations, for instance, to drastic inequalities in access to education, the answer is not as uncontroversial. It is interesting to note that an economist with the same philosophical opinions as Nozick, Milton Friedman, gives an opposite answer to the question posed by Nozick:

Much of the moral fervor behind the drive for equality of outcome comes from the widespread belief that it is not fair that some children should have a great advantage over others simply because they happen to have wealthy parents. Of course it is not fair.[11]

In their practical conclusions, Nozick and Friedman claim the same. However, their theorizing about the fairness or unfairness of the situation is quite different. Friedman thinks that those inequalities are unfair but nothing should be done about them because life is unfair; Nozick thinks that nothing should be done because there is nothing unfair about those inequalities even though they do not correspond to any differences in desert. Without endorsing his practical conclusions based upon the conviction that there is nothing that society may and can do about unfairness of this situation, I think that

Friedman's approach is more convincing. Nozick's position seems to reflect the view that if, for some reason, it is implausible to rectify a certain situation, there is no way in which we can call this situation unjust. I do not see why it should be so, unless we adopt a concept of justice as an all-inclusive social ideal and then the question: "What is a just solution?" equals the question: "What should be done?". A more specific concept of justice, however, does not generate these consequences.

The complexity of social life produces situations in which we confront dramatic conflicts of values: sometimes we must tolerate situations that are unjust because the risks involved in change are too great. If we are unwilling to urge the government to arrange the 'transfer of the swimming pool' from the less to the more deserving,[12] it is not necessarily because we endorse the *status quo* as just but rather because justice is not the only value which is at stake in this whole affair.

2. NATURAL ABILITIES AND DESERT

One of the consequences of the proposition that desert is relevant to a just distribution only in so far as it expresses an actual burden is the conclusion that a person's natural abilities *per se* do not constitute an independent basis of desert in considerations of justice. Admittedly, in reality it is often very difficult to ascertain to what extent someone's effort (considered as a proper measure for a compensation) is due to his innate abilities. In ideal justice, however, desert should be established in such a way that differences in natural assets are not reflected in differential rewards. The question to what extent we can measure the 'inborn' element of one's action is very difficult to answer, but this practical difficulty has no bearing on theoretical moral considerations.

The conclusion suggested above is derived from a more general principle that desert should not be based on things and facts which are beyond a person's control, on circumstances for which a person can claim no credit. Desert is thus 'earned' by a person in the course of his or her conscious action, it is won by the individual himself. To explain this, it may be useful to look at the analogy with criminal punishment. We should not punish a person for his traits of character (for instance, because he is vicious, or aggressive, or unfriendly) but only for his offensive actions. The reasons we do not punish people for their characteristics have to do partly with the social purposes of punishment, partly with the difficuties in obtaining evidence, and also with the problems of personal responsibility. Surely a person has more control over what he *does* than over what he *is*; there is a mediation of human will between personal predispositions and actions. This is not to deny that there are some traits of character which result from deliberate action or inaction by an agent, and if these traits are socially undesirable, morally we may hold a person responsible for them. But, again, the moral source of this responsibility is in what a person has done to acquire them. Likewise, we should not *reward* a person for what he *is* but rather for what he *does*. This strategy is based on a general idea that one of the functions of justice is to nullify, or at least to minimize, consequences of the natural and social lottery which are beyond human control. It has nothing to do with an effort to make all people alike but it is rather an attempt to put justice on a firm, deliberately determined moral basis. It captures our intuitive conviction that justice is something else than the product of caprice of nature or of a social game without any rational or moral justification. Consequently, this idea of justice attempts to make a person the master of his or her place in the social distribution.

A person born more intelligent, more skilful or more beautiful will usually have a better chance than less favoured people of an interesting and satisfying life. It would be silly to ruin these chances in the name of abstract justice; at the same time, however, there is no reason to claim that the person *deserves* those good things of life uniquely on the basis of inborn intelligence, skills or beauty. Perhaps it is more convincing when we approach the issue from another side: a person born less intelligent, less skilful and less able cannot be said to deserve his or her less fortunate or happy life and it is a task of a theory of justice to reflect about what a society can do to compensate this person for undeserved and unearned suffering. To a possible objection that positive *social* obligations of compensation do not follow from the *natural* disadvantages which are of a negative character (absence of skill, capacities etc.), we might answer that society's duty of rectification follows, in this case, not from purely natural deprivations but from the fact that those deprivations are turned by a society into *social* disadvantages and penalties. These social disadvantages are themselves, I believe, culturally-shaped consequences of the existing system of rating, rather than something inevitable in the nature of physical or mental handicaps. That the prevailing views about what is 'normal' and what is 'deviation' express the necessary truth about the nature of things, was never conclusively demonstrated, but only assumed. It is, therefore, a matter of *social* institutions, values and practices that a less gifted person bears additional burdens through no fault of his own.

The proposition that natural assets should be considered as irrelevant for a distribution of goods is sometimes presented as a consequence of the fact that the distribution of natural assets among particular persons is "arbitrary from a moral point of view".[13] I think, however, that this is a misleading formulation of the problem. The distribution of natural assets and endowments is neither in itself arbitrary nor non-arbitrary (in particular, when the adjective 'arbitrary' has negative connotations). There is nothing good or bad about it; it is simply a natural fact which cannot be assessed from the moral point of view because it is totally beyond human control. What may be evaluated as arbitrary or not is the way in which social institutions and practices treat this distribution of natural endowments. The natural distribution is morally neutral but its social use is not. Therefore, it is not the distribution of natural assets but the distribution of social benefits and burdens on the basis of, or in relation to, the natural distribution which may be called arbitrary.

This distinction is worth stressing because the theory of 'the arbitrariness of the distribution of natural assets' has served several critics of distributive justice as an object of criticism and, hence, has made it easier to discredit the idea of redistribution in general. Once we state clearly that an argument about 'arbitrariness' refers to a distribution of rewards, and not of abilities, the anti-redistributive objection falls to the ground. That is why it is important to realize that questions of arbitrariness of distribution, and in consequence those of injustice, may be formulated properly only as to facts and practices which are under human control. Obviously, it would be a confusion to call a thunderstorm 'arbitrary'; it is only to social, human, practices that the complaint of arbitrariness can be relevant.

Still, it does not follow that every human practice or decision which is arbitrary is *eo ipso* unjust. In certain social situations arbitrariness is quite acceptable but this is not to say that this is always the case. For that reason the following example given by Nozick is not adequate to a discussion of the role of natural abilities in just distribution:

If the woman who later became my wife rejected another suitor (whom she otherwise would have married) for me, partially because (I leave aside my lovable nature) of my keen intelligence and good looks, neither of which did I earn, would the rejected less intelligent and less handsome suitor have a legitimate complaint about unfairness?[14]

Indeed, he would not, but that does not prove the point that Nozick wants to make, namely that *in principle* we cannot complain about unfairness of distributions based upon natural abilities which are unearned. The negative answer to Nozick's question is a consequence of the fact that the domain of love, which is the subject of his example (assuming, of course, that love has something to do with marriage) is beyond the scope of distributive justice. Love in general, and romantic love in particular, by its very nature *is* arbitrary (that is, it does not require any 'good reasons', it resists attempts at rationalisation) while the social distribution of such benefits as honours, salaries or leisure — should not be. What Nozick's example shows, therefore, is not that just distribution operates irrespective of the criteria of 'earned' desert, but that in certain areas of life, justice is not a proper standard of evaluation at all. To put it in another way: love is, in certain respects, similar to a gift — it is good to give it but it is not wrong not to give. From this point of view, love and charity belong to a class of supererogatory moral phenomena: we praise the 'givers' but we have no moral right to condemn the 'non-givers', let alone to claim that we are entitled to be given. The question of justice simply does not arise in Nozick's example; the rejected suitor has no claims, he cannot legitimately argue about his desert or need, no rational comparison of his and the other suitor's qualities is relevant here. None of those remedies which would be typical for a sphere of justice fits this case.

The confusion of two distinct problems: distribution of natural assets and distribution of social benefits attached to them, leads some critics to positions that mistakenly attribute rather absurd assumptions to the theorists of distributive justice. As an example, one might consider the following assertion by Alan H. Goldman:

If untalented or unintelligent individuals have no inherent claims upon the talents of others, and I do not see why they should, then it is not demanded, nor perhaps even permissible, that society nullify the distributive effects of these differences.[15]

It seems to me that the second part of the phrase does not follow from the first. It is true, as Goldman states in the first part of the quoted passage, that one cannot have any "claims upon the talents of others": the very idea seems ridiculous. Apart from any other considerations, it is hard to see how these 'claims' could be implemented. The idea, although evidently absurd, is attributed seriously by conservative critics to the theorists of redistribution. In a different part of his book, Goldman finds it necessary to assert that "the less intelligent have no initial right to the time or effort of those more intelligent" and he believes that this principle is sufficient "to offset the claim that we should nullify all effects of differences in intelligence in granting rewards".[16] But this, again, is a case of *non sequitur*: the claim that we should nullify the social distributive effects (in forms of differentiated benefits and burdens) is not necessarily shown to be illegitimate by a principle that we have no right to someone else's talent, time or effort. It is simply a confusion to think that the redistribution of benefits of abilities is based upon or implies the redistribution of abilities themselves. If some of the surplus income is transferred (through the taxation system, for example) from A to B, there is no justification for claiming that A's talents or abilities are encroached on. The only available complaint is that A's right to his income is infringed but, morally speaking, this assumes that A fully deserved his pre-tax income. This may be true but this begs the question.

A popular strategy for discrediting the theory of redistribution (and, in consequence, the principle of compensating for undeserved burdens) consists in identification of the nullification of the *effects* of inborn differences with the nullification of those differences. Friedrich Hayek writes:

The inborn as well as the acquired gifts of a person clearly have a value to his fellows which does not depend on any credit due to him for possessing them. There is little a man can do to alter the fact that his special talents are very common or exceedingly rare.[17]

But why should one try to alter this fact? Surely such an attempt does not follow from the demand for a redistribution of social benefits resulting from unearned, natural distribution of natural abilities. There is nothing in the principle of reward according to desert (based on effort) which suggests the elimination of differences in talents. Implicit in Hayek's argument is the premise that talents exist or are manifested only in so far as they are rewarded. Talents, however, belong to the realm of natural facts and social reward is not a necessary condition of their existence, manifestation and expression.

That is why it is absurd to talk about "nature's unfairness in producing a Marlene Dietrich or a Muhammad Ali".[18] 'Nature', as I suggested before, is neither fair nor unfair. This view is very well expressed in the following words of Rawls:

The natural distribution is neither just nor unjust; nor is it unjust that men are born into society at some particular position. These are simply natural facts. What is just and unjust is the way that institutions deal with these facts ... [T]here is no necessity for men to resign themselves to these contingencies. The social system is not an unchangeable order beyond human control but a pattern of human action.[19]

This is a cogent and powerful exposition of the principles of justice designed to rectify the unfortunate contingencies of nature; yet it is not the most apposite way of expressing this idea to describe the distribution of natural assets as 'morally arbitrary'.[20] Arbitrariness, just as unfairness, is a concept which is inapplicable to caprices of nature. Rawl's inexact formulation gave help to the opponents of redistribution in their effort to discredit the idea of rectification of effects of natural differences. Their view is best expressed in Friedman's: "Life is not fair".[21] But if we accept the view that life, in a natural sense, is essentially neither fair nor unfair, then we must conclude that unfairness starts when we resign ourselves to natural deprivations and treat social ones as their necessary and inevitable extension. Even if, in some borderline cases, the distinction between 'natural' and 'social' is problematical, nevertheless it exists. Friedman tries to blur this distinction suggesting, for instance, that there is no ethical difference between the inheritance of talent and the inheritance of property; if, therefore, we do not complain about children inheriting unequal genetic potential, why should we object to the situation in which children inherit unequal wealth?[22] And yet there is an essential ethical difference between the two cases. The difference consists not only in the fact that inheritance of talent is 'natural' and inheritance of wealth is 'social' (after all, both are equally unearned) but mainly in the fact that the inheritance of talent does not *per se* give any special benefits or privileges in a society (unless it is developed or at least manifested by a person in an effort-consuming activity, in which case it meets the requirements of justice based on desert) while in the case of inheritance of wealth no effort whatsoever is needed to provide a person with real social benefits and advantages over others.

The same conclusion about rewarding on the basis of effort irrespective of natural abilities may be reached if we regard all the benefits stemming directly from the natural abilities, talents, skills and capacities as a part of 'common pool'. This idea, in an even more extreme version, which applies it not to the benefits but to the abilities themselves, was formulated by Rawls:

We see then that the difference principle represents, in effect, an agreement to regard the distribution of natural talents as a common asset and to share in the benefits of this distribution whatever it turns out to be.[23]

Now, if we interpret this metaphor as describing the pooling of social advantages attached to natural talents, and not of natural talents themselves, then Nozick's argument that the common-pool idea "does not take seriously the distinction between persons"[24] breaks down. There is nothing incompatible with the autonomy of individuals in the idea that the fruits of people's natural talents should be shared by all, since those natural talents are not deserved in any way. There is no pooling, sacrificing, sharing, transferring, etc. of talents; they rest where they belong, that is, with individuals. But the benefits attached to them are not a 'natural' matter; they are rooted in the social norms of culture, habits and law. Adam Smith remarks: "The difference between the most dissimilar characters, between a philosopher and a common street porter, for example, seems to arise not so much from nature as from habit, custom and education".[25] There is, therefore, nothing more 'natural' in high rewards for, say, artistic achievements in one society than in disregard for the like achievements in another society. In no way does the first take individual autonomy more seriously than the second. Nozick's argument would be tenable only if social benefits were a part of human personality. But a musician's reputation is not a part of his personal self; even less is his income.

The pooling of advantages derived from natural talents (and from natural talents alone) may be thus viewed as a precaution against the distribution of social goods being influenced by caprice of nature, and as a means of relating a person's share of social goods to the acts which are under his control. Is the idea of a 'common pool' practicable? That is a different matter, with no bearing on the theory of justice. However, Rawls suggests certain applications of his Difference Principle which are fully consistent with the notion of 'common pool' and which are not beyond the scope of the possible (for instance, that resources in education should be allocated in such a way as to improve the expectations of the least favoured). Anthony T. Kronman indicates that "as a practical matter, talent pooling represents nothing more than a system of taxation".[26] For my part, I find a lot of affinity between the 'common pool' idea and Jan Tinbergen's proposal of 'capability tax'. Tinbergen has suggested that taxes should be based on the innate capabilities of individuals rather than on their incomes, so that we do not tax marginal efforts of persons. Accordingly, 'capability taxes' based on complex tests of innate abilities would result in all additional income obtained from extra effort remaining with the individual.[27] Now, abstracting here from all the economic aspects of this proposal, let me point out that it is, in a sense, an application of the principle of 'common pool' of natural abilities. A person's contribution to a social fund would be calculated on the basis of his innate potential and not on the basis of his actual effort. The scheme proposed by Tinbergen would lead to a situation in which only that part of benefits which is a function of a person's abilities (and not of his effort) is taxed.

To this, an important counter-argument has been made that a tax based on native capacities constitutes an infringement of human liberty to choose one's way of life. Charles Fried has argued that just as no-one should be able to claim a greater distributive share on the basis of his greater subjective wants, by the same token no-one should be taxed on the basis of his capacity to contribute.[28] A community, argues Fried, has no right to determine how a person is to develop his or her skills and capacities; the determination of one's life-plan is an essential part of a person's right to self-determination. The liberty to develop some and not other capacities is an aspect of "the liberty to determine a life plan, to choose one's self";[29] by refusing to tax potential contributions, we respect this liberty, Fried says.

> For if we demand of a man that he contribute according to what he might have become, we are saying that this was a choice which was not his to make, while if we assess contributions only on the basis of what a man has chosen to be, we recognize that that choice was entirely his; we respect it.[30]

This is a serious objection and, if valid, it might well identify one of the aspects of the inevitable divergence between the principles of distributive justice and liberty. This objection is not, however, conclusive. For one thing, Fried's suggestion about 'capacity tax' violating liberty to develop one's capacities applies only to cases where there is a gap between what a person could have become (given his/her capacities) and what he/she has actually become. Only then can we say that a community has expressed its opinion about the improper way a person has used his/her native skills. If, however, my development of my capacities corresponds to the potential that these capacities offer, I am not affected by a taxation requirement to contribute according to what I might have become, because 'what I might have become' corresponds to 'what I have actually become'.

At this stage, Fried might reply: even if one has developed his skills in conformity with his innate potential but this decision was affected by his awareness that his taxation contribution would be based on his talents rather than on his actual achievement, then his choice of life-plan was determined by the preferences of the community, hence it was not his, and hence he was not free to choose that life-plan. But this hypothetical argument does not carry much weight. There are various ways by which a society induces people to do one thing rather than another, and we do not necessarily perceive these as violations of liberty. High salaries for scarce qualifications encourage people to develop some of their skills rather than others, and hence influence their decisions about their life-plans but, in the absence of coercion, they do not limit their liberty. Social preferences expressed in salaries, fringe benefits, taxation arrangements etc. are among the factors that affect people's decisions but in so far as people have a genuine choice (that is, when *not* choosing the option preferred by a community does not produce tragic consequences for a chooser), their liberty remains intact.

So the fact that I have developed my skills in conformity with a scheme of preference embodied in a particular taxation system does not mean that my liberty to choose was violated; rather, it may mean that my actual choice was affected, among other things, by these preferences. Now what about these cases, about which Fried seems to be more concerned, where my actual choice of a life-plan does *not* correspond to my potential skills? Well, by the same reasoning as above, I have made my decision freely, knowing in advance that I would be taxed on the basis of my skills, and therefore in the case of not developing them I am losing some extra wealth. If, having developed all my talents, I would reach a level of income X, but in fact I have chosen not to do it and I reach only a lower level Y, then I have to pay tax on a higher level of income (X) than I actually earn (Y). It may or may not correspond to someone's ideas about justice, and my previous argument was precisely that distributive justice *calls for* such taxation because it gives practical substance to the idea of arbitrariness of social benefits based on natural abilities. But in any case it is hard to take such a tax as a serious limitation on one's liberty.

In one way, however, my argument might well be thought to make an arbitrary distinction between those natural endowments which should not be considered relevant to the process of just distribution and those which should be. After all, if someone is born handicapped, then on the basis of the present conception of justice he should be compensated for this undeserved suffering and, thus, brought to a point where the implementation of his life-plans is not drastically more difficult than in the case of other people.

It is perhaps worth noting at the outset that compensation for natural (and other) handicaps is not considered here a matter of 'desert' *sensu stricto* and will be discussed under the heading of 'needs'. Having said this, let me deal with the hypothetical objection about the inconsistency of the conception which in some circumstances prevents consideration of natural endowments as relevant to just distribution and, under other circumstances, demands it. A short answer is available. The irrelevance of natural abilities to just desert is not a fundamental principle in its own right but is a derivative one; it is derived from the more fundamental principle of balance of benefits and burdens. No benefits are 'deserved' when a proposed ground of 'desert' cannot be meaningfully described as a burden, and that is precisely the case of natural abilities, talents and skills. In so far as natural abilities *per se* do not constitute any burden, there is no reason to consider them relevant to just distribution. When, however, the natural lottery results in a substantial disadvantage to a particular individual and, thus, confers upon him burdens which other people do not suffer, then the same principle of balance of benefits and burdens calls for compensatory action by society.[31] There is no contradiction between the 'desert' and the 'needs' aspects of the present theory of justice as far as the role of natural endowments is concerned. Both these are explained by resort to the most fundamental principle of justice: the principle of equilibrium.

The same conclusion is supported by reflecting on the proposition that justice requires that factors which are beyond our control should be eliminated from the determinants of just distribution. Applying this proposition to positive natural assets (such as talents, skills and beauty) yields a result whereby the impact of those assets on just distribution is minimized and, ideally, annulled. In turn, applying this same proposition to negative natural assets (such as physical or mental handicaps) requires positive action to offset the detrimental effects of those disabilities.

3. FREE WILL AND DESERT

As I have suggested, the idea of just desert and, in consequence, of considering differences in natural abilities as irrelevant for reward, is based upon the more general proposition that we do not deserve anything that is completely beyond our control and which we cannot influence in one way or another. But then the troublesome question arises: is there anything that we *can* influence and that *is* under our control? Is there anything in this world that we can claim credit for and, therefore, can we deserve anything? If this is not the case, if the grounds which are proposed here as a legitimate basis of desert (namely: effort) are as much beyond our control as our genetic potential, then the principle of justice based on desert is untenable.

Now, I do not wish to get embroiled here in contemporary controversies over determinism, indeterminism and free will although it is clear that if extreme determinism is correct and everything is predetermined irrespective of our will (either because we have no free will or our free will does not matter) then there is no ground for responsibility and thus for desert. If we cannot ascribe responsibility, we cannot talk of desert.

Numerous writers have spent considerable time and effort in showing that extreme determinism is groundless. One way to approach the question is through the analysis of moral language. It is often submitted that moral language (that is, language of moral duties, obligations, and so on) can be legitimately used only with reference to those actions which are under our control, that is such that before making them, if we had wanted, we could have decided not to undertake them. All 'ought' statements make sense, the argument suggests, only when we believe that the prescribed action is voluntary and it is only for voluntary actions that we can hold people responsible.[32]

The argument that the use of moral 'ought' suggests voluntariness of action is attractive but not conclusive. After all, what we really want to know is whether the very use of 'ought' statements is warranted while the linguistic argument informs us only of what would be the case *if* our use of the moral 'ought' is correct. In other words, this argument says that our use of moral standards implies the assumption about free will but it does not tell us whether our use of moral standards is correct and, consequently, whether this assumption is legitimate. Maybe each time we make moral statements about duties we are committing an error of assuming falsely the existence of free will?

This linguistic argument is not, therefore, decisive but at the same time it should not be neglected. It confirms the obvious truth that usually we behave *as if* free will existed and therefore whenever we prescribe duties, ascribe responsibility or talk about moral 'ought', we behave *as if* people might claim credit for their action. Even if someone comes to the conclusion that whenever we do so, we are in error, this is so strong an intuition that even if it is false, it is an important social fact. However, there are good reasons to believe that it is not false. There are reasons to suppose not only that in our everyday life we behave *as if* strong determinism were not true, but also that it *is* not true. Or at least: that it is not entirely true and in so far as it is not true, our judgments about desert are justified.

It should be noted in the first place that not *any* determinism is incompatible with the doctrine of justice based on desert. Determinism, as such, states nothing more than that all facts, acts and phenomena are determined, that is that they are caused. But to say that everything is determined has nothing to do with the existence or non-existence of free will because some facts, acts and phenomena may be determined by the acts of free will. Determinism in general does not assert that everything is determined by facts which are beyond human control, it only asserts that everything is determined; the nature of causes is another matter. Even if one maintains that all our actions are determined and that not all of them are caused by other human acts, it does not amount to saying that those actions are not free. If I have to decide how to spend my money: on holidays, on a new car or a charity, each of those possible decisions will have its causes which are beyond my control but still the decision will be free and it will be *my* decision. In that sense I can claim credit for my decision, I can be held responsible for it and someone may rightly believe that I deserve a reward (or blame) for my decision.

This general version of determinism is, therefore, not devastating to the doctrine of desert; on the contrary, it provides its necessary condition. In the absence of *any* determinism, and thus of any causality, desert would make no sense since we would not be in a position to state a causal relation between human will and human action, between human action and its effect. Incidentally, also on purely utilitarian grounds, rewarding or punishing according to desert would make no sense in a world without causation: "if everything anyone did depended only on pure chance (i.e., if it depended on nothing) then threats and punishments would be quite ineffective".[33] It is only a strong version of determinism claiming that every act and event is caused uniquely by forces beyond our control which is incompatible with responsibility and desert. However, our everyday experience suggests that it is not true that we have no free will, it is not true that never can we properly say: "I could have acted otherwise" and it is not true that one can never do otherwise than has been done. Experience suggests that there is a whole range of human actions and behaviour, from those where we have virtually no choice (or, even if we have a choice, one of the alternatives would be so destructive that it is *de facto* excluded) to those where our course of action is a result of deliberation taking into account and balancing all pros and cons of possible alternatives in which case we feel that in the final analysis it was our free decision that made us act in that way rather than another.

But what if we are wrong, if the ascription of responsibility and desert in social relations is based on a fundamental error and hard determinism is correct? There is certainly a considerable risk involved in acting 'as if' people had free will while in fact possibly they have not. This risk is particularly evident on the side of 'bad desert': we punish people in the belief that they are guilty of their offences while if there is no free will, there is no guilt either. Of course, criminal law knows various precautions against this danger. All modern legal systems acknowledge numerous instances of non-imputability: in case of mental illness, hypnosis, lack of control of muscular movements and so on and so forth, persons are not punished because they had no free will when committing the otherwise punishable acts. It is, however, irrelevant because we are not concerned here with particular excuses in cases when we know that no free will was involved but rather with a general denial of free will in a human universe, including those cases when people notoriously ascribe responsibility or desert for what they think were free acts.

However, it is conceivable that the problem of free will *versus* hard determinism is philosophically insoluble or, to put it more cautiously, that no answer will be fully convincing. And yet, for practical reasons, we must endorse one view or the other in order to know whether or not our practices of rewarding and punishing on the basis of desert make sense. The only solution to the problem that I wish to offer is, therefore, of a practical nature. Imagine that we mistakenly believe in free will and therefore praise and blame people for their actions without realizing that all these actions are so strongly determined that the agents exercise no free choice over them. But if hard determinism is true then it must be *universally* true and must apply to *all* actions, including actions which are the expression of praise and blame, that is to say, to the very distribution of social benefits and punishments. These are, after all, also human actions, subject to the same laws as the actions that are the object of the assessment. Consequently, if hard determinism is true then both people who *are* praised or blamed and people who *do* praise or blame lack free will. They cannot help punishing and rewarding; the revelation of the truth of hard determinism comes to them as information without any practical significance because their actions (of rewarding and punishing) are beyond their control anyway. The risk of a mistaken belief in the existence of free will is practically nil; the correct answer to this question cannot upset the practice of rewarding according to (alleged) desert. To sum up: either the doctrine of free will is correct and, consequently, our practices of rewarding and punishing for desert and guilt are justified, or this doctrine is false and we cannot avoid rewarding and punishing because we do not have the free will to change existing practices.

And yet, 'unavoidable' does not mean 'just'. A world without free will is a world without justice (in the sense of justice endorsed here). Therefore, if it turns out that, after all, hard determinism is true, or to the extent that it is true, my analysis of just desert would be otiose. Justice-as-desert is justified only in so far as people can freely control their actions.

4. EFFORT OR CONTRIBUTION?

Two main alternative measures of desert are usually suggested: effort or objective contribution. It should be clear from the preceding remarks that I consider effort to be the principal criterion of desert, mainly because 'contribution' or 'success' reflect, among other things, factors which are beyond our control and thus for which we cannot claim any credit. When the airline reservation clerk mistakenly cancels my booking and the plane on which I wanted to fly has an accident, there is no reason why the clerk should feel that he or she deserves my gratitude, let alone reward, although my life was saved. In the distribution of salaries according to productive effects we are indirectly rewarding people for factors which are independent of their own will and effort. Although we often have to assess an objective contribution, we should not take it into account in its own right but rather only in so far as it is the best available measure of actual effort. Consequently, it is a distribution according to contribution only in a derivative sense, for want of any better measure of socially valuable effort.

Let us see what are the principal arguments in favour of the alternative standard of distribution: according to contribution, or effect, or success, or result. The main argument is the Lockeian principle that everyone has a right to the fruit of his labour. "[O]ne has the right to keep what one makes or contributes to a joint venture", claims Goldman.[34] He derives this right from a more fundamental right over one's body: "the rights of individuals over their own bodies seem to indicate rights to what they can produce through the exercise and development of their capacities".[35] Now, this is a remarkable *non sequitur*: I do not see why one right (over the product of our work) is to follow from another (over our bodies). Not only our labour is invested in the product but also other resources to which we cannot claim similar rights: raw materials, know-how, technology, etc. A judgment about our right to a product requires, therefore, a prior judgment about our rights to all those resources and factors which were used in the production of the commodity concerned. This judgment would have to take into account very complex social relationships; for example, if my education was facilitated by someone's taxes, then this taxpayer has contributed (voluntarily or not) to the product of my work, which required certain knowledge on my part. Even if, for the sake of simplicity, we assume that what is at stake here is a product of purely individual labour, there are many factors of production which are results of social co-operation and we cannot simply claim our 'rights' over them in the same way as we can claim rights over our bodies.

The opposite view is suggested by Nozick's formula that things already come attached to particular persons, not as manna from heaven: "The situation is *not* one of something's getting made, and there being an open question of who is to get it. Things come into the world already attached to people having entitlements over them".[36] But what does it really mean to say that things already come attached to people? It is certainly not true in a historical sense because chronologically the existence of 'things' preceded the working out of legal titles over them. There were societies in which 'things' were generally unheld and there are things in the world which have existed and exist quite independently of whether someone holds them or not. Moreover, the view that everyone has a right to the product of his labour or to things which are 'attached' to him can be intelligibly applied only to a very simple production of things. But how are we to apply this principle to a complex industrial structure in which it is virtually impossible to isolate 'products' of particular individuals? And how to apply this standard to professions and activities in which there is no tangible product at all? Both Goldman's view about our rights over our products and Nozick's view that redistribution deprives me of part of things over which I have entitlements, are inapplicable here, anyway in their literal senses, while in a metaphorical sense they become too vague. Take an example of a teacher: what is actually a product of his work and what is 'held' by him? Certainly it is not any tangible thing; what he is entitled to is his salary. But the salary is not a 'thing' which 'came into being already held'; it is a more or less conventional measure of the value of the services that a teacher renders to a community. Hence the scheme: I make a certain product and in consequence I have a right over it, is inadequate here. It is not the case that reward corresponds to the value of my product but rather that the value of my work can be ascertained by my reward. This reward did not come already attached to me nor was it held by me; it was allocated to me on the basis of the value of my work as assessed by someone or by a community. Therefore, when a part of it is deducted in the form of taxation in the framework of a redistributive scheme, I cannot complain that something that was mine was taken away from me since it was never 'mine' in the sense suggested by Goldman and Nozick. And this form of reward is becoming more and more dominant in modern societies. In the case of a growing number of people, rights over their rewards correspond to conventional values regarding the relative importance of their various activities, and not to objective things or products.

If this is the case, one of Nozick's arguments against redistribution breaks down. Nozick considers redistribution through progressive taxation as a transfer of goods from "the man who chooses to work longer to gain an income more than sufficient for his basic needs" (because he "prefers some extra goods or services to the leisure and activities he could perform during the possible non-working hours") to a man who "chooses not to work the extra time". In consequence, the first person has more money but works longer while the latter has less money and works shorter. The trade-off is between the length of leisure and the amount of goods and services one can afford. Hence, the alleged injustice of progressive taxation:

DISTRIBUTION ACCORDING TO DESERT 137

Why should we treat the man whose happiness requires certain material goods or services differently from the man whose preferences and desires make such goods unnecessary for his happiness? Why should the man who prefers seeing a movie (and who has to earn money for a ticket) be open to the required call to aid the needy, while the person who prefers looking at a sunset (and hence need earn no extra money) is not?[37]

Surely this is not what redistribution is about. Society (*any* modern society, for that matter) does *not* consist of these two groups: wealthy, hard-working persons and those who prefer to work shorter hours and be paid less. A unit of actual work does not correspond to a unit of salary; the trade-off is not between more money and less work. The situation in which smaller pay or wealth is a result of voluntary decisions on the part of those who have less costly pastimes is not a typical social situation. The proper conclusion about the inequality of pay is *not* that lower income-earners are less attracted to some sophisticated (and expensive) kinds of leisure but rather that their difficult socio-economic conditions force them to accept whatever salary they are offered. That is why the above quoted reasoning of Nozick is misleading. It is instructive, however, because it shows that the notion of rights over the product of one's work, or over one's holdings, cannot be extrapolated adequately into the sphere of work where no tangible product is attributable to particular producers. Contrary to Nozick's suggestion, a more wealthy person in his example (one who "prefers seeing a movie") did not necessarily derive his right to higher income from his greater effort (and in particular, from a longer period of work, as is implied by Nozick). He had not, therefore, these rights over his pre-tax income which could be derived from the rights over his time or his effort. Nozick's claim that redistribution through taxation is on a par with forced labour and with seizure of "some of a man's leisure" is thus inappropriate: in typical situations, redistribution is designed to rectify the differences resulting from the variety of sources of income or differences in pay for one and the same time-unit of labour; not differences in wealth between those who work more and those who work less.

Finally, let me return to the question of motives which was mentioned at the very beginning of this section. The conception of justice as equilibrium of benefits and burdens explains why the motives and intentions of individuals are relevant for measuring their desert. Not all action beneficial for a society is a ground of desert and beneficial actions of different degree of intentionality should not be credited with the same desert. A noble act done by accident or by error or by omission may give satisfaction to others as useful and beneficial but is not a proper basis of desert for the person who performed the action. Imagine that a doctor gives a placebo (that is, a drug without any chemical and biological effects but designed only to create illusions of relief) to a patient who is, in the doctor's opinion, mortally ill. Subsequently, through processes unknown to and unintended by the doctor but caused by the application of what the doctor considered to be merely a placebo, the patient's health actually improves. The doctor's title to moral praise or gratitude would be very questionable: the absence of particular intention is one of 'disentitling' circumstances.[38] Intention is, therefore, a necessary condition of the moral quality of an act which constitutes the basis of positive desert.

As Christopher Ake points out in his remarkable essay, there is another important reason why motive or intention should be relevant for judgments of desert. Certain intentions may be viewed as an element of the burden itself:

There are certain motives or intentions one can have only as a result of taking upon oneself ... certain responsibilities or obligations, and in the imagery being drawn upon, these responsibilities and obligations are thought of as a kind of weight.[39]

And they are not only so 'thought of'; they often constitute an actual burden. The decision, cited by Ake as an example, to devote one's whole life to finding a cure for cancer, imposes upon the individual actual burdens in terms of hard work, shorter time for leisure, lost opportunities to do more attractive things, even if these burdens are deliberately self-imposed.

5. ARBITRARINESS OF THE PRINCIPLE OF DESERT?

One of the important charges against the doctrine of desert is that inevitably it leads to arbitrary rule. Since in a pluralistic society there is no single, unitary scale of values and, on the other hand, the measure of desert must be based upon opinions as to what is to count as a more and less valuable desert, then someone's (or certain groups') hierarchy of values will have to be imposed upon a society. The argument does not necessarily imply that people will not agree about using desert as a basis of just distribution, but rather that they will not agree about what is to be counted as desert and what are the relative weights of different deserts. The lack of consensus about this latter hierarchy will lead to a situation in which, to use Friedrich Hayek's words, everybody will be "made to fulfil a duty imposed upon him by somebody else" and the rulers will have to "make some unitary conception of relative merits or needs of the different individuals, for which there exists no objective measure".[40]

For one thing, the argument is self-defeating. True, there is no consensus about a scale of deserts, but there is no unanimous approval of pure market distribution either.[41] The requirement of consensus in this context, therefore, cannot be sustained at all in any complex and heterogeneous society. If we abandon, as unrealistic, the principle of consensus, and adopt the principle of majority rule, the whole argument collapses (not surprisingly, Hayek is opposed to the majority imposing its standards of just desert upon the rest of a society). Besides, from the fact that there cannot be consensus about the *measures* of desert it does not follow that we should completely disregard criteria of desert in the distribution of goods. These are two different issues and the existing disagreements about the scale of desert are not *per se* an argument against taking desert into account in distribution. One can well imagine a situation in which *A* disagrees with *B* upon which grounds of desert are more important but, in the absence of consensus, would rather have *B*'s measure of desert adopted in social policy than have desert ignored altogether. In consequence, it is not unreasonable to predict that if *A* cannot have his view on the scale of desert adopted, he will choose the desert-based policy advocated by *B* rather than the abandonment of desert as relevant to distribution. Such a calculus of preferences is justified whenever the intensity of a person's opinion about the importance of desert as such in social distribution prevails over the intensity of this person's opinion about the superiority of a particular scale of deserts. There is, therefore, no reason to believe that disagreements about values of desert entail opting for a market system. However, Hayek appears to take the very existence of market systems as a sign of approval from all those involved in them. Considering a market system as one in which "[e]verybody, rich or poor, owes his income to the outcome of a mixed game of skill and chance", Hayek explains that a high level of welfare is produced because "we have agreed to play that game". He concludes: "[O]nce *we have agreed* to play the game and profited from its results it is a moral obligation on us to abide by the results, even if they turn against us".[42] One is inclined to say in response that a society is not a casino: the stakes are much higher and not everyone agrees to run the risk of losing everything that is essential for his and his family's well-being. In the case of many people participating in and profiting from the market it is simply not true that they "have agreed to play the game". Since economic resources are unequally distributed among different persons, in practice those persons who are involved in transactions are not equally free to reject a proposed exchange.

Be that as it may, the considerations of 'desert' are inescapable in complex modern societies. With respect to a growing number of people in industrial societies the explanation of their wages in terms of marginal productivity and supply/demand relations makes no sense from an economic point of view. The market theory of wages determination holds essentially that their structure may be explained by a demand curve intersected by a supply curve. In the case of teachers, clerks, social workers, managers, public servants and many other people, the notion of marginal productivity is inapplicable in a literal sense. Their wages depend, as Jan Pen notes, not upon supply/demand relations but upon "views on what is right and fair".[43] Certainly, the supply of and demand for various services cannot be ignored; all those white collar workers, teachers and so forth, indirectly contribute to the productivity results. But, as Pen remarks, all that is virtually useless in the explanation of, for example, relations between the salaries of a primary-school teacher and that of a secondary-school teacher. It is impossible to estimate quantitatively the degree to which each of them contributes to the welfare of a society.

This conclusion is supported by a further reflection. While we should not ignore all actual and possible disagreements about the scale of 'just desert' in a society, we should not over-estimate them either. Although no unitary conception of relative importance of merits is to be found in any society where relevant surveys are made, there is no reason to think that the judgments about it are strictly conflicting or that spheres of approximate agreement cannot be established. The search for a full and absolute consensus is, of course, absurd. If, however, we take a less rigorous approach to a consensus, trying to establish only its approximation, hence if we recognize that it exists "when there are no significant amounts of structured disagreement among socially recognizable subgroups of the population in question",[44] we may find in several modern societies empirical proofs of such a structural consensus with regard to distributive justice. The study by Wayne M. Alves and Peter H. Rossi, for instance, provides evidence that in the United States a general agreement exists about the equity of distributions of earnings.[45] This complex and now classical survey in which a representative sample of American adults was asked about the evaluation of incomes of fictional individuals and households described in terms of some typical characteristics such as occupation, education, sex, age, number of children etc., showed a general sphere of agreement on how those factors are rated and their effect on proper earnings assessed. Numerous sociological findings in completely different societies, as in Poland, also show the existence of a certain degree of agreement about just distribution.[46]

6. IMPRACTICABILITY?

It is sometimes suggested that distribution according to desert is not practicable; that however plausible it may be, it cannot be implemented because the grounds of desert cannot be measured, weighed and balanced one against the other. The grounds of desert, even if we agree about what constitutes 'just desert', cannot be measured properly because they are mutually irreducible. How can one weigh the relative importance of physical effort, intellectual or artistic creativity, moral generosity and the like? In particular, it is claimed, we face a totally hopeless task if we try to distinguish between inborn *ergo* unearned propensities for effort and one's own conscious development of personality leading to a valuable result. Yet this impossible task necessarily follows from the conception of justice based on desert. If someone's laziness is a result of genetic factors, then on the basis of this theory he should not be disadvantaged for this reason; no more than someone else should be rewarded for his industrious character, which is a gift of nature. We cannot, however, isolate particular parts of human personality and find out to which degree his actual effort is a result of innate endowments, environmental impact and his conscious effort (which, in turn, is also determined partly by heredity and environment). The problem is so complicated also because those different factors that shape human personality are not distinct and unchanging but rather they mutually interact and influence each other. An attempt to define a precise degree of genetic and environmental influence and the relative role of a person's deliberate effort of self-development is probably doomed to failure because it is the dynamic interplay and mutual reinforcing of those factors that shapes the character, personality and behaviour of human beings.

It seems to me that many of the arguments against distributive justice can be reduced to this argument. However, despite their ostensibly ethical nature, they indicate the practical difficulties of implementing the principle of desert rather than successfully identify an ethical deficiency in the ideal. A good example of such reasoning is provided by Walter Kaufmann. His general proposition is that, in the case of distributive justice, as in the case of retributive justice, we can never say that "justice was done and that everybody got what he deserved".[47] In each case of a distribution "many mutually incompatible solutions are tenable" and, therefore, "a person who received less than he would have received in another distribution that was also tenable could hardly be told that he had received what he deserved, no more and no less".[48] It seems to me that Kaufmann is confusing two distinct sorts of argument, neither of which, for that matter, is totally destructive to the idea of justice-as-desert. The first argument concerns the plurality of possible bases of justice: in particular situations, justice-as-desert may be in conflict with justice based on legitimate needs or justice based on legal entitlements. This is obvious but it only confirms that there can be no single standard of just distribution. Indeed, conflicts of values lead to conflicts of various principles of justice. A choice of one of the precepts of justice, in a particular situation, is based upon a certain hierarchy of values, but it does not follow that a person who has a clear view about his own hierarchy of values is unable to find the right answer about just distribution in a particular case. This argument proves only that there can be no 'absolute', supreme principle of justice based upon criteria of distribution which prevail in all possible situations. There is, however, nothing in this argument which is devastating to a theory of justice in distribution; no more than, for instance, doubts about the criteria for establishing a sphere of personal autonomy are devastatng to the concept of liberty. The choice of a certain basis of distributive justice is usually made to the detriment of another competing basis; often those choices have a tragic character but that is a typical fact about the human condition in general. Kaufmann himself states that "[a]s a rule, wrong clashes with greater wrong";[49] the fact that we may speak of greater and smaller wrongs is proof that one of the solutions is more, and another less just. The choice of a particular basis of just distribution, for example of desert or need, therefore, is difficult but not at all impossible in the framework of a certain hierarchy of values.

The second argument implied in Kaufmann's reasoning concerns the plurality and vagueness of the measures of desert. Doubts arising here are *within* a chosen basis of distribution and not about competing principles of justice. Assuming that we give priority to desert as a legitimate criterion of distribution, in a particular situation, how are we to measure desert? Kaufmann suggests that the task is hopeless; even in relatively simple situations (such as the decision about salary raises at the university) the number and the incommensurability of the criteria make it impossible to reach a just decision. What should be taken into account: teaching or research, unpublished works or publications; if publications, what standards for their assessment should be adopted ("counting pages or words would be rather crude")?[50] In consequence, all this proves to Kaufmann "how *impossible* it is to tell what people deserve, and *it is absurd* to say when one individual gets $1,000; two, $750; one, $500; and one gets nothing, that justice has been done".[51]

I agree that often it is very *difficult*, and sometimes even perhaps *impossible* to say, in the situations of distribution of scarce goods among particular individuals, that the division was just and that it was the only just division. But I do not think it is an *absurd* task. There is a difference between justification of a principle itself and justification of its application to particular instances. The absurdity arises in the first case when the principle makes no sense; when, for instance, a criterion of distribution is clearly irrelevant to a good being distributed. Admittedly, as a function of different hierarchies of values, different principles of distributive justice may seem absurd to different people but this is a normal fact of plurality of moral judgments in human societies. In the second case, that is to say, at the stage of the application of a principle, difficulties may arise with such force that a principle is hardly applicable. Often, for practical reasons, we have little possibility of putting it into practice because we lack sufficient knowledge about how to detect and measure the proposed standard of justice. We can rarely be sure that we have managed to take into account and measured properly all the criteria of justice suggested by our principle; Kaufmann's example about salary increases proves that, and nothing more than that. But the requirement of full and perfect knowledge of all relevant facts is unfair; after all, we can never say that we know everything that is relevant to an action which we undertake and yet we must act upon what we know. This, in itself, does not make our actions irrational. There is, therefore, no reason why we should apply such exaggerated standards to just distribution.

Apart from the deficiencies in knowledge, the main problem with applying the principle of just desert arises with respect to comparative appraisals of the different bases of desert. One should not neglect these difficulties but one should not over-estimate them either. Whenever an appraisal based on moral judgments is made, there is some room for uncertainty and doubt but it does not follow that the actions based upon such an appraisal are always unjustified. In distributive justice based on desert, one has to compare efforts of different types, rank them and compare them with the corresponding rank of standardized rewards. There may be doubts and uncertainties on the way but they do not disqualify the whole enterprise. Just as in the sphere of criminal punishment there can be doubts about the morally proper correspondence between the gravity of a crime and the severity of punishment, so in the case of rewards based on desert, the unavoidable uncertainties do not negate the possibility of a just distribution.[52] We feel that we are justified in our appraisals that one particular desert should count for more than another — no less justified, anyway, than when we pronounce other moral judgments. The fact that desert admits not only the quality of an act but also a degree makes the matter difficult but, after all, most of our moral judgments incorporate appraisal both of kind and degree.

7. COMPENSATORY JUSTICE AND 'STATUS INCONSISTENCY'

The conception of justice advocated in this book is a compensatory one. It is reflected in our main rationale for considering desert only in so far as it expresses actual burden; the hypothetical, initial balance should be restored by the allocation of rewards. Justice is considered here essentially as rectification of injustice resulting from a disequilibrium of benefits and burdens. Naturally, this disequilibrium can be caused by increased burdens in the form not only of physical effort, but also of risk, responsibility and the like. Rewards, and in particular (but not only) wages, are considered as means of achieving an equilibrium and they ought to be devised so as to balance burdens incurred by a person.

The question arises here: is this really a principle of *desert*? When someone is compensated for his more onerous or more risky or more difficult work, is it correct to consider this compensation as a reward for his 'desert'? A negative answer is given by David Miller who argues that "a desert basis consists of personal attributes which are generally held in high regard" while those features of work which serve as a basis for compensation, although they involve 'human costs', are not 'good qualities' displayed by the person in question. Consequently, he says, the principle of compensation is not a matter of desert but "rather an indication of additional factors to be taken into account when rewards are calculated".[53]

Miller's idea of divorcing compensation and desert is tenable only if we grant his premise that typically "desert basis consists of personal attributes which are generally held in high regard". On this assumption it appears that there may be two distinct interpretations of the concept of compensation: as compensation for desert (which Miller, ultimately, refuses to accept) and as compensation for "reduction in the benefit which a man is receiving"[54] (which, for Miller, is a proper understanding of 'compensation'). I believe that this distinction is untenable. If desert is understood as related to a person's intentional *efforts* the results of which are held in high regard then, although certainly this high regard has to do with the fact that such efforts involve a resolute exercise of valuable personal attributes, nevertheless it is not the case that 'personal attributes' *per se* constitute the basis of desert. What makes them relevant to desert is only the extent to which they have been actualized in the effort made, in the conscientious and voluntary activity of a person. As a matter of fact, 'personal attributes' are never sufficient as a basis for desert in their own right; in order to be revealed to others and to be perceived by others, they must be materialized in some effort. For instance, a person's talent as a pianist may be admirable in itself (though available for admiration only so far as manifested in some actual performance), but considered in itself, it yields no judgment about the pianist's 'desert'.

For this reason, Miller's distinction between compensation for desert (when desert is associated with personal attributes held in high regard) and compensation for additional costs incurred by a person (as supposedly distinct from desert) is unjustified. Those personal attributes which Miller associates with desert have to be invested with certain effort before they become a basis of desert and thus this person has actually to incur certain costs. In consequence, I think that on the basis of the concept of desert proposed here, the notion of compensation is fully co-extensive with that of desert. Incidentally, this argument also explains why I use the concept of 'desert' rather than that of 'merit'. Although, in common talk, both notions are used as more or less synonymous, 'merit' suggests some qualities possessed by people, highly valued by society, and as entitling those people to special consideration in distribution of rewards. In the concept of justice endorsed here, no qualities *per se* entitle people to higher rewards; nobody *deserves* more merely by virtue of his or her higher abilities, talents or skills. It is only the amount of burdens incurred in the process of acquisition or use of those abilities which counts in the considerations of desert.

Incidentally, one might envisage the following objection to this attempt at reconciliation of compensation and desert. If A is injured by B's carelessness, we often say that A deserves to be compensated. And why not? And yet, in the case of this example of desert generated by the model of compensation, there is no question of A's valuable characteristics, let alone A's socially valuable effort. So perhaps the latter is not as essential to just desert as it has been suggested so far in this book?

In the first place, it seems that "A deserves to be compensated for his injury" uses 'desert' in a way which was rejected above; that is, as synonymous with formal entitlement.[55] Admittedly, A may claim redress for loss or injury wrongly inflicted on him by B, and he may be entitled to it, but it does not necessarily follow that he deserves it. Desert, for reasons stated above, is a fundamental moral notion which operates irrespective of valid rules conferring entitlements upon people. If, however, one insists that A's moral desert is independent of valid rules, that is, whoever is harmed or injured by someone else, *deserves* to be compensated for the losses incurred, the reply to this is that it all depends on the justness of the prior distribution (that is, before the injurious action). If this distribution had corresponded to just deserts, then *A deserves* to be compensated in the sense that he does not deserve the deprivations to which he has been subjected. This judgment is derivative of (and, thus, not incompatible with) a judgment about desert in terms of socially valuable effort.

The most difficult issue which arises here is, however, *what* should count as grounds for compensable desert. Different theories of job analysis and job evaluation seek to establish lists and ranks of different features of work and relative burdens involved in different sorts of work. Physical effort, amount of time, job environment, risk, responsibility, pressure and so forth are usually thought of as constituting some of those burdens. However, what for some people may be a cost (which therefore increases their total burden), for others may be part of the benefits which they obtain from their work. Responsibility attached to a certain position may be felt by some as a burden, by others as a source of satisfaction; probably most people perceive the responsibility in both ways, with varying proportions of each of those aspects. But each has opposite implications for implementation of the principle of justice as equilibrium; the first interpretation of responsibility leads to demands for higher rewards, the second calls for lower reward (because the rewarding exercise of responsibility is already a part of benefits drawn from work). In this case, in contrast with a conventional wisdom, higher responsibility should be met with diminishing material reward.

Nevertheless, the possibility of so divergent and even opposite interpretations is not devastating for the present conception. A theory of justice takes into account typical situations, and probably it would be right to state that, characteristically, responsibility is rather a source of burden, although one which also involves some degree of personal satisfaction. Burden is not, after all, something that excludes satisfaction; the lack of satisfaction is only one of the forms of burden. In typical situations the burdens of responsibility probably outweigh the satisfaction derived from it. Responsibility may be considered reasonably as a part of global sum of benefits only in so far as it leads to self-fulfilment or personal satisfaction, and not in its own right. There are several types of responsibility, some of them being more conducive to personal fulfilment, others less so. This suggests that it is not responsibility *per se* but its satisfaction-generating elements which should be treated as a part of general benefits. Moreover, a justification of higher rewards for higher responsibility is often based on utilitarian grounds which, although very important, are irrelevant to a theory of justice. Often when we claim that more responsible social positions should have higher rewards attached to them, we argue on *de facto* utilitarian grounds: for example that they should attract more qualified persons. However, the conception of 'just rewards' should ignore utilitarian considerations, although the calculation of optimal reward (from the point of view of both justice and utility) must, of course, take them into account.

Even though the classification of certain attributes of work as burden or benefit may sometimes be difficult, the general idea here is that both sides of the 'calculus' of benefits and burdens should be taken globally. When we think of just reward for a certain work we should take into account the whole package of rewards, including non-material ones, and not only the financial benefits. The totality of social benefits available to a person in a given position should be assessed and compared with the totality of burdens. The monetary return should thus be a complementation of rewards otherwise obtained.

An idea close to that which I am advocating here, can be found in the following words of John Stuart Mill:

> In a co-operative industrial association, is it just or not that talent or skill should give a title to superior remuneration? On the negative side of the question it is argued, that whoever does the best he can, deserves equally well, and ought not in justice to be put in a position of inferiority for no fault of his own; that superior abilities have already advantages more than enough, in the admiration they excite, the personal influence they command, and the internal sources of satisfaction attending them, without adding to these a superior share of the world's goods; and that society is bound in justice rather to make compensation to the less favoured, for this unmerited inequality of advantages, then to aggravate it.[56]

To be sure, Mill does not endorse this idea wholeheartedly as he simultaneously formulates an opposite one (rewards based on talents and skills) in order to reach a conclusion that the principle of utility provides the only possible way of resolving the conflict between those two conflicting conceptions of justice.[57] But it is irrelevant here; what matters is that Mill provides an excellent example of the 'global' approach to compensatory justice. He cites a list of possible non-material rewards enjoyed by persons with higher 'talent or skill': 'admiration', 'personal influence', 'internal sources of satisfaction'. The list may be continued: opportunities of self-development, encouraging and stimulating colleagues, free time, liberty of designing one's plan of work – those sources of satisfaction usually are (although not necessarily) associated with those positions which require higher skills, qualifications and abilities. The point which I wish to make is that they should be taken into account when designing a financial remuneration if the latter is to be seen as a part of a global, aggregate, reward. Adam Smith remarked: "Honour makes a great part of the reward of all honourable professions".[58] When, therefore, a task involves a higher degree of non-material benefits, the salary should be relatively smaller than in the case of a person who incurs a similar amount of burdens but whose non-material rewards (job satisfaction, prestige, and so forth) are smaller. In this sense, material and non-material rewards should be coupled negatively (in case of a similar degree of burdens): a lower degree of non-material rewards should be compensated by a higher salary.

Different elements of reward are viewed here as mutually self-supplementing; those which are more 'manipulable' (for example, salary, length of holidays) serve as a means of compensating for the smaller amount of those elements which are to a lesser extent subject to human influence and design. Again, let me stress, I am abstracting here from the utilitarian arguments about the distribution of rewards. Often, however, utilitarian arguments are consistent with the above argument based on justice: more burdensome occupations should have higher salaries attached to them in order to attract people to those occupations. As Adam Smith observed: "The trade of a butcher is a brutal and odious business; but it is in most places more profitable than the greater part of common trades".[59]

The social structure which would result from the application of this compensatory principle of distribution corresponds to what sociologists and social psychologists call 'status inconsistency', 'rank incongruence' or 'status disequilibrium'. But it is represented in these sciences not so much as a social ideal but, rather, as a descriptive notion (although often with negative flavour). 'Status inconsistency' exists when there is no positive correlation between different rank dimensions and when rankings on different scales (power, money, prestige, etc.) are not in conformity with each other; for instance, when a person ranks high in prestige and low in material position. The opposite situation, namely, when individuals within a group stand in the same rank order in different status hierarchies, is labelled 'status equilibration',[60] 'status in-line-ness', 'status crystallization'[61] or 'status congruency'.[62] Sociological surveys concerning status incongruence in small groups have shown that some stereotypes about its allegedly negative consequences (aggression, increased tensions, weakened motivations for good performance) are unfounded. On the contrary, Stuart Adams has provided evidence for a conclusion that lack of congruence may be an effective motivator for productivity, although it deteriorates when status incongruence increases.⁶³ It should be noted, however, that his assertions referred to a very specific small group (bomber crews undergoing training for combat duties) and are not necessarily adequate for a global society. In a more general context, Melvin M. Tumin has expressed doubts as to "whether any reward system, built into a general stratification system, must allocate equal amounts of all three types of reward ⁶⁴ in order to function effectively, or whether one type of reward may be emphasized to the virtual neglect of others".⁶⁵ Be that as it may, this is a matter of efficiency, not of justice.

An idea similar to the principle that justice requires higher salaries for otherwise less rewarding work, has been expressed (in a quite different context) by a Polish sociologist, Wlodzimierz Wesolowski. When discussing the prospects for social equality in the socialist societies, he has suggested two possible approaches to the problem. Under the first approach, equality consists in the reduction of differences *within* particular dimensions of stratification (for example, reducing the distance from 'high' to 'low' positions as far as the incomes are concerned). The second, 'multi-dimensional', approach is concerned with the "congruence of certain attributes among strata of socialist society" and gives rise, for instance, to the question: "Is the level of income ... synchronised with the levels of education and prestige"?⁶⁶ In consequence, this second idea of equality calls for a lack of synchronisation of particular dimensions of inequality, for a "decomposition of attributes of social position".

Now, this idea seems to be contrary to conventional wisdom which usually disapproves of situations of status inconsistency, sometimes even in terms of injustice. Offhand, it might seem that it is unjust if a person having a higher education earns less than an uneducated one or if a lower position in the hierarchy of power has a higher salary attached to it. The more rigid the social structure of a society is, the stronger are norms against rank inconsistency; in societies of relatively high social mobility situations of incongruence are not viewed as something necessarily abnormal or unjust.

It should be noted, however, that even in the advanced societies which display high social mobility, the view that justice requires status equilibrium is widespread.⁶⁷ It is also true that situations of status disequilibrium are likely to produce negative psychological consequences on the part of those who feel 'deprived': when, for example, a university professor is to be paid less than an industrial worker. Situations of status disequilibrium can lead to aggression in certain conditions, although sociological and psychological evidence shows that this is not necessarily so.⁶⁸ But a theory of justice should aim at the correction of moral opinions when it considers these opinions unjustified; when, for instance, the very fact of rank disequilibrium is seen as a sign of injustice. There is no reason, in terms of justice, why particular dimensions of inequality should be synchronized; if, on the contrary, a compensatory idea of justice may be found plausible, then necessarily it will lead to incongruencies in status. Although certain dissatisfaction may be understandable in those cases, this need not be viewed as a result of injustice. On the other side of the coin, injustice may be perceived when, in the situation of perfect status consistency, the worst-off person in one hierarchy is necessarily and inevitably the worst-off from every point of view.

It is often assumed, for instance, that a high degree of education should be reflected in a higher salary. Indeed, there is convincing statistical evidence of a strong positive correlation between education and earning.[69] But what justice-related argument can be invoked in favour of this rule, except the bad argument that greater capacities call for greater pay (which is unacceptable under the present theory of justice because of the irrelevance of natural abilities to desert, and also because higher education is not necessarily a symptom of higher abilities)? One of the popular arguments is that education may be seen as a sort of 'investment' and, in consequence, a 'burden' incurred voluntarily by a person in view of his or her future benefits. To be sure, there is an immediate appeal in the idea that "not only unpleasant and hazardous work but also terribly responsible positions and functions requiring extensive preliminary training deserve compensation".[70] But, on the basis of the compensatory theory of justice proposed here, in what sense can this 'investment' be viewed as a 'burden' which calls for compensation? I doubt whether the process of education can be considered as a particular burden when compared with other alternative situations, and it seems also that jobs which require higher education usually are more rewarding in a non-material sense. If that is true, and it seems to me to be a general rule, then this 'educational' element of a job should be seen rather as one of rewards and not as a burden to be balanced by some additional benefits of a different nature.

This is not to deny that in particular exceptional situations the successful pursuit of higher education may require considerable effort and even involve the sacrifice of more lucrative and attractive positions. However, I find the general argument that higher salaries may be defended on the basis of an 'investment' in studies unconvincing, since students, in general, are a rather privileged social group as far as the enjoyment of various social benefits is concerned. It is worth recalling in this context Tumin's arguments against the theory that a training period involves sacrifices and, hence, calls for additional benefits.[71] If those sacrifices are identified with the costs of training[72] then, Tumin notes, these costs are generally borne by the parents of the youth undergoing training and, in consequence, the parents' ability to pay for the training of their children is part of the differential *reward* that those parents received for their privileged position in society. If, however, those 'sacrifices' are identified with the surrender of earning power during the training period, then it is manifest in all modern industrial societies that the average earnings of age peers who *did* go into the labour market for a period equal to the average length of the training period are easily earned back by university graduates in the first decade of professional employment, over and above the earnings of their age peers who were not trained. There is, therefore, no justification (in terms of alleged 'sacrifice') for the wage differentials during the remaining twenty or so years when the university graduates earn far more than their unskilled age peers. In addition to this, the numerous non-financial privileges enjoyed by students and not available to their wage-earning peers (prestige, greater opportunity of self-development, enjoyment and entertainment) make the thesis about 'sacrifice' even less tenable. The argument about higher pay for a higher degree of education might, therefore, be maintained only on utilitarian (and not on desert-related) grounds but there are good reasons to believe that higher pay is not the decisive incentive for people being attracted to positions which require high qualifications and which are likely to retain most of the quality of 'internal job satisfaction'. Such positions probably will be filled even if they do not offer any particular financial advantages because their other attributes are sufficiently attractive.

The controversy about the role of education in the determination of pay demonstrates, once again, that in particular cases it is difficult to distinguish between those job attributes which are elements of global benefits and those which constitute burdens. Schematically, however, such a distinction may be made: in typical situations effort (in either the physical or the mental sense), responsibility, burdensome job environment, monotonous and repetitious work, may be considered as burdens; salary, social prestige, degree of satisfaction, security, chances for initiative, self-development and freedom – as benefits. The measurement, in particular of non-material elements of reward, is very difficult in practice although not impossible in principle. Different surveys concerning job satisfaction and the relative weight of particular factors of jobs (such as, for example, growth, challenge, interest), as assessed by employees, bring approximate answers to questions about what people view as particularly important rewards drawn from their employments.[73] Admittedly, it is very difficult to compare these non-material values with financial rewards and to find a correspondence between both; it is not, however, a totally hopeless task. Jan Tinbergen proposed an interesting method for establishing the relative importance of various material and non-material elements of a job. Relations between salaries of different jobs are just when A, who knows both the income and the character of B's job, would not swap his job with B, nor would B with A. If either would, it means that his income must be increased to a point when he finds an income-job mix attractive enough to stick to his work.[74] By a complex method of questionnaires we may establish approximately what are the conditions of trade-off between job satisfaction and pecuniary rewards. By asking people whether they would change their job if the salary were to be decreased by a certain percentage, whether they would change their job if they were offered a more attractive one but less financially rewarding or if their jobs were to become more difficult but better paid, and so on and so forth, we may perhaps arrive at certain indications of the relative value which people attach to material and non-material elements of benefits that they enjoy.

The injustice of the situation in modern advanced societies, both in the East and in the West, consists in the fact that, more often than not, different rankings of hierarchy are closely correlated. There is usually a strong congruence of rankings of pay and status ('status' which expresses, to a certain degree, non-material benefits). It is a rule (not without exceptions) that a person enjoying high prestige, high work satisfaction and high position in the power structure is at the same time very well paid; on the other side of the coin, jobs which have no 'internal' or non-material benefits attached to them, are usually worse paid. This creates a cumulative process of adding insult to injury and of strengthening social stratification. These two rankings are mutually reinforcing: the high 'status' often serves as an independent argument about the need for higher pay. A recent study of wage determination in England reports several instances in which status has been held to be an actual determinant of pay:

In general, the status hierarchy coincided with the national job-rate structure; but where the methods and the organization of work conferred upon different groups of workers rewards which were not regarded as commensurate with the status of the job performed, there was adjustment of earnings to fulfil expectations.[75]

Also Jan Pen notes in his analysis of distribution of incomes that the higher status is often regarded as a sufficient reason for higher pay.[76]

Furthermore, there is a feedback process in status/pay relationships; the other side of the phenomenon of pay being *moulded* by status is the fact that status is often *measured* by pay. In hierarchical societies the fact that a given job is well paid is one of the important determinants of its prestige. The general correlation between status and pay produces a situation in which the former is, *inter alia*, determined by the latter. This may be illustrated by the statement of the chairman of an organisation of British engineers, quoted in a sociological study about the distribution of incomes, who demanded "the need for something to be done about salaries as one leg of a campaign to upgrade engineering and its public image generally".[77] And George Caspar Homans, in his classic study on the employees of Eastern Utilities Co., quotes one of the ledger clerks (otherwise satisfied with his job) as saying: "We ought to get just a couple of dollars (a week) more to show that our job is more important [than that of other employees]".[78]

8. DESERT AND THE PRINCIPLE OF COMPETENCE

So far I have been discussing distributive justice as if it applied to all the good things of life which are socially distributed and allocated. Such an indiscriminate approach is not adequate, of course, at the level of the more detailed analysis. In particular I will suggest that, while justice based on desert (and desert understood essentially as based on effort) should be applied to the distribution of rewards for work done, for sacrifice, effort, time, etc., it does not apply to a distribution of jobs themselves. The adoption of standards of distributive justice with respect to the former (i.e., distribution of rewards) does not imply necessarily the adoption of those same standards with respect to the latter (i.e., distribution of positions).

One might object at this point: if a theory of justice is to be universal, it should have its principles applied to all scarce goods which are distributed socially and which are sought by people. Interesting, satisfying, pleasant and important jobs are typical examples of such scarce goods; why should we not apply the principles of justice to the distribution of those jobs? In this way, the argument would naturally reduce *ad absurdum* the principles of compensatory justice themselves; no reasonable person could claim that in a well-ordered society the allocation of jobs and positions should be based on compensatory criteria and that, for instance, the least able people should be hired for the most responsible jobs in order to have a general balance of benefits and burdens restored. This argument, therefore, would lead to the following dilemma: either the principles of compensatory justice are not valid because they lack the attribute of universality or they produce absurd results when applied in practice. Either way, this argument would appear to discredit the principles of compensatory justice.

The simplest line of defence would be the following: although the principles of compensatory justice outlined above are universally valid, nevertheless when applied to certain spheres of social life, they produce more detrimental effects in terms of social utility than in other spheres. The sum of negative effects (in utilitarian terms) of these principles applied to an allocation of employment would most certainly prevail over the amount of benefits in terms of justice. Hence, it is not the ethical absurdity of application of these principles to hiring but the negative result of the calculus of pros (in terms of justice) and cons (in terms of utility) that allows us to abandon them when designing the procedures and criteria for hiring persons to jobs. Although we can say, with a considerable plausibility, that the application of those principles to the sphere of salary fixing would not undermine the whole structure of a well-ordered society (we might reasonably hope that, notwithstanding less impressive wages, the most responsible jobs would be taken by the most qualified people because of the non-material rewards attached to them), it would be a fair guess that if those principles were to be applied to the process of hiring, we would end up with the least competent people in the most responsible positions and that would undermine the proper functioning of any society.

Be that as it may, this analysis won't do, since considerations of utility have no bearing upon the consideration of justice in the present theory. The same conclusion, however, may be reached in another way. There *are* differences between job placement and income distribution important enough to justify the application of different sets of distributive principles.[79] There is no contradiction between, on the one hand, the claims that incomes should be an instrument for moderating or even nullifying the effects of natural or social contingencies and, on the other hand, the proposition that there are no sufficient reasons why the distribution of those jobs should be also of compensatory character. From the point of view of a standard of desert, its application to income distribution is fully justified because the job is *already* done, an effort has been already spent. Here the application of compensatory justice is legitimate because we try to restore a balance which is actually upset by the fact that someone has had to spend time, effort and energy in doing something socially valuable. The situation is different, however, at the stage of job placement and that is why the application of the notion of desert there is not as convincing as in the first situation. When we say that X deserves a certain job, we do not usually mean that it would be just to hire X on the basis of past sacrifice of his (although this meaning may be sometimes employed) but rather that he is the most qualified person of all the candidates and, therefore, that there are reasonable prospects that he will be a good and efficient employee (past experience, of course, is usually taken into account, but as a basis for predicting future usefulness of a person). This, however, as I have pointed out earlier, is not a correct use of the notion of 'desert' which is necessarily past-oriented; one cannot be said to 'deserve' something on the basis of the probable future utility of a proposed distribution.[80] This is, therefore, a utilitarian argument, not an argument about justice. We sometimes use the statement "X deserves that job" in yet another meaning: that on the basis of some formal promises or valid rules X is the one who should be hired for that position; when, for example, X meets in the highest degree of all candidates the set of formal conditions listed in an advertisement for a job. But then it is on the basis of 'entitlement' and not of 'desert' that X should be given that job and, again, as I stated earlier, those two criteria do not necessarily coincide.[81]

In consequence, I think it is fair to say that job placement does not fit the general pattern in which the categories of 'desert' are applicable and thus should not be governed by the principles of justice-as-desert. This conclusion is supported by a further reflection. Income distribution is uncontroversially and undoubtedly a distribution of benefits. It obviously fits the scheme of balance of burdens and benefits as a form of the distribution of benefits. But this is not necessarily true of job placement; while in some circumstances it may be regarded by some people as allocation of rewards, it can be also (and often is) viewed as distribution of burdens. After all, for most people work is essentially an important burden, a necessary means of assuring the material basis for their own and their family's life. From the fact that in non-slave societies hiring is not compulsory it does not follow that it is always *de facto* voluntary, in a non-legal sense. With this ambiguity of the meaning of 'job' in mind it should appear as very far from obvious that the allocation of jobs is to be always considered on the 'benefits' side of the benefits/burdens calculus. This is why the allocation of jobs is not necessarily a subject-matter of the oonception of justice as a balance of benefits and burdens although, as I have proposed earlier, some attributes of jobs should be considered as elements of benefits and of burdens. But a job, as such, is not a single element of this calculus which may be simply put on one side; it is, rather, an aggregate category which should be separated into its different elements before we apply the principles of justice to it.

It is evident, therefore, that there is no essential conflict between the principle of hiring the most competent and rewarding on a compensatory basis. These are two distinct issues and the difference between them justifies application of different standards. Accordingly, the idea that higher skills required in a job call for a higher salary has no justification in the theory of justice endorsed here in so far as higher skills do not necessarily represent higher effort, whether effort in the job or effort in acquiring the qualifications for it.

9. THE ROLE OF DESERT

At the outset I have mentioned that desert is not the only standard governing a just distribution and that desert-related considerations do not exhaust the scope of considerations of justice. There are certain burdens which cannot be described adequately as 'desert' in the strict sense of the word but which it would be unjust to ignore and to fail to compensate them with social benefits. That is why identifying distributive justice with "getting what one deserves"[82] is unjustified and leads to a watering down of the specificity of desert considerations. It often happens that distributive criteria other than desert (such as formal entitlements or basic human needs) override those of desert. In those cases the assertion "X does not deserve it" does not necessarily imply "X should not get it" or "X should be deprived of it".

Considering all things, one must conclude that desert is but one of several grounds of just distribution. However, one should not push this point too far: while desert is not *the* criterion of justice, it is nevertheless an extremely important criterion; indeed, an essential one. It is the only basis of just distribution which is necessarily and inherently connected with, and justified by, moral praise for the action of a particular individual. In other justice-related considerations this association is an accidental rather than a necessary one. In the case of needs we appeal to our feelings of sympathy or of pity but not necessarily to any moral praise of the needy. We base our claim of just distribution, in those cases, on respect for an individual as a member of the general class of human beings, not on respect for the particular individual for what he has specifically done. Nor, in case of arguments based on rights and entitlements need we argue about the moral qualities of the beneficiary of a distribution: the reasons are of an institutional and formal nature rather than being directly moral. It is only in the case of desert that moral praise for the particular individual is expressed in the act of distributive justice. It is, therefore, an important embodiment of the conception of a human being as an individual and as an autonomous moral agent. It is only in the case of desert that a person is awarded certain benefits because of his individual, socially valuable effort. That is why a valid conception of desert must assume the view of persons as autonomous moral individuals; we reward for desert because we believe that what a person has done was under his or her control and that it was socially valuable.

In a word, distribution according to desert is important because it tries to introduce a conscious moral element into human affairs. It wants to base the distribution of scarce goods on principles which are intelligible, relevant and deliberately chosen by a community; it rejects the view that a social distribution should be a matter of uncontrollable and impersonal forces, an "outcome of a mixed game of skill and chance".[83] By demanding the elimination, or reduction, of the impact of uncontrollable factors (such as genetic endowment or social position at birth) upon the distributive shares, this theory of desert appeals to a certain view about human freedom. A free person should, as much as it is possible, be the master of his (or her) own fate; hence, his situation should not be a function of factors which are totally beyond his control. This is, ultimately, what justice-as-desert is all about: an attempt to make a person's situation dependent upon his own free choices, and to liberate, to the largest possible extent, people from the operation of uncontrollable forces in a social distribution. It is a protest against the reduction of social life to a game or to a lottery, and it is a defence of the relevance of morality to social allocation of desired goods.

CHAPTER 6

NEEDS AND JUSTICE

Under the theory of justice as a balance of benefits and burdens, needs are relevant to just distribution only in so far as they express actual burdens, not in their own right. To the extent to which unmet, important needs are a burden in one's life and constitute an important impediment to achieving one's life-plans, they should be considered as creating a disequilibrium of benefits and burdens. But it is not the existence of *any* needs that is a proper reason for compensatory action. It is not even the existence of any *important* unmet needs that is a sufficient reason for a compensation. After all, the need for love, self-respect or self-realization is important but the fact that it is unmet is not a sufficient reason for social compensation. On the other hand, unfulfilled needs for basic food or shelter or education or medical protection give rise to a legitimate claim for their provision because it is typically within human power to satisfy those needs in the course of social action and, as long as they remain unsatisfied, a person suffers major obstacles in his life, including obstacles to his individual action in satisfying all his other needs. The main difficulty lies, of course, in determining which important needs, when unmet, constitute such a burden as to justify collective intervention leading to a restoration of the equilibrium. Only some needs call for such action; the indiscriminate treatment of all needs as requiring satisfaction in the name of justice would, besides everything else, put seriously in question the possibility of distribution according to desert which, as I have suggested earlier, has primary importance.

Claims to special treatment on the basis of some important needs are independent of claims based on desert. In case of people who are handicapped, chronically ill, homeless and so on, their claims to justice in the form of special treatment are not based on moral desert, strictly speaking. When, for example, Joel Feinberg says:

A man with a chronically sick wife or child *deserves* compensation since through no fault of his own he has a greater need than others; and the same is true of the man with a large number of dependents[1]

he is using the notion of desert in a broader sense than one advocated in this book. Neither having a sick wife, nor a large number of dependents, is a ground of desert in a strict sense of the word, but rather of special needs. It is the existence of those needs that calls for action in the name of justice, although not in the name of justice-as-desert.

1. BASIC NEEDS

Different needs have different status with respect to a theory of justice. I submit that only basic needs unquestionably require social intervention for the sake of justice, irrespective of desert considerations. Only those needs may be said to constitute obviously and inherently a burden such that their satisfaction is a necessary condition of a person being able to realize and fulfil his or her other needs and desires.

There are various ways of defining the things which constitute basic needs. Some writers link them with survival: their lack presents most important threats to life and prevents a person from engaging in professional activity or from making use of available means to protect life.[2] Consistently with the intuitive notion of 'basic', basic needs are considered to be for things in the absence of which "a person would be harmed in some crucial and fundamental way".[3] The basic character of certain needs is often defined by their universal and general character: those needs are simply "present in all men".[4]

Those different approaches to 'basic needs' seem to define rather clearly areas of these needs: they are closely related to a minimal level of subsistence, to the fundamental conditions of biological and social life. Vague though it is, Rodney Peffer's description seems to me to point out this aspect properly: basic needs are related to "those things which we require if we are to survive and to have any sort of a life worth living".[5] But, at the same time, this formula suggests that there is some room for cultural variation in defining the level of 'basic needs'; in so far as they represent something more than bare survival, they are determined by social standards which vary in different societies. Those standards are certainly determined by prevailing life-styles, general moral ideas and also by the productive capacities of the economy. For instance, criteria of what shelter is basic vary as a function of, among other things, the wealth of a society; not only because a more affluent economy can provide people with more comfortable housing but also because it tends to favour life-styles and attitudes in which higher quality housing is considered 'basic'. The relationship between the economic capacities of an economy and the standard of basic needs is not, therefore, direct and simple: the fact that, say, objective economic conditions in India are not sufficient to provide everyone with food does not justify the conclusion that people there do not have a 'basic' need for food.

This does not cast doubt on the general assertion of a certain relativity of basic needs. One should, however, be very careful about the limits of this relativity and one should not push this argument too far. An excessive emphasis on social or cultural relativity leads to a situation in which the limits of what is 'basic' are located either too low or too high. The first instance is illustrated, I think, by the views of S. I. Benn and R. S. Peters. They stress that 'basic needs' are "governed by a social norm" and that there is no universal standard of need. For example, if basic needs are linked with health protection, it is because "the social norm is a state of health. Where poor sight is common and spectacles rare, there would be no basic need for spectacles".[6] But, being governed by social norms, basic needs are necessarily related to a standard of needs which are actually satisfied already for a majority of the population:

'Basic needs' are thus a function of the general living standards of the community in question, which yield norms like 'subsistence level', or 'a decent standard of living'. In any community there is a certain income (the median) enjoyed by the most numerous income group, which sets the minimum standards of expectation of that community. It comes as something of a shock, therefore, when we encounter in our community people well below that standard. We call them 'the needy', because they lack what the overwhelming majority enjoy – they fall below the norm.[7]

I am not convinced by this argument. Do we call some people 'needy' only on the basis of general standards of this community as enjoyed by the most numerous group? It seems to me that often we apply the criteria of needs, or even of 'basic needs', irrespective of whether or not the standard necessary to their satisfaction is already attained by the most numerous group in this society. According to the terminology proposed by Benn and Peters, it would be always an error to say that the majority of people in a given society have their basic needs unmet. But such an assertion does not strike me as internally inconsistent. I do not find any absurdity in saying that a certain society fails to provide satisfaction of basic needs for most of its members and I do not see any clear reason why such a complaint could be made correctly with respect to a minority only (unless, of course, this comparison involves a judgment by reference to some other, or more all-inclusive, community, in which case the relativist conception is no longer as 'relativist' as its advocates believe). Even if standards of 'basic needs' are determined socially and culturally, this determination is visible in relation to an observer's standards of assessment of basic needs in a given society rather than as a function of what "the overwhelming majority enjoy". Below a certain level, 'basic needs' are simply biologically determined and the margin of relativity is very narrow:

most economists, for instance, do not have problems understanding what is meant by basic housing unit for a family in a particular country, or by survival values of nutrition.[8] If people are starving, then this fact *has* something to do with their basic needs grounded in regular features of human life, irrespective of whether the overwhelming majority suffers hunger or not.

Over-emphasis on the relativity of basic needs may also lead to a situation where the level of what is 'basic' is located too high, from the point of view of common sense. The reason for this is that the extreme relativist concept of 'basic needs' is concerned only with *relative* deprivations and with inequalities, without paying any attention to the harm caused (in absolute terms) to people whose needs are unmet. If we adopt a criterion of basic needs which is described solely in terms of welfare distribution, for instance by considering as 'needy' everyone whose income is less than half of the society's median income, the inevitable consequence of such an approach is that there will be always the same proportion of needy persons in society, even if the general standard of living rises, in absolute terms, twice, five times or ten times. This seems to me to be a counter-intuitive notion which stems from the rejection of objective ingredients (that is, ingredients related to deprivations stated in absolute and not in relative terms) of 'basic needs' and which confuses the idea of satisfaction of needs with the idea of equitable distribution.[9] A statutory prohibition, in California, against the attachment by creditors of the family TV set, presumably because it is recognized as a necessity,[10] seems to be a good example of such an unreasonable relativisation of 'basic needs'. Frank Michelman observes that, in societies where private car ownership is prevalent and where the distances between residential areas and work-places are long, "a private car may become, in practice, a critical factor in employability and in general mobility"[11] and that leads to recognition of private automobiles as basic needs. Yesterday's luxuries are transformed into today's necessities, we are told. But we must impose some limits on what is to be counted as 'basic' or else the concept of 'basic needs' will fall under its own weight. That is why the argument of the 'rising minimum' should not be pushed too far.

The exaggerated stress on the variability and relativity of 'basic needs' may lead to questioning of the usefulness of this notion, to suggestions about the impossibility of their more concrete determination. Charles Frankel, for example, without completely rejecting the notion, asks two questions about 'elementary human needs': firstly, what is the list of those needs? (as to which he remarks: "That it is an indefinitely expandable list is at least suggested by recent history"), and secondly,

What do we have in mind when we speak of 'satisfying' a need? How far does the term 'satisfaction' go? Granted that all men need a minimal amount of food, how pleasant should the food be, how varied, how bountiful?[12]

Now, any morally laden notion may be reduced *ad absurdum* in an analogous way, although probably this was not Frankel's intention. The questions he asks are not easy to answer and certainly there may be controversies about practical matters in particular societies to do with the boundary between basic needs and luxuries. There is, undoubtedly, some room for cultural variation in defining 'basic needs'. For instance clothing, apart from providing protection against the climate and other aspects of the environment, fulfils also other functions: it is usually necessary to meet certain customary clothing standards before people can play a normal role in society. But the existence of borderline cases and of socio-cultural relativity as to what is 'basic' does not suggest that the notion does not make sense or that it is totally incapable of specification. Apart from all the cultural relativities, there are certain attributes of human beings *qua* members of the same biological species which determine the uncontroversial sphere of basic needs (for example, below a certain level of calory intake, starvation and damage to vital organs occur); there are also socially determined needs (e.g., for a basic education) without satisfaction of which meaningful life in a society is seriously impeded. Furthermore, I do not think that disagreements about what needs are basic are so significant as Frankel suggests, although certainly there are disagreements about the moral principle that a community has a duty to satisfy the basic needs of all its members.

The distinction between basic and non-basic needs is of particular relevance to a theory of justice as equilibrium for it sets up the boundaries of needs-based claims of justice. Over and above the minimum, a just distribution should be based on other principles of justice and, in particular, upon the principle of desert. It follows, therefore, that attempts at discrediting this distinction are at the same time directed against the compensatory conception of justice in so far as it postulates distribution according to basic needs. One example of such a criticism of this distinction may be illustrated by an argument of Robert Nozick's. Criticizing the view that medical need is the only proper criterion for the distribution of medical care, Nozick suggests ironically, that similarly "the only proper criterion for the distribution of barbering services is barbering need" and then defends a barber's liberty to offer his services according to his own criteria, for example "to those he most likes to talk to". Reducing the whole argument to absurdity, Nozick asks: "Need a gardener allocate his services to those lawns which need him most? ... In what way does the situation of a doctor differ?"[13]

It seems that it does differ in a very important way, indeed. Even abstracting from the obviously misleading, and not very serious, example of a gardener having to offer his services to "those lawns which need him most", the relations: barber-customer and doctor-patient are of a completely different nature because in the latter, *basic* human needs are involved, while none are in the former. There are good reasons why an individual should have, irrespective of his financial abilities or of his moral desert, legitimate claims against the community to medical care (within the limits of the technical and financial capacities of this society).[14] Some will argue about it in terms of the right to life; others will appeal to a general duty to render aid to people in situations of terminal danger; I, for one, will argue in terms of prerequisites for desert-considerations. Be that as it may, we are, as a matter of principle, unwilling to allow the allocation of scarce medical resources merely on the basis of the prevailing distribution of wealth in society precisely because these resources are so crucial for protection of central human values, that is to say, of human life. Now, the claims about medical care are not addressed to any particular doctor but, rather, to the community as a whole and it is up to this community to organise the medical care in one way or another. The doctor's right to proper remuneration should not be neglected either but those rights are not necessarily in conflict with people's needs to have their health protection assured. The obligation to provide medical care does not fall on doctors *qua* particular individuals but rather on the community as a whole. It has to be decided between the community and doctors how to reconcile the satisfaction of basic human needs for medical care with the rights of doctors.

At the same time, there is no similar justification for claims against society concerning, say, 'barbering needs' (to use again Nozick's example). More generally, there are three main reasons for asserting that a community has no duties with respect to the satisfaction of other than basic needs; that, in other words, the problem of satisfying non-basic needs is beyond the scope of principles of social justice. First, at some point distribution according to needs necessarily must conflict with distribution according to desert. I have argued in the former chapter in favour of the fundamental character of distribution according to desert and, even though the satisfaction of basic needs has priority, this is so because no one can meaningfully have chances to deserve something unless his basic needs are met. In this sense, a satisfaction of basic needs is a prerequisite of any reasonable application of the principle 'to each according to his desert' (I will return to this point later). But, beyond the minimum of basic needs, an attempt to distribute goods according to needs in general would seriously impede distribution according to desert.

The second reason for the claim that non-basic needs do not create any social duties in terms of justice is that needs beyond a certain minimum are extremely vague. As we have seen, although basic needs are not a very precise notion, within a particular society there may be a degree of agreement about what needs are most basic. It is almost impossible, however, to define the modes of application of 'higher', non-basic needs, such as the need for leisure, self-realization, satisfaction, cultural self-development and so on. Moreover, it is unclear whether the means for satisfaction of these higher needs are distributable at all. Satisfaction of basic needs for food, shelter or security is a problem which can be solved through social distribution: when something is given to an individual, the need is met. But this is not necessarily the case with the needs for self-fulfilment etc.; by their nature, they cannot be simply 'met' (through the act of distribution) by a community. True, society can distribute some resources which help to satisfy these needs but this distribution is never a sufficient guarantee of the satisfaction of those needs. This satisfaction depends more on the individual concerned than on the society. After all, if we distribute food to a hungry person, we know that his needs are met but when we allocate places at universities to some of the candidates, we cannot be sure that their needs for self-fulfilment will be satisfied. In consequence, even though needs for self-esteem, self-realization or love may be held to be extremely important, it is hard to see how a society can be said to have any duties with respect to the direct satisfaction of those needs.

This leads me to the third reason for restricting the theory of justice to basic needs. The only way of rescuing the concept of non-basic needs from the objection of vagueness is through the emphasis on the 'objectivist' interpretation of these needs, as contrasted with the subjective wants. Indeed, the distinction between 'needs' and 'wants' is generally accepted in the modern theoretical literature about needs. One of the essential criteria of this distinction is that needs are determined not only by the fact that they are felt by someone but in addition (or even independently) by reference to some objective tests. Accordingly, when we make statements about someone needing something, we suggest not only (and, in certain interpretations, not even necessarily) that this person wants it or desires it, but also that this object of actual or potential desire is conducive to some ends and values, judged as important and positive by an observer who makes statements about those needs. Need is not merely a psychological state; it is an aim which can be attributed to a person on 'objective' grounds, independently of the actual realization of those needs by a person.[15]

This distinction between objective 'needs' and subjective 'wants' is sometimes presented as the distinction between so-called 'true' and 'false' needs. An important line of critique of modern consumer society is based on such a distinction. What is actually desired by people, and what they consider to be their needs is, according to this critique, essentially influenced by the ruling interests in the given society and is a part of the general scheme of domination. An explicit illustration of the contrast between 'false' and 'true' needs on a similar basis is given by Kai Nielsen:

[W]here the needs in question are also 'true needs' or 'genuine needs', we are speaking ... of needs which answer to the pervasive interests of human beings. True needs answer to such interests, false needs do not; rather false needs are those things that people come to want and feel they must have as a result of social stimulation and ideological indoctrination and would not otherwise feel such ... attachment to or concern about.[16]

It is hard to deny that the very distinction between 'true' and 'false' needs has some rational nucleus in it, that human needs are often artificially stimulated and that, as a result of this stimulation, people start to think that they need something that otherwise they would not. But when applied to a theory of social justice, the distinction between 'true' and 'false' needs (or between objective needs and actual wants) is fraught with practical dangers. A theory of justice which demands a distribution according to needs but at the same time clearly distinguishes between those needs which are 'true' and those which are 'false' (although actually shared by some people), inevitably must end up with an agency that will decide which needs deserve the attribute of being 'true' or 'genuine'. To be sure, a certain degree of social evaluation of claims is necessary in the case of any other principle of justice as well, for instance, when we have to assess what should be counted as desert and what are relative values of different deserts. But it is only in the case of the claims based on needs that the explicit distinction between what is actually felt by people and what 'objectively' merits a positive evaluation, is so clear and straightforward. In the case of judgments of desert, we stop short of imposing upon those who disapprove of them, any standards of 'what is really good for them'; we are merely stating what effort is beneficial for a society, and we try to influence human activity accordingly. So no paternalistic aspiration is implied in the attempts to base social distribution on the standards of desert. However, in the case of distribution according to needs (all needs, that is), we are inevitably substituting our judgment for the judgment of recipients about what they really need. We are, therefore, denying in practice that they are the best judges of what is best for them.

This danger of paternalism is symbolically illustrated by the fact that in justifying a distinction between 'true' and 'false' needs, authors often appeal to examples about children. Thorstein Eckhoff writes that "[i]n this, partly normative, sense a child may need medicine which he does not like, while he is not considered to need sweets which he does like".[17] Christian Bay states:

[A]nyone who has ever dealt with young children must for practical purposes recognise that what children must have, or need, may or may not correspond to what they demonstrably want. Clinical psychologists and social workers in their work routines know that the same can be true of adults. Only liberal social scientists, plus the vast constituencies of citizens who have been taught that constitutional democracy should always prevail, appear to be blind to this particular part of common sense.[18]

The last phrase in Bay's passage suggests why this "part of common sense" is dangerous when applied to political practice, including the operations of social justice. Treatment of children is not a proper model for general rules for just distribution in a society. A model of just distribution in which someone is to decide what the subjects 'really need' and to distribute medicines rather than sweets when his childish subjects mistakenly think that they need the latter, requires indeed the rejection of the view that "constitutional democracy should always prevail". In this model, a citizen's conviction that he is the supreme judge of his needs is a pure illusion: he falsely takes his wants for needs. Human wants will merit the honorific title of 'true needs' only when people become fully rational: when they will be able *themselves* to distinguish between their true needs and the temptations which lead to false needs. In this sense, the idea of true *versus* false needs is associated with a certain normative view about human rationality. This is expressly stated by Kai Nielsen who writes that "talk of needs, including talk of 'true needs', is to be seen as an integral part of a conception of what it is to be a thoroughly rational person or a fully reasonable human being".[19] Unless individuals live up to this ideal of "a thoroughly rational person", their actual needs obviously have a similar status to those of children and Bay's distrust for constitutional democracy is fully understandable in this case.

Again, I do not deny that there *is* a meaningful distinction between needs and wants or, alternatively, between true and false needs. Many people eventually recognize themselves that what they were seeking in the past was not really in their interest and did not correspond to their needs. But if the opposition of 'true' or 'genuine' needs and actual but 'false' needs is to be one of the pillars of the conception of justice, then it obviously advocates (or, at least, gives a justification for) a disregard for what people actually want, seek and demand. It presupposes a distinction between what I actually want and what I should want, between what I am seeking and what is really in my best interest, between what I think that I need and what I really need (and what I would need were I more 'rational' and more 'responsible'). This danger is much less obvious in the case of adopting only *basic* needs as the standard for distribution, since the gap between 'objective needs' and subjective wants at the level of subsistence conditions is very unlikely.

2. BASIC NEEDS AND DESERT

I have already argued against excessive relativism in identifying 'basic needs' but at the same time it is necessary to admit that those needs cannot be determined in an absolutely objective manner. On the basis of this argument some social thinkers reject the legitimacy of distribution according to basic needs: since we cannot define their scope objectively, any measure of 'basic' needs must be relative and, in consequence, arbitrary. This implies, therefore, an imposition upon a society of a hierarchy of values which is not necessarily and not usually shared by all its members.

This argument is advanced by F. A. Hayek with respect to medical protection. He rejects the view that "medical needs are usually of an objectively ascertainable character".[20] We can always think of an additional effort and an additional amount of resources that can be spent in each situation of medical need and therefore there must be some method to put a lid on it. Hence, there is an alternative: either the limits of those resources will be determined collectively (in the form of a public health service) or they will be influenced by the financial capacities of the patient. Hayek clearly opts for this second method, as being less arbitrary:

Somebody must always decide whether an additional effort and additional outlay of resources are called for. The real issue is whether the individual concerned is to have a say and be able, by an additional sacrifice, to get more attention or whether the decision is to be made for him by somebody else.[21]

The idea that an individual should have a say about additional resources devoted to his medical treatment, and be able to obtain more attention "by an additional sacrifice", is somewhat troublesome: what about persons who are unable to make this additional sacrifice to secure more money for that treatment? Leaving aside this question, the point here is that Hayek's argument takes it for granted that there cannot be any agreement on the reasonable measure of satisfaction of needs (in this case: of needs for medical protection). He suggests that when a decision is made for a person "by somebody else", it always involves arbitrariness and imposition of someone else's values upon that person. But that is not necessarily true. Probably most of us would agree that, in a situation of scarcity of resources, a person suffering from yellow fever should be given priority over someone needing a cosmetic operation or contact lenses. There is an element of objectivity in the assessment of the hierarchy of basic needs and the hierarchy of their satisfaction: the more directly needs are related to subsistence, the more basic they are and, therefore, the higher priority they should have when the decisions about distribution of resources are made.

But even in less clear-cut situations than the choice between treatment of yellow fever and fitting contact lenses, the possible disagreements over the hierarchy and priority of needs do not necessarily undermine the whole idea of social distribution according to basic needs. Hayek's argument has the following structure: since people disagree among themselves about the priority of needs, we should abandon the social duty to satisfy basic needs because its implementation must involve the imposition of someone's hierarchy of needs upon other people. But the conclusion does not necessarily follow from the premises concerning disagreement; people may disagree on the *measures* and hierarchy of particular needs but, at the same time, agree on the *principle* of the satisfaction of basic needs. The argument runs similarly to that on desert: I do not like having your hierarchy of basic needs imposed upon me, but I would rather have this situation than that of complete disrespect for basic needs in social distribution. To take Hayek's example, I may disagree with the way the public medical service distributes its resources, but I still think it is a lesser evil than not to have any public medical service at all and to distribute health resources solely on the basis of patients' capacities to pay.

But the more general question remains: even if we leave aside moral disagreements about the priorities of needs that have to be satisfied, are there any 'objective' grounds for judging which needs are more basic and which are less? Previously, I have proposed the general principle that it is relevance to subsistence that dictates such an objective hierarchy of needs. This commonsense opinion seems to be confirmed by behavioural studies and, in particular, by the well-known theory of needs put forward by Abraham Maslow. He argues that human needs are arranged in a hierarchy of 'prepotency' which means that "the most prepotent goal will monopolise consciousness and will tend of itself to organise the recruitment of the various capacities of the organism".[22] Maslow lists five sets of basic needs in the order of their priority: physiological needs, safety, love, esteem and self-actualisation. Now, the actual list, the hierarchy of needs, and their classification as basic may be controversial. But one thing seems to be obvious and it is relevant to ethical judgment about the place of needs in a theory of justice: needs are arranged in a hierarchy of prepotency and "the appearance of one need usually rests on the prior satisfaction of another, more prepotent need".[23] To be sure, humans should not be seen just as animals; one could therefore argue that the so-called higher needs are equally essential for a life worth living. Granted. But in order to have a worthwhile life, one must have a life in the first place. The very emergence of certain needs is conditioned largely by the satisfaction of the more basic ones. This is confirmed both by everyday experience and by clinical experiments; for instance, in the situation of starvation or semi-starvation people are usually dominated by the thought of food and all other, higher desires succumb to the hunger drive.[24] This suggests that satisfaction of those 'basic needs' is a condition of all other needs: not only of *satisfaction* of those other needs, but also of *emergence* of those needs.

From the point of view of a theory of justice this conclusion is of great importance: the failure to satisfy basic needs is such a heavy burden in a person's life that he is unable to participate normally in social co-operation and to become the subject of other principles of justice. In particular, if we agree that justice-as-desert is of fundamental ethical importance, then we must also conclude that only those people whose basic needs are satisfied are 'eligible' for desert considerations. One cannot be said to deserve something, one cannot even try to do something which may be counted as grounds of desert, without having basic needs satisfied first. This simple observation suggests a plausible justification for the principle of satisfaction of basic needs within the theory of justice where desert is the fundamental principle of distribution. This observation also explains the relationship between the principle of desert and the principle of basic needs. Implementation of the latter is the condition of the application of the former: questions of desert do not even arise where basic needs are not satisfied. The principle of desert remains the fundamental moral principle of justice but it can be meaningfully put in force only when the basic needs of all members of the community are satisfied.[25] Distribution according to desert when basic needs of some are unmet is not genuine because some people haven't got an opportunity to deserve anything. They are prevented, due to these deprivations, from developing their life-plans with this minimal degree of autonomy which makes 'desert' possible. Not only are their aspirations destroyed but also all the resources available to them have to be used in their struggle for subsistence. Desert has been defined in this book as expressing socially valuable effort but a starving person has to spend all his effort in order to satisfy his basic needs in the first place.

3. NEEDS AND RIGHTS

The principle that the satisfaction of basic needs should have priority over all other distributive principles suggests that people have *rights* to the satisfaction of their basic needs. To say that those claims have priority over other claims, and that they have a special weight overriding the weight of other claims, practically amounts to saying that these claims are based on a person's rights. The proper way to elucidate the view that basic needs give birth to rights is to examine the principal criticisms that have been made of it. The nature of the three counter-arguments that I will discuss is similar: they all attempt to show that the concept of rights based on basic needs would require a significant transformation and distortion of the traditional concept of a right. They attempt to show that the notion of basic-needs-as-rights is qualitatively different from rights which are less controversial, such as property rights or rights to physical security. To apply the concept of 'rights' to claims for recipience of means necessary to the satisfaction of basic needs would, then, constitute a misuse of the language of rights.

The importance of these arguments is not merely terminological. By asserting that rights to the satisfaction of basic needs are not genuine rights, they advocate the view that a community has no obligation to meet its members' basic needs or, at least, that this obligation is of lesser importance than the protection of 'classical' rights. My strategy will be to show that there is nothing about rights of recipience which makes them relevantly different from other, non-controversial rights. I will show that the three features by virtue of which rights of recipience are frequently denied the status of 'rights' are equally manifested by other rights which are not questioned *qua* rights. These features, therefore, cannot serve as a test for distinguishing genuine rights from non-rights. If my arguments are correct, the refusal to recognize rights to the satisfaction of basic needs as genuine rights is based on a false reading of the nature of rights in general. The main thrust of my argument will be negative: I will show not so much that rights based upon basic needs *are* rights indeed but rather that there is nothing about them which makes them ill-suited to constitute genuine rights. But, although essentially defensive, when this argument is combined with the assertion of the priority of satisfaction of basic needs over other just claims, it goes a long way toward demonstrating that people indeed have genuine rights to the satisfaction of their basic needs.

First, it is sometimes suggested that the effective satisfaction of people's needs (including basic needs) would often require violation of some existing rights (for instance, property rights); therefore, it cannot constitute a right itself. This opinion is expressed in Nozick's conception of rights:

> The major objection to speaking of everyone's having a right *to* various things such as equality of opportunity, life, and so on, and enforcing this right, is that these 'rights' require a substructure of things and materials and actions; and *other* people may have rights and entitlements over these. No one has a right to something whose realization requires certain uses of things and activities that other people have rights and entitlements over.[26]

This last phrase implicitly assumes that there can be no real conflicts of rights: in those cases one of the conflicting 'rights' is not a genuine one. If *A* claims he has a right to *X* and *B* claims he has a right to something that requires a use of *X*, then one of those putative 'rights' is not a true one, Nozick suggests. The primacy is given in such cases to property rights:

> Other people's rights and entitlements to *particular* things ... and how they choose to exercise these rights and entitlements fix the external environment of any given individual and the means that will be available to him.[27]

But it seems to me that this view mistakenly identifies the very existence of a right with the absolute weight of this right. For Nozick, it is impossible to violate one right in the application of another right because one of those 'rights' is not a genuine right. His theory of rights rests upon the assumption that it is not possible for rights to conflict with each other and that if someone has a right to a thing, no-one else can have rights with respect to that thing. But surely the possibility of occasional conflicts of rights is compatible with the very notion of a right. Even if we consider such classical and noncontroversial rights as the right to free speech (as distinguished from the rights of recipience, which are defended in this Section), we see that they are not 'absolute'; for example, a right to free speech can be in conflict with the right not to be maliciously slandered by newspapers. We have to decide which right to uphold in preference to the other, but this fact does not negate the existence of any of these rights. It suggests only that neither of them is absolute: in order to apply one of them, it may be necessary to infringe another. Each person's enjoyment of his rights can limit the exercise of rights by others. The decision about the hierarchy of rights depends on a particular hierarchy of values but the suggestion that if one of the rights is effectively overriden by another then the first one is something less than a 'right', is not justified. Rights correspond to protected interests and, since interests have to be balanced against each other, the exercise of various rights will involve mutual balancing in cases of conflict. It is commonplace that sometimes we must place limits on the exercise of one right in order to make the application of the other right possible, and this is a notion which can be perfectly well accommodated in the general framework of a theory of rights.

Rights are rights if they have a certain 'threshold weight' against claims based on other considerations, such as utility. According to Dworkin's well-known formula of rights as trumps: "If someone has a right to something, then it is wrong for the government to deny it to him even though it would be in the general interest to do so".[28] But this is a test of rights *versus* utility, not of rights *versus* other rights. For any right there may be other rights (or other moral claims) of greater importance. There is no reason to think that all rights have exactly the same weight and, therefore, that conflict between rights is conceptually impossible. As Dworkin points out, "the Government has a reason for limiting rights if it plausibly believes that a competing right is more important".[29]

Judith J. Thomson makes a useful terminological suggestion dealing with the situation in which the exercise of one right has to be limited in order to make the attainment of another, more important, goal possible.[30] She proposes to distinguish between the 'infringement' of a right and the 'violation' of a right. Suppose, she says, that someone has a right that such and such shall not be the case. Now, we *violate* this right when we bring it about that it is the case and, at the same time, if we act wrongly. But we *infringe* this right when we bring it about that it is the case and, at the same time, our action is not wrong. The example she gives is the following: a child will die if he is not given a particular drug immediately; the only available bit of this drug is locked in a case which is in the house of someone who is out of town and cannot be asked for his consent. Breaking into his house and getting the drug *infringes* the owner's right but does not *violate* it because "a child's life being at stake, we do not act wrongly if we go ahead; that is, though we infringe a number of your rights, we violate none of them".[31] Thomson's example is not devised specifically for a conflict between two rights but, more generally, for a conflict between a right and an important social purpose (which may well be another right but may not be so; actually Thomson does not make it clear whether the justification of the infringement of the owner's property right in her example lies in the child's *right* to life).

Obviously, the infringement/violation distinction fits well our argument that the exercise of a right may be curtailed without impugning the validity or the existence of this right. And, let me add, her clarification of the language of rights is not mere academic pedantry. In the case of violation of a right, the right-holder may legitimately complain about the wrongdoing of those who violated his right; hence, there are grounds for punitive action. In the case of mere infringement, there is an obligation to make good the damage caused to the right-holder (in Thomson's example, the damaged gate, the destruction of the box which contained the drug, the value of the drug, etc.) but this reparation has no punitive element whatsoever because no wrong had been committed. The duty of making good the owner's harm is justified because there is no reason why the right-holder should incur the costs of achieving the legitimate goal which justified the infringement of his right. But this inringement was not, on balance, wrong; therefore, the reparation does not involve any moral criticism of those who did infringe the right in question. It is consistent with the general principle that moral blame is not a necessary condition of the obligation of reparation.[32]

Secondly, the notion of rights to satisfaction of basic needs is sometimes rejected on the basis that they require a particular positive action (rather than merely forbearance) on the part of individuals, society or the state. Therefore, it is assumed implicitly that rights exist only when correlated with a duty to refrain from acting in certain ways; in other words, that rights are typically guaranteed by non-interference on the part of someone else. This view is expressed in the very first phrases of Robert Nozick's book:

Individuals have rights, and there are things no person or group may do to them (without violating their rights). So strong and far-reaching are these rights that they raise the question of what, if anything, the state and its officials may do.[33]

This suggests clearly that rights are of such a nature that their violation consists only in some positive acts, in 'doing something'. They are violated when a person or a group *does* something to me. Rights, in this formulation, demand constraints on what others may do *to* me; it is not envisaged that rights may justify claims upon others to do something *for* me.[34] If all rights had this structure, then rights of recipience would not have the status of real 'rights' because they are violated when someone fails to do something, not when someone does something to me. Their denial has the form of non-action (that is, failure to provide people with particular goods, such as food, shelter, health care, or the income needed to buy them). Rights of recipience are correlated with positive acts, not with omission of action.

This point, though important, is insufficient to show that rights of recipience are not rights. There is no reason why we should limit the notion of rights only to those which are correlated with negative duties. Even in the case of some non-controversial rights (which are not rights of recipience), a positive action is sometimes needed in order to ensure the application of the right. There are rights which are generally recognized as rights *par excellence*, and which cannot be reduced to a demand simply to be left alone. For example, the right to a fair trial requires certain things to be done by those who have duties to protect this right: to provide a fair jury, an attorney, to observe the proper procedures and so on. In order to protect rights to physical security, positive steps must be taken with regard to police forces, guards, penitentiaries etc. Similarly, in the case of citizens' right to vote, the positive duty of the government to make all the necessary electoral arrangements comes to mind first, and the duty not to interfere with the voters' actions presents itself as the derivative concept. Hence, there is nothing in the concept of a right and in a general theory of rights which confines the notion of rights only to those rights which are coupled with the negative duties of non-interference.

To this, one might say perhaps that the right to a fair trial, to physical integrity, to vote etc. is correlated only with negative duties of non-interference with the implementation of this right. The positive duties of the State to make positive arrangements safeguarding fair trials, bodily integrity of citizens, proper voting procedure and so on, correlate with the expectations by citizens that the above-mentioned rights will be protected, rather than with the rights themselves. These expectations may or may not be described in terms of 'rights'; in any case, they are distinct from the rights which are the proper object of protection. Let us take the example of the right to physical security. This right, so the argument goes, is violated only when another person or a group actively invades the person's bodily integrity: when the right-holder is beaten, mugged, raped or otherwise abused. This right seems, therefore, correlated only with the negative duty *not* to do certain things to a person. However, the positive duty of the State to provide effective police protection corresponds to a right (or, under the other interpretation, merely to an expectation) to have a right to physical integrity protected. If the State fails to fulfil this positive duty, the argument concludes, it does not violate anyone's right to physical security, but only the right to protection against those who violate (or who would like to violate) one's physical security.

Such an argument can be made, and has been made.[35] If correct, it inflicts a serious blow on the observation that 'classical' rights correlate with a mix of positive and negative duties and, hence, it undermines my defence of rights to recipience which themselves are correlated with positive duties. However, there are good reasons to believe that this argument is incapable of seriously challenging the concept of basic-needs-as-rights.

In the first place, while it seems rather easy to draw the line between the right itself and its protection parallel to the negative/positive distinction with respect to the right to bodily integrity, it would be much more difficult (if not impossible) to repeat this operation with respect to some other 'classical' rights, such as the right to vote or the right to fair trial. Take the first of these two rights. A reasoning analogous to the argument about the right to physical integrity would have to identify a right distinct from the right to have all the necessary electoral arrangements provided for by the State. This other, more fundamental right, would have to be correlated only with negative duties. But I fail to see what such duties there can be. If these are duties not to interfere with the voting process, then certainly they are derivative from the more fundamental positive duties to organise this process. Otherwise, we would reach the conclusion that what the State is doing is protecting its citizens against the possible harmful actions by other citizens who might wish to interfere with the act of voting. True, but how can they interfere with something which did not take place because of the hypothetical failure of the State to initiate the process? We cannot, therefore, identify a right coupled with negative duties before we describe a right coupled with positive duties. So the argument about the right to physical integrity, that I have cited above, has insufficient weight as far as the theory of rights is concerned.

Secondly, even if violation of a right itself is distinguishable from failure to protect this right, it does not follow that the positive duty to protect a right is not correlated with a right. In order to undermine seriously the idea of positive rights, one would have to show that the positive duty of protection of rights corresponds with something less than a right: perhaps a 'legitimate expectation' or something of that sort. But this begs the question. Such an argument is not necessarily implied by the above-mentioned reasoning about physical integrity. We might as well infer from it that we have two types of rights of equal (or comparable) importance: a right to security and a right to protection from assault on our security.[36]

And thirdly, this distinction itself is questionable. Surely, one can split the protection of physical integrity into two (or more) distinct rights: why not? After all, these are merely words, and we can do with them whatever we like. But what is the practical significance of such a terminological operation? Well, the identification of two separate rights is meaningful when we believe that they correspond to two distinct types of protected benefits. After all, rights do constitute benefits, or interests, or advantages. Whatever else they may be, rights are typically protected interests of members of a society. But what interest might someone have in his physical security distinguishable from protection of this security? If, indeed, we can conceptually separate a right to security from a right to protection of security, I suggest that such a separation would be artificial in the extreme since people would have little practical interest in seeking the former one in isolation from the latter.[37] When people are concerned about their bodily integrity, they are concerned about its protection; when they demand the observance of their right to security, they do not distinguish between the right to being left alone and the right to being protected in this autonomy by those who are in charge of citizens' security.

So the argument that 'classical' rights (as opposed to rights to satisfaction of basic needs) are coupled with negative duties does not withstand close examination. Moreover, an argument has been made that, under some circumstances, the rights of recipience are correlated not so much with the positive duties of allocating certain goods to a right-holder, but rather with the duties of protecting him against those who would otherwise harm him. The description of this duty sounds more 'negative' than 'positive'. Henry Shue illustrates this duty with a story about a village in a Third World country where malnutrition has been caused by a contract requiring an owner of land (in exchange for a salary) to shift from cultivation of black beans to production of flowers for export.[38] What had been needed, in order to protect the subsistence rights of people in the neighbourhood, was a legal system which made these contracts unenforceable. Society, in this case, is not obliged to 'give' anything; it is rather obliged to see to it that people are protected from harmful acts by other people. "The request is not to be supported but to be allowed to be self-supporting on the basis of one's own hard work", says Shue.[39] The upshot of all this is that since neither 'classical' rights are coupled with unequivocally negative duties, nor are rights to the satisfaction of basic needs always correlated with positive obligations, the positive/negative duty distinction fails to provide a test for the notion of right.

Incidentally, it also follows from the above that the notion of rights of recipience is consistent with the idea that rights imply 'side constraints' upon actions to be taken.[40] Side constraints prohibit certain types of behaviour which may adversely affect the position of other people. This characterization fits well the notion of rights of recipience in so far as we believe that there is a course of action available in a society in order to provide needy persons with means necessary to their survival. Side constraints stemming from rights to satisfaction of basic needs require the elimination of those types of behaviour which make satisfaction of basic needs by others impossible. True, basic-needs-as-rights *are* incompatible with that notion of side constraints which restricts them to constraints upon positive action only, as opposed to constraints upon the whole range of behaviour (including non-action). But if my previous argument was correct, there is no reason to believe that human rights can be violated only through positive action, and never through inaction. What is important is to make sure that it is within the scope of human behaviour to observe other people's rights. Whether this behaviour takes the form of action or forbearance is irrelevant as a criterion of the existence of a correlative right.

The opposite view has been advocated on the basis of the Kantian principle of treating a person as an end, never as a means to other people's ends. It has been argued that if we force someone to sacrifice for the benefit of others, we use him as a means of bringing benefit to others. To hold "that some persons have to bear some costs that benefit other persons more" allegedly presupposes the view that there exists one social entity which "undergoes some sacrifice for its own good".[41] This, of course, does not respect the separate identity of particular individuals.

To this two answers are available. First, the idea that we should enforce sacrifices on one person whenever these sacrifices are outweighed by another person's benefits, indeed violates the concept of individual rights. To make the use of rights contingent upon such a utilitarian calculus would make the whole notion of rights spurious. Fortunately, the concept of rights-to-basic-needs comes nowhere near making such a claim. It is not the balance of benefits and losses that dictates a duty of redistribution. This duty is dictated by the fact that it is within the power of human beings to remove the most urgent threats to the subsistence of others. Rights impose side constraints upon the use of resources when the channelling of some of these resources towards the more needy persons would help meet their basic needs. Secondly, and more importantly, to talk about 'sacrifices' (and thus about treating the 'givers' as means to the recipients' aims) would make sense only if by an independent argument it might be shown that the putative 'givers' have absolute rights over the resources which they control before redistribution. In other words, the absolute notion of private property would have to be defended first, before the argument that redistribution involves sacrifices by some. So the argument of libertarians about forced sacrifices and treating people as means in the redistributive transfers begs the question. In a complex society, where people are mutually interdependent, and where the satisfaction of B's basic needs may depend on a transfer of surplus from A, the imposition of such a transfer calls for no larger sacrifice than the imposition upon A of a duty to abstain from mugging B.

The *third* objection to the idea that rights of recipience (as far as satisfaction of basic needs is concerned) are rights *sensu stricto* consists in pointing out the links between the protection of those putative rights and some material conditions of their satisfaction which are by no means universally attained. In certain societies the satisfaction of those needs is simply impossible due to insufficiency of resources; therefore, ask the critics, what sense would it make to say that people have rights to something that objectively cannot be implemented?[42]

One possible reply would be by showing that there is no reason to restrict the 'justice constituency' to one society or one country. Even if there are societies which are unable to meet the basic needs of all their members, such possibilities exist if the material resources of the entire world are taken into account. By 'justice constituency' I mean a collection of individuals among whom a just distribution is to be made.[43] Within such a group the principles of justice operate according to one and the same scale: equal desert is rewarded with equal benefits etc. The justice constituency provides a framework for the comparison of individuals for the purposes of distribution of benefits and burdens; if various sub-groups within one justice constituency are rewarded according to different scales, justice requires transfers of resources up to the point where distribution is made uniformly.

I do not propose to discuss the problem of the justice constituency in detail here. But it is obvious that our moral obligations of justice follow upon the fact of community. The criteria for the constituency of justice are more rigorous than those for constituencies underlying other moral principles. For instance, we may have certain duties towards strangers (duties of non-infringement of their bodily integrity, duties to prevent something very bad from happening to them if it is in our power to do so, etc.) but it is hard to conceive of duties to distribute justly within an amorphous crowd which does not constitute any real community. We face, therefore, the task of identifying meaningful justice constituencies and, in particular, the question whether or not the 'world community' meets the criteria for a justice constituency. But before we address this question, we had better realize that this is largely an empirical matter related to the actual structure of interdependence in the international political and economic system. The principles of justice cannot themselves dictate where to draw the line: it is *also* a matter of knowledge about the existing scale of interdependence, decision-making, autonomy and divisions of the world system.

Now it seems obvious that nation-states in the modern world are becoming increasingly interdependent. This mutual interdependence is based on a complex network of economic, political and cultural processes which operate across national frontiers; the level of interaction among the individuals and groups in different parts of the world has reached such a degree of intensity that talk about 'a world community'[44] or about 'a universal, although underdeveloped, society of mankind'[45] seems to be justified, not as an expression of idealistic wishful thinking, but as a statement of observable facts. This global interdependence has numerous dimensions. For one thing, transactional exchange of economic goods through international trade has reached a level in which a significant proportion of world output passes through foreign trade. From these contacts, common standards and practices have emerged and have been formally stated in bilateral and multilateral treaties. On the political level, the global threats stemming from the nuclear arms race, the environmental degradation and the depletion of natural resources, have caused a rapid increase in intensity of international political contacts. It also has led to increased (though insufficient) roles played by the United Nations and other international organizations. One has also to note the significance of regional integration blocs, such as the European Economic Community which is progressively abandoning the traditional absolutist notions of state sovereignty and adopting supranational modes of decision-making. As a result of these trends, world politics no longer correspond to the traditional model of self-sufficient and mutually independent nation-states. On the cultural level, we have reached an unprecedented degree of global mass communication through radio, TV, press, tourism etc. The proliferation of human contacts has led to what some call 'supranational professionalism'[46] — an emergence of permanent patterns of interaction between various kinds of professional groups in different national societies. This is particularly true of scientific circles with the 'invisible universities' integrating the specialists in a given area in different countries.

This highly unsystematic and far from exhaustive list shows that the use of the notion of 'world community' is justified, and that McDougal, Lasswell and Reisman are right when they claim that "[t]he inhabitants of the contemporary globe are ... the members of a 'group', not merely an 'aggregate', since they share a sufficiently high frequency of perspectives and interaction".[47] If this is true, then the argument about a world-wide dimension of distributive justice is on solid ground. If the inhabitants of the world constitute a world community, they all share the duty of helping to assure a minimum human existence for everyone else. Thus, the correlative duty of the rights to satisfaction of basic needs can be meaningfully identified. Since within the least developed countries resources are often insufficient to satisfy basic needs of all the inhabitants, this correlative duty amounts, in practice, to "a duty on all richer states to afford means for ensuring a minimum level of subsistence for the men and women of all countries".[48] Such a *moral* duty stems from the existence of the world community and from the availability of means to satisfy the basic needs of all. Moreover, according to some international lawyers, the UN member-states have committed themselves to a *legal* duty to create reasonable living standards both for their own peoples and for those of other countries.[49]

The actual forms of transfer of resources needed to achieve this aim are outside the scope of this book; what matters is that, if we take account of the overall planetary resources, there are sufficient means available to satisfy the basic needs of all the inhabitants of the world. Achievement of this goal would require the establishment of a new economic order based on important changes in the nature of economic relations between the highly industrialised and the less developed countries. Important progress could be achieved through the restructuring of international trade: the Charter of the Economic Rights and Duties of States recognizes the importance of trade in promoting economic development and it calls for special preferences for developing countries.[50] But surely much more is needed than reshaping world trade; in order to achieve an international redistribution of resources, larger flows of aid and capital investment, programs for pooling and making available managerial and economic skills, transfers of know-how, technical assistance etc. are necessary. For instance, as far as world hunger is concerned, particular studies show that the achievement of adequate food supply in the poorest countries is a perfectly feasible task.[51] Increasing domestic food production and providing adequate food storage and information in developing countries would require a significant transfer of financial resources designed to boost these countries' domestic investments, to provide raw materials, educational facilities and trained personnel and to induce population planning programs. This would require concerted action by major nation-states, international organizations and private corporations to finance these investments by credit arrangements or by direct transfers.

Incidentally, let us note that justice constituencies may well exist at different levels with different degrees of intensity. Strong links of interdependence within nation-states do not exclude the existence of interdependence on the world-wide level as well as interdependence on a local level. This corresponds to the 'multi-layer' concept of society, which envisages social processes as ocurring in a number of territorial 'layers'.[52] Hence, it may happen that distributive justice at the level of city, state or region coexists with world-wide injustice. However, in so far as the world community *is* a significant justice constituency, the sufficiency of resources on a planetary scale provides an answer to the objection against the rights to satisfaction of basic needs on the grounds that they are impossible to satisfy.

But to those who find this answer unsatisfactory, or lacking in persuasive power, there is fortunately another argument available to uphold rights of recipience *qua* genuine rights. As was already noted, basic needs are relative (within certain limits), and this relativity is a function of, among other things, the availability of resources in a given society. They do not represent any constant figure: growing economic capacities result indirectly (through the transformation of life styles, habits, etc.) in a growing level of 'basic needs'. This relativity seriously weakens the general argument considered here, namely the argument that basic needs do not give birth to rights if they are not attainable universally. It would be, admittedly, objectionable to claim that an individual has rights to receive certain goods and services which it is impossible to provide. But there would be no such problems in saying that an individual has a right to the most extensive amount of goods and services (up to the level of his basic needs) within the limits of the productive capacity of his society. He cannot demand it of a society and his fellow-citizens that they do the impossible, but he can demand that they do their best. Consider this proposition:

It may be asking the impossible to demand social security for all human beings, but every society can, and perhaps should, provide "that degree of social security made possible by its available resources".[53]

In other words: there is no need to stress the relativity of rights to the satisfaction of basic needs[54] because this relativity is already involved in the notion of basic needs. The right to satisfaction of basic needs is *not* relative or merely declaratory, but the basic needs themselves *are* relative.

However, this relativity lies within certain clear limits. There was an argument in my previous remarks on basic needs which was directly opposed to an exaggerated stress on the relativity of basic needs; I cannot, therefore, rely too heavily on their relativity now. To the degree to which those needs *are* relative, the argument about a dubious character of rights based on them is objectionable; at the same time, this degree of relativity of basic needs is restricted. But there is a second argument which may bring us out of this unattractive alternative: either basic needs are relative, or they do not give rise to rights. The fact that there are no practical means of implementing certain rights in a given society, at a given time, is not necessarily a good reason to say that they fail to meet the conditions of rights *sensu stricto*. In other words, there is no inherent contradiction between saying that I have a certain right and at the same time admitting that it cannot be exercised for some practical reason, such as scarcity limitations. After all, the existence of rights is not identical with the existence of the material means for their implementation. For instance, the right to freedom of the press, including a right to publish a newspaper, is not denied by the fact that some people have little or no means to print their own newspapers. They still have the right, but they do not have the capacity to use this right. There is no conceptual contradiction between both parts of this last phrase: if we identify the very existence of a right with the means of exercising it, we will end up by identifying those societies in which freedom of the press is legally or politically restricted with those in which the economic means of putting in practice some of the benefits of freedom of the press are unequally distributed. Both these cases have some practical negative consequences, but they cannot be treated on the same footing.

By the same token, rights to satisfaction of basic needs do not presuppose the existence of all the practical means for their implementation in each and every situation. The fact that a putative right fails to meet a test of practicality is not a sufficient reason to deny to it the status of a right. My right to police protection calls for, among other things, action that ought to be taken by the police if my car is stolen. I have a right that the police undertake all possible and reasonable actions. However, this right does not include the attainment of the final goal: finding my car. The achievement of this goal depends on many contingent factors (quality of police equipment, qualifications and energy of police officers, etc.) as well as on luck. My right consists in a claim that they do their utmost, within limits of possibilities, to find my car; I cannot have any claim on the police to actually find my car. But this is not a reason for refusing the status of a right to my claim. We may argue similarly about economic rights of recipience, related to the satisfaction of basic needs: the fact that not always can my basic needs be effectively satisfied (because of underdevelopment, natural disaster etc.) does not deprive my claims of the status of rights. I have a right to demand that my society do its best, within the limits of possibility, to satisfy those needs.

We see, therefore, that all three main arguments against viewing rights to a satisfaction of basic needs as rights *sensu stricto* hinge upon conditions of the concept of 'rights' which it would be hard or unreasonable to apply even in the case of uncontroversial or 'classical' rights. Therefore, they are not proper arguments against 'economic rights' either.

CHAPTER 7

PREFERENTIAL TREATMENT

The two previous chapters outline the principles of perfect justice: a society displaying them is a perfectly just society. The part of the conception of justice sketched there belongs to what John Rawls calls 'ideal theory'; it assumes that principles of justice "will be strictly complied with and followed by everyone".[1] Ideal theory is always utopian. It is a *useful* utopia in that it provides us with a vision of the world to be sought, yet it is a utopia because it will never be attained fully. We need also, apart from the 'ideal theory', a conception of how we should react to already existing injustices. 'Non-ideal theory' avoids the need to resort to the Rawlsian 'strict compliance' condition. It starts with the assumption that the world in which we live is essentially unjust. This Chapter is concerned with a particular part of such 'non-ideal theory' regarding the distribution of social benefits; it is, therefore, useful to discuss it before we turn to the question of a distribution of burdens in the next Chapter. Preferential treatment is an emergency device: it gives redress to victims of injustices committed in violation of the principles of desert and/or of basic needs, which have been discussed earlier in this book. It tries to remove some of the consequences of existing injustices rather than to build a perfectly just society. In a perfectly just society, there will be no rationale for preferential treatment.

There is no gap between 'ideal' and 'non-ideal' parts of the theory of justice. Preferential treatment is an extension of the general conception of justice into less favourable conditions. The compensatory conception of justice demands that people who have suffered gross discrimination in access to important goods should be given special treatment; society should help them obtain access to those goods and compensate them for past discrimination. If particular individuals have suffered unusual burdens, those burdens constitute an obvious obstacle to the satisfaction of their needs and to undertaking efforts which may be rewarded on the grounds of desert; it is, therefore, a postulate of justice as equilibrium that preferences should be accorded to them in order to rectify past injustices. These preferences should be viewed as an attempt to offset those burdens that are arbitrary from a moral point of view and unjustified from the point of view of the principle of balance of benefits and burdens.

1. THE PROBLEM

Programs of preferential admissions to universities are of particular importance and so they are a convenient focus for the discussion of the principle of preferential treatment in general. What makes the distribution of educational opportunity so crucial is that so much else is distributed along with educational opportunity; education plays a key role in defining a person's place in the social structure. In all advanced societies, the level of education determines, to a certain degree, income, occupation and prestige. There is, for instance, a direct relationship between the extent of education and lifetime earnings [2] In a word, the distribution of educational opportunities determines, to an important extent, the distribution of many other social opportunities.

The best known example of preferential treatment in access to universities is offered by contemporary practice in the United States. It has resulted in an enormous amount of books and articles analysing various legal, political and ethical aspects of programs designed to reduce the effects of racial discrimination. But the problem, of course, is not confined to the United States and to racial groups; there are many other countries in which affirmative action programs (including preferential admissions programs) were established. In Poland, in the mid-sixties, the universities began to award extra points at entrance examinations to children of workers and of peasants. Every applicant coming from a working-class or peasant family had a fixed number of 'bonus' points added to his grade points. The amount of the addition has been computed with the goal in mind of admitting a higher percentage of students coming from these social groups. This system has been generally criticized as unjust and ineffective, and is in any event a failure: in 1981 there were, for example, only 8% of peasants' children in tertiary education institutions in Poland (while almost 30% of the population was employed in or supported from work in agriculture). The failure probably occurred because the system was based on false empirical foundations: social deprivations and discriminations in Poland do not correspond to the ideologically moulded notion of 'class' distinctions between workers, peasants and intelligentsia. Access to universities is unequal as a result of socio-economic inequalities which are much more complex than so-called 'class' distinctions.[3]

By way of another example, there have also been demands for a system of educational preferences for Aborigines in Australia. A recent report by a Federation of Australian University Staff Associations points out that only

0.3% of Aborigines continue to tertiary studies (compared with over 2% of the general population) and that this disproportion can be remedied only by 'positive discrimination measures'.[4] Although there is no uniform scheme in operation, several Australian universities (for example, the University of New South Wales and Macquarie University in Sydney) operate special schemes for admission of persons of aboriginal descent.[5] Other universities in Australia, for instance the University of Sydney, make provision for educationally or socially disadvantaged persons to be given special consideration in admission, without any particular group being singled out.

Of course, preferential treatment programs are not confined to access to higher education: there are preferential programs in the United States for the Black population in the field of housing or for women and Blacks in that of employment. Likewise, affirmative action programs in Australia have been implemented with the aim to foster greater representation of Aborigines and other minority groups in the public service.[6] A number of Black African countries have adopted programs of 'corrective equity', taking measures to promote the fairer representation of different racial groups in the public service and in educational institutions.[7] India has undertaken a wide range of preferential treatment initiatives towards classes of citizens considered to be socially and educationally deprived, such as former 'untouchables'. These actions include preferences in employment and in education: for example, reservation of government jobs and places in state-run educational institutions for 'backward classes', supplementation of scores in merit exams, exemptions from certain tests required of all other employees for promotion.[8]

My arguments here will not concern any particular, actual program of preferential treatment; I do not want to defend any specific program. The fact that I will be referring mostly to the American example is not to be taken as evidence of my conviction that American programs are free from deficiencies. I am interested here in the ethical justification of a *principle* of preferential treatment and nothing else. I want to reflect on the principle that once we have correctly identified a group of people who have been significantly discriminated against in the past, or who are deprived of opportunities which are important for access to a particular good, compensatory justice requires some preference to be accorded to the members of the group in the distribution of the good in question. It is only this type of 'preferential treatment' that I will be discussing in this Chapter. The reason for this limitation is simple: this type of 'preferential treatment' is the most controversial and is subject to the strongest criticisms; if it proves defensible then, *a fortiori*, milder preferences are also justifiable.

For the purposes of this Chapter, I shall take 'preferential treatment' to be synonymous with what is often called reverse, benign, compensatory, or positive discrimination. It is based upon the principle that in the processes involving selection, admission or distribution of important opportunities, preference should be given to the persons singled out on the basis of those very characteristics which have been used in the past to deny them equal treatment with respect to the selection, admission or distribution in question. I shall deliberately avoid using the catch-phrase 'reverse discrimination' because the very notion of 'discrimination' carries negative connotations while 'preferential treatment' sounds morally neutral. If 'discrimination' is understood as "treating people differently when they are similar in the relevant respects or treating them similarly when they are different in relevant respects"[9] then one of the arguments of this Chapter will be that 'preferential treatment' is not discriminatory because it treats differently people who are indeed different in relevant respects. 'Discrimination' denotes an unjustified distinction yet whether or not 'preferential treatment' is justified remains to be shown and must not be 'resolved' by a definitional fiat. And also, I will not examine the argument that preferential treatment introduces inequality before the law, since I have dealt with this issue, in a slightly more general context, earlier in this book.[10]

It should be noted that the type of 'preferential treatment' which I have described above constitutes but a part of a generic notion of 'affirmative action'. Affirmative action can operate without preferences at the point of admission, selection or distribution; it can be carried on, for instance, through priority being given to a particular group in welfare expenditure. When, say, the Australian government provides special grants for health programs designed to alleviate the depressed conditions of Aborigines (whose health standards are well below those of white Australians) then this 'affirmative action' does not raise any special moral issues comparable to those raised by preferential treatment, apart from the routine questions of the appropriateness of the goal and the effectiveness of the scheme. Although schemes like this one reflect certain 'preferences', nevertheless they do not give rise to moral problems related to a situation of one applicant being turned away because another applicant is admitted on grounds other than traditional notions of competence. 'Preference' in the Aboriginal health grant is given at the taxpayer's expense and not at the expense of someone whose expectation of obtaining a particular benefit is frustrated; the cost imposed on a group that is not a recipient of the scheme is so mild as to be insignificant from a moral point of view.

There may be various other types of 'affirmative action' which do *not* involve preferences. For instance, special training programs for minority-group applicants before their admission to a university are designed to improve their qualifications but do not involve any preferences at the point of admission.[11] Advertising of vacancies in the ethnic language newspapers merely broadens the channels of information about the available positions; it helps members of ethnic minorities to obtain information about jobs and to apply for them along with other groups without, however, any preferences at the point of hiring. These are examples of 'facilitatory' measures which are part of the concept of affirmative action in a broad sense but which do not constitute preferential treatment as it is understood here because they do not involve any preference in the process of selection itself. Consequently, they present no special problems for moral or legal theory.

Programs of preferential treatment use various techniques of preferences. They can establish special 'quotas', that is, a fixed number of places reserved for minority applicants who have been singled out as disadvantaged or discriminated against.[12] They can set up 'goals' or 'targets' which aim at increasing the representation of underprivileged groups and, thus, allow decision-makers to take into account minority status as a positive factor in the consideration of applications.[13] Extra points can be awarded to the members of such groups in the admissions process[14] or there may be a requirement that for each successful non-minority applicant there must be one minority applicant admitted.[15] There are preferences which operate irrespective of comparison of qualifications of candidates: the preference is given to a minority applicant even if he is not as qualified as the best qualified non-minority applicant. On the other hand, there are schemes which award preference to the applicant from the nominated group 'all other things being equal', that is to say, if he is equally as qualified as the other best qualified candidate.[16] The differences between these methods may be very important in practice. After all, the distinction between 'quotas' and 'goals' was crucial in Justice Powell's opinion in *Bakke* where he struck down as unconstitutional the Davis Medical School special admissions program for reserving a 'quota' for minority applicants while, at the same time, upholding the validity of preferential 'goals' of increasing minority representation.[17] However, from our point of view, these are merely cosmetic distinctions which do not affect the very principle. The moral status of 'quotas' is the same as one of 'goals' or extra points or of any other preferential technique since all these techniques provide a competitive edge for the people singled out as victims of past discrimination. As Justice White stated, "[i]n any admissions program which accords special consideration to disadvantaged racial minorities, a determination of the degree of preferences to be given is unavoidable".[18] Now, the method of according this preference and the actual degree of preference need not worry us here. We are interested in the moral defensibility of the general principle of preferential treatment and not in the appropriateness of this or that technique. My argument is that these preferences should be seen as a method of restoration of the group to a status of equality with other social groups; extra benefits for a group otherwise discriminated against or deprived of important opportunities is a form of 'evening the score'. The principle of balance of benefits and burdens is relevant here since special burdens give an additional weight to the claims for social benefits. I will argue in favour of preferential treatment along restorative lines: it is a restoration of an equilibrium of benefits and burdens. In support, and by way of example, reference will be made to preferential admission programs to higher education.

2. UTILITARIAN ARGUMENTS

Before the compensatory arguments are discussed, I will consider briefly the main utilitarian arguments for and against preferential treatment. In general, most arguments about preferential treatment may be qualified as either compensatory and, therefore, past-oriented, or utilitarian and future-oriented. Although I treat the first kind of argument as decisive in this debate, I think it would be a mistake to ignore the utilitarian arguments altogether. This is partly because certain arguments which have the appearance of compensatory reasoning in fact appeal to utilitarian notions.

Utilitarian arguments consider preferential treatment essentially as a means of achieving important social goals: welfare, social harmony, more even representation of different social groups in important positions and the like. Incidentally, let me remark that the above-mentioned distinction between considerations based on justice and considerations based on utility does not coincide necessarily with the distinction between past-oriented and future-oriented approaches.[19] The first distinction is fundamental and has to do with the very nature of justification; the second is merely a matter of formulation of argument. The compensatory justice argument may be reformulated in terms of the future state of affairs: we want not only to compensate some groups for their *past* deprivations but we also want to bring about a *future* shape of society such that these groups will have a fairer access to important goods and positions. Arguments about the 'past' and the 'future' are closely interconnected; it is impossible to define what is the *future* gain from the point of view of the criterion of justice without understanding a society's *past* burdens, discriminations and deprivations. An example of an argument in favour of preferential treatment in terms of justice but at the same time with the future-oriented formulation is offered by Dworkin's essay on reverse discrimination. He approves of reverse discrimination on the basis that it makes the community as a whole better off, but at the same time 'better-off community' is understood in an 'ideal' sense, as a more just society.[20] This argument, at the same time justice-based and future-oriented, is clearly distinguishable from the utilitarian arguments which are also future-oriented but not justice-based, for instance, arguments in favour of or against preferential treatment advanced in terms of the quality of education or quality of services rendered in a society.

The main utilitarian argument put forward in favour of preferential treatment is that it is the only way to interrupt a cycle of disadvantage for underprivileged groups.[21] The deprivations suffered by some groups discriminate against them in their access to education and training they need to qualify for desirable jobs; this discrimination tends to perpetuate all other deprivations. Preferences offer the only way out of this vicious circle, it is claimed, and the advantages connected with the promotion of a traditionally deprived group prevail over the disadvantages of discrimination against groups that have not suffered similar deprivations.

The force of this argument depends, however, on our evaluation of the aim fostered by the preferential treatment program. That there is more equality in a society as a result of this program is not a sufficient *utilitarian* justification because equality is not a value in itself. If, however, 'more equal society' is considered to be valuable *per se*, then this is no longer a utilitarian argument. It boils down to a general assertion about the moral value of equality and, as such, is vulnerable to all the traditional criticisms of egalitarianism which I need not restate here.[22] I, for one, can see much sense in egalitarian argument about preferential treatment but I also see that it requires further justification which transcends utilitarian theoretical frameworks. In turn, the value of this argument in utilitarian terms depends on other values fostered by a more equal society, for instance, more social harmony and social peace, less frustration and aggression, more co-operation with fewer tensions and so on. To the extent that these values are considered important parts of a general utilitarian social good, the argument about breaking the vicious circle of disadvantages seems to be a valid one.

The problem is more complex than only this. It still must be shown that preferential treatment programs are likely to foster harmony, integration and social peace. Those categories are not easily verifiable and it is by no means obvious that empirical evidence can clearly support the argument in favour of preferential treatment. There are important counter-arguments which are not to be neglected. Alan Goldman, for instance, questions the whole notion that preferential treatment for minorities really favours harmony and integration; the reason for his doubt about it is that "others know that the treatment *is* preferential".[23] In consequence, he says, the non-members of the preferred minority will feel that some people are getting undeserved benefits which are not available to members of other social groups. The persistence of such feelings will slow down the whole process of integration of the previously disadvantaged groups with the rest of a society; as a result, there will be "more friction and resentment than that inevitable from residual bigotry".[24] It is worth noting that the argument about preferential treatment as reinforcing bigotry is quite popular. R. A. Posner notes that "[t]he characteristics that university admissions officers associate with black people ... are the same characteristics that the white bigot ascribes to every black".[25] The reason for this is that, as Posner explains, benevolent discrimination reinforces racist stereotypes about blacks being lazy, unintelligent and, hence, unable to make it to the universities without preferences. It is also claimed that any racial distinction, no matter whether it discriminates against or in favour of the underprivileged minority, is inherently divisive and tends to invoke the prejudices of both non-minorities and minorities. This alleged 'divisiveness' is often taken for granted. For example, the Supreme Court of California stated in *Bakke* that "[t]he divisive effect of such preferences needs no explication and raises serious doubts whether the advantages obtained by the few preferred are worth the inevitable cost to racial harmony".[26]

The moral force of this argument, however, hinges upon the prior argument about justice or injustice of a particular program. The very fact that someone (or a particular group) is given preferential treatment is not a sufficient cause of prejudices and divisiveness; this only happens when people are not convinced about the fairness of the treatment. Preferences for handicapped people usually do not foster prejudice and frictions since people think that the preferences are justified. Similarly, if a community is aware of real and important deprivations suffered by a certain group, there are no valid grounds for resentment. If this resentment is felt by some members of the community out of bigotry and prejudice, there is no reason why the community has to resign itself to those feelings and treat them as an important obstacle to the proposed solution. In practical terms, the disapproval of the proposed preferences by the majority raises important policy problems in a democratic state. But from a moral point of view, surely the validity of arguments in favour of equalizing access to education or employment does not depend on the approval of these arguments by those who benefit from existing inequalities. One of the legitimate tasks of political philosophy is to explain that preferences for some deprived groups in a society are justified and that opposition to them is an act of bigotry. The whole argument about fostering prejudice, bigotry and divisiveness evaluates preferential programs not on the basis of what they really entail but, instead, in terms of how they are perceived by those people who are denied the advantages of these programs. As I have already suggested in a slightly different context,[27] it is simply not appropriate to build a theory of justice on the purported perceptions by a part of the population regarding what is just. The speculations about the effects of preferential treatment upon social prejudices and attitudes are no substitute for justification of a particular policy. Similarly, a Gallup poll showing disapproval of preferential programs by the majority[28] is not an argument in the moral debate but rather provides an additional illustration of the problem. In sum, the divisiveness argument about preferential treatment is a derivative one: it cannot stand on its own because its plausibility depends upon prior evaluation of the justice or injustice of preferential treatment.

The other argument, made frequently, and which is closely related to the previous one, is that preferential treatment 'stigmatizes' the preferred minority. The knowledge that someone's promotion, recruitment or admission is a result of preferential treatment may "unfairly stigmatize those members of the groups who receive it, especially those who could have obtained their positions without it"[29] and place on them "a stamp of inferiority".[30] This 'stigma' argument is being understood in two distinct ways. First, it is maintained that preferential treatment stigmatizes members of the minority in the eyes of the general public, fostering prejudice, imposing a badge of inferiority, and thus causing greater difficulties for the minority students who have to make a special effort "to impress others with their competence".[31] Secondly, the 'stigma' argument sometimes points out the consequences of preferential treatment for the consciousness and self-perception of the members of the preferred minority themselves: their frustration, loss of self-respect, pride and incentive. I shall distinguish between those two aspects of the 'stigma' argument because they raise quite different questions.

As far as the 'stigma' in the eyes of the general public is concerned, it again depends upon the general public being convinced about the unfairness of the whole arrangement. There is no reason to think that *any* preferential treatment will be judged as unfair and, hence, that *any* preferential treatment will cause a 'stigma' effect. After all, certain preferences for war veterans do not stigmatize them as inferior. If the rest of the community recognizes that the present deprivations suffered by a certain minority are not a result of its inferiority but of "a long history of discrimination, economic impotence and cultural deprivation"[32] and that the only fair solution is now to accord to this group some preference which will help it overcome the results of the past discrimination, no 'stigma' is necessarily produced by this program. Of course, the more educated and more convinced about the fairness of such an arrangement the society is, the less likely is the 'stigma' effect to occur. After all, the process of stigmatization consists in distorting and stereotyping differences between the members of a society. As Erving Goffman says, "[a] stigma ... is really a special kind of relationship between attribute and stereotype ... "[33] and by constructing the ideologies of stigma, we often "rationaliz[e] an animosity based on other differences, such as those of social class".[34] There is no reason to take stigmas for granted, as something inevitable and unremovable, for they are the product of the representation of actual social differences in a false light. The fact of preferential treatment, in itself, does not imply anything about the inferiority of those to whom the preferences have been granted. Such inference is the product of interpretation and persuasion. As Goffman says further: "This differentness [of the stigmatized] itself of course derives from society, for ordinarily before a difference can matter much it must be conceptualized collectively by the society as a whole".[35] In this context, it is worthwhile to mention the recent findings that a majority of the white population in the United States holds unrealistic beliefs about the opportunities available to blacks.[36] Most white Americans tend to deny structural limits to the educational and employment opportunities of blacks and they regard blacks as having better than average opportunities due to affirmative action. Conversely, the general conviction that invidious discrimination in the past is the source of the present underrepresentation of certain groups in higher education, is the best way to overcome 'stigmas'. As has been pointed out with respect to the American racial problems:

Governmental use of benign racial classifications may destroy blinding myths by teaching people that race is indeed a factor of great importance in our society and that many people are now disadvantaged because of past and continuing racial discrimination.[37]

This phrase may well be applied to many other forms of societal discrimination, not only racial ones. It suggests also that the stigma argument is based upon a double standard: the governmental use of distinctions in according preference is condemned as likely to foster stigmatization, but stigma inevitably produced by the actual perpetuation of the deprivation and underrepresentation is tolerated.

As far as the second aspect of the stigma argument is concerned, namely that the beneficiaries of preferential treatment are likely to view themselves as inferior, the easiest way to deal with it is to say that if alleged losses of self-respect by the members of a certain minority were really significant then one would expect this minority to protest against the programs of preferential treatment. There do not appear to be the protests of this kind on any major scale in the case of preferential treatment programs discussed here. Although in the United States some black intellectuals oppose these programs,[38] the black minority as a whole and its representative spokesmen support such policies. "[M]inority admissions programs are far more the product of minority insistence than the tardy manifestation of white conscience", says Derrick A. Bell, Jr.[39] The stigmatizing effect for those groups evidently is not perceived by them as significant enough to outweigh the benefits of those programs.

However, even if there is an element of truth in the 'stigma' argument, and even if preferred minority members have good reason to feel frustrated by the procedures of their access to certain important places in a society, one might suggest that these minorities are stigmatized even more when they are drastically underrepresented in education, administration, professional life, and so on. Is not this underrepresentation (which has, as we know, its roots in past invidious discrimination) likely to produce stereotypes of minorities as being inherently less intelligent, able, clever, and laborious? In consequence, it is likely also to affect the self-perception of the group members and to deepen their sense of hopelessness. As Hardy Jones observes, with regard to these groups that traditionally had enjoyed privileged positions in a society: "There is hardly much rational self-respect on the part of persons whose good qualifications derive heavily from discrimination against others".[40] This argument may be reversed: there are no great chances for self-respect on the part of persons whose hopes of attaining prestigious and significant social positions are much lower than is the case of members of other groups.

The other major argument about preferential treatment concerns the effects of those programs upon professional and academic standards. In particular, with regard to education, it is often claimed that recruitment of students on any other basis than their competence (understood as knowledge, intellectual capacities, and so on) must result in the lowering of general standards of education. This will produce, in turn, the lowering of professional standards, for instance of legal or medical services. Anyone who needs help, it is claimed, wants the best available lawyers and physicians, not the lawyers and physicians selected through a process which disregards competence and qualifications.

This argument may be valid and yet it may not be decisive: we may agree that a lowering of academic and professional standards is not too high a price to pay for justice. We should not, however, take this argument at face value. It is correct only under the condition that its specific assumptions about competence and merit are accepted. In the first place, it assumes that various tests, grades, selection exams, and so on, constitute accurate measurement of qualifications and academic merits. This may or may not be the case. As a matter of fact, the argument is frequently made that qualifications are very inadequately tested by various grade averages or test scores and that these grades and scores are very inaccurate, in more than one sense, in predicting an applicant's success. Not only are the grades at the entry point an imperfect indicator of success at a tertiary level but also they do not constitute good predictors of professional success. But even leaving aside this complication caused by a possible hiatus between academic success and professional success, it is clear that grades and scores are not sufficient measures of qualifications. There are various personality factors (of 'non-cognitive' nature) which are relevant to potential success in school and/or in a profession. As one writer observes, "people do not qualify for medical training the way a Girl Scout qualifies for a merit badge — by tying certain knots — or the way a discus thrower qualifies for a gold medal".[41] It, therefore, comes as no surprise that such unquantifiable and apparently non-academic qualities as compassion, leadership potential, unique work experience, maturity, ability to communicate with the poor, and so on are considered to be important for successful students.[42] None of these qualities can be measured by the standard ability tests but, at the same time, a candidate exhibiting these characteristics may become a much more successful lawyer or physician than a marginally more able fellow-candidate. The departure from the strict principle of merit (the principle which demands that whoever scores higher in ability tests, wins the competition) may serve the aim of improving professional standards. Besides, it is by no means definitively settled that the only aim of professional schools at universities is to produce professionals in their particular fields. As R. Kent Greenawalt notes: "A [law] school might well, for example, admit a student it thought had great potential for political leadership, though believing he might perform less well as a lawyer than some rejected applicant".[43] The adoption of this aim, which does not strike me as blatantly irrational, will result in the use of other selection criteria, in addition to academic merit.

Be that as it may, I do not propose to rest my argument categorically upon this point: after all, it might be argued that some very refined tests are the least objectionable of all the imperfect criteria of selection. However, before I introduce the principal objection to the argument that preferential treatment brings about lowered standards, a simple observation may be useful in this context. The less than perfect composition of a student body does not lead necessarily to a lowering of the quality of education in *absolute* terms. If anything, it may lead to a lowering of standards in *relative* terms, that is, in comparison with the highest possible level imaginable under the existing circumstances. But the actual level of education, even if not as high as it could be in the absence of preferential admissions, may still be as high as, or even higher than, previously. In consequence, it will not lead to a lowering of professional standards. The 'less qualified' does not mean 'unqualified'. This point is ignored by many critics of preferential admissions who frequently talk about 'unqualified' or 'unprepared' students without making a reservation that these are merely relative descriptions.[44] The universities which operate preferential admission programs may easily protect themselves against the danger of admitting 'unqualified' students; after all, preferential admissions are quite compatible with the setting of minimum standards of competence. Universities use 'cut-off points' below which they will not admit students; employers utilize tests which determine whether an applicant can perform a job. All those above a certain level are qualified and marginal differences in scores rarely matter. In the case of many employment positions, any candidate who meets the basic requirements is equally qualified to do the job and no additional skills will enable him to do it better. The same argument applies to university admissions. And yet, in the situation of a relative scarcity of these positions, "the selection process inevitably results in the denial of admission to many *qualified* persons".[45] Therefore, as long as basic standards are observed, those admitted preferentially are not 'unqualified', and perhaps even not 'less qualified' than those who had scored better on competence tests. That preferential admissions have very little detrimental effect upon academic standards, is demonstrated by practical experience. It lends support to the view that preferentially admitted students usually catch up quickly with the rest of their peers and do not push the general level of education down.[46] That is why warnings about incompetent lawyers and physicians, as a result of preferential admissions, have to be taken with scepticism.

However, the main counter-argument to the 'lowered educational standards' thesis has to do with the very notion of the standard of education. Even if one agrees that some of the favoured minority students are less qualified, in the academic sense, than those who could have been admitted had only the test grades been taken into account, the very presence of minority students at the university is an important positive factor of the quality of education. If university education is understood not only in a narrow professional sense but also as a means of learning about one's own society and as a practical study in community life, a diversity of a student body becomes an important condition of the quality of education. A great deal of learning occurs through contacts among students; the presence of a significant number of minority students, as a consequence of preferential admission, helps to expose students to different social and cultural backgrounds. In certain fields of studies it may be considered as a part of the professional studies themselves: in law, sociology, political science, and so on. In all these fields where the knowledge of one's own society is a part of professional qualifications, it is especially valuable. As Chief Justice Vinson of the United States Supreme Court has observed: "[t]he law school, the proving ground for legal learning and practice, cannot be effective in isolation from the individuals and institutions with which the law interacts".[47] Let us add that this need for broad cultural and social experience is important not only in the social sciences and law: it seems to be a significant part of the learning process in the university in general.

The argument about the importance of having a diverse student body is often opposed on the grounds that ethnic or racial differences are not the only significant social differences; therefore, one should not limit attention to these only. This is certainly true: racial diversity is only one feature in a range of possible indicators of the overall diversity of a student body. It is also true that in various societies the importance of ethnic divisions varies. In racially homogenous societies racial distinctions are socially insignificant and, therefore, they are irrelevant to the quality of the teaching process. This is misunderstood or ignored by those critics who attack the argument about the importance of a diverse student body and the effect it has on the quality of education. Alan Goldman suggests that this argument can be challenged on utilitarian grounds. He asks: "Is it true that one learns better in a racially, ethnically, or sexually mixed atmosphere? Do students in Sweden then learn less than those in New York?"[48] Probably not, but it is irrelevant. What is important is that students in Sweden live in a different society from those in New York. For various reasons, race is a much more important social characteristic in the United States than in Sweden. Students in Sweden, even if there is no racially mixed atmosphere at the university, do not necessarily lose an important experience which reflects something significant about their society; students in New York do. This aspect of university education which is linked not so much with professional qualifications but rather with a general knowledge of one's society and its different social and cultural backgrounds, cannot be determined in isolation from the social environment of a university; hence the difference between Sweden and the United States. It is the whole concept of a university education which is essential to this argument: if one adopts the broader concept of the goals of a university education, then diversity in the student body corresponding to significant social pluralism is an important condition in the quality of education.

3. EQUAL OPPORTUNITY AND PREFERENTIAL TREATMENT

The upshot of the previous discussion is that utilitarian arguments about preferential treatment are not conclusive. One could hardly claim categorically that they support the case for or against preferential treatment. Utilitarian considerations give arguments both to the partisans and opponents of preferential treatment; a more fruitful area of moral controversy is, therefore, elsewhere. It seems to me that what is decisive is the moral argument in favour of or against preferential treatment as a rectification of past discrimination in consequence of which members of particular groups were disadvantaged and their chances of access to some valuable positions, reduced. What is essential about this argument is the implicit use it makes of the notion of equal opportunity. Since both partisans of preferential treatment and its opponents appeal to the ideal of equality of opportunity, it will be necessary to devote some attention to this concept and to see what are its implications for the argument about preferential treatment.

The real controversy about equality of opportunity arises when some sections of society suffer deprivations or discriminations yet there are no formal, legal, restrictions on their access to desired positions. Is such a situation consistent with the principle of equality of opportunity or not? The answer to this question depends, obviously, on one's understanding of that principle. At first blush, we are inclined to suppose that equality of opportunity occurs when particular groups and persons face no obstacles or barriers in their access to higher positions in a society. Although not everybody can become a factory manager or a medical student, no one should be *a priori* excluded from the competition for these positions and no one should be discriminated against in the competition. But surely there is more to it than that; after all, *any* distribution of limited resources or positions must be based on certain criteria, and any formulation of the criteria for distribution will inevitably disadvantage certain groups; namely, those who satisfy the criteria to a lesser extent than others. Any standard of admissions, promotions, awards and distributions "will place certain candidates at a disadvantage as against others".[49] If, for instance, ability is considered as a criterion for admissions to universities, it automatically places those less able at a disadvantage. There is nothing unreasonable in this remark of Dworkin's: "Suppose an applicant complains that his right to be treated as an equal is violated by tests that place the less intelligent candidates at a disadvantage against the more intelligent".[50] The standard reply to this applicant would be: the criterion of intelligence is *relevant* to the selection of students and, therefore, even if it puts you at a disadvantage, it is not unfair. Now, I leave aside the question whether the criterion of intelligence (granted that we have the means of measuring it) is relevant indeed and whether it is the only relevant criterion. Let us assume, for the sake of this argument, that this is the case. This does not carry us any further in the elucidation of the idea of equality of opportunity; it is one thing to say that opportunities are distributed on the basis of *relevant* criteria and quite another to say that these opportunities are *equal*. These are not identical propositions.

In particular, it could be argued that the judgment about the relevance of distributional criteria is utilitarian in nature: it concerns efficiency and not equality. Consider the following example. The commander of a bombing squadron has to choose one of his pilots for a particularly difficult and important mission. He makes his selection by considering which pilot is the most experienced, the most physically fit, the best prepared at the moment and so on. Obviously, these are relevant grounds of selection and they will necessarily put some of the pilots at a disadvantage (assuming that there are many who wish to undertake the mission). But from the fact that the criteria are the most appropriate it does not follow that we judge this selection in terms of 'equality of opportunity'. We do not ask ourselves whether all of the pilots had equal training, equal past experience and equal physical abilities. No issue of equality is involved here and the judgment about the relevance of criteria is based solely on the considerations of efficiency. I do not see great differences between this example and the selection of university candidates on the basis of their abilities. If we say that this criterion is the most appropriate or relevant, it is not because it establishes any sort of equality among the applicants but because we think that, by its application, we will obtain the best results in terms of social utility. For instance, we believe that universities will produce the best possible graduates who, in turn, will be able to render the best possible services to the community. It does not express our judgments of justice but, rather, it is founded upon the criteria of efficiency. Views about relevance are influenced here by ideas about utility; those are the real grounds of assertions about 'equality of opportunity' when the criteria established are considered relevant. This line of reasoning about 'equality of opportunity' is, in a word, a realm of utility and not of justice.

If we want to have stronger grounds for our assertions about equality of opportunity, we should reflect not only on the proper choice of selection criteria but also on the social chances of satisfying those criteria. To return to our example about the bombing squadron: one of the reasons why we were unable to evaluate the commander's decision in terms of 'equality of opportunity' was that he did not take into account the pilots' opportunities to acquire the qualifications necessary for the mission. This was not relevant because we assume that the commander's decision should have been based solely on the grounds of efficiency. The success of the mission was all that counted. If, however, we postulate the principle of 'equality of opportunity' as relevant to social selections or distributions, we usually want to treat it as something else than pure efficiency criteria; we suggest that the selection is not only (and not necessarily) the most useful, but rather that it is the most fair. We should, therefore, satisfy ourselves that all the applicants had equal possibilities for acquiring those qualities which are considered as relevant to the distribution in question. This is what Bernard Williams had in mind when he suggested that equality of opportunity

> requires not merely that there should be no exclusion from access on grounds other than those appropriate or rational for the good in question, but that the grounds considered appropriate for the good should themselves be such that people from all sections of society have an equal chance of satisfying them.[51]

This suggests that the principle of equal opportunity has a complex, 'multi-level' structure. Its implementation depends upon people having equal chances to satisfy a criterion of selection, but those equal chances depend on previous equal chances in the acquisition of the chances to satisfy this condition ... , and so on, and so forth. For instance, equal opportunity in obtaining a particular position depends on equal opportunity of studying at a good university, and that depends in turn on equal opportunity to study in a good secondary school, and that depends ... , etc. Each time, in order to discern equal opportunity, we must step back to a previous stage, when the opportunities to acquire qualities needed at the present stage have been distributed. If we pursue this regression to the first decisive factors, we end up with the conclusion that perfect equality of opportunity requires not only an equal family encouragement and environmental influence, but also equal genetic endowment. This may sound absurd, but it only proves that it is absurd to demand *perfect* equality of opportunity. On the other hand, it suggests that the concept of equality of opportunity is taken in an extremely narrow sense if it is limited only to the last link in the chain, that is to say, if we are interested only in the application of a relevant standard to a selection process without inquiring into differential chances of acquiring qualifications defined by that standard. In consequence, it is not correct to classify as 'equality of opportunity' a situation in which some people are excluded from obtaining a certain good on 'appropriate' grounds when the possibilities of satisfying them were clearly unequal.

From this point of view, it is very important to consider not only the distribution of opportunities to acquire certain qualifications but also to see whether those opportunities are not correlated significantly with other unequal opportunities, although the latter formally are not established as relevant in the distribution of a good in question. This problem is illustrated by the following example given by Bernard Williams:

Suppose that in a certain society great prestige is attached to membership of a warrior class, the duties of which require great physical strength. This class has in the past been recruited from certain wealthy families only; but egalitarian reformers achieve a change in the rules, by which warriors are recruited from all sections of the society, on the results of a suitable competition. The effect of this, however, is that the wealthy families still provide virtually all the warriors, because the rest of the populace is so undernourished by reason of poverty that their physical strength is inferior to that of the wealthy and well nourished. The reformers protest that equality of opportunity has not really been achieved; the wealthy reply that in fact it has, and that the poor now have the opportunity of becoming warriors – it is just bad luck that their characteristics are such that they do not pass the test. "We are not", they might say, "excluding anyone *for* being poor; we exclude people for being weak, and it is unfortunate that those who are poor are also weak".[52]

Williams properly describes this answer as cynical although there is one aspect in which the hypothetical wealthy, in his example, are right: it would be disastrous to have an army consisting of weak, unfit men. But that only shows that the genuine ground of reasoning in this case is of a utilitarian nature: the cynicism starts when the official justifications for those grounds of selection and exclusion are given in terms of equality of opportunity. Even if no one is excluded from the selection process *for* being poor, it is clear that when being poor and being weak are closely interconnected and causally linked, those who are poor are in fact excluded. Likewise in university admissions: even if no one is excluded for being black or for living in a small remote village with a poor school and no library, when criteria of ability or knowledge are linked with those circumstances then those who are black or who live in rural areas are in fact excluded or discriminated against. This may still be found an insufficient reason for granting them preference but such a refusal will be made not on the basis of equality of opportunity but on the basis of efficiency.

Let us now return to the question of equal educational opportunities. It is a notorious fact that in all modern societies those opportunities are influenced strongly by the social position of a child's parents. This influence has various forms: as an influence of differential levels of parental encouragement, housing conditions, quality of primary and secondary schools, general life-style of a given social class. There is unquestionable empirical evidence showing that educational opportunities are strongly determined by social stratification.[53] The very fact of underrepresentation of underprivileged groups at universities is an indication of a high likelihood of societal discrimination. The statistical underrepresentation of certain groups or minorities raises the presumption of discrimination: unless it can be shown to the contrary, it can be recognized that this underrepresentation is due to reduced opportunities. Statistical evidence is, therefore, a *prima facie* indicator of discrimination.[54]

To be sure, one must not overestimate the significance of the statistical evidence in this regard. I do not take statistical underrepresentation to be conclusive evidence of invidious discrimination; it is rather a fair guess based upon wide historical experience suggesting that, more often than not, underrepresentation is a result of discrimination. It does not follow that each and every instance of underrepresentation is caused by discrimination. It may well be true that a particular social or ethnic group has special aptitudes for, or interests in, particular disciplines and occupations. Their over-representation in those fields does not necessarily mean that other groups are victims of discrimination. A particularly high percentage of Italians running pizza restaurants does not indicate that other groups are discriminated against. On a slightly more serious note, Richard Posner may well be correct in suggesting that, for instance, medical aptitude and interest is not evenly distributed among racial and ethnic groups in the United States. In consequence, "the failure of blacks to achieve proportionate representation cannot automatically be ascribed to the history of discrimination against them".[55] No, not automatically. To equate 'automatically' every fact of statistical underrepresentation with the past group discrimination would be a grave error, indeed. Similarly, it would be erroneous to measure the extent of invidious discrimination by numerical representation of particular groups in the universities, business or government. Statistical imbalance may well be the result of factors that have little or nothing to do with discrimination yet which are relevant to processes of selection and recruitment. Thomas Sowell points out, for instance, that median age differences among American ethnic groups account for significant variations of these groups' representation in adult jobs.[56] He observes also that many important differences among ethnic groups reflect historical differences which have their sources in diverse traditions and cultures of these groups.[57]

But one must not protest too much. Statistical imbalances do not *prove* anything, but nonetheless they should not be totally ignored. We know, for instance, that underrepresentation of American blacks in important, prestigious and lucrative positions in a society is, by and large, due to past invidious discrimination. This explanation is not necessarily correct in each and every case of underrepresentation, but as a rule of thumb it works reasonably well. Imbalances such as those cited by Justice Marshall in *Bakke*, that is, in life expectancy, average income and unemployment figures,[58] can hardly be explained by the lower 'aptitudes and interests' of blacks. Even if it is true that, for example, prevailing family models in black communities in the United States do not emphasize the importance of formal education to the same extent as some other ethnic groups, these attitudes themselves are products of the long history of discrimination. As for the hypothesis about lower capacities, it is extremely doubtful whether such proof can be made since even poor biological inheritance may be a result of the poor environmental conditions of the group. The lower average IQ of the members of the group may be the result rather than the cause of its underprivileged position in a society.[59]

This suggests that the principle of equality of opportunity, if viewed more broadly than when restricted to the last link in the chain of stages in a person's life, requires taking into account those different social opportunities to acquire qualifications relevant to the distribution or selection in question. Equality of opportunity calls for a differential approach to candidates or applicants, unless it can be shown that their chances of acquiring competence were similar. It is, therefore, a consequence of the principle of equality of opportunity that those with inferior initial capacities of obtaining the types of competence required, should be treated in a more favourable way;

otherwise their opportunities are unequal. This is how John Rawls defines 'genuine', as opposed to formal, equality of opportunity. Discussing the principle of redress, he says:

[T]he principle holds that in order to treat all persons equally, to provide genuine equality of opportunity, society must give more attention to those with fewer native assets and to those born into the less favourable social positions. The idea is to redress the bias of contingencies in the direction of equality.[60]

Thus, the principle of compensation is *required* by the principle of equality of opportunity, not contradicted by it. Equality of opportunity demands equal treatment of those who had equal opportunities to acquire a qualification demanded; the other side of the coin is that those with unequal opportunities should be treated unequally and should be compensated for the handicaps imposed upon them if those handicaps result in reduced competitive chances. If the social system is unable to abolish the differences resulting in unequal opportunities to acquire valuable qualifications, it should at least compensate for those differences in order to approximate the genuine equality of opportunities. In this context, preferential treatment is a method of equalizing opportunities. As Felix E. Oppenheim says, "giving certain minorities extra points is a device which helps them reach the common starting line".[61]

4. GROUPS AND INDIVIDUALS

But is it to *minorities* that we should give those 'extra points' which Oppenheim mentions or rather to particular *individuals*? In this Section I will discuss one of the most common objections against preferential treatment programs: that they confer benefits upon groups and not individuals. Many writers among those who criticize preferential treatment programs admit that they would not object to individual compensations. For example, Alan Goldman approves of actions taken "to compensate individuals who themselves deserve it on grounds of actual prior discrimination or denial of equal opportunity" but

with regard to groups that are defined only according to some shared characteristic, that have no official representative bodies, whose members have no formal interaction, and whose individual members may suffer harms from injustices that do not necessarily affect others, compensation can be owed only to the individual members who have been harmed and not to the groups as a whole.[62]

Preferential treatment programs, the argument goes, tend to benefit indiscriminately all the members of the favoured group, irrespective of the actual discrimination or deprivation suffered by them. It is a far cry from acceptance of the duty to compensate a particular individual (about whom we know precisely that he was denied a job or place at the university on a discriminatory basis) to the claim that all the members of the group are entitled to preference. Goldman, who is prepared to accept reverse discrimination in favour of *individuals* who have been overtly discriminated against in the educational system or in employment, rejects all forms of *group* reverse discrimination. "Certainly not all members of these groups [women and blacks] have been unjustly denied a job or a chance at a decent education — the type of harm that may call for reverse discrimination as compensation in kind".[63] It has been also suggested that group preferences tend to select those individuals who least deserve compensation relative to other members of the same group. Judge Krishna Iyer of the Supreme Court of India has warned that the benefits of preferential promotions "are snatched away by the top creamy layer of the 'backward' caste or class, thus keeping the weakest among the weak always weak and leaving the fortunate layers to consume the whole cake".[64]

For the sake of clarity, I will distinguish between two types of arguments advanced by opponents of group preferential treatment. The first type rejects group preferential treatment as unjustified on the grounds that a group is not an entity which may have moral claims, needs, merits or deserts; in a word, that it is not a proper subject of moral rights and obligations. The second, more pragmatic, type of argument points to the dangers of over-inclusion and under-inclusion when those entitled to preferential treatment are defined on a group basis.

The first type of argument may be best illustrated by an article by George Sher who asserts that groups cannot be reasonably said to have 'merits' or 'needs'. Referring, in particular, to racial and sexual groups, Sher convincingly points out the absurdities resulting from ascribing 'merit' or 'needs' to groups and concludes that "such groups do not fall under the principle of distributive justice at all".[65] There is certainly an initial appeal in the idea that groups do not 'deserve' or 'need' anything except in a metaphoric sense. Groups do not qualify for 'desert' or 'merit' because they are not capable of 'acting' in a literal sense of the word. Groups cannot 'need' anything because they do not experience the various states of comfort or discomfort which are presupposed by the notion of needs. However, group preferential treatment need not rely upon the assumption about group merits or group needs. In most of the cases, with important exceptions to which I shall refer later, preferential treatment is justified not on the basis that a group as a whole 'merits' compensation but rather that its *members* have been discriminated against and that compensation is owed to them. Group characteristics are only an indicator, which may be accurate or not, of discrimination or deprivation suffered by particular members of the group. In so far as this indicator is accurate, that is to say, in so far as there is a strong correlation between membership of the group concerned and actual discrimination, past or present, the group characteristics play a useful role in defining a class of particular individuals to whom preferences should be given.

It is appropriate, at this point, to make a distinction between two types of justification for group preferential treatment: distributive and collective. The group characteristic is used distributively when it defines a property which may be attributed to each of the group's members; it is used collectively when a group property is attributed to a group as a whole and is not reducible to characteristics of its particular members.[66] Sher's reasoning constitutes an effective rebuttal only of the collective arguments about preferential treatment. However, the bulk of arguments in favour of group preferential treatment are based upon group characteristics in the distributive sense. Group preferential treatment is usually argued for on the basis that compensation is due to particular persons who have been wronged and, as these deprivations are correlated with group membership, persons who have been wronged are *identified* through their group membership. This identification may be correct or incorrect: this is a matter to be verified empirically in particular cases. For instance, when it is claimed with regard to the United States that "[b]eing black can ... become morally relevant in distinguishing between those individuals who are members of the group to whom reparations are owed and those who are not",[67] this may be confirmed by empirical evidence or not. In any event, 'being black' is taken in this phrase to be a method of identifying those individuals to whom reparations should be given. With regard to such an obviously 'distributive' group approach, Sher's argument against group preferential treatment is simply irrelevant.

It should be observed that the collective approach to group characteristics against which Sher's argument is indeed directed, should not be entirely rejected. True, we must be circumspect in applying collective group characteristics but it does not follow that we are never justified in doing so. There may well be situations in which a group, as a whole, has been wronged or discriminated against; in these cases a group characteristic is something more than an indicator of particular individuals who are most likely to have suffered consequences of discrimination. When people are discriminated against because of their membership in a given group and not because of their individual characteristics, then the collective approach is justified. When the fact of being a member of a certain group is a sufficient ground for discrimination, then it is directed against a group as a whole and against all its members *qua* members of the group.[68] Classifications that single out minority groups for the purposes of redress are, in these cases, fully justified.

To be sure, such a collective rather than a distributive approach requires proof that the past discrimination was directed against the group as a whole; it seems that it is proper, in this case, to place the burden of proof on those who demand group preferential treatment on a collective basis. An institutionalized system of racial inequality, such as apartheid, would provide an example of such past discrimination that justifies a collective approach to group preferences. One may consider also cases where stereotypes and prejudices against an ethnic group create such a general social climate that each and every member thereof is necessarily touched by it and suffers negative group identity as a result. This type of 'collective' justification of group preferential treatment is expressed well in the words of Justice Marshall: "It is unnecessary in 20th Century America to have individual Negroes demonstrate that they have been victims of racial discrimination; the racism of our society has been so pervasive that none, regardless of wealth or position, has managed to escape its impact".[69]

In the cases when such collective past discrimination can be found, the so-called 'reversal test' proposed by Alan Goldman as a method of evaluation of preferential treatment, is clearly inadequate. This test, as applied to the American preferential treatment programs, "calls upon us to judge whether a white male in similar circumstances ... would deserve preferential treatment in the context in question".[70] It is applicable to distributive group preferential treatment but in the cases of collective arguments such a test is simply not available: if the individuals have received discriminatory treatment because of a group characteristic, the non-members of the group cannot be thought of as being 'in similar circumstances'. If, for instance, one can claim that discrimination against blacks in the United States had a collective, rather than a distributive character, then 'a white male in similar circumstances' is a contradiction in terms: relevant circumstances here include race.

More often than not, however, it is a distributive sense which is attached to arguments about group preferential treatment. Preferences are demanded for a member of a particular group not because he is a member of this group but because it is a fair estimate that he was discriminated against or deprived of equal opportunity. In the distributive sense, group membership is not a justification of the preference but an index of probability of past discrimination or deprivation. James W. Nickel proposes to distinguish between a 'justifying basis' and an 'administrative basis' for preferential treatment programs: being a member of a group does not justify the preferences but it indicates the features correlated with those which actually do justify such preferences. For example, "since almost all American blacks have been victimized by discrimination it would be justifiable to design and institute programmes of special benefits for blacks".[71] Such programs, Nickel adds, are justified in terms of the injuries that nearly all of the recipients have suffered, not in terms of their race. We see, therefore, that this justification is based mainly on the considerations of practicality and administrative convenience: it is much easier to detect the feature of 'being black' than that of 'being deprived of equal opportunity'. The higher the correlation between the administrative basis and the justifying basis, the smaller is the risk that the program will result in unfair over- and under-inclusiveness. In other words, the smaller is the risk of producing benefits for a large number of people who had not suffered any discrimination (over-inclusiveness) and of disregarding the legitimate claims of those who had been discriminated against (under-inclusiveness).

This empirical correlation between the justifying and the administrative basis is of particular importance: much of the philosophical and legal discussion of preferential treatment has been concerned not with the moral weakness of the principle but with the defects of particular programs in which this correlation is not sufficiently high. However, the fact that the administrative basis is not identical with a justifying basis is not a sufficient reason to reject the principle of preferential treatment. The demands to abolish all 'proxy' features in preferential treatment programs (that is, features which indicate the existence of another feature which is a real justification of preferences) would not only cause immense administrative problems but also would be inconsistent with the nature of the discrimination which is intended to be eradicated. As was clearly illustrated by Williams's example about warriors,[72] discrimination can be effected without indicating openly its real basis but through a criterion of classification which is linked with the actual ground of discrimination. In the example given by Williams, poverty was the real basis of discrimination, and physical weakness was merely a 'proxy'. Similarly, racial discrimination can be instituted by 'proxy', without mentioning race as a basis of classification. In 1971, the United States Supreme Court considered whether the Civil Rights Act of 1964 prohibited an employer from requiring a school diploma or an educational test where such requirements were unrelated to job performance and resulted in a limitation on the number of blacks employed.[73] Title VII of the Act prohibits the differentiation among employees on the basis of their race, color, religion, sex or national origin. The Court held that if the use of tests results in a statistical decrease in the number of minority employees then the burden of proof is shifted to the employer who has to show that the tests are job-related. The Court concluded also that the absence of discriminatory intent "does not redeem employment procedures or testing mechanisms that operate as 'built-in headwinds' for minority groups and are unrelated to measuring job capability".[74] Another example of such discrimination 'by proxy' is the setting of such an age requirement which indirectly discriminates against women. In England, a woman complained to an industrial tribunal that a condition of appointment to the particular position in the civil service requiring that the candidates should be under 28 years of age discriminated against her on the ground of sex. She maintained that women have greater difficulty in complying with the upper age limit of 28 than do men because many women in their twenties are having children or looking after children. By the time they feel able to apply for a job, it is too late. The Employment Appeal Tribunal agreed that this condition of appointment was discriminatory because "the condition is one which it is in practice harder for women to comply with than it is for men".[75]

We see, therefore, that sex discrimination need not operate through the explicit use of sex criteria, just as racial discrimination can be effected without mentioning race. Some anti-discriminatory statutes prohibit such indirect discrimination.[76] The lesson to be drawn from this for the purposes of affirmative action is rather obvious: if invidious discrimination can operate effectively 'by proxy', then sometimes it may be necessary to eradicate it 'by proxy'. If, say, 'being uneducated' works as a surrogate for 'being black' in the invidious discrimination, then 'being black' should be used as a surrogate for 'being discriminated against' in a preferential treatment program. Or, to take again Williams' example about warriors, 'being weak' serves as a proxy in the discrimination against the poor, and 'being poor' may serve as a proxy for 'being discriminated against'.

To what extent this use of surrogate features is justified depends on the degree of correlation between the 'proxy' feature and the characteristic which is represented by the 'proxy'. It is with regard to this matter that the second major argument against group preferential treatment is relevant. According to that argument, preferential admissions, selections and distributions are necessarily over- and under-inclusive; in other words, when individuals to be compensated are singled out by their group membership, not *all* the deserving and not *only* the deserving obtain preference. My initial answer to this charge is simple: it depends on the empirical correlation between the justifying basis and the administrative basis of preference, that is, between the fact of discrimination and group membership. This is a question of fact that can be resolved by evidence. If this empirical correlation is low and the property which is the administrative basis of the preference does not indicate accurately those who suffered discrimination or deprivation, then it is simply a bad preferential treatment program. But this is an empirical matter and not a matter of principle; the fact that some preferential treatment programs are deficient does not provide an argument against the principle of group preferences. It may be argued, for instance, that in the United States being black is a relatively accurate indication of deprivation in educational opportunities. If that is so, race may be a relevant indicator of previous discrimination or deprivation. If most black children, in a certain school district, received an inferior education because they were excluded from white schools in one way or another, a measure that requires remedial classes for all black children is a reliable means of overcoming the hardship resulting from past discrimination. By the same token, preferential treatment designed to help Aborigines in Australia contains very little risk of benefiting those individuals who had not experienced consequences of discrimination. As an Australian legal scholar notes: "There are few middle class Aborigines and this avoids immediately over-inclusion as a major problem".[77]

So much for the argument about over-inclusiveness. The charge of under-inclusiveness is more serious. It is sometimes claimed that preferential treatment gives insufficient protection to problems of less vocal minorities and, in particular, to disadvantaged members of a group which is, as a whole, well off and therefore is not given preference.[78] The charge is often justified but again, it does not necessarily upset the principle of a group preferential scheme. It is important to bear in mind that such programs must not be viewed as universal devices for eradicating the results of discrimination against all members of a society or of deprivations suffered by all its members. Those programs are established in order to overcome the consequences of some typical deprivations: they compensate *some* of the victims of *some* social wrongs. There is no reason why some others, who were also discriminated against, should not be compensated on another basis. As Hardy Jones puts it: "The fact that not every injustice can be rectified should not make us feel justified in compensating no one".[79] Group preferential programs strike at harm where it is thought to be most acute. To require that a single program remedy all aspects of a particular social discrimination or none at all might preclude the law from undertaking any program of correction. If the critic of such a scheme takes the problem of under-inclusion as an argument against the *principle* of group preferential treatment, this must be because he presupposes a curious moral proposition that we should not try to compensate for *any* harm to the victims of discrimination unless we can compensate for *all* injustices. Preferential treatment programs try to compensate some groups which were discriminated against in a significant way: their members suffered forms of discrimination which were typical, because related to their group membership. This is not to say that other claims to compensation should be ignored.

The argument about over- and under-inclusiveness of group preferential treatment is useful in so far as it indicates the need for a high correlation between the administrative and justifying basis. In certain cases, a bad choice of the administrative basis results in a general failure of the program. For example, this was essentially the case in Poland, where the basis of preference in university admissions was established in an arbitrary way, according to so-called 'class' criteria, and this did not reflect properly the real social discriminations and inequalities in access to education. Critics of the existing scheme argued convincingly that more complex criteria, taking into account family income, place of habitation, educational disadvantages at the secondary school level and so on, would express more correctly the obstacles one has to overcome on one's way to the university.[80] This problem of proper identification of the group characteristics of those to whom the preferential treatment is due may be illustrated well by the case of preferential programs in India.[81] The Indian Constitution provides in Section 16(4) for preferences in favour of "any backward class of citizens which, in the opinion of the State, is not adequately represented in the services under the State". In 1953, India's President appointed a Backward Classes Commission charged with the responsibility of determining criteria for social backwardness. The Commission's report, submitted two years later, categorized over two thousand castes or communities as backward and announced guidelines for 'backwardness' relying mainly on the criterion of caste. The report was met with strong criticism and, ultimately, was rejected by the Parliament. The task of determining the criteria of 'backwardness' was then assumed by the Supreme Court of India. In a series of decisions, starting with the landmark case *Balaji v. Mysore*,[82] the Court established a complex set of indicia of 'backwardness' which included poverty, occupation and place of habitation. In order to avoid the risk of overbroad designation of 'backward classes', the Court approved the imposition of income ceilings for State preferences, thus excluding affluent citizens from the benefits of preferential programs even if, by other standards, they would fall into a favoured group of citizens.

This suggests to me that the problem of under-inclusive and over-inclusive classifications can be solved through a more refined designation of group characteristics of those who should receive preferences. To reject the very principle of group preferential treatment on the basis that some of the existing programs do not properly identify the scope of the recipients, would be an example of throwing the baby out with the bathwater. The alternative, suggested by the critics of group preferential treatment, is to consider each candidate individually and accord preferences only when specific acts of past discrimination against this particular individual are established: "reverse discrimination is ... justified in order to compensate specific past violations of ... rights or denials of equal opportunity".[83] Let us leave aside here the question of the costs of such a procedure which may require the recruitment of a whole army of investigators, inquiring into past acts of discrimination or denial of equal rights. Even if such a practice were to be justified on the grounds of justice, probably the costs resulting from under- and over-inclusiveness of group programs would be smaller than costs of individual investigation. But this is not the main point: the issue of costs and administrative convenience is not decisive in matters of justice. What is important, however, is that even if we agree to preferential treatment solely on an individual basis, we still have to establish general criteria of what is to be counted as past discrimination (or relevant deprivation) and how it is to influence the preference accorded. The absence of such general criteria would lead to total arbitrariness: if the admission officers were instructed merely to accord preference to those who had been deprived of equal opportunity in the past, it would lead to a situation in which not rules but whim were decisive. The existence of rules excludes a case-by-case basis for solving problems. Strictly speaking, 'individual' treatment is, in its extreme version, incompatible with treatment by means of law: law considers typical situations and prescribes typical remedies. If, however, the administrators of preferential programs are given the general guidelines about those deprivations which justify particular kinds of compensation and hence about distinctions which can be incorporated in their decisions, it leads inevitably to a 'group approach'; those meeting the conditions described by a preferential treatment program, constitute a group of recipients of preferential treatment. Now, it is rather unimportant whether it is a 'group' in a sociological sense which exists irrespective of the preferential treatment provisions (for example, an ethnic group), or a 'class' in a merely statistical sense (for instance, all those earning under a certain minimum), or even a class established on the basis of multiplicity of traits (for instance, all divorced women earning under a certain minimum and living in big cities). There may be different ways to answer the question: "Who should be given preference"?, but the answer: "All those who deserve it on individual grounds" is insufficient as far as legal regulation is concerned. Such a 'guideline' would simply mean that the admission committees are left to their own devices as to how to decide the selection of candidates. If a pattern of selection emerges, it becomes clear that the use of those committees was simply a roundabout way of saying that *they* are to make the legal guidelines concerning the criteria of preferences and there is nothing to prevent us from assessing these criteria. If, however, no pattern of decision can be discerned, one may suspect that the admission committee is mindless or arbitrary.

5. 'VICTIMS' OF PREFERENTIAL TREATMENT

Finally, I would like to consider what is probably the most serious charge against preferential treatment, and certainly the most emotionally and psychologically persuasive one. The arguments discussed so far may be said to take into account only one side of the coin: that of the beneficiaries of the preferences. This is not the whole story, however. For each preferred person there is one rejected, for each preferentially admitted black there is a DeFunis[84] or a Bakke.[85] A distribution of scarce goods is a zero-sum-game or something similar to it: in order to give we have to take. The generosity of preferential programs, it is argued, is at the expense of other innocent persons who have to pay for it in the currency of frustrated expectations. It seems natural that the opponents of preferential treatment tend to stress the situation of its 'victims' while its partisans are more concerned about the recipients of preferences. This last viewpoint expresses the general conviction that, in practice, social justice is principally a matter of those 'worse-off' since those 'better-off' take care of themselves quite successfully. But this populist intuition, when reflected in a more comprehensive conception of justice, becomes vulnerable to criticism as imputing double standards and disrespect for individual rights. That is why, in this last part of the chapter about preferential treatment, I would like to turn to the 'victims' part of the argument.

The starting point for the argument in question is that "[f]or every less qualified person who is admitted to a college, or hired for a job, there is a more qualified person who is being discriminated against, and who has a right to complain".[86] At this point one could argue, of course, that there is a relatively simple solution to this dilemma: both 'a more qualified' and 'a less qualified' could be admitted. One way of doing that, so far as university admissions are concerned, would be to increase the number of admission places, reserving the additional ones for members of the disadvantaged groups and financing the extra facilities out of the public purse so that the costs of compensation would be distributed evenly among the whole community. True, but there always comes a point at which the scarcity of resources makes it impossible or unreasonable to increase further the number of places available. It is only at this point that the serious moral debate about preferential treatment begins. If we could increase the number of positions indefinitely, the question of distributional criteria would not arise at all. Whenever such criteria are in operation, there will be some who will complain about their lower chances of acquiring the necessary qualifications and, if preferences are accorded to them, others who are 'more qualified' will inevitably fail to gain admission.

On this basis, several arguments in defence of alleged victims of preferential treatment are formulated. It is claimed, for instance, that if a discrimination is societal and can be attributed to the social structure in general, it is inequitable to charge a few individuals, who are innocent, with the cost of compensation. The costs of compensation, we are told, should be assigned either to the perpetrators or to the beneficiaries of injustice; when it is not possible, these costs should be distributed evenly among the entire community. In particular, it is argued that those who effectively pay the costs of preferential admissions (that is, the rejected non-minority applicants who would have been admitted in the absence of special admission schemes) are the least likely to have benefited from the past discrimination against others, let alone to have been engaged actively in such discriminatory practices.[87] In consequence, it is often claimed that preferential treatment violates the rights of those who have to bear its burdens; for example, in the United States, the rights of "most qualified white males, who are not liable for past injustices".[88] On the extreme side of the 'victims argument', preferential treatment is compared to shooting hostages[89] or Nuremberg laws.[90]

These are serious charges. Let us try to consider them without emotion, although the frustration of a white applicant in the United States, or a member of 'intelligentsia' in Poland, refused a place at the university because, respectively, a 'less qualified' black or worker's child was admitted, is something very human, natural and understandable. However, emotion and frustration are not good advisers in reflections about what is just and what is not just. For a moment, let us take the 'victims argument' at its face value, accepting the assertion that preferential treatment results in deprivations for nonmembers of a preferred group, and that they are being discriminated against. Even if it is true, the general calculus of gains and costs may still result in a conclusion that those discriminations and deprivations are reasonable costs for the rectification of other, more oppressive, discriminations and deprivations. After all, we have to compare the degree of one injustice with that of another. To discriminate is unjust, but to tolerate the existing discrimination or deprivation is also unjust. A failure to establish preference devised to assure genuine equality of opportunity may be a greater injustice than to establish such a scheme; failure to practise preferential treatment may be more unjust than practising it. The very fact that we merely abstain from doing something does not release us from moral responsibility in so far as it is within our power to prevent existing injustices. This argument is answered sometimes by saying that no injustice can be justified by a desire to rectify another injustice. J. A. Passmore rejects the contention that "injustice in selection is so serious a form of injustice that it demands reparation in the form of preference in selection", and he says:

[T]his argument, fully set out as 'civil injustice in [sic] so serious a form of injustice that it demands compensation in the form of committing acts of civil injustice', contains the same moral absurdity as: 'killing is so terrible a crime that the killer must be killed'.[91]

I must confess that I do not see anything particularly shocking about this supposed 'absurdity'. It is an unfortunate truth about the human condition that we do not always make choices between good and bad but often between different degrees of bad. There is nothing 'morally absurd' about situations where we have to infringe one moral principle in order to save another; when, for instance, we prefer to lie in order to diminish someone's suffering or *vice versa*. This allegedly 'morally absurd' situation reflects the tragedy of human life in which conflicts of values are part of our world and in which to act morally often means to choose a lesser evil. The same applies to the realm of justice: not always do we have the luxury of choice of an absolutely just solution against an unjust one; sometimes a just act consists in the choice of a less unjust solution.

If a putative justification of preferential treatment rests upon the moral priority of the rectification of existing injustice over the prevention of another act of injustice, then the defence of 'victims' in terms of their infringed rights would add much weight to their claims and could possibly reverse the moral priority in their favour. Indeed, the argument that preferential treatment violates the rights of those 'more qualified' but rejected, is a familiar line of criticism of preferential treatment.[92] For my part, I doubt whether anyone's rights are violated in such a case, although some expectations may be frustrated. What rights of non-members of a preferred group may be said to be violated? The right to be admitted to a university? Not really, no-one has an intrinsic right to become a student (otherwise, any selection procedure would violate rights of those not admitted).[93] The right to be selected only on the basis of one's intellectual capacities as measured by tests and grades? It is hard to see why such a *prima facie* right should exist; I see no plausible argument that selection on the exclusive basis of knowledge is a matter of *right*. The right to be treated equally, the right to equal opportunity? Yes, but I have tried to show that, in the process of selection and distribution, the principle of equal opportunity requires a differentiated treatment and that to link it with the tests of abilities is a matter of utility rather than of equality. Hence, even if non-preferred applicants are deprived of *something* by the process of preferential admissions, it is doubtful whether their *rights* are violated. Therefore, the issue raised by preferential treatment is *not* one of the rectification of injustice by the means of violation of rights. Rather, it is a matter of balancing one injustice against another.

Now, if we have to choose between an injustice affecting adversely the minorities systematically discriminated against and an injustice against a traditionally dominant group, there is a good deal to be said for choosing the latter. Certainly, it is hard to argue that preferential treatment for blacks in the United States or Australia endangers seriously the self-esteem, confidence and motivation of the white majority.[94] Measures undertaken in order to upgrade a social group which is in a particularly disadvantaged situation seem to justify the inevitable injustices imposed upon those who in all other regards are better off. The measures which are unjust towards a dominant group do not perpetuate prior unjust deprivation and they do not confer privileges upon an already overprivileged group. If indeed it is an injustice, it is an injustice based upon the expedient of choosing a lesser evil. Of course, it would be better if we did not have to frustrate expectations of anyone but, alas, such a painless course of action is rarely available.

The argument that it is unjust to make non-minority members pay for the compensation assumes so far that they have not engaged in, or benefited from, past discrimination. But this assumption is not unquestionable. The argument that the costs of compensation should be paid only by the perpetrators and/or beneficiaries of past discrimination is not a sufficient reason for rejecting group preferential treatment programs such as, for example, preferential admissions for the blacks in the United States. In societies where various groups suffer reduced opportunities of access to, say, education, as a result of past discrimination, the rest of society enjoys unearned advantages in this access. The non-members of the disadvantaged group benefit from the very fact that the group has received discriminatory treatment, irrespective of their actual active involvement in the acts of discrimination. The test for these benefits has the structure of a counter-factual argument: if there were no past acts of deprivation or discrimination and thus the minority were better off than it actually is, would the non-minority members be in an equally advantageous position now and would they have the same access to the positions sought by them? If it can be argued that, in the absence of past discrimination against a group, the rest of society would be in a less advantageous position with respect to the opportunities in question, this would suggest that the non-minority members benefit from the past discrimination. The argument could be made, for example, that in the absence of past discrimination there would be a larger pool of qualified minority candidates for university studies. Consequently, the probability of an average non-minority applicant being admitted would be lower than it actually is. Even if a particular person did not commit any specific act of discrimination, his position in a society may give him special advantages as compared with others. Reverse discrimination is, then, the removal of an unfair advantage to which he is not entitled. It does not need to be shown that, for instance, a white applicant "has inherited profits from his father's discrimination against blacks"[95] to prove that he is benefiting from the unequal position of blacks. What *is* relevant is the question whether he has actually benefited from unequal educational opportunity. If this is the case, then his right to equal opportunity is not violated by the preferential treatment, because his opportunity *before* the treatment was better; this is, therefore, a situation of unequal treatment of unequal cases.

Consequently, it is incorrect to claim that, for example, in race-conscious preferential admissions, non-members of the race which is preferentially treated are excluded *because of* their race. Justice Stevens has made this observation: "[t]he University [of California at Davis], through its special admissions policy, excluded Bakke from participation in its program of medical education because of his race".[96] But, strictly speaking, this is not true. Bakke was not excluded *because of* his race. Rather, he was excluded because his examination results were not good enough. True, he had to pass more stringent examinations than black applicants, but this is because it could be reasonably presumed that he had had better opportunities to obtain the qualifications necessary for medical students. Ultimately, his combined qualifications, measured by tests scores *and* by other considerations (that is, those considerations related to his prior opportunities to acquire qualifications) did not outweigh the combined qualifications of other applicants. Those other applicants who proved to be more successful than Bakke, included the preferentially admitted applicants. Bakke scored better in the Medical College Admissions Tests than some of the admitted blacks, but this was only a part of the measurement of his qualifications and, all things considered, he proved to be less qualified than the persons who displaced him. The conclusion is that he was not excluded because of race but because of insufficient qualifications in the broad sense of the word.

If this argument sounds somewhat demagogic, the following example might be usefully considered. In a particular factory, all male manual workers are expected to fulfil onerous tasks, including carrying heavy objects, while women are released from this type of work and are directed to duties which do not require the same physical strength. Now, imagine that a male worker consistently refuses to carry heavy boxes and, in consequence, is sacked. He cannot complain that he has been fired *because of* his sex. He has been fired because he was not doing a job which was reasonably expected of him. At the same time, it is true that those expectations were directly influenced by sex considerations. By the same token, Bakke was rejected not because of his race, although his race was instrumental in shaping the reasonable expectations of the selection committee. He did not live up to these expectations and he should not have blamed anyone but himself for his failure.

Thus, at the end of the day, the controversy about preferential treatment boils down to the controversy about the concept and criteria of qualifications. In the discussions about preferential admissions to universities, opponents of these programs assume that abilities and skills, as revealed by test grades, are the only relevant criteria of the decision about who should become a student in a situation of scarcity of places. I have attempted to show that the principle of equal opportunity requires taking other criteria into account as well; those other criteria supplement the criterion of ability which still remains the central criterion. If I have suggested that social opportunities of acquiring qualification should be taken into account, it is because they could be relevant to the acquisition of skills and abilities. But now I should like to go a step further. Certainly, the question of skills is essential from the point of view of the desirable professional standard of university graduates. But this is not an absolute and not the only approach which is relevant to the purposes of higher education. Education, besides serving utilitarian social purposes, plays an essential role in human self-development; it is an important condition of self-realization for those who see it as part of their life-plans. If this approach is taken towards the aim of education, then the problem of skills and abilities becomes much less relevant. The purpose of assistance in self-development is equally well served in the case of an exceptionally talented person as it is in the case of a mediocre one. The self-realization of both cannot be measured by one and the same scale: each of them gains as much as he is capable of using and developing. Above a certain basic level of qualifications, without which a student cannot obtain any benefits from participating in classes, the difference between 'a less qualified' and 'a more qualified' candidate is not relevant from the point of view of attaining those broad purposes of tertiary education. True, in a situation of scarce resources, some criteria for limiting the access to education must be found. But if we consider self-development as an important aim of education, then it is by no means obvious that skills are the only proper criterion for such limitation.

Consider criteria for limitation of the access to culture. Probably no-one would suggest that when the demand for opera tickets exceeds the number of seats available, musical skills or theoretical knowledge of music on the part of theatre goers should be taken into account in the distribution of tickets. Some will propose an increase in prices of tickets up to the level of equilibrium between supply and demand, others will call for a distribution on a first-come, first-served basis, or through a lottery. The superiority of these methods of distribution over distribution on the basis of musical tests stems from the very purposes of opera performances. Both the most sophisticated connoisseurs and the musical illiterates will draw some satisfaction from this cultural experience: it will help in the self-development of each within everyone's individual scale of potentiality. *Mutatis mutandis*, the same applies to education. The difference is that in the case of education, utilitarian goals are much more urgent and obvious. But in so far as inner satisfaction and self-realization are also important aims served by an educational system, selection solely on the basis of skills is hardly justified. Selection on meritocratic grounds is justified by considerations of efficiency and utility; they are important, probably the most important, but not the sole aims of education.

One final point. A charge is frequently made that preferential admissions programs try to remedy the effects without curing the cause. For instance, it has been argued with regard to the 'preferential points' in Poland that the proper way to equalize opportunities is through equalization of the level of education in rural areas with that of big towns. Instead of giving 'extra points', so it is argued, we should see to it that no-one is denied good primary and secondary education in the first place. Similar arguments are made also in the context of racial relations in the United States: the proper way is to equalize educational opportunities and not to accord preferences when it is already too late. There is a great deal of truth in this argument. Preferential treatment does not cure causes, it operates only in the sphere of consequences. But this approach does not contradict the other: it is important to try to eliminate causes of discrimination but it is also important to rectify consequences where this has not been done. Equalization of the quality of schools is a task for generations — what of today's teenagers? In his opinion in *Bakke*, Justice Blackmun said: "I yield to no one in my earnest hope that the time will come when an 'affirmative action' program is unnecessary and is, in truth, only a relic of the past".[97] It would be better if there were no circumstances which give rise to compensatory treatment but if, alas, they exist, why should the just claims of people who actually suffer these consequences be ignored? By the same token, one might say: it would be better if, instead of compensating some workers for their onerous work, we should rather see to it that each job is equally pleasant and satisfying. True as it is, it does not make actual claims for compensation unfounded. Future goals are not sufficient remedies for past and actual deprivations.

CHAPTER 8

PUNISHMENT AND THE THEORY OF JUSTICE

1. DISTRIBUTION AND RETRIBUTION

The general scheme of thinking of justice as equilibrium is applicable not only to a distribution of goods which are sought by men in a society but also to distribution of punishments. There is no reason to think that these two fields of application of justice should be governed by completely different sets of moral principles. If the balance of benefits and burdens is to constitute an essential theoretical framework for social justice, it can be applied both to a distribution of advantages (in order to balance the increased amount of burdens) and of punishments (to balance undeserved benefits gained by the criminal). In both cases, the acts of social justice are responses to those facts and actions which may be described as benefits and burdens. Both fields of social justice can be considered as the proportional relations between inputs and outputs: in the case of distributive justice, the inputs are deserts and needs; in the case of retributive justice, the inputs are crimes.

Now, this 'symmetry' of distributive and retributive justice must not be taken for granted. Although it seems to me that there is a good *prima facie* case for believing that the just distribution of benefits and burdens should be governed by the same general principles, there are also important views to the contrary. In this Section, I will consider one objection to the idea of 'symmetry' of distributive and retributive justice, an objection which seems to be particularly significant. My task here will be modest: to rebut the objections to the symmetry of distribution and retribution, rather than to provide a positive argument in its favour. If these objections turn out to be unfounded, the way will be cleared for the application of the principles of distributive justice to the sphere of punishment.

In his 'Theory of Justice', John Rawls rejects the view that distributive and retributive justice are 'converses' since, he says, distributive justice lacks the specific moral basis which is essential to retributive justice. Legal punishments, Rawls argues, correspond to moral wrongs: "those who are punished for violating just laws have normally done something wrong", hence "a propensity to commit such acts is a mark of bad character, and in a just society legal punishments will only fall upon those who display these faults".[1] The distribution of advantages is not, according to Rawls, a 'converse' of punishing. The principles of justice propounded by Rawls, and in particular his 'difference principle', do not require that the distribution of benefits should correspond to moral worth or moral desert; in a well-ordered and just society there is "no tendency for distribution and virtue to coincide".[2] Justice requires that each obtains his due; what is a person's due, is defined by the structure of a just scheme and not by this person's desert. Therefore, if a distribution satisfies the Rawlsian principles of justice then it is just irrespective of the relations between the moral worth of a person and the distributive shares. To sum up, Rawls's argument about the asymmetry of distributive and retributive justice relies upon the argument that, in the case of the first, the moral value of an act (or of a person) is irrelevant whereas in the case of the latter, moral wrong is a prerequisite of a just punishment.

In one sense, Rawls misrepresents the nature of retributive justice: when he contrasts it with distributive justice, he refers to the assessment of the moral worth of an individual which is, allegedly, made in the case of just punishment but absent in the distribution of social benefits. But whether indeed "a propensity to commit [criminal] acts is a mark of bad character" is a contentious matter and is, at any rate, irrelevant to the justification of the infliction of punishment. It may well be true that most criminals punished for their crimes have what Rawls calls 'bad character' but this is by no means a necessary truth. The validity of punishment is not contingent upon the 'bad character' of the offender. As a moral proposition, it is almost universally accepted that punishments are for what a person *did* and not for what a person *is*.[3] Also in this Chapter, a theory of punishment will be proposed which totally abstracts from the evaluation of the character, and 'moral worth', of the offender.

So if the presence of the evaluation of 'moral worth' is to be a test for the similarities between theories of distributive and retributive justice, symmetry is complete: neither one relies upon these assessments. For it is needless to add that our theory of desert is not concerned with the 'moral worth' of an individual, but with his socially valuable effort. But perhaps the Rawlsian asymmetry thesis would be tenable in its less radical version, that is, when applied not so much to people's worth but to the moral assessment of their actions? A slightly more plausible reformulation of his thesis would have it that distributive justice operates irrespective of the moral assessment of human actions which constitute the basis of distribution, while moral reprobation of a criminal act is a necessary condition for a just punishment. Now this thesis is tenable provided that one holds a theory of distributive justice purged of the notion of desert, or of other similar notions which refer to "some appropriate relationship between what a person has done or what he is now and the benefits that he receives or the costs that he bears".[4] I have been arguing that the concept of desert is a fundamental moral notion in a theory of justice, that it cannot be reduced to a mere application of valid rules of distribution and that relating distribution of goods to personal desert is an expression of a particular concept of human freedom. More specifically, it is a consequence of the view that a person's situation in a society (including his share in a distribution of goods) should be shaped, as much as it is possible, by the factors over which this person has control.

Perhaps the controversy about the 'asymmetry thesis' reaches its limits at this point: Rawls has a desert-free theory of distributive justice and so, within the framework of his theory, asymmetry between retribution and distribution occurs. In the theory propounded in these pages, there is obviously no reason for such an asymmetry. And this statement of different positions might be sufficient for my needs at this juncture of the argument. But it should perhaps be added that, in so far as Rawls writes off the notion of desert, his theory of justice is rather eccentric. Both in our immediate, and in more considered judgments of justice, most of us tend to think of desert as a relevant (if not *the* relevant) ground of a just distribution.[5] As morality is not a matter of counting heads, this cannot add any weight to the arguments about the moral validity of desert, and yet it can be perhaps regarded as one of these fixed points in our moral landscape that constitute a starting point for the reflective equilibrium. Also, oddly enough, very similar moral grounds to those upon which I have supported the concept of desert based on effort underly the Rawlsian rejection of desert. The difference principle, which states that socio-economic inequalities are allowed only on condition that they are to the benefit of the least advantaged, expresses an attempt to nullify the effects of natural contingencies and accidental social circumstances. In this book, desert-based-on-effort, in order to correspond to the actual burdens incurred by an individual, calls for screening out, in the calculus of desert, those factors over which a person had no control, including natural assets and social place at birth. In this very important point, both the theory of desert and Rawls's difference principle converge. So perhaps, after all, the rejection of the notion of desert by Rawls is not wholehearted; perhaps this notion, rejected when Rawls sketches the 'asymmetry thesis', returns through the back door? Consider this: "[T]he difference principle gives some weight to the considerations singled out by the principle of redress; and since inequalities of birth and natural endowment are undeserved, these inequalities are to be somehow compensated for".[6] It seems to me that in order to deem some inequalities undeserved, one must have a conception of what the deserved allocations would be. A negative assessment of injustice presupposes a positive notion of justice.[7] Likewise, a judgment of the undeserved presupposes a view of positive desert: if a certain mode of treatment is declared undeserved, it can only be on the basis of a prior conception of what is required by desert considerations. So it seems that a general view about individual desert (although not identical with the worth of a person) underlies Rawls's theory.

To this, the following response could be made: Rawls, throughout his book, uses the notion of 'desert' in two different senses: as denoting a fundamental principle of distribution (which he rejects) and in a derivative sense, as a concept of legitimate expectations relative to existing social rules.[8] The justness of these rules, and in consequence the validity of 'desert' in a derivative sense, depends on whether or not they conform with the more fundamental principles of justice, and in particular with the difference principle. This argument would rescue Rawls's theory from the supposition that it implicitly presupposes 'desert', because whatever 'desert' appears here, it is merely derivative and so identical with legitimate expectations. But this defence will not do because the difference principle incorporates the idea of moral arbitrariness of natural and social contingencies. It is hard to see how one can accept the difference principle without requiring to nullify those contingencies; Rawls himself affirms that this principle "represents ... an agreement to regard the distribution of natural talents as a common asset and to share in the benefits of distribution whatever it turns out to be."[9] And further he adds: "No one deserves his greater natural capacity nor merits a more favourable starting place in society. ... The basic structure can be arranged so that these contingencies work for the good of the least fortunate".[10] This suggests to me that the class of 'the least fortunate', which is a part of the difference principle, includes those with lesser natural capacities, or worse social position at birth. And if we couple this observation with the statement that these inequalities are 'undeserved', and also with the idea that 'the undeserved' presupposes a positive conception of desert, then in consequence it turns out that the notion of 'desert' which Rawls uses is in fact not merely secondary, because it is inherent in the difference principle itself. In other words, it is not *merely* by reference to valid rules that a person can be said to deserve something under Rawls's theory, but also these very rules presuppose a particular idea of desert.

Finally, it should be noted that some of Rawls's arguments against the primacy of desert are ineffective against a theory of justice which takes seriously the distinctiveness of justice and efficiency. Arguing against 'moral worth' as a criterion of just distribution, Rawls observes:

> Surely a person's moral worth does not vary according to how many offer similar skills, or happen to want what he can produce. No one supposes that when someone's abilities are less in demand or have deteriorated (as in the case of singers) his moral deservingness undergoes a similar shift.[11]

This argument holds neither against desert based on moral worth, nor desert based on effort. What it shows is that the operation of a competitive market economy does not produce by itself results consistent with rewarding for 'moral deservingness'. The curves of supply and demand may dictate the proper salaries in a free market situation, and a free market may be indeed the most effective system of production, but this is irrelevant to considerations of justice in distribution. The dictates of justice-as-desert may not (and most probably, do not) coincide with the dictates of effectiveness. But this is a problem for an overall theory of an ideal society, not for a theory of justice.

The upshot of all this is that the rejection, by Rawls, of the principle of desert, does not seem to be complete and genuine, but even if it is genuine, it rests upon some unconvincing arguments, and even if they were convincing, this rejection is contrary to prevailing moral intuitions, and even if it does not matter, this is not a view shared by the theory of justice advanced in this book. Each of these statements is sufficient to dispense with the thesis about moral asymmetry between distribution and retribution.

2. PUNISHMENT AND EQUILIBRIUM

The general justification of punishment is analogous to that of rewards: it is a method of restoring an overall balance of benefits and burdens. Criminal justice is concerned with the distribution of rights among members of a society: in particular, rights to life, liberty, security, property. All these rights are considered as benefits, even if in some cases some individuals do not have the actual means to enjoy them. But even then, the very existence of these rights is a benefit. Although members of a community can be dramatically unequal in many other respects, in a well-ordered society people are equal at least in this respect that all of them have the same basic rights guaranteed by the rules of the criminal law.

The use of those rights does not occur in isolation from the rights of others. The enjoyment of a particular right by a person may be limited by the enjoyment of another right by another person. Therefore, rights secured by criminal law are most often correlated with other people's duty not to interfere with the exercise of recognized rights. This is a prerequisite for the effective use of a right; it may be implemented only if others restrict their activities or, exceptionally, if others do specific things prescribed by the law (for example, render aid in situations of peril). This self-restraint which is a precondition for the effective enforcement of rights, can be perceived as a burden. Indeed, it is a limitation on the freedom to do as one wishes. If such freedom is a benefit, its limitation is obviously a burden. Not everyone perceives it constantly as a burden; most people do not consider their duty to refrain from murder, assault or rape as an actual inconvenience. They do not feel constrained or deprived of anything because they think that even under the conditions of unrestricted liberty they would not like to act in this way. But this psychological fact is irrelevant here; the point is that those restraints that are prerequisites for the effectiveness of rights can be presented reasonably as burdens upon a person's life since they cut off a range of options which would be otherwise available to him.

Now, the harm inflicted on another person by an offender constitutes the infringement of that other person's rights to liberty, life, property etc. By infringing those rights, the offender intrudes upon the enjoyment of one's liberty and, thereby, he oversteps the bounds of his own sphere of liberty in such a way as to limit his victim's liberty. In consequence, the distribution of rights secured by the criminal law is changed; the legally recognized frontiers between the offender's and his victim's spheres of autonomy are changed to the detriment of the latter. The *status quo* with regard to liberties of those particular members of society is upset since the offender has arrogated to himself part of his victim's sphere of liberty. He has acquired some of his victim's benefits and he has renounced some of his own burdens (namely, burdens of self-restraint). The offender has arrogated benefits without bearing the burden of self-restraint and, in consequence, the general balance of benefits and burdens has been upset.

It is a requirement of justice that this balance be restored by a redistribution of burdens. If an offender arrogated an excessive sum of benefits, the equilibrium will only be restored when he suffers more burdens than would normally be required to safeguard the enjoyment of rights by other people. Just as with the distribution of benefits, in which case additional rewards correspond to desert (or to unmet basic needs), in the case of punishments the burdens inflicted by a society correspond to the degree of illegitimate benefits gained by the offender. The aim of punishment is to restore the equilibrium of benefits and burdens and not to restore the previous *status quo*. What has been done, often cannot be undone. But the illegitimate benefits gained by the offender can be nullified by inflicting him with burdens. It is a redistribution after the wrongful distribution has taken place.[12]

So far I have been describing only one aspect of 'doing justice' after a crime, that is removing the unfair advantages from the criminal. But there is, of course, another side to it: restitution for the victim. The 'equilibrium of benefits and burdens' model provides the justification for compensating the victim for his suffering and loss. The upsetting of the equilibrium produces undeserved benefits for the criminal and, at the same time, unfair burdens for his victim. Justice, therefore, calls for both restitution and punishment. These are two distinct aspects of 'doing justice' after the crime has been committed: they are related to each other and yet they are distinct. For one thing, a theory of punishment which is only a part of a broader notion of criminal justice is interested in the harm inflicted upon a criminal rather than in the benefits to be restored to the victim. For another, and more importantly, the problem of punishment raises more controversial moral issues than that of restitution since any deliberate infliction of harm upon human beings (in particular, if it is done on behalf of the community as a whole) requires stronger moral justification than the act of allocating benefits to them. This is why I will not discuss the victim's aspect of criminal justice in this Chapter; it remains important but, at the same time, rather uncontroversial.

The most serious criticism that might be made, and that actually has been made, about this conception of punishment is that criminal behaviour simply does not fit the scheme of benefits and burdens: neither is law-abiding conduct necessarily burdensome, nor is crime always advantageous to the criminal. I should like to demonstrate that this criticism is unfounded. As to the first part of this argument, I have already pointed out earlier that self-restraint *is* burdensome as compared to unrestricted liberty, irrespective of whether we perceive it so or not. If unrestricted liberty gives me all those options that I have in the situation of self-restraining behaviour and, in addition, some extra options, then it is an advantage irrespective of whether I really want to experiment with these extra options or not. After all, any restriction eliminates certain options available to a person. To realize that prohibitions resulting from criminal law do diminish the legitimate scope of action, one needs only to compare the range of lawful behaviour with a hypothetical state of affairs in which there was no criminal law at all. We do not have, therefore, to enter into the troublesome calculus of counting the options available, or comparing the relative importance of particular options, in order to conclude that criminal law restricts an absolute freedom to do as one pleases. To have a choice is better than not to have it: to have a choice between aggressive and peaceful behaviour is more advantageous to an agent than not to have it. Even if one does not consider seriously taking advantage of the possibility to act aggressively, the very existence of the choice is the advantage in itself. Therefore, in order to hold that self-restraint is burdensome as compared with unrestricted liberty, one does not have to presuppose a Hobbesian theory of human nature [13] and to suggest that we all *actually* "suffer a burden in abstaining from the core crimes of murder, rape, arson, robbery, and burglary".[14] It is a purely conceptual calculus and not an empirical fact of human predispositions.

More serious is the second part of the argument: that not all crimes bring benefits to the criminals and that the gravity of the crime (as reflected in the severity of punishment) is not a function of the benefits acquired by the criminal.[15] Now offhand it seems that only some crimes may benefit the criminal; the most characteristic is the crime of theft. The wrongful redistribution brought about by the thief may be redressed by restitution but restitution is not a punishment. The criminal punishment for theft is not intended to restore the stolen property to the victim. Thus even in the case of such an 'advantageous' crime as theft, the punishment cannot be understood as a restoration of the balance of benefits and burdens, the argument goes, because the punishment is meted out irrespective of whether or not the fruits of illegal activity are removed from the thief.[16] Furthermore, there is a wide range of crimes that do not benefit the criminal: careless driving, rape or assault may or may not bring the offender non-material benefits. It may happen that someone has great fun while driving carelessly, or that someone derives sexual gratification only while raping another person, or that someone genuinely enjoys beating other people, but these are contingent benefits which do not constitute the necessary element of the crime. We punish a careless driver or a rapist irrespective of whether they derived any satisfaction from their illegal behaviour or not. Moreover, the punishment is not necessarily proportionate to the amount of satisfaction derived by the criminal: a rapist who felt sexual satisfaction need not be punished more severely than one who did not.

At first blush, this seems to be a very powerful criticism of the present conception of punishment. It relies, however, on a misunderstanding as to the nature of benefits acquired by the criminal. The major value protected by the criminal law is the immunity of citizens from interference within precisely defined limits. This immunity can be enjoyed only on the condition that other people observe self-restraint. It is *this* burden which is imposed by criminal law in the first place. The fundamental benefit that a criminal acquires from violating the rules of criminal law is a benefit of non-self-restraint, that is to say, a benefit of freedom from burdens imposed by the criminal law. All other benefits are contingent and incidental: financial gains, psychological satisfaction, sexual gratification and so on. They may or may not occur but the fact that they have not occurred in a particular instance does not necessarily make us unwilling to inflict a punishment on the offender. The separation of restitution and punishment presupposes a moral view which condemns the act of non-self-restraint irrespective of its more tangible consequences.

Once this notion of benefit produced by a crime is accepted, the counter-argument about 'non-advantageous' crimes collapses. At the same time, we can dispense with the argument that benefits are not proportionate to the generally perceived gravity of a crime. If one accepts the present notion of what are the fundamental benefits of a crime then it is simply not true that, as it is alleged by Goldman, "crimes against property often bring more benefits to their perpetrators than do more serious crimes against persons (crimes involving violation of more precious rights)".[17] Crimes against property may bring more *financial* benefits to the perpetrators than murder or rape, but such financial benefits are only of a contingent nature as far as crime is concerned. The fundamental benefit, that is, the benefit of non-self-restraint, is a function of the violation of the protected sphere of liberty. Within this sphere, some values are regarded more highly than others. Human life is usually considered as more important than property, although this hierarchy of values varies in different cultures. Be that as it may, criminal law reflects the hierarchy of protected values: the more precious the value, the bigger the benefit of non-self-restraint acquired by the criminal. The intuitively just principle that more serious crimes should be punished more heavily is not, therefore, violated by the proposition about punishment as a restoration of the balance of benefits and burdens. The present notion of the benefits of autonomy which are distributed and safeguarded by the rules of criminal law necessarily implies that the relative importance of the sphere of autonomy violated by a criminal constitutes a measure of the advantages which he derives from his act. Under this conception, it is a mere tautology to say that a more serious crime brings about more benefits of non-self-restraint to the perpetrator: the 'seriousness' of the crime is actually measured by the degree of intrusion by the offender into the protected sphere of autonomy of another person.

Another argument which could be deployed against the present conception of punishment concerns actions normally regarded as criminal but which have been committed unintentionally. A person acting under duress, or while insane, has a good defence. But it could be argued that he nonetheless does obtain benefits out of his action. For instance, an insane woman by killing her tyrannical husband may benefit from her action after all. So it would appear that there are situations in which the criminal law fails to restore the balance of benefits and burdens since the principles of responsibility cannot be accounted for in terms of the conception of punishment proposed here. But this argument again relies upon the misconception concerning the nature of relevant benefits. An insane person, or a person acting under duress, does not *act* in any sense which might be regarded as enjoyment of his freedom. The benefits which are acquired by a criminal are the benefits of unrestricted liberty, yet this state of affairs does not occur in the case of an insane killer, or a person acting under coercion. In their cases there is no broadening of their freedom. In no way were the constraints on their actions reduced. For that reason, punishment in such cases is unjustified. Far from being incompatible with the common defences, the equilibrium model of punishment provides a justification for taking these defences into account so that a judge does not impose extra burdens on a person who actually had not acquired extra benefits.

At this point the following observation could be made: if the judge's role, in imposing punishment, is to deprive the criminal of unfair benefits, then perhaps the punishment should be less severe if the criminal has already suffered some burdens as a result of his offence? Suppose a thief broke his leg in the course of committing a crime, or rapist was caught during the escape by a member of the victim's family and was severely beaten. Should not the punishment take into account those burdens already suffered by the offender in the course of events related to a crime? Apparently, the balance of benefits and burdens would call for such a reduction of the sum of the burdens inflicted by the verdict.

This may well be a correct implication from the 'balance' model of punishment. The 'official' punishments pronounced by judges and enforced by the state have, as one of their functions, to eliminate and replace self-help; they are substitutes for privately administered revenge.[18] For various reasons which are too obvious to discuss, legal punishment is a more appropriate reaction to a crime than a vendetta or lynching by a mob. But if the criminal has already suffered the burdens resulting from a vendetta, then the balance has already been restored, at least partly. Surely the official judicial system should discourage privately imposed revenge but once it has occurred, the burdens inflicted thereby must not be ignored. A similar reasoning might be made with respect to the example of a wounded criminal or, say, with respect to a defendant who has suffered great moral pain due to the publicity given to his case by the mass media. This pain constitutes a burden and therefore reduces an overall amount of the benefits he has acquired through his crime.

Interestingly enough, judges and juries, as the case may be, *do* tend to take the wrongdoer's suffering into account in sentencing. It was noted, with respect to the American legal system, that a criminal's suffering weighs heavily on the minds of judges and juries.[19] Circumstances such as accidental injury during the crime, lengthy pretrial detention or brutal treatment by the police may convince the jury that the criminal has already 'paid for his crime' before he was even brought to trial. Likewise, the criminal code in West Germany allows the courts, under certain circumstances, not to impose punishment at all if the crime had very serious results for the offender himself.[20] This idea, referred to as *'poena naturalis'*, or 'natural punishment', seems to reflect something deeply embedded in our moral sense. This is confirmed also by the empirical studies of social psychologists who have examined the effect of the criminal's suffering upon the community's views about just punishment. The respondents were asked to indicate their opinions about the appropriate punishment after being presented with various versions of the same crime. In one version the criminal suffered physical damage following his crime and in the other he did not. The results clearly confirm the view that the suffering of the criminal is regarded as relevant to the severity of punishment: the more the defendant was said to have suffered after the crime, the smaller the prison sentence mock judges gave him.[21]

The final charge which might be made against the 'balance of benefits and burdens' theory of punishment is of a different nature. It is sometimes argued that if punishment indeed aims at restoring the balance of benefits and burdens then it should take into account not only the redistribution of benefits and burdens produced by the criminal act but also the disequilibrium *before the crime*. Very often criminals are, before committing their crimes, in a very disadvantaged social situation. It happens often that they are poorer or more oppressed than the rest of the community. The crime, the argument goes, may then be considered as restoring, not upsetting, the balance of benefits and burdens. If this is so, punishment brings back the former disequilibrium. As Alan Goldman says, "punishments are often imposed upon those already unfairly low on the scale of benefits and burdens. To represent them as having unfair advantages over others is ironic at best."[22]

This criticism essentially misses the point for the same reason as the other criticisms discussed above: it misrepresents the nature of benefits and burdens which are relevant to the operation of criminal law. It should be noted that criminal law covers a rather narrow area of protected values: independence of persons from interference by others with their bodily integrity, with their property, and so on. It leaves outside its area of concern certain important spheres, such as for example, the sphere of economic well-being. Criminal law, limited in scope as it is, builds upon the equality only of those benefits and burdens which relate to non-interference with human autonomy and the other values protected by criminal law. There are many other benefits and burdens which are distributed in a society in a manner inconsistent with the principle of equilibrium but they are irrelevant to the discussion of punishment.[23] As far as the benefits and burdens which *are* relevant to criminal punishment are concerned, it is not unrealistic to presuppose basic equality. This is equality with respect to a very narrow area of human values, yet this is all we need for a theory of punishment. For example, if the criminal code prohibits murder, and thus establishes a regime for the protection of human life from physical interference, then in so far as this rule is observed, all are *equally* free from such interference and all bear an equal burden of self-restraint.

But where does this argument stand if the law itself imposes unequal burdens of self-restraint? It may happen that a criminal law imposes some of its prohibitions on certain social groups only, or that it inflicts much harsher punishments for the same crimes committed by the members of particular groups. At this point, the argument about initial inequality of benefits and burdens must be reconsidered. The discussion in this Chapter relied so far upon a presupposition that the criminal justice system is basically just; that is to say, it imposes equal benefits (of freedom from interference) and burdens (of self-restraint) upon all people under the jurisdiction of the system. Only under such circumstances can punishment be considered as restoration of equilibrium. But if this condition is not met, and if the law itself imposes drastically unequal benefits and burdens upon its subjects, then the justification of punishment becomes untenable. If, for instance, the law reduces blacks to a position of slaves and requires them to obey their white masters, then it is the law itself that perpetuates the imbalance of benefits and burdens.[24] The 'crime' of disobedience, in this situation, does not justify the punishment. Far from upsetting the balance of benefits and burdens, disobedience aims at redressing the existing imbalance.

3. RETRIBUTIVISM

Such an approach to punishment locates the present conception of punishment in the group of theories usually characterized as 'retributivist'. In opposition to utilitarian theories which justify punishment in terms of its beneficial consequences, retributivism claims that criminal guilt is the sole reason for punishment, regardless of considerations of social utility. If, therefore, the theory of punishment as restoring balance of benefits and burdens belongs to the family of retributivist theories, it is necessary to discuss some general problems of retributivism and to examine the main objections against it.

Retributivism is based upon the principle that criminal guilt justifies punishment, both in terms of determining a class of persons who should be punished and in the measurement of punishment. Guilt deserves punishment for the sake of justice. As to this, it has sometimes been suggested that the retributivist theory avoids a justification since it is a mere affirmation that it is good to punish the guilty. Benn and Peters maintain that the retributivist theory is either based on 'utilitarian reasons in disguise' or belongs to "assertions of the type 'it is fitting (or justice requires) that the guilty should suffer'. For to say 'it is fitting' is only to say that it ought to be the case, and it is just this that is in question".[25] The conception of punishment as restoring the balance defends itself against this charge. Even if 'it is fitting' equals saying 'it ought to be the case', the phrase 'justice requires' is not identical with 'it is fitting' or 'it ought to be the case'. It gives an answer to the question: Why ought it to be the case? It is a moral reason for, not the equivalent of, the statement that it ought to be the case. It is not the only possible reason; there may be also utilitarian ones. But to say that requirements of justice do not provide any ethical reasons independent of utilitarian ones is to underestimate the moral status of judgments of justice. Benn and Peters say that to accept retributivist justification of punishment is "to deny the necessity for justification; for to justify is to provide reasons in terms of something else accepted as valuable".[26] But an appeal to the principles of justice *does* provide us with reasons for punishment which are more substantive than the vague assertion that 'it is fitting' if justice is understood in a more precise way than an overall desirability of a particular practice.[27] If justice is regarded as a specific virtue of institutions, then to say 'justice requires' is not a mere expression of preference but provides good reasons for a proposed practice.

In the discussions about punishment it is often stated that the relations between guilt and punishment are of a logical and not an ethical nature, that *ex definitione* we can punish only those who are guilty and that 'punishment of the innocent' is a contradiction in terms. If this observation is correct, retributivism is not concerned with justification of the punishment but only with the meaning of the word 'punishment'. Hence, a justification still has to be found. This point was emphatically made by Anthony Quinton:

> It is not ... that we *may* not punish the innocent and *ought* only to punish the guilty, but that we *cannot* punish the innocent and *must* only punish the guilty.... The infliction of suffering on a person is only properly described as punishment if that person is guilty. The retributivist thesis, therefore, is not a moral doctrine, but an account of the meaning of the word 'punishment'.[28]

It is true, Quinton adds, that suffering similar to that which is inflicted upon criminals can be inflicted as well upon innocent people but then it is not punishment, properly speaking, but rather a case of 'judicial error or terrorism'. The proof that Quinton gives for this assertion has to do with our linguistic intuition: punishment is always *for* something. To say: "I am going to punish you for something you have not done" is, for Quinton, an absurd (rather than morally wrong) statement.

A long discussion about the logical *versus* moral aspects of 'punishing the innocent' followed Quinton's essay;[29] I will not go into details of this discussion here. However, the general point is important for a defence of retributivism. If Quinton's arguments are correct, the retributivist justification for punishment in terms of guilt and desert is clearly insufficient. If the main retributivist thesis about the necessary connection between guilt and punishment is merely an explanation of the meaning of the word 'punishment', then obviously it cannot provide us with any substantive justification for the system of punishment.

First of all, the unconditional assertion by Quinton that properly the infliction of suffering can be called punishment only when a person is guilty, cannot be maintained without serious qualifications. What of judicial errors? If a jury is convinced of the guilt of the defendant, it seems proper to say that he will be punished even though he has not committed any crime. If the proper characterization of official infliction of suffering as 'punishment' were dependent on whether this decision is just or not, the notion of 'unjust punishment' (apart from the cases of excessive punishment of the guilty) would be nonsense. And yet it is not a terminological error to say: "It was an unjust punishment, I am sure X was innocent". It does not appear as a contradiction in terms. Moreover, it would not be reasonable to call the infliction of suffering 'a punishment' as long as we believe the defendant guilty and then to stop calling it 'punishment' after we learn about his innocence. We still continue to think of it as a punishment, even though unjust.

There were some theoretical attempts at refinement of Quinton's general thesis. Antony Flew, for example, suggests that the proposition about the logical impossibility of punishing the innocent refers to a system of punishment and not to particular cases. A system of punishing people who have not committed any offences cannot be called a system of punishment, maintains Flew. However, this does not exclude the use of this term "in single cases [of punishing people who had broken no laws] and providing these do not become too numerous".[30] But, as K. E. Baier has shown, the solution to the problem does not lie in statistics. If a system of inflicting suffering on scapegoats is not a system of punishment, then individual cases of making scapegoats suffer cannot be characterized as punishments either. A system of punishing people does not lose its character of 'punishments' just because, in a given society, the police are inefficient and the judges are corrupt so that frequently innocent people are punished. Consider this example by K. E. Baier:

In Ruritania, everyone who has been punished during the last year or the last ten years may have been innocent, for in Ruritania the judges and jurymen and the police and prison authorities are very inefficient and very corrupt. A system of punishing people does not turn into a system of inflicting unpleasantness on scapegoats, simply in virtue of the fact that in this system innocent people happen frequently to get punished.[31]

The criteria of something being 'punishment' are, therefore, of an institutional and formal nature. They do not depend on whether punishment is justified or not. The punishment does not have to pass a test of justice in order to 'deserve' the title of punishment. When an infliction of suffering is decided by legal agencies, in conformity with certain 'secondary rules' which confer a power of adjudication upon those bodies, then it is a punishment irrespective of whether or not any breach of law has occurred as charged. If breach of law has not taken place, it is a wrong punishment yet it is a punishment. The existence of criminal guilt is a condition of *just* punishment, not of punishment as such. Many people in Ruritania were placed in prison without actually having committed the crimes they were accused of; but they were judged and sentenced *as if* they had committed those crimes. The motivations of the judges are irrelevant in this respect. Perhaps they really were convinced of the guilt of the defendants, or perhaps they were bribed, or perhaps they were forced to hand down unjust verdicts by the politicians who wanted to harass their opponents thereby. The only thing that matters is that their verdicts were recognized as punishments under the valid legal rules in Ruritania.

What would be the use of restricting the term 'punishment' only to punishments inflicted on the persons who are actually guilty? When a person is sentenced in the course of a 'show trial', and we know that he is innocent, do we conceptually gain anything by refusing to call it 'punishment'? After all, there is nothing honorific in this term. When the victim of a show trial is executed, it is different from the case of an assassination of a political rival without resort to any legal forms and procedures. The results for the victim are the same but the political and legal mechanisms of the situations are different. Bukharin was punished, Beria was killed; it is irrelevant that Bukharin was less guilty than Beria. A refusal to apply the term 'punishment' to corruption of justice results in a denial that punishments can be abused by political power. There is a difference between punishing Slansky and the assassination of President Sadat; the refusal to admit this disregards the fact that law can be and is often used as an instrument of political persecution. In the same way as unjust law is still a law, unjust punishment remains punishment whenever it is an act of application of valid legal rules in a given legal system.

The solution to the problems of punishment does not, after all, lie in terminology. The question: 'Should guilt be required as the basis of punishment?' is a substantive moral question and should be given a substantive answer, not a definitional one. If this question seems to be nonsense, and if the answer seems to follow from the definition, the question may be reformulated and we may ask, along with K. G. Armstrong: "Why shouldn't we do to the innocent that which, when it's done to the guilty, is known as punishment?"[32] In this somewhat clumsy manner we avoid the answer that guilt is part of definition, not of justification, of punishment. It is a matter of fact that in some situations some people are tempted to inflict, through legal mechanisms, painful measures upon other persons irrespective of their guilt. The 'definitional stop'[33] does not provide us with any guidance about these situations and the substantive issue still must be faced. What we want to know is whether it is morally right or wrong to punish innocent people. It would be possible, of course, to adopt a terminological convention in accordance with which punishing the innocent is called, for instance, 'telishment', or in which we have to use the lengthy phrases about "inflicting on innocent people that which is called punishment when inflicted on the guilty".[34] I do not see any reason for doing so. In common language it is not a mistake to talk about 'unjust punishment' when the innocent defendant is sentenced. Accordingly, it is not a case of linguistic error to ask why we should not punish the innocent. The connection between guilt and punishment is not a logical necessity but a moral postulate. If someone asks: 'Why was Bukharin punished?', the answer: 'To begin with, he was not punished . . .' is hardly satisfactory. His suffering was thought to be, and was perceived as, a punishment, unjust as it was. There is no reason for moral theory to disregard this linguistic intuition.

The question of the relevance of guilt to punishment is not to be solved by definitional methods for the further reason that it applies not only to the determination of who should be punished but also to the measurement of punishment. The retributivist thesis about the fundamental relevance of guilt to punishment not only delimits the scope of those who deserve punishment but also provides moral grounds for penalty-fixing. The retributivist thesis objects to punishment of the innocent as well as to the excessive punishment of the guilty. This is a substantive moral principle which cannot be derived from a definition. That is why retributivism *is* a moral theory about the justification of a punishment, and not only a terminological explanation of what the word 'punishment' means.

The principle that punishments should be proportionate to crimes is one of the essential postulates of the retributivist theory. This idea of proportionality is often the main target of criticisms addressed against retributivism. Crime and punishment, the argument goes, are incomparable and incommensurate, there is no common denominator which would make it possible to calculate this proportionality. As Henry Weihofen has observed: "Crime and punishment are different things, and cannot be equated. You can take a life for a life, but beyond that there is practically no room for the principle of equation to operate."[35] But this argument misses the point. It is conceived as an argument against the retributivist theory yet it is relevant only with respect to *lex talionis* which is not a necessary conclusion of retributivism. Retributivism demands proportionality, not equation. Likewise, in the case of just rewards we are not paying with goods similar to these which constitute a basis of desert but with certain typical, standard prizes according to a certain scale. So in the case of punishments, we restore a balance with those means that are at our disposal. Even when it is possible to return like for like, there is no reason to act in this way. The principle of proportionality is not a surrogate for an equation but is a principle in its own right. Restoring the equilibrium means neither restoring a *status quo* (hence, restitution is not necessarily an ideal of punishment) nor paying like for like. Justice operates with the help of transformation rules which determine a conversion of one set of values into another. A scale of good deserts is compared with a scale of rewards and a scale of offences with a scale of punishments.

The principle of proportionality operates always within a certain system of values that help to convert the seriousness of the offence into the severity of punishment. Relative severity of particular punishments corresponds to the relative gravity of offences. There is, naturally, room for subjectivity; hence, there may well be disagreements about the relative severity of appropriate punishments for particular offences. Many anti-retributive discussions of punishment fasten almost entirely on this point and it is claimed that no reasonable conversion of the seriousness of crimes into measures of punishment is possible. Walter Kaufmann asks: "[H]ow could one possibly establish what a man deserves for seducing a child, for raping a child, or for arson or treason?"[36] This is one of the reasons he gives for the view that there is no just punishment for any crime. The whole idea of meting out justice, Kaufmann says, is irrational and the "frightening task of weighing alternatives"[37] is hopeless. Another author claims also that "[i]t is totally arbitrary to fix six days, or six weeks, or six months, as the just sentence for stealing say, an old raincoat worth 37s. 6d".[38]

But is it really 'totally arbitrary'? Would anyone consider as 'arbitrary' the proposition that the punishment for rape should be more severe than for stealing a raincoat? By postulating the degree of criminal guilt as the basis of punishment, the retributivist theory requires that there be a proportionality between crimes and punishments (the graver the crime, the more severe the punishment) and that the punishment be commensurate to the crime. The first postulate, of proportionality, is merely comparative: it does not imply any scale of punishments in absolute terms, it neither decides where the minimum punishment should commence nor where the maximum punishment should be set. But surely this is not enough. It is not sufficient to compare a scale of crimes with *any* scale of punishments. The requirement of commensurability imposes constraints upon the mildness or severity of particular punishments for particular crimes; for instance, our feelings of justice would probably be offended if rape were punished by a one dollar fine even if the penalties for less dangerous crimes were even more lenient. As I have argued before,[39] this moral judgment is still comparative although to reach it, the comparison of two scales (a scale of crimes and a scale of punishments) is not sufficient. We also compare the treatment of the guilty with the treatment of the innocent and we conclude presumably that the degree of burdens (imposed through punishment as compared with acquittal) does not correspond to the amount of benefits of non-self-restraint incurred by the criminal. This judgment relies upon a certain hierarchy of values which helps us compare the severity of punishment with the gravity of a crime. But this is not peculiar to a theory of just punishment: the problem of the need to resort to a system of substantive judgments about the relative importance of various harms and benefits is endemic to a theory of justice as a whole. As we can never be certain about an absolute validity of such judgments, it follows that we can never be sure that any particular system of punishments is absolutely just. It should not come as a surprise, and it should not deter us from approximating the justness of such a system. At the extremities of the scale of proper punishments, there are certain things we *know*: we know that a fine of ten dollars is inadequate as a punishment for murder, and we know that life imprisonment is too much for petty theft. There may be doubts and disagreements as to less extreme cases but they do not undermine the validity of the principle of retribution.

Incidentally, critics of retributivism tend to exaggerate the degree of disagreement about the appropriate scale of crimes and of punishments. It is true that "[d]ifferent cultures vary enormously in their ranking of offences"[40] but this is not relevant here because what matters is the level of agreement *within* a particular culture. And there is no evidence supporting the assertion that, say, in the United States "it would be impossible to achieve anything like a consensus on the relative seriousness of different crimes and the just punishment".[41] As a matter of fact, empirical studies show that there is considerable agreement in the United States and other countries on the ranking of seriousness of crimes.[42] Be that as it may, the practical disagreements about the measures of appropriate punishment do not constitute a case against the very principle of retribution just as the disagreements about the measures of appropriate wages do not discredit the very principle of rewarding according to desert.

One of the frequent charges against retributivism is that it postulates harsh, severe or even inhuman punishments. Indeed, criticism of retributivism is often based upon resentment against the cruelty or severity of particular criminal and penal systems. Henry Weihofen compares retributivism with 'primitive urge for vengeance', 'vindictive punishment and terror', 'hate'. He asserts also that "[t]here is no proof that the public is as thirsty for vengeance" as retributivism allegedly assumes.[43] But there is nothing in the retributivist theory which justifies demands for severe, let alone cruel, punishments. Historically, the utilitarian approach to the theory of punishment was often linked with humanitarian penology and was aimed against cruelty in punishment — but this is a contingent matter. John P. Conrad writes: "it is one thing to lay down a bloodless principle; it is another thing to contemplate the sanguinary quality of punishment as it has been administered throughout the history of Western civilization".[44] A theory of punishment should distinguish between these two things: between a principle and its historical forms of application and misapplication.

It is sometimes claimed that retributivism is needlessly severe in that it does not leave any room for mercy.[45] Now we should be careful when talking about 'mercy' to ensure that the word is used properly. Mercy, strictly, means that a judge, or whoever else has the power of imposing punishments, decides to impose less than just punishment.[46] But we often talk about 'mercy' referring to cases of more lenient punishment than that dictated by the strict application of law for reasons which, we feel, *are* relevant to justice-considerations. When, for instance, a judge shows 'mercy' by acquitting, or by punishing less severely, a person who has committed a criminal act in the heat of the moment, then it is not genuine 'mercy' at all because the extenuating circumstances make the crime less severe. In this case, irrespective of whether the particular system of criminal law allows for considering those circumstances or not, we feel that, morally, the crime is not as grave as the same crime committed with premeditation, and therefore justice requires a less severe punishment. Or, to take another example, if a judge shows 'mercy' by punishing less severely a criminal who has brought upon himself some harm or suffering as a result of his crime, then again a less severe punishment is demanded by the requirements of justice because of the burdens imposed, or self-imposed, upon the criminal before trial.[47] These are not cases of mercy but of justice, and occasional departures by the judge from the strict application of legal rules may be dictated by his notions of justice and by the inevitable distance between them and the legal rules which are incapable of grasping all possible factors relevant to the degree of guilt. Genuine mercy occurs when, notwithstanding the dictates of justice, a judge imposes a less severe punishment. Now whether, and when, mercy is justified is a matter outside the scope of a theory of justice. The retributive theory is about *just* punishment but it does not say that punishments should always and without any exceptions be just. It says only what conditions must be met *if* a punishment is to be just. But there is no reason why we should be always just; we must consider the conflicts between justice and other criteria. Mercy is a departure from the principles of desert on grounds other than justice considerations. When a 75-years old, sick criminal is punished less severely than others whose guilt is exactly the same, it is unjust but it may be right.

Retributivism determines standards of justice in punishment but it does not claim that justice should be the only standard of punishment.

Retributivism is the only theory of punishment which takes the notion of human responsibility seriously because it justifies punishment solely on the basis of acts and situations which were under the control of the perpetrator concerned. Only those facts which are believed to be free human acts are relevant in assessing guilt and deciding about punishment; all circumstances independent of the offender are considered as irrelevant. An offender is treated as a free individual who has the right to be held responsible for his actions; in so far as he is actually not free, he is not liable and should not be punished. This is an analogous principle to rewards on the basis of desert. Conscious human effort, which is under a person's control, is the sole appropriate moral basis of just reward.

This also explains why the retributivist theory is, in principle, opposed to criminal punishment based on strict liability, that is, when the only relevant fact for a guilty verdict is that the defendant has actually committed an act proscribed by the criminal law. In these cases, the defendant incurs criminal liability although he was ignorant of the factors which rendered his conduct criminal, even though his ignorance is not attributable to any default on his part.

But perhaps we should not dismiss the moral validity of strict-liability punishments too hastily for, after all, there may be some place for them within the retributive theory. In the remaining part of this Section, I will briefly discuss this issue mainly because of its highly contentious nature, and also because of the suggestions that the only available justification for strict criminal liability derives from the utilitarian theory of punishment.[48] Against these suggestions, I maintain that there is an interpretation of strict-liability offences possible which does not violate the retributivist principle of punishment.

Consider the following typical examples of strict liability in English and American criminal law. A bar owner sold drinks to a drunken person who had given no indication of insobriety, and without being aware that the person so served was drunk.[49] A person sold drugs without knowing they were narcotics.[50] A seller of cattle feed unknowingly misrepresented the percentage of oil in the product, relying on the analysis made by a reputable chemist.[51] One possible way of reacting to these 'punishments without guilt' would be to say that strict criminal liability is an example of unjust, immoral and unjustified legal repression.[52] Another reaction would be to suggest that strict liability, unjust as it is, may be nevertheless justified on the basis of convenience and utility: either because of difficulties in proving guilt in certain classes of cases[53] or because it serves well the aims of deterrence.[54] These last two points are controversial. For one thing, administrative convenience should not justify the suspension of the principles of natural justice in the criminal process; difficulty of proof is too weak an argument in the matters of justice. As for the deterrence argument, the aims of deterrence can hardly be served by punishing involuntary actions. And it is rather disturbing to read that "the disadvantage of inflicting a fine on a morally innocent defendant is more than counterbalanced by the social gain in securing the observance of certain minimum requirements".[55]

But there is yet another approach to strict liability available, which leads to different conclusions. Sometimes it is claimed that strict liability is justified on the basis of much higher risk involved in certain activities or individual actions. Persons undertaking those actions are aware, in advance, that much higher standards of care are required than usual. They cannot complain of the unfairness of a strict-liability regulation because they undertake the activity voluntarily and they were warned about the risk and degree of liability; they also know that it is not physically possible to exclude a minimum possibility of harm. They have a choice: they can take the risk assigned by the law or not. Those who decide to run a risk and to embark on such business as sale of food or of drugs know in advance that "he who shall do them shall do them at his peril and will not be heard to plead in defense good faith or ignorance".[56] The seller of drugs knows that the usual degree of care is not enough in his profession and that lack of moral guilt is not an adequate defence when it comes to criminal liability resulting from the wrong chemical composition of his products. *Theoretically*, it was possible for him to control the quality of his products. He might have employed another chemist, or he might have double-checked his analysis. *Under normal circumstances*, it would not be reasonable to expect him to do so and that is why he can be regarded as morally innocent. However, the circumstances were not 'normal': the special risks involved in the activity required a special degree of care.[57] The failure to apply this degree of care justifies the ascription of guilt to the defendant: he has acquired the illegitimate benefit of not spending enough time and effort in order to exclude a probability (however minimal it was) of imposing unfair burdens upon others.

If we accept this line of justification of strict liability then apparently there is no *qualitative* difference between strict liability and offences involving negligence as far as the relations between criminal liability and moral guilt are concerned.[58] The difference is rather of degree: in the case of strict-liability offences, such as those cited above, the degree of care expected in high risk situations is much higher than in the cases of criminal negligence where the standards of care of 'a reasonable man' are typically applied. The courts, in the strict-liability decisions, presuppose that it *was* within the power of the defendant to control his behaviour and to avoid the criminal result although in order to do so, he would have had to apply an unusually high standard of care, higher than that of 'a reasonable man'. Unusual circumstances call for an unusual standard of care. But this standard is not so high as to be beyond the possibility of human compliance; legal rules do not, and should not, impose "an unattainable standard of accuracy".[59] What is important for the present argument is that, even in the strict-liability cases, the defendant must have had at least *some* control (minimal as it might be) over his action and some means of reducing the risk.

4. RETRIBUTIVIST FALLACIES

To say that the 'balance of benefits and burdens' model of punishment is retributivist, and to defend the general principle of retribution, does not commit one to the endorsement of every conception of retribution in the theory of criminal justice. In particular, there are three special versions of retributivism which seem to be highly objectionable: the theory of punishment as 'annulment', the theory of the 'right to be punished' and the 'expressive function' theory of punishment. It needs to be shown that they do not necessarily follow from the general principle of retribution.

The first retributivist doctrine that I will mention here is the idea that punishment annuls the wrongdoing. This doctrine has two versions. One of them treats 'annulment' in a literal sense: restitution is thought to be an essential function of punishment. It is sometimes claimed that the offender's debt is to the victim, not to society. He should be, therefore, required to compensate the victim. The attainment of other goals, traditionally attributed to punishment, should be incidental to reparations paid to the victim.[60] But rarely is such a restitution possible: what is done cannot be undone. There are many types of crimes that by their very nature cannot be annulled and the *status quo ante* restored: treason, murder, rape. Punishment is distinct and independent of restitution; restitution is a matter of the losses of the victim, punishment is a matter of illegitimate benefits of the offender. Hence, punishment restores the equilibrium of benefits and burdens by imposing an additional burden upon the criminal without necessarily bringing any benefits to the victim.

In the second version of the annulment theory, 'annulment' is understood in a juridical, rather than factual, way. Consider this:

> Any criminal offence may be said to be *legally* annulled if all the just claims created by that offence are as nearly completely satisfied as possible. . . . [A]n offence considered as a legal act – an act performed within a system of just demands – can be legally annulled under the aegis of rightfully inflicted punishment.[61]

But this very Hegelian interpretation of punishment seems to use the term 'annulment' in a loose and metaphorical sense. Punishment 'annuls' the crime only in this sense that it is a legitimate reaction to the crime. This interpretation is, therefore, merely a reformulation of the general retributive thesis about the justification of punishment. At the same time, it is hard to see what sort of 'just claims' are created by an offence apart from restitution claimed on behalf of the victim and from public claims that the law enforcement bodies punish the offender. The proposition about legal annulment of the crime does not seem to offer any explanation or justification for punishment different from the general retributivist thesis.

The second retributivist doctrine that I will discuss here, appeals to the 'criminal's right to be punished'. This idea merits closer examination if for no other reason than the fact that it was advanced by Herbert Morris who at the same time advocates the view that punishment restores the balance of benefits and burdens. It is, therefore, important to refute the possible suggestion that these two ideas: the idea of punishment as restoring the balance and the idea of criminal's right to be punished, are intrinsically and necessarily interconnected.

The main aim of Morris's highly influential paper is to demonstrate the moral superiority of punishment over non-punitive measures, notably over therapy. As a starting point, he submits four fundamental propositions:

> first, that we have a right to punishment; second, that this right derives from a fundamental human right to be treated as a person; third, that this fundamental right is a natural, inalienable, and absolute right; and, fourth, that the denial of this right implies the denial of all moral rights and duties.[62]

But, in the course of his article, Morris also suggests a weaker interpretation of the right to punishment. In one place he suggests that 'a right to be punished' is identical with a person's 'right to all those institutions and practices linked to punishment'.[63] But surely there are several important differences between the first and the second 'right'. Throughout most of his argument Morris seems to adopt a strong version of a 'right to punishment', as being equivalent to a right to be punished for the offences a person has committed. He unequivocally declares that his argument is "not just for a right to a system of punishment, but for a right to be punished once there is in existence such a system".[64] The right to be punished is interpreted by him as a fundamental one and a right to a system of punishment as one of its derivations. I will argue that these are two distinct notions and that the notion of 'a right to punishment' is untenable while a right to all the institutions and practices linked with punishment (that I will call 'a right to a system of punishment') is indeed an important right *per se*, irrespective of the validity of an alleged 'right to be punished'.

There are three major reasons why 'a right to punishment' cannot be properly called a right, while 'a right to a system of punishment' can. First, the concept of rights suggests certain benefits or advantages for the bearer of those rights. It seems to be counter-intuitive to conceive them in such a way as to bring disadvantages to those who have them. "It is an odd sort of right whose holders would strenuously resist its recognition", writes Quinton.[65] This is probably the most obvious reason why the concept of 'right to punishment' is untenable. This problem does not arise, however, in the case of a right to a system of punishment. The institutions of punishment, including the guarantees of fair trial, give a person obvious advantages as compared with situations in which those institutions are absent. Admittedly, the understanding of 'punishment' proposed here does not require actual respect for the principles of fair trial: an unjust punishment is still a punishment. One may ask, therefore, what is the advantage of having the institutions of punishment without having guarantees that actual punishments will be just? The answer is that the very institution of punishment, as a legal reaction to criminal act, is more advantageous to individuals than any alternative way of dealing with offenders. As Morris has convincingly demonstrated, the system of punishment is superior to a system of therapy for offenders because it treats them as responsible persons and not as objects of manipulation. A system of therapy is incompatible with a right to be held responsible. It may be necessary for those persons who actually are not responsible for their actions because of insanity; in such cases it involves the treatment of people who have no free will and cannot exercise a choice between obedience and disobedience to the law. But to establish a system of therapy which treats all criminals as *ipso facto* irresponsible humiliates them, and deprives them of all those opportunities and safeguards related to a fair trial which are available in a system of punishment.

Secondly, it seems to be an attribute of every 'right' *sensu stricto* that its holder may waive the implementation of his right. A right involves a choice; there can be hardly a duty to use one's right. If one is compelled to exercise his 'right', or punished for failure to do so, it makes better sense to say that he has a *duty* to act in a particular way. This is one of the reasons why I have claimed that a right cannot be construed in such a way as to constitute a burden. If, in a particular situation, I think that the enjoyment of my right is not advantageous, I may renounce it. In a word, a holder of a right has control over its implementation, and may influence its use by his own conscious actions. Again, this attribute of 'a right' does apply to 'a right to a system of punishment' but not to 'a right to be punished'. An offender has no choice with regard to the latter; the enforcement of the punishment does not require his consent.[66] However, in the case of the procedural rights connected with the system of punishment, he may choose not to use his rights of defence, he is entitled to refuse to lead any evidence in his defence, he may abandon all those privileges which are offered to him by the procedures leading to the punishment. Such actions do not result in the denial of the guarantees granted by the principles of 'natural justice' or 'due process of law'. In case of inalienable rights, such as the right to liberty or to due process of law, a person may surrender the enjoyment of his right but it does not result in the waiving of the right itself since it does not cancel other people's correlative duties. The judge, jury and officials are still bound by their duties which correspond with the defendant's right, though its effective use has been surrendered. The fact that the defendant behaves as if he had no right to fair trial does not permit the judge to draw any legal consequences from it in order to abrogate the principles of fair trial. The defendant still has a choice, at any time he may resume and implement his rights. From this point of view, the right to a system of punishment is the same as any other right, for instance, a right to liberty. It is within everyone's power to renounce the use of the right but no-one else is relieved of a correlative duty to respect that person's liberty. The object of a waiver is the *use* of the right, not the right itself. But the possibility of such a waiver is not available in the case of the alleged 'right to be punished'.

The third difference between the two 'rights' is related to the general test of something being a 'right' or not; namely that it cannot be easily overridden by the considerations of general good or social utility. Rights, as Ronald Dworkin suggests, have certain threshold weight and cannot be defeated by an appeal to collective goals, unless these goals are of special urgency. It does not follow, Dworkin says, that the state is never justified in overriding a right but, rather, the right may be overriden only when it is necessary to protect a more important right or "to prevent a catastrophe". An alleged right which can be overriden by a mere calculus of net gains is not a genuine right.[67] Now it should be noted that this notion of rights as 'trumps' applies to a 'right to a system of punishment' but does not apply to a 'right to be punished'. As far as the latter is concerned, the practices of amnesty, mercy or release on parole are examples of situations when considerations of social good, expediency or humanitarianism prevail over the alleged 'right to be punished'. But the considerations of public good should not be allowed to prevail over the right to a system of punishment. This right implies the inadmissibility of letting considerations of utility override the principles of a fair trial. Dworkin's test for something being a 'right' is highlighted most clearly in his discussion of moral rights: "[A] man has a moral right against the state if for some reason the state would do wrong to treat him in a certain way, even though it would be in the general interest to do so".[68] Now, it is wrong for the state not to provide a person with a fair trial even though social benefits would follow from this denial. Hence, it is wrong to override the right to a *system* of punishment. Yet, it is *not* wrong to release a prisoner on parole, or to declare an amnesty, and so to override the alleged 'right to be punished'. A right to a system of punishment passes Dworkin's test, an alleged 'right to be punished' does not.

There is a distinguishable but related claim that every punishment is, in a sense, self-imposed by the offender; that the criminal brings the punishment upon himself. The idea derives from Kant who suggested that "the undeserved evil which any one commits on another, is to be regarded as perpetrated on himself".[69] In Kant this idea was connected with a view that the criminal threatens the social order and thus, indirectly, harms the conditions for his own existence. For example, a thief makes property insecure in general, therefore he also deprives himself of security in his own property. Within these limits this idea appears plausible. It becomes questionable when extended to include the view that punishment is a product of the criminal's will and that it is self-imposed. This view is restated (somewhat hesitantly) by Morris who finds "some plausibility in the exaggerated claim that in choosing to do an act violative of the rules an individual has chosen to be punished".[70] Morris derives the plausibility of this view from the fact that punishments are publicized and defences respected but it seems to me to be much too weak a foundation for the obvious fiction of the criminal choosing to be punished. More often than not, criminals do their best to avoid punishment. Nor does this take account of crimes of negligence where the construction of implicit consent of the criminal to his punishment is obviously inapplicable.

But even in the case of intentional crimes, the very fact of the penalties being publicized in advance does not, in itself, provide a good moral reason for imposing them. If I publicize a warning: "I shall kill anyone who steals fruits from my garden", it does not give me any moral right to kill a thief, much less does it support the argument that he has chosen to be killed.[71] The formula of 'a criminal bringing the punishment on himself' may have, at best, a causal but not a moral meaning; it may be another way of saying that the act of punishment is causally one of the end-results of the crime. But this formula is clearly irrelevant as a moral theory for justifying the punishment.

The third retributivist doctrine which I would like to dispute is the theory that sees the main function of punishment in its expressive role or symbolic significance. The main justification of punishment is alleged to be the "emphatic denunciation by the community of a crime";[72] it is seen as "a formal and solemn pronouncement of the moral condemnation of the community"[73] and "a means of expressing disapprobation or condemnation of the acts of those who offend".[74] Now, if all the assertions about symbolic or expressive function were confined to empirical observations about functions actually played by punishments, they would be probably hardly problematic although I doubt if one could treat the expressive aspect as a necessary element of each act of punishment and, consequently, as a constitutive element of its definition.[75] After all, one can well imagine punishments which are kept secret: 'a secret punishment' is not a terminological nonsense and yet it is hard to see how a symbolic reprobation on behalf of the community can be expressed in secret. To be sure, it might be argued that a judge who is pronouncing a secret punishment expresses, in his capacity as a representative of the state, a symbolic denunciation of the offender, even if the rest of the community is unaware of this fact.[76] This would be an effective line of defence of the expressive theory; it would disconnect the act of punishment from *social* condemnation and restrict it to condemnation by a particular official. But this is not exactly what most proponents of the expressive theory claim. The sentence, they say, is pronounced by a judge on behalf of the community; it is a *public* condemnation as it expresses public censure. "Even floggings and imposed fastings do not constitute punishments ... where social conventions are such that they do not express public censure", says Joel Feinberg commenting upon the distinction between 'reprobative hard treatment (punishment)' and the same treatment without reprobation.[77]

With these reservations, the theory of the expressive function of punishment seems to *describe* rather correctly the functions usually played by punishments: they indeed, apart from everything else, express moral condemnation. The retributivist theory which I have in mind now is not limited to empirical observation, however. It postulates the expressive condemnation as the fundamental *raison d'être* of punishment; it is a normative, and not a descriptive, theory. As such, the expressive theory of punishment is questionable. For one thing, from the point of view of the theory of punishment as a restoration of the balance of benefits and burdens, expressive reprobation must be seen as something contingent, accidental and secondary. In some cases, expressive reprobation may be in itself a part of the burdens imposed upon a criminal when, for instance, the punishment consists in the publication of the name of the offender and of information about his wrongdoing. Not every punishment has this aspect; indeed, very few punishments have a symbolic character *per se*. For instance, in penalties by way of imprisonment, symbolic reprobation is not an element of the burdens inflicted upon the prisoner by the judge.

If reprobation and expressive condemnation were to be the fundamental justification of punishment, would not present forms of punishment be disproportionately harsh methods of expressing this reprobation? After all, fines, prison cells or electric chairs are not merely symbolic; they lead to actual human pain and suffering. Pain and suffering are not necessary if the only reason for punishing the criminal is that a community wishes to pronounce solemnly the moral condemnation. Ceremonial denunciation will do.[78] A theory of expressive function, in its normative aspect, seems to propose an ethical aim which is grossly inconsistent with the methods employed; the logical implication of this theory would be to postulate punishments limited solely to verbal condemnation. Unorthodox as it is, the only way of rescuing the expressive theory of punishment would be to postulate, with Neil MacCormick, that criminal punishments may be free from a coercive element and confined to the emphatic denunciation of the crime.[79] Since such a denunciation constitutes a burden imposed on the wrongdoer, and in so far as it is possible to communicate real disapproval to him without imposing any pain upon him other than that resulting from moral condemnation, the expressive theory of punishment can be reconciled with the theory of punishment propounded in this Chapter. But rarely do the partisans of this theory of punishment take such a radical step. To the contrary, most proponents of the expressive theory of punishment claim that both the reprobation *and* the 'hard treatment' must be taken as necessary parts of the definition of punishment.[80] At any rate, it is clear that the concept of punishment as a restoration of the balance of benefits and burdens need not entail any symbolic condemnation or reprobation. Symbolic condemnation is but one of the possible burdens imposed upon the offender. The criminal law may well choose sanctions which do not express any symbolic condemnation and yet those sanctions constitute burdens imposed upon the offender.

5. UTILITY AND PUNISHMENT

The utilitarian theory of punishment emphasizes its beneficial consequences, in the sense that both the general justifying aim of punishment and criteria of penalty-fixing are grounded in the value of the predicted consequences of punishment. Punishment is justified in so far as it tends to reduce the occurrence of crimes and, more particularly, discourages those contemplating criminal acts, has a salutary effect on the individual punished and prevents further crimes. Criminal punishment is justified because, and in so far as, its good effects outweigh the suffering of the convicted person.

A relatively simple response to the utilitarian theory would be that deterrence, prevention and reform are irrelevant from the point of view of justice. It is a reflection of a more general truth that there is no necessary connection between the criteria of utility and those of justice. The usefulness of punishment does not imply its justness; it may be the case that a just punishment is, at the same time, effective from the point of view of the aims postulated by utilitarians, but this is merely a coincidence. To say that a punishment achieves certain aims and to say that it is a just punishment, is to make two different and mutually independent statements. The utility of a punishment depends either on factors which are beyond the criminal's control (deterrence), hence which cannot be relevant to questions of justice, or on factors which *are* related to the offender, but with reference to his future, not to his past, and which are again irrelevant to matters of justice because no-one's desert can be ascertained on the basis of some future acts or states of affairs.

A society in which the system of punishments efficiently deters potential criminals, reforms the convicted offenders and prevents them from committing further offences is not necessarily a just society although it is probably a very safe society. The fact that a disproportionately harsh punishment has effectively reformed a convict does not make this punishment just; the fact that another punishment has failed to deter other offenders does not make it unjust. There is nothing odd in saying that a punishment is efficient yet unjust or just yet inefficient. Since a just punishment is not necessarily a useful punishment, usefulness as well as justice should be taken into account when designing the standards of proper punishments. The retributive theory does not state what punishments should be imposed but what punishments are just. H. J. McCloskey is right when he says that "[s]ometimes it is morally permissible and obligatory to override the dictates of justice".[81]

At this point the whole argument may seem to have become merely semantic. One can very well imagine the following reply by a utilitarian: "I concede that what I am trying to justify is not a *just* punishment but a proper punishment. What really matters is to answer the question about proper standards of punishing, that is, the question about why we should punish people and how we should punish them. Even if a retributivist proves that only retributivism is compatible with justice in punishments, he still has to prove that justice is the ultimate virtue of punishments and that punishments should be just rather than useful".

Now, it is true that so far the argument has only been about justice. This is, however, not the least important of arguments about punishment and the argument that only retributivism is fully consistent with justice must not be dismissed too lightly. After all, there are good reasons why we should be just, and there are also good reasons why punishments should be just. True, justice is not the only standard of a good society and, consequently, justice is not the only standard of a proper punishment. Principles of justice are of fundamental, although not absolute, moral importance. This importance stems from the links between the principle of desert and respect for human persons. This importance is reflected in our linguistic habits: it would be odd and unacceptable to suggest that proper punishments need not be just. When deciding about appropriate punishments, we usually first take into account the considerations of guilt (and, thus, decide about the conditions of a just punishment) and only later (if at all) do we modify this decision by other considerations, such as utility, benevolence, mercy. Those considerations are relevant, but the initial focus is always on the criteria of just punishment.

Utilitarians claim that an appropriate punishment should serve three main purposes: it should deter others who might commit a crime, it should reform or rehabilitate the offender himself and it should protect society at large from people who are likely to commit further crimes. These three aims are identified by utilitarians as the main justifying aims of punishment. Let us consider deterrence first. It should be noted that 'deterrence' strictly speaking is not equivalent to a broader concept of 'general prevention' understood as "the ability of criminal law and its enforcement to make citizens law-abiding".[82] This effect of general prevention may result not only from deterrence but also from the educational functions fulfilled by law.

Law creates inhibitions against committing crimes not only by the frightening examples of the punishments actually imposed but also by the moral force ascribed to legal principles, whether embodied in statute law or in judicial precedents. But from the point of view of a theory of punishment, what counts is general prevention resulting from deterrence, in the form either of the actual infliction of harm or of the threat of punishment as perceived by potential offenders. The educational role of law envisaged as pure persuasion about what is wrong and what is right is irrelevant here; when it is, however, associated with threats of punishment it becomes indistinguishable from deterrence.

I leave aside the question of the effectiveness of deterrence. This is a controversial matter and about which criminologists have reached no final conclusion. But even if we admit that deterrence works effectively, and that punishments do discourage people from committing crimes, there are important arguments against treating this as a fundamental justifying aim of punishment. One of the most frequent charges is that if deterrence is an important aim of punishment, then there is no reason why we should avoid punishing the innocent. In his well-known essay, H. J. McCloskey has convincingly argued that "[w]e may sometimes best deter others by punishing, by framing, an innocent man who is generally believed to be guilty".[83] Utilitarians usually reply that punishing the innocent is an ineffective deterrent and, therefore, is incompatible with the utilitarian creed.[84] But this pragmatic reply contains a very weak argument. For one thing, the supposed ineffectiveness of punishing the innocent, pointed out by the utilitarians, is a result of the fact that the general public *knows* that the accused is innocent. But we do not have to presuppose this condition; we might as well imagine a situation in which the general public is convinced, however falsely, about the defendant's guilt. Secondly, and more importantly, effectiveness of the punishment is an empirical matter. To pursue this issue is a task for the sociology of law and not for moral theory. For the purposes of moral argument, we may well imagine a society in which, due to the high rate of certain types of crimes and due to the incompetence of the police in controlling these crimes, the best deterrent effect could be attained by the deliberate punishment of an innocent person who is generally considered to be guilty. In reply, the utilitarians would have to demonstrate that punishment of the innocent is inadmissible *even if* it could be shown to produce beneficial results. As McCloskey correctly remarks: "whether or not unjust punishments are in fact useful, it is logically possible that they will at some time become useful, in which case utilitarians are committed to them".[85]

After all, there are several examples in history where innocent people have been punished as a means of deterrence for others. It is not absurd to say that, in some circumstances, a punishment inflicted upon innocent people may turn out to be an effective deterrent.

In practice, a more important question is that of deterrence by excessive punishment of the guilty rather than that of punishing the innocent. That is not merely an academic question: there have been several cases of exemplary punishments, unusually harsh for reasons of deterrence. This is consistent with the utilitarian theory: the prospects of effective deterrence stand in no relation to the gravity of a crime. The deterrent effect is a function of several variables which are independent of the seriousness of a crime. For instance, it seems obvious that the commission of premeditated crimes may be more effectively deterred than those committed in the heat of passion. But this distinction has nothing to do with the gravity of those crimes. The expected effectiveness of deterrence has no correlation with the degree of guilt of a punished person. The principal charge against deterrence as an important factor in penalty-fixing is, therefore, that the criminal is treated as a means toward other people's ends; he is merely a device used in order to give others a lesson. He is paying for something that is beyond his control. The fact that certain crimes are particularly frequent in a given society has nothing to do with the guilt of a particular criminal; to take it into account while punishing him, is to take into account factors irrelevant to his guilt.

The reform of the criminal is considered by utilitarians as another important aim of punishment. This aim is presented in two distinct versions. The first type of reform theory tries to justify punishments essentially in their present form by their alleged function of reforming criminals. Even if additional proposals for changes of methods of punishment are made, in particular in the way of penitentiary reforms, it is envisaged that current patterns of punishment as known and as practised will be maintained. Accordingly, the thesis is that imprisonment or other typical punishments are justified by the aim of reforming the offender. However, it is unlikely that a person can be reformed and re-educated by being deprived of his liberty and other rights. "[P]ain or fear of pain, being a non-moral motive, cannot bring about moral improvement".[86] Surveys show, indeed, that the overall results of various correctional treatment programs are disappointing.[87] The point is, however, that even if in some cases punishments may produce some positive changes in the personality of the offender, it is not the punishment *per se* which produces them but reform measures accompanying the punishment. This fact should be welcomed, but we had better realize that it is not a part of the nature of punishment itself. If a criminal is reformed while serving a sentence, he is reformed by something other than by the punishment, and even in spite of it. Even if the reform of a criminal is a justifiable aim, it is the aim of something other than punishments; those reformatory measures do not constitute a part of the institution of punishment.

If reform were the supreme aim of the punishment, there would be plausible ground for demanding the abolition of punishments and their replacement with purely reformatory measures. This conclusion is reached by the second, more radical, version of the reform theory. It demands that punishment be replaced by the treatment of offenders in a manner analogous to therapy in cases of sickness. This suggested alternative to punishment has been widely criticized in legal and philosophical literature;[88] there is no need to elaborate on it here. Criminals, according to this view, are considered to be sick rather than guilty and, therefore, they should be cured and not punished. Just as it is irrational to punish a man for, say, pneumonia, it is irrational to punish people for their pathological, anti-social acts which "have their roots in social conditions and the consequent impact on individual personality".[89] In such cases (the argument goes) what is needed is "evolving techniques for social control utilizing what we know about the forces that control human behaviour".[90] This will lead to the replacement of an irrational institution of punishment by a scientific, rational system of eliminating crimes, a system controlled by psychiatrists rather than by lawyers.

This idea, as we see, is based on the view that the criminal is insane and irresponsible for his actions. The very fact of crime is taken to be sufficient proof that the agent suffers from a disease which is beyond his control. But this is, of course, untrue. There are offensive actions committed by sick people who cannot be held responsible for what they do and there are offensive actions committed by persons who are sane and who understand what they are doing. It is one thing to try to cure persons who actually are irresponsible, and it is another thing to believe that the very act of committing an offence is proof of insanity. Crimes are committed sometimes by very rational and sane people; there is no reason to presuppose that criminal action is a product of a sick mind and there is no evidence that delinquents are significantly different psychologically or emotionally from the rest of the population.

The third utilitarian aim of punishment is prevention, or making it impossible for the criminal to commit further offences. Of course, this aim may be attained by some punishments only. It certainly applies to such penalties as the withdrawal of a driving licence but these punishments are rather marginal and unimportant. An obvious preventive role is played by capital punishment or exile, but they raise very substantial objections of a humanitarian nature. They also appear to be disproportionate methods to attainment of the aim of prevention: it is like destroying a factory in order to prevent pollution. As far as the most typical punishment is concerned, namely incarceration, it is an efficient preventive measure but limited in time: eventually, offenders are released. Moreover, if prevention is to be the main justification of punishment, there would be no sense in maintaining the principle of proportionality of punishment to criminal offence. The likelihood of repetition of a crime is not a function of the gravity of the crime committed. Evgenii Pashukanis, one of the most radical exponents of the utilitarian approach to punishment, explicitly states that there is "the contradiction between the rational goal of the protection of society – or the re-education of the criminal – and the principle of the equivalence of punishment".[91] The formal principle of justice: 'treat like cases alike', is incompatible with the utilitarian theory of punishment which allows unequal punishments for similar offences if the prospects of attaining the proposed goals of punishment are different.

6. RETRIBUTIVISM AND UTILITARIANISM RECONCILED?

It does not follow from this critique of the utilitarian approach to punishment that deterrence, reform of the criminal and prevention are undesirable functions of criminal policy or that they should be given no weight in the debate about appropriate punishments. However, they cannot constitute the supreme justification of punishments but rather they are to be seen as the desirable by-products of a system of punishment. We may hope that just punishments will help to attain the utilitarian goals, and we should adopt methods which maximize the likelihood of achieving them. Yet, if justice is considered to be the basic criterion of proper punishments, utilitarian considerations should be taken into account in so far as they do not conflict with the just verdict and sentence based on guilt.

In practice, this leaves some room for utilitarian considerations in the design of the *forms* of punishment.[92] The retributive theory requires that the burden be imposed upon those who have appropriated illegitimate benefits by violation of the rules of criminal law. It requires also that the burdens imposed by the judge be commensurate with the benefits of non-self-restraint enjoyed by the offender. But the retributivist demands go no further; the retributivist does not make a distinction between a fine, compulsory labour or imprisonment as long as these burdens are equally commensurate with the crime. If one form of punishment is just while another form of punishment is equally just and, in addition, brings about beneficial social consequences, the latter punishment should be, obviously, chosen. The withdrawal of a driving licence may be equally burdensome for an offender as short-term imprisonment; the retributivist will give no guidance as to which of these penalties should be chosen but utilitarians may have a lot to say in favour of one or the other penalty. The appropriate decision should, if possible, maximize both justice and effectiveness. There is, therefore, ample room for the application of utilitarian considerations in the decision about the appropriate punishment within the limits of justice as determined by the retributive criteria. Conceptually, though, the retributivist and the utilitarian are guided by distinct and irreconcilable criteria.

This view presupposes that, with regard to the conceptual aspects of punishment, there is an intrinsic conflict between retributive and utilitarian views. There is, however, a theory which tries to reconcile retributivist and utilitarian approaches by demonstrating that they address very different sets of problems and that they apply to different situations. If this were to be correct, a large portion of this Chapter would appear pointless. The supposed contradiction between retributivism and utilitarianism would turn out to be based on a misunderstanding and, in particular, on an erroneous identification of two different problems to which retributivism and utilitarianism try to give answers. A compromise between utilitarianism and retributivism is possible, it has been argued, because these two theories give answers to different questions: utilitarianism justifies the system of punishment in general while retributivism justifies infliction of punishments on particular persons. The difficulties which inevitably arise from trying to make one answer do for both questions, may be overcome when one distinguishes between the questions of rules or practices (utilitarianism) and of their particular application (retributivism).

The best exposition of this distinction is given by John Rawls:

We might try to get clear about this distinction by imagining how a father might answer the question of his son. Suppose the son asks, 'Why was *J* put in jail yesterday?' The father answers, 'Because he robbed the bank at *B*. He was duly tried and found guilty. That's why he was put in jail yesterday'. But suppose the son had asked a different question, namely, 'Why do people put other people in jail?' Then the father might answer, 'To protect good people from bad people' or 'To stop people from doing things that would make it uneasy for all of us; for otherwise we wouldn't be able to go to bed at night and sleep in peace'. There are two very different questions here. One question emphasizes the proper name: it asks why *J* was punished rather than someone else, or it asks what he was punished for. The other question asks why we have the institution of punishment: why do people punish one another rather than, say, always forgiving one another?[93]

My objection to this argument is that, although these are indeed two different questions, their relevant difference lies in something other than the point which Rawls makes and that the true difference does not warrant this reconciliation of utilitarianism and retributivism.

When a son, in Rawls's example, asks his father "Why was *J* put in jail?" it may be understood as the question: "What were the ethical grounds of putting *J* in jail? On the basis of what principle was he put in jail?" The father's answer: "Because he was duly tried and found guilty" makes sense only if we have antecedently accepted the principle that people who are found guilty should be punished. The son's question refers therefore not to the particular case of *J* in isolation but rather to the case of *J* in its character as an exemplification of a general principle. On that account, no satisfactory answer can be given to it without appealing to a general principle. This principle applies, by its very nature, to the general practice and not only to particular cases.

In order to test this assertion, let us assume that, after having asked the question "Why was *J* put in jail?", and after having obtained the answer "Because he was found guilty", the son asks: "So what?". Annoying as it is, the question is far from being nonsensical. The already-given answer "Because he was found guilty" does not provide any self-evident and manifestly good reason for *J*'s imprisonment; it is satisfactory only if we accept prior validity of the principles regarding guilt and punishment which underly the general practice of punishing people who are guilty. Now, to the question "So what?" the father might answer "It is proper that we put those who are guilty of robbery into gaol". He may go on and try to justify this principle on retributive, restitutive, utilitarian or any other grounds but it is clear that the retributivist moral discourse does not stop at the level of particular cases, and that the answer about *J*'s guilt is far from being satisfactory in itself.

Let us take now the other question asked by the son in Rawls's dialogue: "Why do people put other people in jail?". The father's answer, "To protect good people from bad people" makes sense *not* only with respect to general practices, contrary to what Rawls suggests. The analogous answer could be plausibly given to the question "Why was *J* put in jail?". The answer could be then: "To protect other people from him". The aims of protection and prevention which, according to Rawls, can be used only as the justification of a general practice, turn out to be equally relevant to justification of individual instances of punishment.

This suggests that the contrast between the two answers lies in something other than the general/particular distinction because each of these answers may be formulated in such a way as to fit the question put either in particular or in general terms. Both utilitarian and retributive theories may be employed as justifications of the institution of punishment as such and of the infliction of punishment on particular persons. If one agrees with the father's justification of putting J in jail (in Rawls's example), there is no reason why this agreement stops short of endorsing a general principle justifying punishments on the basis of guilt. The reasons given for the imprisonment of J ("because he was found guilty") are closely linked to there being some justification for the general principle of punishing the guilty. We see that, for someone who accepts this argument, the justification of a particular act of punishment is retributive, but so it also is of the general practice of punishing those who are guilty of violating the criminal law. On the other hand, if one finds the father's reasons for the institution of punishment satisfactory ("to protect good people . . . "), there is no reason why the same satisfaction stops short of the conclusion that particular acts of punishment should be determined by the aim of prevention.

There is no discrepancy between the justification of the general practice and of particular cases because the general practice is an aggregation of particular instances. In consequence, the distinction: utilitarian/retributive does *not* parallel the distinction: general rules/particular acts. There is no reason to think that the fact that legislators and judges participate in the legal process at its different stages, enables them to follow different sets of principles. The general principles apply to particular cases, individual cases mould general principles. This is particularly manifest in Common Law jurisdictions where the distinction between law-making and judicial decisions is not as clear-cut as in Civil Law systems. But even in statutory law, where the frontiers are more precise between the general and the individual in law, both legislators and judges must make their moral options about the principles of punishment; and in particular, they must decide about the relative weight of justice and utility in punishment.

POSTSCRIPT

CHAPTER 9

BEYOND SOCIAL JUSTICE

The aims of this book were twofold. First, my aim was to demonstrate the relevance of the categories of social justice to legal theory. I have attempted to show that the principles of legal justice cannot stand on their own unless based upon an antecedently accepted set of judgments about social justice. Accordingly, my second aim was to propose and defend a particular conception of social justice.

The inevitable corollary to the proposition that social justice constitutes a specific social value rather than an all-encompassing ideal is the conclusion that it is not the only important virtue that a legal system, or a social system, can exhibit. A perfectly just society might still not be an ideal society. It was stressed in various contexts in this book that justice must be always balanced against other important social values. The problems of these trade-offs lie outside the scope of a theory of justice, yet no comprehensive legal (or social) philosophy can ignore them. In these last pages, I shall discuss some problems arising out of the conflicts and trade-offs between the principles of justice, on the one hand, and the ideal of liberty and utilitarian goals, on the other. This will be followed by concluding remarks about the role of a theory of justice.

1. JUSTICE AND LIBERTY

Since liberty is an important social good sought by people, social justice may be viewed as a standard for the distribution of liberty among members of the community. However, if we leave aside this aspect of social justice, we must conclude that there are no intrinsic conceptual links between the distribution of liberty and the distribution of other social goods governed by the principles of social justice. Besides, social justice as a *distributive* principle is indifferent to the total *aggregate* level of liberty in a society. The question of choice between a more and a less free society is, therefore, outside the scope of a conception of social justice which is concerned with liberty (as well as with any other important social goods) only in its distributive aspect.

This is why the First Principle of Justice in Rawls's theory is problematic *as a principle of justice*. The principle is: "Each person is to have an equal right to the most extensive total system of equal basic liberties compatible with a similar system of liberty for all". Rawls supplements this principle with a priority rule stating that "liberty can be restricted only for the sake of liberty" (and not, for instance, for the sake of economic gain, or economic justice, or fair equality of opportunity). This means, in Rawls's words, that "a less extensive liberty must strengthen the total system of liberty shared by all" and that "a less than equal liberty must be acceptable to those with the lesser liberty".[1]

Many critics of Rawls have argued convincingly that so categorical a priority principle is far too rigorous. They have argued that exclusion of any trade-off between liberty and socio-economic justice is implausible when the loss of liberty is infinitesimal and gain in terms of socio-economic justice very big.[2] Here, I am not concerned with the moral attractiveness of the priority of the First Principle over the Second (which governs the distribution of other primary goods) but I am concerned rather with whether it is a principle of justice at all. It appears that the First Principle is properly a principle of justice only in so far as it demands *equal* basic liberties. In its aggregative aspect, when it calls for "the most extensive liberty compatible with similar liberties of others" it is not a principle of justice in so far as we maintain our general definitional stipulation that justice is about distribution and is not concerned with the size of the total amount of social good. For Rawls, a situation in which liberty is equal for all, but less extensive than it might be, is unjust unless it works for the benefit of other, more important, liberties; the condition is that, on balance, there must be a gain for individual liberties.[3] But why is this principle to be considered a matter of justice?

Imagine that a particular liberty of citizens is more limited than it might be: for instance, no-one in a given country is free to acquire foreign newspapers legally and, in addition, the reception of foreign radio broadcasts is 'jammed'. This limitation upon free flow of information and ideas is not justified by any gain in terms of other types of liberty; it is an arbitrary decision made by a despotic government. Let us assume further that the enforcement of this prohibition is stringent and total: even the highest ranking members of the government have no access to foreign news. I would call this illiberal, oppressive or authoritarian but not unjust. Injustice would arise only if some of the citizens were allowed this particular liberty and the others were not, without any good reason for the differentiation. However, in Rawls's theory it is a case of 'injustice' if equal restrictions on liberty cannot be shown to work for the sake of liberty itself. In making this point, Rawls is departing from his own general formula that justice is a specific social virtue and that "[s]ocial arrangements generally, may be ... liberal or illiberal, ...

as well as just or unjust".[4] In the example considered above, an illiberal arrangement is, according to Rawls's theory, *ipso facto* unjust by virtue of the inclusion of the First Principle of Justice (and more specifically, of its 'extensiveness' clause) into the conception of justice.

My argument may be defended only under a particular condition: that comparative aspects of the First Principle (equal liberty) and aggregative aspects (the most extensive liberty) are separable. The upshot of my argument is that the aggregative principles with respect to liberty (as with respect to any other social value) are not principles of justice. But is it possible to distinguish the aggregative aspect of liberty from the distributive one? Rawls appears to think so; he says that "[t]he basic liberties may be either less extensive though still equal, or they may be unequal".[5] If this is true, and if there is no necessary link between extensiveness and distribution of liberty, then the idea of the Principle of Liberty as a principle of justice is untenable. The only way to rescue this idea is to defend Rawls *malgré lui* by linking 'extensiveness of liberty' with its 'equality' in such a way that a case of less-than-extensive liberty is at the same time *necessarily* a case of unequal liberty. If such reasoning is tenable, then the 'extensiveness' clause of the First Principle could be considered as *both* an aggregative and a distributive principle; hence, its place in a conception of justice would be justified.

It seems to me that such a defence is possible. However, although it rescues the principle of equal liberty *qua* a principle of justice, it comes at significant expense to other aspects of Rawls's concept of liberty, and so would likely be resisted by Rawls himself. I will try to show that only by assuming it, can the principle of liberty be sustained in the theory of justice. Let us return to our example of liberty of speech and press (being limited by a legal ban on all foreign newspapers). Imagine, again, that the government lifts this ban but sets the price of all foreign newspapers at such a level that most people in this society cannot afford to buy them. Now, if we had a theory of liberty which holds that such an actual inability on the part of an individual to buy a newspaper limits his freedom, we might well conclude that 'less-than-extensive liberty' (that is, less than the most extensive possible under the given circumstances) is *eo ipso* unequal liberty.

What concept of liberty would be necessary in order to make such reasoning valid? Before I answer this question, it should be noted in the first place that a conceptual scheme dividing various notions of liberty into 'positive' and 'negative' is unhelpful to our argument. Much philosophical discussion has been concerned with demonstrating that any type of 'positive' liberty can be formulated in a 'negative' way: as absence of constraints which are themselves of a negative character; for instance, freedom to study is freedom from constraints preventing study. Liberty to do X is, at the same time, absence of restrictions which exclude X. As Gerald C. McCallum pointed out in his classic essay, every full statement about freedom has a form: "X is (is not) free from Y to do (not to do, become, not become) Z"; the distinction between so-called negative and positive freedom does not vindicate two kinds of freedom but emphasizes two different aspects of a particular freedom.[6] I also believe that a distinction between legal and non-legal factors is not helpful in identification of those constraints which do and those which do not affect liberty; as has been demostrated previously, various essentially non-legal constraints may be expressed in a legal form.[7] What is important here is the identification of the structural character of factors affecting the presence or absence of freedom, the identification of the nature of constraints which are considered as decisive of freedom. Is it only a specific act by another person (or government) which can frustrate my freedom? Or are conditions which effectively allow me to take advantage of opportunities offered by my freedom also relevant to discussion about the existence of freedom? Am I free to eat only when there is no one to prohibit it by physical coercion or when, in addition, food is available to me?

The merits and demerits of both concepts have been widely discussed in the literature.[8] For my part, I see a good deal of sense in a broader idea of freedom, where the means of actualizing opportunities offered by freedom are included in a list of factors determining whether freedom is absent or present. The main argument for this concept might proceed like this. Freedom is a valuable thing, and its value is significant. To be sure, abuses of freedom may turn out to be detrimental and freedom often must be traded-off for another goal; in some situations even basic freedoms should be curtailed. But typically freedom is good: the sense of freedom raises positive, rather than negative, emotions. Yet, the notion of freedom as a *prima facie* significant and positive value is hardly tenable if we excluded from the notion of freedom those factors which enable people to enjoy its value. In other words, if freedom is a positive value, then a distinction between the conditions affecting the value (or worth) of freedom and conditions of freedom itself is illegitimate.[9] Within this perspective, conditions determining the actual exercise of liberty must belong to a category of factors definitive of liberty. If freedom to eat is valuable then the same conditions which curtail the value of this freedom, restrict the freedom itself. Absence of food leads to the absence of freedom to eat, not merely to absence of the value of this freedom. It does not seem rational to speak of freedom which cannot be exercised since it is not rational to attach value to an ideal which exists independently of the prerequisites for its worth. The worth of freedom lies in the ability to exercise it and, since freedom is worthy, its existence is determined by the ability to exercise it.

Now, if we recognize factors determining the worth of freedom, together with the absence of external coercion, as constituting freedom itself, we might attempt to show that, in the case of certain freedoms, a less-than-extensive freedom is, at the same time, an unequal freedom. We would have to inquire into the meaning of 'less-than-extensive': less-than-extensive as compared with what? The principal point of reference is an analogous freedom of other people: if my freedom could be made more extensive without frustrating the analogous freedom of others, then it is actually less-than-extensive. But if each marginal increase of my freedom results in a reduction of similar freedom for someone else, then my freedom is at the optimal point; it is the most extensive possible. If factors decisive of the worth of freedom are considered as decisive of freedom itself, then the extensiveness of freedom affects the equality of freedom. To take our newspapers example: if the freedom of Alex to read foreign newspapers is affected by (among other things) whether he can afford to buy them, then the most extensive freedom for Alex, Brian and Charles requires equal distribution of purchasing power. Otherwise, the stronger economic position of Alex over Brian and Charles will diminish the possibilities of Brian and Charles to use their freedom to buy foreign newspapers in the most extensive way compatible with the similar freedom of Alex (for instance, because Alex will be able to buy all the available stock, or because his superior financial position will make it possible to increase the price of newspapers and thus eliminate Brian and Charles from the market without diminishing the total financial profit of the distributor). In other words, less-than-extensive freedom (in so far as its socio-economic factors are concerned) occurs whenever the socio-economic conditions of its enjoyment are distributed unequally. Therefore, this particular aspect of less-than-extensive freedom is an unmistakable symptom of unequal freedom. Whenever a particular freedom is less-than-extensive in this aspect of freedom which consists in the conditions of enjoying its value, the sources of this incompleteness lie in an unequal distribution of those conditions. In this sense, a 'less-than-extensiveness' clause in the Principle of Liberty could be related to an 'inequality' clause in this Principle.

However, even if the reasoning proposed above offers an opportunity to defend the principle of equal and most extensive liberty *qua* a principle of justice, Rawls's notion of liberty does not lend itself to this explanation.

Rawls explicitly rejects those constraints which, as I suggested above, are decisive of liberty itself, and places them outside the scope of his notion of liberty. He maintains that if someone is unable to use his rights or opportunities due to, say, poverty, this does not affect his liberty but only the worth that this liberty has for him. In this conception there is a clear distinction between liberty and the worth of liberty (a distinction which the previous argument rejects explicitly). Rawls says: "Freedom as equal liberty is the same for all ... but the worth of liberty is not the same for everyone. Some have greater authority and wealth, and therefore greater means to achieve their aims".[10] Within this notion of liberty I see no grounds for holding it as a principle of justice, unless 'justice' is understood as an over-arching ideal of the 'good society', going far beyond distributive matters. In any event, those three issues cannot hold at the same time: (1) justice as a distributive ideal, (2) the concept of liberty within which its existence is unaffected by socio-economic constraints determining the value of liberty, (3) the most-extensive-liberty principle as a principle of justice.

The incorporation of the principle of liberty into a conception of justice precludes talk of conflicts and trade-offs between justice and freedom. Intuition suggests that a certain degree of liberty has to be sacrificed sometimes in order to achieve more justice or *vice versa*. Intuition suggests also that absolute liberty cannot coexist with absolute justice, that in order to establish an absolutely just society we would have to have total control over transactions and distributions. Maintenance of substantive justice would require a large authoritative machinery of enforcement, maintenance and supervision of distributions. The implementation of any pattern of just distribution must involve a permanent interference with people's free transactions. On the other hand, voluntary and free exchange of trade between people will not bring about an overall pattern of distribution corresponding with a just scheme. Absolute freedom of action would mean also freedom to benefit from, and act towards, unjust distribution. Although speculations about absolute freedom or absolute justice have little practical value, nevertheless they indicate that freedom and justice are distinct ideals. Sometimes they are interrelated and mutually reinforcing; extreme lack of freedom tends to generate injustices, extreme injustices lead to limitations in freedom of those who are badly off. Be that as it may, freedom is not a part of justice, although it is a part of a global vision of a good society. This independence of freedom and justice also exists on the level of individual actions and transactions; a free action may lead to unjust results, one may adhere to unjust contracts freely because of ignorance, or because another alternative was even worse. A free bargain is not always a just one; criteria of justice transcend those of individual free will. Criteria of justice are ascertained by a third party, they are not at the mercy of the subjective feelings of those involved in an exchange.

2. UTILITY AND JUSTICE

For similar reasons we should avoid confusing the considerations of justice with those of utility. True, in making an optimal decision we should take into account both types of criteria. However, in order to weigh them each against the other (in a situation of conflicting demands) we need to have principles of justice which do not incorporate considerations of utility. When I speak of 'utility', I use the word in a broad sense; perhaps it would be better to speak of 'aggregative' principles or 'consequentialist' ones. The point is that considerations of distributive justice are distinct and independent of considerations of the good produced as a consequence of taking an action or following a rule: this 'good' might be defined in terms of a global amount of happiness, satisfaction or preferences, maximization of utility, perfection of human nature, aesthetic satisfaction and so on. Maximization of good, however understood, may or may not be the consequence of just distribution. Brian Barry's distinction between aggregative results and distributive principles[11] is very useful; justice is of a distributive nature and there is no necessary connection between the distribution of a good and its maximization. Just as the beneficence of an action does not necessarily result in justice, so no necessary connection operates the other way round: the just action is not necessarily the most beneficent or useful one.

Practical experience offers innumerable examples of conflict between demands of utility (maximization, efficiency, expediency, etc.) and justice. The principle of the just wage requires that remuneration correspond with effort, or with qualifications, or with productivity, or with all those three elements combined. Without entering into what really should constitute a ground for just remuneration,[12] one thing is certain: justice requires, at a minimum, that those who satisfy those criteria equally, should be paid equally. Yet for various utilitarian reasons we may decide on differentiation of wages without relation to effort, success or competence. In order to attract people to particular, socially important, positions it may be necessary to offer higher salaries than justice would require. One might argue that usually utilitarian considerations will coincide with justice considerations: if it is necessary to attract people to particular employment with higher salaries, there must be something about those jobs that people consider less attractive than in other jobs, *ergo* increase of pay is not simply an incentive for people to apply for the job but also a compensation for the unattractiveness of the job. Hence, we enter the realm which is characteristic of justice considerations. However, this need not be so: it is conceivable that some positions should be filled very quickly (for instance, because of requirements of economic management or of national security) and there is no other efficient means to achieve this end than to offer high salaries, not commensurate with effort or qualifications. Here, the link between utilitarian and justice-based criteria is contingent and incidental. We have seen that similar is the case of just punishment, as distinct from useful punishment.

Much of the utilitarian effort directed towards incorporating the principle of justice into utility has proved to be unsuccessful. The most significant one, undertaken by John Stuart Mill in the fifth chapter of his *Utilitarianism*, has been widely discussed and commented upon in the literature and there is no need to go over this same ground again. Let me only comment upon one of Mill's arguments, leading to a general conclusion that requirements of justice are built into the utility principle and that "justice is a name for certain moral requirements which, regarded collectively, stand higher in the scale of social utility".[13] The argument which I wish to take up here concerns conflicting and irreconcilable judgments of justice in the distribution of financial benefits and burdens. Mill gives two examples: one about "co-operative industrial association" and the second about "repartition of taxation". In both of these cases he cites perfectly respectable yet diametrically opposed views about just distribution. With regard to the first example, he demonstrates that both a distribution according to skill and the egalitarian distribution, which is aimed at offsetting the benefits accrued from unequal skills, can be supported by good moral arguments in terms of justice. It is just to compensate the less favoured for unmerited disadvantages and it is also just to reward the more efficient worker with higher remuneration. The arguments cited by Mill, both in favour of and against remuneration proportionate to skill, sound persuasive and clever. Yet, they cannot be reconciled. Mill asks:

Who shall decide between these appeals to conflicting principles of justice? Justice has in this case two sides to it, which it is impossible to bring into harmony, and the two disputants have chosen opposite sides: the one looks to what it is just that the individual should receive, the other, to what it is just that the community should give. Each, from his own point of view, is unanswerable, and any choice between them, on grounds of justice, must be perfectly arbitrary. Social utility alone can decide the preference.[14]

He argues analogically about the second example. There is a good case for proportional taxation but also for progressive taxation and even for equal taxes in absolute terms (since "a dealer should charge all customers the same price for the same article, not a price varying according to their means of payment").[15] Mill argues again that there is no other way out of this dilemma but by recourse to a principle of utility. "From these confusions there is no other mode of extrication than the utilitarian".[16]

But is this conclusion really warranted by the previous argument? What the argument shows is that, in typical issues of distribution, there may be proposed various *prima facie* reasonable and intelligible conceptions of just distribution. But this does not mean that, at the end of the day, all of them will remain equally justified after closer moral scrutiny. I have argued in Chapter 5 that, with respect to the first of Mill's examples, the compensatory answer is more justified in terms of justice than a 'meritocratic' one. Now, my argument may be valid or not but the very fact that several, mutually incompatible and not nonsensical views on just solutions are available, does not exclude the fact that one solution may be better than the others. The situation with the second example is similar: the fact that all three answers cited by Mill (proportionate, progressive, and equal taxation) may lay claim to merit does not mean that each one of them is equally plausible.

However, even if after citing two or three alternative answers to a particular question about just distribution we find ourselves in a total ethical stalemate, this still would not substantiate the conclusion that utility is a good criterion of *justice*. Utility may be a helpful tie-breaker when we are undecided about the choice between different solutions which, although incompatible, seem to be equally just. Recourse to utility is an appeal to a value other than justice. If both courses of action, A and B, seem to be equally just, then it is better to follow A which is just and, *on top of that*, useful, rather than B, which is just but counter-productive. But A does not become more just by virtue of its efficiency; it becomes closer to an optimal decision which, ideally, should meet both the requirements of justice and of utility.

Utilitarians appear to be more convincing when they openly admit that justice is a foreign concept to their moral system; if a decision based on utilitarian criteria is just, so much the better, but its justness is not built into its utility. That is the view of J. J. C. Smart:

The concept of justice as a *fundamental* ethical concept is really quite foreign to utilitarianism. A utilitarian would compromise his utilitarianism if he allowed principles of justice which might conflict with the maximization of happiness (or more generally of goodness, should he be an 'ideal' utilitarian). He is concerned with the maximization of happiness and not with the distribution of it.[17]

To be sure, Smart admits that certain ways of distributing the means of happiness may bring about more happiness than others; he is concerned with the maximization of happiness itself while the proper object of social distributions is the *means* leading to happiness. To distribute ten apples equally among ten children results in a greater overall happiness than to give all ten apples to one child and disregard the remaining nine children. However, even if we leave aside all the notorious problems in calculation of happiness, it is openly admitted by Smart himself that this remark (about distribution being relevant to maximization) is about an empirical and contingent fact, rather than about a necessary, inherent link. This observation hinges upon our knowledge of marginal decreases in satisfaction: each succeeding apple gives a child marginally less satisfaction than the previous apple. Yet, it need not be so; the satisfaction of being a monopolist may be so great that it will outweigh the total sum of satisfactions felt by equally endowed members of the community. Be that as it may, we need not get embroiled in these controversies here. The version of utilitarianism propounded by Smart makes it clear that just distribution (or equal distribution) is relevant to the utilitarian calculus only in so far as it is conducive to the maximization of total output and not by virtue of its being part of the utilitarian principle.

Smart's further remarks also justify a suspicion that a consistent utilitarian is insensitive to the problems of distribution as such. Consider this:

If a utilitarian is given the choice of two actions, one of which will give 2 units of happiness to Smith and 2 to Campbell, and the other of which will give 1 unit of happiness to Smith and 9 to Campbell, he will choose the latter course. It may also be that I have the choice between two alternative actions, one of which gives − 1 unit of happiness to Smith and + 9 units to Campbell, and the other of which gives + 2 to Smith and + 2 to Campbell. As a utilitarian I will choose the former course.[18]

This argument is, of course, unacceptable from the point of view of a theory of justice, so long as justice is considered to be a distributive principle. The essential question asked by a theory of justice is not related to an overall output. The question is whether a proposed distribution is justified by something about Smith and Campbell that we accept as a basis of reward. For instance, does Smith deserve his − 1 and Campbell his + 9? We might also ask the question whether − 1 is not beneath an acceptable minimum for a decent human life.

To digress for a moment, this last question is conspicuously absent from those comparisons between various courses of distribution which are meant to prove that a more inequalitarian distribution is preferable to an equalitarian one if it leads to higher levels of overall welfare. Smart's example is − 1, + 9 as compared with + 2, + 2. Lauchlan Chipman declares his preference for 5, 4, 3, 2 over 3, 3, 3, 3.[19] Alan H. Goldman chooses 4, 4, 4, 3 over 2, 2, 2, 2.[20] Plausible though these choices are, three simple objections indicate their limitations. First, what is important for a theory of justice is neither the total aggregate, nor the equality of shares but a justification of the distribution in terms of justice-relevant grounds, such as desert. Secondly, examples such as those quoted above are rather abstract intellectual exercises; in practice it is hard to imagine that, in given circumstances, taking two courses of distributive action may result in differences of total output such as 15 : 8 (Goldman's example) or 10 : 4 (Smart's example). And thirdly, the persuasive force of these examples is strongly reduced by the fact that they leave aside the dramatic problem of a minimum, while we know that minima for decent human life exist. Imagine that a minimum for decent existence is located in Smart's example at the level of − 0.5 or, in Chipman's example, at the level of 2.5. Would the more productive alternative (in terms of aggregate output) still be intuitively preferable to a less productive one which did not sacrifice anyone's basic requirements of a decent life?

Although (as we have just seen) the critics of redistribution often misrepresent the conditions of justice/utility trade-offs, it is indisputable that justice, understood in purely distributive terms, is independent of, and often in conflict with, considerations of beneficial consequences of an action to be taken. There is no reason why the requirements of efficiency should be incorporated into the demands of justice although the optimal decision should take both into account. Once we have construed the principles of justice and the principles of efficiency as distinct from each other it becomes obvious that, in real life, we should make decisions which satisfy both types of standards. It is impossible to conceive priority rules for resolving, once and for all, cases of conflicting demands: it seems that in some situations principles of justice should take precedence over those of efficiency, if both cannot be implemented equally (say, in the criminal process); while, in other situations, the principles of efficiency should prevail over those of justice (for instance, in the distribution of burdens among soldiers in a military unit). The just rule is *prima facie* right but rightness, all things considered, requires transcending the principles of justice. In practical decision-making, the principles of justice are (and should be) supplemented by various other principles (including those of utility) to make up an overall set of criteria of a good decision. Very few people would subscribe unconditionally to a maxim *"fiat iustitia, pereat mundus"*; we want to render justice but without thereby compromising the vital interests of mankind. If justice can be done without causing any losses, so much the better for justice. If not, we face one of those tragic choices which are of the essence of our lives. However, criteria and conditions for balancing justice with other considerations, including those of utility, are outside the framework of a theory of justice.

This, of course, also applies to law. We all want law to be just but law has various social functions that are not necessarily consistent with its justness. To most people the question: "Can unjust law ever be justified?" sounds almost a nonsense and begs an unconditionally negative answer.[21] However, this reaction seems to assume implicitly a very broad concept of justice, identical to an overall ideal of good law (and then, of course, a statement that unjust law is never justified is merely a tautology). If we wish to sustain consistently the concept of justice as a distributive ideal, we will probably have to reach the conclusion that law which distributes benefits or burdens unjustly may sometimes be justified because of the exigencies of social life. We need not go as far as Hobbes and affirm that the utility of law is its only important virtue.[22] Certainly it would be an odd compliment to say to a legislator: "this is a very useful and beneficial legal act, the only problem with it is that it is very unjust". However, in some circumstances, the evil of injustice may be overridden by the good achieved or even greater evil avoided.

Consider two famous cases of the United States Supreme Court concerning discrimination against American citizens of Japanese extraction during World War II (after Pearl Harbour). In *Hirabayashi v. United States*[23] the Court considered the constitutionality of a curfew order imposed on American citizens of Japanese ancestry. Under an Executive Order authorizing the taking of measures to prevent espionage and sabotage, the commander of a West Coast military area issued on March 24, 1942, an order requiring all persons of Japanese ancestry, resident in the area, to be in their places of residence daily between 8 p.m. and 6 a.m. In *Korematsu v. United States*[24] the order under scrutiny went much further: the Civilian Exclusion Order of May 3, 1942, directed that all Japanese should be excluded from described portions of areas considered as military ones. Petitioners complained that these Acts were unconstitutional because (among other things) they involved racial discrimination. The validity of both Acts was sustained by the Supreme Court.

The arguments of the Court, in both judgments, clearly stress expediency as the main motive justifying such measures. In *Hirabayashi* the Court admits that a great many Japanese-Americans were loyal American citizens and that they were beyond suspicion of committing acts of sabotage or espionage. However, efforts by Japan to establish a fifth column in the United States were not to be excluded and the overriding aim of the Act in question was to safeguard the military area, at a time of threatened invasion by the Japanese forces, from the danger of sabotage and espionage. It is unfortunate, the Court says, that the curfew hit many loyal and innocent people; however, the urgency did not permit a distinction, on an individual basis, between those who deserved this treatment and those who did not. As Mr. Justice Douglas put it:

The sorting process may indeed be as time-consuming whether those who were disloyal or suspect constituted nine or ninety-nine per cent. And the pinch of the order on the loyal citizens would be as great in any case. But where the peril is great and the time is short, temporary treatment on a group basis may be the only practicable expedient whatever the ultimate percentage of those who are detained for cause.[25]

The supremacy of principles of expediency over those of justice was brought out even more clearly in *Korematsu*. The restrictions were applied on a racial basis because of the "[p]ressing public necessity".[26] The Court openly admits that the restrictions were determined by future-oriented considerations, not necessarily related to facts about the particular persons who suffered harm: "Korematsu was not excluded from the Military Area because of hostility to him or his race. He *was* excluded because we are at war with the Japanese Empire, because the properly constituted military authorities feared an invasion of our West Coast and felt constrained to take proper security measures".[27] This is a significant confession. Although the Court falls short of admitting its disregard for justice, the above-quoted words of Justice Douglas show that the burden was distributed not on the basis of justice but on the basis of efficiency. If the answer to the question: "Why was Korematsu ordered to leave his place of residence?" is: "Because the United States was at war with Japan", the irrelevance of this answer, in terms of *any* conception of justice, is evident. The war between the United States and Japan is not something *about* Korematsu which may justify imposition of a burden upon him. However, it is relevant as a future-oriented, utilitarian, consideration (it is possible that the presence in the area of any Japanese, including Korematsu, might in the future endanger important military interests of the United States).

The dissent of Justice Jackson is significant in this regard. If the military authorities believed that these restrictions were useful, Jackson says, then it is their responsibility to impose them and it is not up to the court to judge the wisdom of such a decision. However, it is up to the court to decide on its legality and, according to Jackson, the military order in question was clearly unconstitutional. Yet, the interesting aspect of his reasoning is that he does not say that the military commander was *wrong* when issuing this order; he simply did not act legally. In some circumstances, however, expediency may prevail over constitutional considerations. Jackson says: "When an area is so beset that it must be put under military control at all, the paramount consideration is that its measures be successful, rather than legal".[28] However, it is one thing when a military officer sacrifices legality for the sake of expediency (and Jackson openly avoids disapproval of this act) and another, when a judge endorses it as a legal rule. These are two separate actions, generated by different principles: "[A] commander in temporarily focusing the life of a community on defense is carrying out a military program; he is not making law in the sense the courts know the term. He issues orders, and they may have a certain authority as military commands, although they may be very bad as constitutional law".[29] Emergency is a short period, law maintains its validity much longer. If a judge gives his sanction to rules applied in an emergency period, then he creates abnormal law for normal times.

A military order, however unconstitutional, is not apt to last longer than the military emergency. Even during that period a succeeding commander may revoke it all. But once a judicial opinion rationalizes such an order to show that it conforms to the Constitution, or rather rationalizes the Constitution to show that the Constitution sanctions such an order, the Court for all time has validated the principle of racial discrimination in criminal procedure and of transplanting American citizens. The principle then lies about like a loaded weapon ready for the hand of any authority that can bring forward a plausible claim of an urgent need.[30]

I suppose that, without the risk of grave misrepresentation, we may read Jackson's adjectives 'legal' and 'constitutional' as identical with 'just'. After all, his view of law is not merely positivistic: when he says that considerations of success in wartime should prevail over legal criteria, he really means that success considerations should override those of justice. For a positivist, the military commander's orders (issued on the basis of Executive Orders and Congressional Acts) *were* law; they were binding rules of behaviour addressed to citizens and backed with State coercion. But they were not just: they imposed burdens upon people with regard to the utility of those measures, not on the basis of their justification in terms of justice. Whichever construction we choose: Jackson's (military order in question was unconstitutional but necessary) or positivistic (military order was constitutional though, alas, unjust), one thing is sure: considerations of justice and utility do *not* go hand in hand in this case. Facing such a dilemma, a judge does not disapprove of a commander's actions but he cannot endorse them either; the latter has efficiency in view, the former is guided by considerations of justice.

3. THE IMPORTANCE OF JUSTICE

The substantive principle of justice advocated in this book is based on a very simple moral intuition: that justice is incompatible with the rule of dumb luck and, hence, that we do not deserve anything that comes to us as a result of circumstances over which we do not have any control. It was argued that this general intuition (which applies both to the distribution of negative and positive goods) underlies many of our actual social and legal practices. It was argued that to be coherent, these practices presuppose the ideal of a hypothetical balance of benefits and burdens. It was also argued that this ideal, when combined with the above-mentioned intuition, gives special weight to the principle of desert based on effort, the principle of satisfaction of basic needs, and the retributive principle of punishment.

This moral intuition is very simple, and perhaps may seem to many banal, and yet it generates a very radical conception of distributive justice. 'Radical' in the sense that if we consistently acted upon it, our societies would be fundamentally different from what they are now. The prevailing distributions, in particular of economic benefits and burdens, that have come to be taken for granted in our societies, would have to be radically altered in order to match this conception. But the label of 'radicalism' does not trouble me. For one thing, although some of the *consequences* of this conception may seem radically different from what most people accept (for example, those consequences described above as 'status inconsistency'), its *premises* are not iconoclastic at all. On the contrary, they are deeply embedded in our actual moral thinking. As I have suggested before, legal practices of compensatory benefits for undeserved suffering do express this very moral intuition. Social psychologists have demonstrated that the belief in a just world deeply permeates our thinking and our behaviour: we usually like to see moral sense in the way happiness and tragedy are distributed among people. When our experience contradicts this belief, when we encounter undeserved suffering, we usually tend to re-establish the moral order, either by trying to reduce the effects of the unjust suffering or by 'reinterpreting the event' which may lead us to condemning the victim. Melvin J. Lerner describes numerous experiments in which the witnesses to the 'suffering' of the innocent reinterpreted the whole event in such a way as to blame the victims for their misfortunes and made them appear to 'deserve' their suffering.[31] Although this may cast important doubts on our moral integrity when we are confronted with unpleasant facts which contradict our moral principles, nevertheless it shows that, as a rule, we are reluctant to allow sheer chance to determine the way in which important burdens and benefits are allocated amongst people. Also, sociologists surveying opinions about rules of distributive justice encounter views indicating that material benefits should be proportional to actual effort, rather than based on arbitrary factors such as social place at birth.[32] So, in fact, the conception of social justice discussed here is largely inspired by our actual, current moral views.

One should not, however, over-emphasize this point. It has been stated earlier in this book that the conformity of moral principles with actually accepted community standards is not a proper test of moral legitimacy of these principles. One may, perhaps, distinguish two different approaches to this problem. One approach, which for brevity we may call 'external', refuses to attach any weight to the fact of acceptance of certain rules by a community; this fact, though important from a practical point of view, has no relevance to the reasoning about the plausibility of proposed principles. In the words of Michael Walzer, it is the view that "the political philosopher must separate himself from the political community, cut himself loose from affective ties and conventional ideas".[33] The 'internal' approach postulates working within the system of community standards in order to organize familiar principles and ideas into an overall coherent conception. In one of his recent articles, John Rawls says:

> The aim of political philosophy, when it presents itself in the public culture of a democratic society, is to articulate and to make explicit those shared notions and principles thought to be already latent in common sense; or, as is often the case, if common sense is hesitant and uncertain, and doesn't know what to think, to propose to it certain conceptions and principles congenial to its most essential convictions and historical traditions. . . . The real task is to discover and formulate the deeper bases of agreement which one hopes are embedded in common sense, or even to originate and fashion starting points for common understanding by expressing in a new form the convictions found in the historical tradition by connecting them with a wide range of people's considered convictions: those which stand up to critical reflection.[34]

The second part of this quotation clearly begs the question: it is not obvious why the aspiration of political philosophy should be to discover the bases of agreement behind conflicting views. Leaving aside the question of the likelihood of detecting such an agreement (in particular, in "the public culture of a democratic society" to which Rawls's statement applies), the asserted task of political philosophy is far from being self-evident. With similar plausibility one might propose the opposite aim: that is, to reveal the genuine and irreconcilable conflicts of basic moral theories behind the apparent consensus. I do not propose to advocate this latter view about the role of political philosophy but I cannot accept the aims suggested by Rawls as the only legitimate ones. And yet, there is an important insight in the first part of the above-quoted passage: that the political philosopher should work, as it were, from the inside and try to articulate, interpret and rearrange the principles which are congenial to the political culture of which that philosopher is a part.

This 'internal' approach need not, and most probably will not, lead to the moral consensus envisaged by Rawls. But this does not undermine the validity of the 'internal' approach. Having accepted the inevitable plurality of moral conceptions in their societies, political philosophers may still find good reasons to work from within the system in a more limited sense. They may try to identify and articulate *some* of the principles or practices congenial to their political culture and then try to arrange them into a coherent conception which (even if in many respects opposed to many accepted practices) will nevertheless be presented as an extension of those principles and convictions which people do accept though they fail to follow them through to their proper conclusions. There are at least two reasons supporting such an 'internal' approach. First, its persuasive effectiveness is much higher than in the case of principles proposed 'from outside', from the position of total detachment of a philosopher from the community. Secondly, and more importantly, when a philosopher proposes a theory of justice with the view to its use in judging, and possibly reshaping, law, it must be remembered that law is a social enterprise within which people arrange their affairs with each other, and therefore it would be appropriate if a philosopher proposing a system of just law could relate it to at least some of the familiar and accepted principles and moral convictions. It may well happen that this will turn out to be impossible: that a philosopher's views will be completely at odds with everything that a community, whose ideas are studied, believes and practices. But one cannot say this unless one has made an account of these actual ideas, practices and convictions.

In any event, this book obviously is not a neutral description of how most people actually think. It is not an essay about how societies actually confront the situations of social distributions of benefits and burdens under the circumstances of relative scarcity. Rather, with the above qualification about the 'internal approach', it advocates a particular conception of justice which follows from the basic principle about desert being related only to things over which a person can have control. If we accept this principle in *some* circumstances, then perhaps we should take it as a universal principle controlling our social distributions (if not, we must be able to pinpoint the relevant differences between those situations in which this principle operates, and those where it does not). Unless this principle is rejected, the other distributional rules described above, which follow from it, must also be accepted, if we want to be consistent in our moral conceptions. But if someone rejects the principle itself, there is little reason why he or she should accept its consequential rules.

However, if the general principle of distributive justice proposed here is accepted, it does not vindicate, in itself, any particular rules or decisions about any particular distributions. Principles of justice require interpretation through a theory of the good before they can be enforced, but they do not stipulate any *particular* theory of the good. Theory of justice, such as advocated here, postulates a substantive principle controlling distribution of benefits and burdens, but in itself it does not say what relative weight should be assigned to particular benefits and particular burdens. It says, for instance, that if the coal-miner's effort is higher, and his job-satisfaction lower than the respective effort and job-satisfaction of a university teacher, then the former should be more highly paid. But it does not say whether indeed the burdens imposed by a miner's duties are higher than those of a teacher. And it does not prove that pay is indeed a benefit, just as it does not say what increment in pay is commensurate with the loss in job-satisfaction. Or, to take another example, the present theory of justice cannot conclusively demonstrate that a rapist should be punished more severely than a tax evader: such a demonstration would have to rely on an assessment of the relative importance of the values infringed (and consequently, the amount of benefits of non-self-restraint). Further, if we wanted to propose more specific types and measures of punishment (say, a specific sentence of imprisonment for a rapist, a fine for a tax evader), we would have first to accept as valid the judgments about the relative burdens inflicted on persons subjected to different types of punishment.

Therefore, to answer questions about particular distributions of particular benefits and burdens among particular persons, it is not enough to have a theory of distributive justice. One must have a theory about what things are good which will provide measures of the grounds of distribution (such as effort, basic need, gravity of a crime) and also measures of the goodness (or badness) of the things to be distributed. It is clear that the theories of the good held by particular people in a given society vary immensely, and still much more do they vary between societies. A theory of justice may ignore these differences: it provides merely a general form which is to be filled in with a conception of the good by whoever uses this theory. That is why concrete implications of one and the same theory of justice may be very different as a result of different theories of goodness. But a legislator who is about to enact a just law, cannot disregard a theory of the good because he must give particular answers to the questions about proper distributions. This is *his* problem. It is also a problem for his political theory to decide to what extent the current views about relative measures of the good (and 'the bad') shared by the members of his society should determine his own judgment. A democratic legislator is bound, within the limits imposed by the theory of democracy that he accepts, by the current views of what is good and what is bad. But even then, he cannot be sure that the particular distributions will be just, for an addressee of his decision may hold an eccentric, or a non-typical, theory of the good. A criminal may think that, after all, prison is not all that bad. What, typically, is considered as suffering, may be a matter of indifference, or even a source of enjoyment for him. And yet, law has to use some typical standardized measures in its operations. Fortunately, a theorist of justice does not have to solve these problems. He acts like a law-maker who uses open-ended terms such as 'equity', 'reasonableness', 'due care', and who leaves it up to a judge to fill in the meaning of these terms in particular cases. This privileged position of a theorist of justice is made possible by the fact that 'social justice' is an ideal of a high level of generality: it is a 'meta-good' for it dictates the distribution of other, more specific, social goods.

It will be, perhaps, prudent to state a caveat at this point. When we are saying that the enforcement of a theory of justice requires knowledge about particular views in a society about what people consider to be good for them, it does not commit us to any philosophical theory of the good understood, for instance, as an intrinsic moral quality of certain things or acts. In this philosophical sense, a theory of the good is not identical with description of actual human desires, interests and aspirations. It is also important to note that, although we talk about justice as a 'good' thing in a loose sense (that is, as something to which a positive moral assessment may be attached), nevertheless a theory of justice is not part of a theory of the goodness in a strict sense. It is, rather, part of the conception of the rightness, that is, of the set of moral norms about the acts that ought to be done. As W. D. Ross has pointed out, statements about rightness are not identical with statements about moral intrinsic goodness. In his interpretation,

> when we ask what is the general nature of morally good actions, it seems quite clear that it is in virtue of the motives that they proceed from that actions are morally good. Moral goodness is quite distinct from and independent of rightness, which ... belongs to acts *not* in virtue of motives they proceed from, but in virtue of the nature of what is done.[35]

Within this distinction, a theory of justice clearly fits a broader notion of a theory of rightness. An act is 'just' irrespective of its motives; according to the theory proposed here, its justness depends only on whether or not the resulting distribution conforms to the pattern of equilibrium of benefits and burdens. That is why our judgments of social justice do not necessarily imply (though typically they will) moral praise of those who brought about a just distribution.

From the statement that a theory of justice belongs to a broader conception of rightness, it follows that only from the point of view of this broader theory, questions about trade-offs between justice and other social ideals can be meaningfully dealt with. Now it has been a constant topic in our discussions that justice is a *specific* social ideal, and though it is important, it is by no means the only or the supreme social ideal. Hence, the rules of justice themselves cannot prescribe what should be done when justice conflicts with other social goods. This is a matter for a theory of good society, not for a theory of justice. 'Doing justice' is important, but 'doing the right thing' may sometimes require some degree of injustice.

What procedures should be employed to decide about the proper mixture of justice and other social virtues? It is easier to say what procedures are *im*plausible. One proposed method was a 'lexicographical' (or a 'lexical') order, that is, such a hierarchy of values in which we can move on to implement a lower value only after a higher value has been fully implemented.[36] But, first, this method is obviously counter-intuitive: often great increments of a 'lower' value justify a sacrifice of a very slight amount of a higher value, especially given the law of diminishing marginal utility, that is to say, when we operate in a situation of a high absolute level of satisfaction of the 'higher' value. Secondly, and more importantly, the 'lexicographical' order does not provide any solutions to the problem of trade-offs, but rather eliminates the problem altogether. We want to know how to define the optimum mixture of social goods, and this is exactly what 'lexicographical' order proscribes.

An alternative procedure is to construct a matrix of causal and consequential variables which reflect various types of social ideals. One can define, for instance, the main components of justice, freedom and welfare, and then try to see how the presence of (or an increment in) any of these variables affects the other variables.[37] So far so good. What is missing is some procedure which will help us to decide whether, and how much of, one good compensates for a loss of some quantity of another good. The matrix of variables perhaps facilitates the proper way of asking this sort of questions, but it does not provide any answers.

And yet, we do constantly 'trade off' justice against liberty, or welfare. These are difficult moral decisions but in a practical world we cannot avoid them. All good things do not go together, and we have to trade off gains in one social good against losses in another. What a theory of justice can demand is that, before we define the optimum mixture of them, we should first clearly realize what justice, and other social ideals, would require. For the sake of clarity in our moral reasoning, we should avoid amalgamating various social ideals: social justice should not be confused with other social virtues if we are to decide about choosing among them, or about trading them for one another. We can plausibly propose the standards of justice, efficiency, liberty, democracy etc., but I am hesitant about the existence of morally convincing general theories for proposing the mixture of these ideals. At any rate, they are beyond the range of a theory of justice. But this statement is not so much an expression of perplexity as a reflection of a plurality of ultimate moral principles which, in practice, have to be weighed against each other and which, when contemplated theoretically, do not cohere into some "ultimate, all-reconciling, yet realizable synthesis".[38] This view about social morality corresponds to Isaiah Berlin's 'pluralism'[39] or, in a more recent formulation, to James Fishkin's 'ideals without an ideal'.[40] However, while for Fishkin this "plurality of principles without a unified vision" is "the most honest response to the true difficulties of distributive justice",[41] for my part I suggest that the conflict occurs between the principles of distributive justice and other principles, with the result that there can be no single ideal of a good society.

Perhaps one procedure that a theory of justice can insist on is that in our actual moral reasoning we should first consider what justice would require and only afterwards modify the rule by considering other social ideals. This is, I suppose, a proper way for a judge in a criminal trial to proceed: the considerations of deterrence, reform and prevention work as modifiers of the verdict determined by the principles of justice, and not the other way round. This procedure seems to be justified by the centrality of justice (as understood here) in expressing human independence from factors which are beyond human control. But, of course, the centrality of justice hinges upon the ethical value of this particular ideal which in itself will remain here undefended.

One final remark. From the statement that justice is an important social good it does not follow that it is, and always will be, equally important in every human society. Justice, as a distributive notion, is important when the necessity of distributing scarce goods arises. In other words, the circumstances which make justice an important value are such that desired goods fall short of the claims that people make. If all people could satisfy all their claims and desires without exhausting the available supply of distributable goods, the principles of distributive justice would become unimportant.

This claim has been often expressed in a stronger form, that is, that in the situation of abundance or superabundance, the 'circumstances of justice' do not obtain at all. This is, among others, the position of Rawls[42] who follows the well-known analysis of Hume.[43] To this, it has been counter-argued that, first, some goods are intrinsically scarce (such as political power, positions of authority) and, secondly, that even in a situation of abundance, claims of justice are meaningful to the degree to which they are based on desert (for "it may be unjust for an individual to possess some good even if no one else is thereby deprived of the opportunity to possess the same or equivalent good").[44] While the first point is largely irrelevant,[45] I agree with the latter: it makes sense to talk about just or unjust distributions even if the total available for distribution exceeds the totality of valid claims. But the principles which control the distribution are really *important* only when it is necessary to adjudicate between conflicting claims in a situation of scarcity. Put another way, the principles of justice are meaningful but relatively unimportant in a situation of abundance. This can be compared to the ideal of security in a non-threatening situation. This ideal of security is meaningful, and we can intelligibly state the principles dictated by the postulates of security, but their social importance is rather low in a community where no-one threatens other people anyway. Likewise, in a situation of abundance we are still able to say what the principles of distributive justice require, but we do not need them as badly as in a situation of scarcity.

Abundance and scarcity are described with reference to a relation between the claims people make and the amount of goods available. This suggests that the importance of justice is a function not only of the amount of goods in absolute terms, but also of the subjective attitudes of people who make claims on those resources. Consequently, we can well imagine very affluent societies in which the importance of distributive justice is very high because people want more than is available to satisfy them and, conversely, relatively poor societies in which the prevailing self-discipline, or altruism, or disinterestedness in material goods effectively reduces the level of conflict of claims. Consider the following example. The ancient Chronicle of Sri Lanka which goes back to the third Century B.C., *The Mahavamsa*, describes the construction of Ruanwelli — one of the oldest and largest shrines in Ceylon. At a certain stage of the construction, when the master-builders were about to commence making the relic-chamber, the king

> made it known: 'Work shall not be done here without wage.' At every gate he commanded to place ... very many garments, different ornaments, solid and liquid foods and drink withal, fragrant flowers, sugar and so forth, as well as the five perfumes for the mouth.
>
> 'Let them take of these as they will when they have laboured as they will.' Observing this command the king's work-people allotted (the wages).[46]

This historical account illustrates two things. One, that relative abundance makes justice unimportant but not meaningless. Judgments of justice could be made with respect to the builders of Ruanwelli with similar precision as with respect to the more competitively oriented recipients of wages, but the importance of these judgments in regulating human affairs was much lower. Second, that abundance is as much a matter of availability of resources as of human attitudes. The principles of justice are important in societies in which people's desires prevail over the capacities of meeting them. One may regret the lack of altruism or of self-discipline but the business of justice is to regulate the allocation of goods among people as they are, with all their imperfections. It may well be that in an ideal society it will be possible to do without justice, and without law. It is also possible that there have been, or there are, such admirable communities. In this sense, the importance of justice may be of a historical and parochial character. At this point, a theory of social justice ends and utopia begins.

NOTES

INTRODUCTION

¹ F. A. Hayek, *Law, Legislation and Liberty*, Vol. 2 (London: Routledge and Kegan Paul, 1976), p. 97, footnote omitted.
² *Ibid.*, p. 97.
³ Robert Nozick, *Anarchy, State, and Utopia* (New York: Basic Books, 1974), p. 183.

CHAPTER 1

¹ For a not dissimilar account of concept/conception distinction, see John Rawls, *A Theory of Justice* (Oxford: Clarendon Press, 1972), pp. 5, 9–10; see also Ronald Dworkin, *Taking Rights Seriously* (London: Duckworth, 1978), pp. 134–136. On definitions of ethical concepts, see Richard Robinson, *Definition* (Oxford: Clarendon Press, 1950), pp. 165–170.
² Dworkin, *op. cit.*, p. 135.
³ Aristotle, *The Nicomachean Ethics*, V, 1.15–2.12 (trans. F. H. Peters).
⁴ John Stuart Mill, 'Utilitarianism', in *Utilitarianism, On Liberty, Essay on Bentham*, ed. by Mary Warnock (London: Collins, 1962), p. 306.
⁵ Rawls, *op. cit.*, p. 9.
⁶ See Chapter 4.2.
⁷ In Chapter 9.1.
⁸ Iredell Jenkins, *Social Order and the Limits of Law* (Princeton: Princeton University Press, 1980), p. 324.
⁹ Henry Sidgwick, *The Methods of Ethics* (Chicago: The University of Chicago Press, 1962; Ist. ed. 1874), pp. 265–266.
¹⁰ Brian Barry, *Political Argument* (London: Routledge and Kegan Paul, 1965), p. 44.
¹¹ Joel Feinberg, *Social Philosophy* (Englewood Cliffs: Prentice-Hall, 1973), pp. 98–99, and in a much more developed form in his essay 'Noncomparative Justice', in *Rights, Justice, and the Bounds of Liberty* (Princeton: Princeton University Press, 1980), reprinted from *The Philosophical Review* (1974). Subsequent references in brackets in the main text discussing Feinberg's views are to the pages of this essay.
¹² Phillip Montague, 'Comparative and Non-Comparative Justice', *Philosophical Quarterly* **30** (1980), p. 132.
¹³ This example of 'absolute' (as opposed to 'comparative') principle of justice is given by Barry, *op. cit.*, p. 44 in connection with p. 96.
¹⁴ See pp. 160–161 below.
¹⁵ See pp. 178–181 below.
¹⁶ Barry, *op. cit.*, pp. 96 and 44.
¹⁷ Rachel Karniol and Dale T. Miller, 'Morality and the Development of Conceptions

of Justice', in Melvin J. Lerner and Sally C. Lerner, eds., *The Justice Motive in Social Behavior* (New York and London: Plenum Press, 1981), p. 76.

[18] See Wojciech Sadurski, '"Non-Comparative Justice" Revisited', *Archiv für Rechts- und Sozialphilosophie* 69 (1983), pp. 504–514, esp. 505–507.

[19] Eugène Dupréel, *Traité de morale*, Vol. 2 (Bruxelles: Presses Universitaires de Bruxelles, 1967; 1st ed. 1932), pp. 485–491.

[20] Friedrich A. Hayek, *Law, Legislation and Liberty*, Vol. 2 (London: Routledge and Kegan Paul, 1976), p. 31.

[21] Friedrich A. Hayek, *New Studies in Philosophy, Politics, Economics and the History of Ideas* (London: Routledge and Kegan Paul, 1978), p. 58.

[22] See excellent discussion by John Kleinig, 'Good Samaritanism', *Philosophy and Public Affairs* 5 (1976), pp. 382–407, esp. pp. 391–398.

[23] John Stuart Mill, 'On Liberty', in *Utilitarianism . . . , op. cit.*, p. 137.

[24] Aristotle, *op. cit.*, V, 2.12.

[25] See Chapter 8.1. below.

[26] James Gordley, 'Equality in Exchange', *California Law Review* 69 (1981), p. 1589.

[27] Georges Burdeau, *Traité de science politique*, Vol. V (Paris: Librarie générale de droit et de la jurisprudence), p. 89.

[28] *Halsbury's Laws of England* (London: Butterworths, 1977), 4th ed., Vol. 18, p. 344. On the development of this doctrine in the United Kingdom, see S. M. Waddams, 'Unconscionability in Contracts', *Modern Law Review* 39 (1976), pp. 369–393.

[29] *Wood v. Abrey* (1818) 3 Madd. 417, at p. 423 *per* Leach V. C.

[30] *Fry v. Lane* (1888) 40 Ch.D. 312, at p. 322 *per* Kay J.

[31] *Horwood v. Millar's Timber and Trading Co. Ltd.* [1917] 1 K.B. 305, 311.

[32] This Act has been replaced by the Consumer Credit Act (1974).

[33] *Contracts Review Act*, 1980 (N.S.W.), s.7(1). See John Goldring, Joan L. Pratt, D. E. J. Ryan, 'The Contracts Review Act (N.S.W.)', *University of N.S.W. Law Journal* 4 (1981), pp. 1–16.

[34] *Tasman Dry Cleaners (Balmain) Pty. Ltd. v. Diamond* [1960] N.S.W.R. 419.

[35] *A. Schroeder Music Publishing Co. Ltd. v. Macaulay* [1974] 3 All E.R. 616.

[36] *Ibid.*, at p. 623. See also *Lloyds Bank Ltd. v. Bundy* [1974] 3 All E.R. 757.

[37] See Lord Denning M. R. in *Clifford Davis Management Ltd. v. W.E.A. Records Ltd.* [1975] 1 All E.R. 237, a case concerning two musicians who signed an evidently unfair contract with their manager. He said (at p. 240): "They were composers talented in music and song but not in business. In negotiation they could not hold their own".

[38] *U.S. v. Bethlehem Steel Corp.*, 315 U.S. 289, 326–328 (1941), Frankfurter, J., dissenting.

[39] See a recent powerful restatement of this proposition by Anthony T. Kronman, 'Contract Law and Distributive Justice', *Yale Law Journal* 89 (1980), pp. 472–511.

[40] *Scott v. U.S.*, 79 U.S. 443, 445 (1870). On the recent development of this doctrine in the U.S., see particularly M. P. Ellinghaus, 'In Defense of Unconscionability', *Yale Law Journal* 78 (1969), pp. 757–815 and John E. Murray, 'Unconscionability: Unconscionability', *University of Pittsburgh Law Review* 31 (1969), pp. 1–80.

[41] *Frostifresh Corp. v. Reynoso*, 52 Misc. 2d 26, 274 N.Y.S. 2d 757 (Dist. Ct. 1966); 54 Misc. 2d 119, 281 N.Y.S. 2d 964 (Sup. Ct. 1967).

[42] *Campbell Soup Co. v. Wentz*, 172 F.2d 80, 83 (3d. Cir. 1948).

[43] See, e.g., note 38 above.

NOTES

[44] See, e.g., Richard E. Epstein, 'Unconscionability: A Critical Reappraisal', *Journal of Law and Economics* 18 (1975), pp. 293–315 and Arthur Allen Leff, 'Unconscionability and the Crowd – Consumers and the Common Law Tradition', *University of Pittsburgh Law Review* 31 (1970), pp. 349–358.
[45] Thomas Hobbes, *Leviathan*, ed. by C. B. Macpherson (Harmondsworth: Penguin, 1981, 1st ed. 1651), p. 208.
[46] Matthew, 20.1–16.
[47] Frankfurter, J., in 315 U.S., pp. 326–327 (quoting Holmes, J.).
[48] Abbott, C. J., quoted with approval by Frankfurter, J., *ibid.*, p. 327.
[49] Ronald Dworkin, *op. cit.*, chs. 2–4, 13.
[50] Hobbes, *op. cit.*, p. 388.
[51] John Austin, *Lectures on Jurisprudence or the Philosophy of Positive Law* (London: John Murray, 1920, 1st ed. 1832), p. 108.
[52] Hans Kelsen, *What Is Justice?* (Berkeley: University of California Press, 1971), p. 430.
[53] John Finnis, *Natural Law and Natural Rights* (Oxford: Clarendon Press, 1980), in particular pp. 363–366.
[54] Lon L. Fuller, *The Morality of Law* (New Haven: Yale University Press, 1972, 1st ed. 1964), pp. 33–39.
[55] *Ibid.*, p. 133.
[56] Rawls, *op. cit.*, p. 59.
[57] This example is discussed by Feinberg in *Social Philosophy, op. cit.*, pp. 106–107.
[58] L. L. Fuller, 'Positivism and Fidelity to Law', *Harvard Law Review* 71 (1958), p. 474.
[59] Fuller, *Morality* ..., *op. cit.*, p. 39.
[60] *Ibid.*, p. 39.
[61] *Ibid.*, p. 96.
[62] See also Peter P. Nicholson, 'The Internal Morality of Law: Fuller and His Critics', *Ethics* 84 (1974), pp. 307–320.
[63] H. L. A. Hart, *The Concept of Law* (Oxford: Clarendon Press, 1961), p. 206.
[64] See A. M. Honoré, 'Social Justice', *McGill Law Journal* 8 (1962), p. 82.
[65] Dupréel, *op. cit.*, pp. 485–489; D. D. Raphael, *Justice and Liberty* (London: Athlone Press, 1980), pp. 80–93; Sidgwick, *op. cit.*, p. 293; Chaim Perelman, *The Idea of Justice and the Problem of Argument* (London: Routledge and Kegan Paul, 1963), p. 63.
[66] 315 U.S., pp. 325–326.
[67] See Julius Stone, *Legal System and Lawyers' Reasoning* (Sydney: Maitland Publications, 1968, 1st ed. 1964), pp. 263–267.
[68] W. J. Wagner, 'Equity and Its Socialist Equivalent in the Polish Legal System', *Review of Socialist Law* 1 (1975), pp. 151–169.
[69] Quoted *ibid.*, pp. 156–157.
[70] 315 U.S., pp. 312–313.
[71] Hans Kelsen, *General Theory of Law and State* (Cambridge, Mass.: Harvard University Press, 1946), p. 410 (trans. A. Wedberg).
[72] Dworkin, *op. cit.*, chs. 2–4 and Appendix.
[73] *Ibid.*, p. 342.
[74] Ronald Dworkin, ' "Natural" Law Revisited', *University of Florida Law Review* 34 (1982), p. 165.

[75] Dworkin, *Taking...*, *op. cit.*, p. 66.
[76] *Ibid.*, p. 342.
[77] *Ibid.*, p. 102.
[78] *Ibid.*, p. 102.
[79] *Ibid.*, p. 65.
[80] See, in particular, Neil MacCormick, *Legal Right and Social Democracy* (Oxford: Clarendon Press, 1982), ch. 7.
[81] Dworkin, *Taking...*, *op. cit.*, p. 126.
[82] See, e.g., Norman P. Barry, *An Introduction to Modern Political Theory* (London: Macmillan, 1981), p. 119.
[83] Rawls, *op. cit.*, p. 86.
[84] See also William Nelson, 'The Very Idea of Pure Procedural Justice', *Ethics* 90 (1980), pp. 502–511.
[85] Rawls, *op. cit.*, p. 86.
[86] *Ibid.*, pp. 85–86.
[87] *Ibid.*, p. 85.
[88] In the following pages I discuss *legal* procedural justice, but of course the concept of 'procedural justice' is broader: it may be applied to an account of procedures governed by any rules, not necessarily legal. 'Due process of law' and 'natural justice' (in the technical meaning of this last term) are therefore narrower concepts than 'procedural justice' but I think that conclusions drawn from the exploration of those concepts may be applied to procedural justice *tout court*. On the other hand, the American doctrine of 'due process of law' also contains certain principles of a substantive rather than procedural character (liberty of contract, right to privacy, etc.) but this need not bother us here: we take it as an illustration of procedural principles and discuss it here only in so far as it imposes constraints on procedure.
[89] David Resnick, 'Due Process and Procedural Justice' in J. Roland Pennock, John W. Chapman, eds., *Due Process, Nomos XVIII* (New York: New York University Press, 1977), p. 213.
[90] *Ibid.*, p. 213.
[91] Rupert Cross, *Evidence*, Australian Edition by J. A. Gobbo (Sydney: Butterworths, 1970), p. 288.
[92] See *Ibid.*, pp. 497–499.
[93] *Hawkins v. United States*, 358 U.S. 74, 75 (1958).
[94] Carl J. Friedrich, 'Justice: The Just Political Act', in Carl J. Friedrich, John W. Chapman, eds., *Justice, Nomos VI* (New York: Atherton Press, 1963), pp. 27–28, 43.
[95] Clarence Morris, 'Law, Justice and the Public's Aspirations', *ibid.*, p. 189.

CHAPTER TWO

[1] Arnold Brecht, *Political Theory* (Princeton: Princeton University Press, 1970), p. 136.
[2] Alf Ross, *On Law and Justice* (London: Stevens & Sons, 1958), p. 274. See also Hans Kelsen, *What is Justice?* (Berkeley: University of California Press, 1971), pp. 4, 11, 295–296.
[3] The subsequent parenthesized references in the text are to John Rawls, *A Theory of Justice* (Oxford: Clarendon Press, 1972).

NOTES   289

⁴ Ronald Dworkin, 'The Original Position', in Norman Daniels, ed., *Reading Rawls* (Oxford: Basil Blackwell, 1975), p. 18.
⁵ Examples of such confusion and, in consequence, unjustified criticism of Rawls: Allan Bloom, 'Justice: John Rawls vs. the Tradition of Political Philosophy', *The American Political Science Review* 69 (1975), pp. 648–662; David Lewis Schaefer, *Justice or Tyranny? A Critique of John Rawls' 'Theory of Justice'* (Port Washington: Kennikat Press, 1979), pp. 39–41.
⁶ John Locke, *Two Treatises of Government* (Cambridge: Cambridge University Press, 1970), II, 104.
⁷ *Ibid.*, II, 114–121.
⁸ Jean-Jacques Rousseau, *The Social Contract and Discourses*, translated by G. D. H. Cole (London: J. M. Dent & Sons, 1973), p. 165, emphasis added.
⁹ Thomas Hobbes, *Leviathan*, ed. by C. B. Macpherson (Harmondsworth: Penguin, 1981), p. 229.
¹⁰ James Buchanan, *The Limits of Liberty* (Chicago: The University of Chicago Press, 1975), p. 26, emphasis added.
¹¹ *Ibid.*, p. 25.
¹² *Ibid.*, pp. 23, 28.
¹³ *Ibid.*, p. 167.
¹⁴ *Ibid.*, p. 73.
¹⁵ John Rawls, 'Kantian Constructivism in Moral Theory', *The Journal of Philosophy* 77 (1980), pp. 523–524.
¹⁶ *Ibid.*, p. 523.
¹⁷ See Chapter 4.1.
¹⁸ Rawls, 'Kantian Constructivism . . .', *op. cit.*, p. 518.
¹⁹ H. J. McCloskey, *Meta-Ethics and Normative Ethics* (The Hague: Martinus Nijhoff, 1969), chs. 4 and 5.
²⁰ *Ibid.*, p. 143.
²¹ See Richard Brandt, *Ethical Theory* (Englewood Cliffs: Prentice Hall, 1959), pp. 192–196: John Hospers, *Human Conduct* (New York: Brace & World, 1961), pp. 539–540.
²² R. M. Hare, 'Rawls' Theory of Justice', in N. Daniels, *op. cit.*, p. 84.
²³ On the distinction between normative and meta-ethical intuitionism, see Jonathan Harrison, *Our Knowledge of Right and Wrong* (London: Allen and Unwin, 1971), pp. 74–76.

CHAPTER 3

¹ See, e.g., Friedrich A. Hayek, *Law, Legislation and Liberty*, vol. 2 (London: Routledge & Kegan Paul, 1976), in particular pp. 85–88.
² I have deliberately omitted, at this stage of discussion, a third sense in which equality may be applied to law: social equality as promoted by the application of differentiated legal rules. This notion of equality is, in a sense, 'external' to the quality of law itself.
³ John Stuart Mill, 'Utilitarianism', in *Utilitarianism, On Liberty, Essay on Bentham*, ed. by Mary Warnock (London: Collins, 1962), p. 301, emphasis added.
⁴ Richard E. Flathman, 'Equality and Generalization, a Formal Analysis', in J. Roland

Pennock and John W. Chapman, eds., *Equality, Nomos IX* (New York: Atherton Press, 1967), p. 49.
[5] Hans Kelsen, *What is Justice?* (Berkeley: University of California Press, 1971), p. 15.
[6] *Railway Express Agency v. New York*, 336 U.S. 106, 112 (1949).
[7] Jean-Jacques Rousseau, *The Social Contract*, trans. by H. J. Tozer (New York: Washington Square Press, 1974), pp. 34–35.
[8] See Chaim Perelman, *The Idea of Justice and the Problem of Argument* (London: Routledge & Kegan Paul, 1963), pp. 36–41 and *passim*.
[9] See a recent decision of the U.S. Supreme Court upholding the constitutionality of the registration of males and not females for potential conscription: *Rostker v. Goldberg*, 453 U.S. 57 (1981).
[10] *Ibid.*, pp. 76–83 (Rehnquist, J., majority opinion).
[11] *Ibid.*, pp. 93–106 (Marshall, J., dissenting).
[12] Note, 'Sex, Discrimination, and the Constitution', *Stanford Law Review* 2 (1950), p. 720.
[13] In Pennock and Chapman, eds., *op. cit.*, pp. 267–269.
[14] See Julius Stone, *Human Law and Human Justice* (Sydney: Maitland Publications, 1965), pp. 325–330, more fully developed in *id.*, 'Justice Not Equality', in E. Kamenka and A. E.-S. Tay, eds., *Justice* (London: Edward Arnold, 1979). See also Flathman, *op. cit.*, pp. 50–51.
[15] Friedrich A. Hayek, *The Constitution of Liberty* (Chicago: The University of Chicago Press, 1960), p. 154.
[16] *Ibid.*, p. 154. I thank Lauchlan Chipman for his comments on this subject.
[17] Jan Wawrzyniak, *Równość obywateli PRL* (Warszawa: P.W.N., 1977), pp. 116–21.
[18] J. C. Smith, *Legal Obligation* (London: The Athlone Press, 1976), p. 124.
[19] *Ibid.*, pp. 124–125. To be fair to Smith, I should mention that further on he introduces the notion of 'equality *under* the law' which requires that the conditions of rules be relevant (*ibid.*, pp. 128–129) and which corresponds to what I identify here as a third model of non-discriminating classification. But this does not alter my observations about his interpretation of 'equality before the law' which still is an example of a '*per se* theory'.
[20] M. J. Harkins III, 'Affirmative Action: The Constitution, Jurisprudence and the Formulation of Policy', *Kansas Law Review* 26 (1977), p. 89, emphasis added.
[21] "[S]ome elements such as social class . . . , though in theory neither hereditary nor unchangeable in the sense that race is, may in fact depend very much on the luck of birth and may often be changed only with difficulty", Note, 'Developments in the Law: Equal Protection', *Harvard Law Review* 82 (1969), p. 1167.
[22] Ronald Dworkin, *Taking Rights Seriously* (London: Duckworth, 1978), p. 227.
[23] See Note, 'Sex, Discrimination, and the Constitution', *op. cit.*, p. 717.
[24] See Kathryn L. Powers, 'Sex Segregation and the Ambivalent Directions of Sex Discrimination Law', *Wisconsin Law Review* (1979) pp. 81–82. However, while condemning particular protective labour laws of the beginning of the 20th Century in the United States, she notes that "some feminists, certain labor unions, and social reformers lobbied for these laws in order to protect women workers from sweatshop conditions", p. 81.
[25] *Schlesinger v. Ballard*, 419 U.S. 498 (1975).
[26] *Ibid.* at 508, Stewart J. delivering the opinion of the Court.

NOTES   291

[27] See John D. Johnston, Jr., 'Sex Discrimination and the Supreme Court — 1975', *U.C.L.A. Law Review* 23 (1975), pp. 243–244.
[28] Ruth Bader Ginsburg, 'Gender in the Supreme Court: The 1973 and 1974 Terms', *Supreme Court Review* (1975), p. 7.
[29] E.g. the civil service laws which require certain levels of intelligence as measured by civil service examinations for certain jobs, see Note, 'Developments in the Law: Equal Protection', *op. cit.*, p. 1174.
[30] E.g. the army regulations which refuse induction to those who are without all their limbs, see *ibid.*, p. 1174.
[31] *Plessy v. Ferguson*, 163 U.S. 537, 559 (1896), (Harlan J., dissenting).
[32] *Edwards v. California*, 314 U.S. 160, 185 (1941) (Jackson J., concurring).
[33] *Loving v. Virginia*, 388 U.S. 1, 11 (1967).
[34] For a more detailed discussion of the issue of preferential programs, see Chapter 7.
[35] *Regents of the University of California v. Bakke*, 438 U.S. 265 (1978).
[36] See, *inter alia, McLaughlin v. Florida*, 379 U.S. 184, 191–2 (1964); *Bolling v. Sharpe*, 347 U.S. 497, 499 (1954).
[37] On "the marginally suspect nature of classification by sex" see *Commonwealth v. Daniels*, 243 A.2d (Pa 1968), *noted* in *Harvard Law Review* 82 (1969), 921, 923. See also *Craig v. Boren*, 429 U.S. 190, 197 (1976). To be sure, the Supreme Court has been more equivocal in categorizing sex classifications as 'suspect' than it has been with regard to racial classifications. In *Frontiero v. Richardson*, 411 U.S. 677 (1973), four justices declared that suspect classification analysis is appropriate for sex discrimination cases, but two of them later departed from this doctrine. Nevertheless, other U.S. courts have often relied upon *Frontiero* in treating sex as a suspect classification requiring the strict scrutiny test, e.g., *Johnston v. Hodges*, 372 F. Supp. 1015 (E.D. Ky. 1974).
[38] See Note, 'Developments in the Law: Equal Protection', *op. cit.*, p. 1174, n. 61.
[39] *McDonald v. Board of Election Commissioners*, 394 U.S. 802, 807 (1969). It should be noted, however, that in the U.S. jurisprudence it is still highly controversial whether certain classifications based on wealth related categories (e.g., payment of a fee to a State) should be invalidated *solely* because of their adverse impact on the poor or *also* because they involve 'rights of fundamental importance'. See Gerald Gunther, 'The Supreme Court, 1971 — Foreword: In Search of Evolving Doctrine on a Changing Court: A Model for New Equal Protection', *Harvard Law Review* 86 (1972), p. 10. See also Note, 'Developments in the Law: Equal Protection', *op. cit.*, p. 1126.
[40] *Cramer v. Virginia Commonwealth University*, 415 F. Supp., 673, 681 (1976); see also Powell, J., in 438 U.S. 265, 295 (1978).
[41] Alexander Bickel, *The Morality of Consent* (New Haven: Yale University Press, 1975), p. 133.
[42] See Paul W. Taylor, 'Reverse Discrimination and Compensatory Justice', *Analysis* 33 (1973), pp. 177–182.
[43] See James W. Nickel, 'Discrimination and Morally Relevant Characteristics', *Analysis* 32 (1972), pp. 113–114.
[44] Flathman, *op. cit.*, p. 59.
[45] Joseph Tussman and Jacobus tenBroek, 'The Equal Protection of the Laws', *California Law Review* 37 (1949), p. 346.
[46] *F.S. Royster Guano Co. v. Virginia*, 253 U.S. 412, 415 (1919), (Pitney, J., delivering the opinion of the court), emphasis added.

⁴⁷ Note, 'Developments in the Law: Equal Protection', *op. cit.*, p. 1115, emphasis added.
⁴⁸ *Morton v. Mancari*, 417 U.S. 535 (1974).
⁴⁹ Stone, *Human Law . . . , op. cit.*, p. 102, emphasis added.
⁵⁰ *Railway Express Agency v. New York*, 336 U.S. 106, 113 (1949).
⁵¹ This distinction between fundamental notion of equality and derivative 'equality in law' corresponds to Dworkin's distinction between 'treatment as an equal' and 'equal treatment', *op. cit.*, p. 227–228.
⁵² For the distinction between 'respect' and 'praise' regarding distributive justice, see W. G. Runciman, *Sociology in its Place* (Cambridge University Press, 1970), pp. 201–221.

CHAPTER 4

¹ In Chapter 2, Section 2. Note that 'reflective equilibrium' in moral argument has nothing to do with the 'equilibrium of benefits and burdens' that is advanced here as a substantive principle of justice.
² Joel Feinberg, *Doing and Deserving* (Princeton University Press, 1970), p. 93, emphasis added. See also Lars O. Ericsson, *Justice in the Distribution of Economic Resources* (Stockholm: Almqvist & Wiksell, 1976), p. 140.
³ Bruce A. Ackerman, *Social Justice in the Liberal State* (New Haven: Yale University Press, 1980), p. 248.
⁴ See John Rawls, *A Theory of Justice* (Oxford: Clarendon Press, 1972), p. 20.
⁵ *Ibid.*, p. 49.
⁶ See Elaine Walster and G. William Walster, 'Equity and Social Justice', *Journal of Social Issues* 31 (1975), No. 3, pp. 21–43.
⁷ This formula was recently outlined (with respect to desert and need) in an excellent article by Christopher Ake, 'Justice as Equality', *Philosophy and Public Affairs* 5 (1975), pp. 69–90.
⁸ Kurt Baier, *The Moral Point of View* (Ithaca: Cornell University Press, 1958), p. 205.
⁹ Ake, *op. cit.*, p. 72.
¹⁰ See Chapter 2.
¹¹ Subsequent parenthetical references in the text of this chapter are to page numbers of Rawls's *A Theory of Justice, op. cit.*
¹² See Chapter 9.1 below.
¹³ In Chapter 7.3.
¹⁴ Richard A. Posner, *Economic Analysis of Law* (Boston: Little, Brown and Co., 1972), p. 218. See also Norman Daniels, 'Equal Liberty and Unequal Worth of Liberty', in Norman Daniels, ed., *Reading Rawls* (Oxford: Basil Blackwell, 1975), p. 254.
¹⁵ Michael Don Ward, *The Political Economy of Distribution* (New York: Elsevier, 1978), pp. 166–168.
¹⁶ F. A. Hayek, *The Constitution of Liberty* (Chicago: University of Chicago Press, 1960), p. 299.
¹⁷ See also Christine Swanton, 'Is the Difference Principle a Principle of Justice?', *Mind* 9 (1981), pp. 415–421.
¹⁸ See Chapter 9.2 below.

[19] See Chapter 5.2 below.
[20] John Rawls, 'The Basic Structure as Subject', in A. I. Goldman, J. Kim, eds., *Values and Morals* (Dordrecht: D. Reidel, 1978), p. 64.
[21] See also *ibid.*
[22] See, in particular, Tom L. Beauchamp, 'Distributive Justice and the Difference Principle', in H. G. Blocker, E. H. Smith, eds., *John Rawls' Theory of Social Justice* (Athens: Ohio University Press, 1980), pp. 132–161.
[23] Rawls, 'The Basic Structure . . . ', *op. cit.*, p. 47.
[24] *Ibid.*, pp. 65–66.

CHAPTER 5

[1] See Section 4, this Chapter.
[2] Joel Feinberg, *Doing and Deserving* (Princeton: Princeton University Press, 1970), pp. 59–60, n. 8.
[3] David Miller, *Social Justice* (Oxford: Clarendon Press, 1976), p. 89.
[4] See, e.g., Alan Zaitchik, 'On Deserving to Deserve', *Philosophy and Public Affairs* 6 (1977), p. 382.
[5] See John Rawls, *A Theory of Justice* (Oxford: Clarendon Press, 1972), p. 314.
[6] See Chapter 1.3.
[7] J. A. Passmore, 'Civil justice and its rivals', in Eugene Kamenka, Alice Erh-Soon Tay, eds., *Justice* (London: Edward Arnold, 1979), pp. 28–29.
[8] Robert Nozick, *Anarchy, State, and Utopia* (New York: Basic Books, 1974), p. 161.
[9] Feinberg, *op. cit.*, pp. 57–58. See also John Kleinig, *Punishment and Desert* (The Hague: Martinus Nijhoff, 1973), p. 59.
[10] Nozick, *op. cit.*, p. 238.
[11] Milton Friedman, *Free to Choose* (Harmondsworth: Penguin Books, 1979), pp. 167–168.
[12] Nozick, *op. cit.*, p. 238.
[13] Rawls, *op. cit.*, pp. 311–312.
[14] Nozick, *op. cit.*, p. 237.
[15] Alan H. Goldman, *Justice and Reverse Discrimination* (Princeton: Princeton University Press, 1979), p. 12. See also Michael J. Sandel, *Liberalism and the Limits of Justice* (Cambridge: Cambridge University Press, 1982), p. 145.
[16] Goldman, *op. cit.*, pp. 43–44, comp. Nozick, *op. cit.*, p. 237.
[17] Friedrich Hayek, *The Constitution of Liberty* (Chicago: University of Chicago Press, 1960), p. 94.
[18] Friedman, *op. cit.*, p. 169.
[19] Rawls, *op. cit.*, p. 102. See also Albert Weale, *Equality and Social Policy* (London: Routledge & Kegan Paul, 1978), pp. 36–37.
[20] Rawls, *op. cit.*, pp. 311–312.
[21] Friedman, *op. cit.*, p. 168.
[22] *Ibid.*, p. 168.
[23] Rawls, *op. cit.*, p. 101.
[24] Nozick, *op. cit.*, p. 228 (in this phrase, Nozick echoes Rawls's arguments against utilitarianism).

[25] Adam Smith, *An Inquiry into the Nature and Causes of the Wealth of Nations* (London: J. M. Dent, 1929), p. 14.
[26] Anthony T. Kronman, 'Talent Pooling', in J. Roland Pennock, John W. Chapman, eds., *Human Rights, Nomos XXIII* (New York: New York University Press, 1981), p. 66. Kronman notes, however, several practical complications and difficulties in applying the 'common pool' concept to taxation.
[27] Jan Tinbergen, *Income Differences* (Amsterdam: North-Holland Publishing Co., 1975), p. 63.
[28] Charles Fried, *Right and Wrong* (Cambridge, Mass.: Harvard University Press, 1978), pp. 143–150.
[29] *Ibid.*, p. 150.
[30] *Ibid.*, p. 147.
[31] See Chapter 6.
[32] See Frederic Vivian, *Human Freedom and Responsibility* (London: Chatto & Windus, 1964), esp. pp. 127–128.
[33] J. J. C. Smart, 'Free Will, Praise and Blame', in Gerald Dworkin, ed., *Determinism, Free Will, and Moral Responsibility* (Englewood Cliffs: Prentice Hall, 1970), p. 209.
[34] Goldman, *op. cit.*, p. 43.
[35] *Ibid.*, p. 43.
[36] Nozick, *op. cit.*, p. 160.
[37] *Ibid.*, p. 170.
[38] See Eric D'Arcy, *Human Acts* (Oxford: Clarendon Press, 1963), p. 125.
[39] Ake, *op. cit.*, p. 86.
[40] F. A. Hayek, 'The Principles of a Liberal Social Order', *Politico* 31 (1966), p. 611.
[41] There are several studies providing evidence for this statement with respect to different countries. See, for instance, Stefan Nowak, 'Values and Attitudes of the Polish People', *Scientific American* 245 (1981), n. 1, pp. 23–31, esp. pp. 24 and 27–28; Guillermina Jasso and Peter H. Rossi, 'Distributive Justice and Earned Income', *American Sociological Review* 42 (1977), pp. 639–651.
[42] Hayek, 'The Principles...', *op. cit.*, p. 614, emphasis added.
[43] Jan Pen, *Income Distribution* (London: Allen Lane, 1971), p. 97.
[44] Jasso and Rossi, *op. cit.*, p. 649.
[45] Wayne M. Alves and Peter H. Rossi, 'Who Should Get What? Fairness Judgments of the Distribution of Earnings', *American Journal of Sociology* 84 (1978), pp. 541–564.
[46] See Nowak, *op. cit.*
[47] Walter Kaufmann, *Without Guilt and Justice* (New York: Peter H. Wyden, 1973), p. 72.
[48] *Ibid.*, p. 71.
[49] *Ibid.*, p. 74.
[50] *Ibid.*, p. 76.
[51] *Ibid.*, p. 77, emphasis added.
[52] See Edmund L. Pincoffs, 'Are Questions of Desert Decidable?', in J. B. Cederblom and William L. Blizek, eds., *Justice and Punishment* (Cambridge, Mass.: Ballinger, 1977), pp. 75–88.
[53] Miller, *op. cit.*, pp. 112–113.
[54] *Ibid.*, p. 111.
[55] See Section 1 of this Chapter.

NOTES

[56] John Stuart Mill, 'Utilitarianism' in *Utilitarianism; On Liberty; Essay on Bentham*, ed. by Mary Warnock (London: Collins, 1962), pp. 313–314.
[57] See pp. 268–269 below.
[58] Smith, *op. cit.*, p. 89.
[59] *Ibid.*
[60] Emile Benoit-Smullyan, 'Status, Status Types and Status Interrelations', *American Sociological Review* 9 (1944), pp. 151–161.
[61] George Caspar Homans, *Sentiments and Activities* (New York: Free Press of Glencoe, 1962), p. 94.
[62] Stuart Adams, 'Status Congruency as a Variable in Small Group Performance', *Social Forces* 32 (1953), pp. 16–22.
[63] *Ibid.*
[64] The list of rewards, which is referred to by Tumin, includes "those things which contribute to (a) sustenance and comfort, (b) humor and diversion, (c) self-respect and ego expansion" (my footnote – W.S.).
[65] Melvin M. Tumin, 'Some Principles of Stratification: A Critical Analysis', *American Sociological Review* 18 (1953), p. 392.
[66] Wlodzimierz Wesolowski, *Classes, Strata and Power* (London: Routledge & Kegan Paul, 1979), p. 114.
[67] See Edward E. Sampson, 'Studies of Status Congruence', in Leonard Berkowitz, ed., *Advances in Experimental Social Psychology* (New York: Academic Press, 1969), esp. pp. 240–241, 247–248.
[68] See Johan Galtung, 'A Structural Theory of Aggression', *Journal of Peace Research* 1 (1964), pp. 95–119, esp. pp. 98–100.
[69] Table 7.9 in Henry Phelps Brown, *The Inequality of Pay* (Oxford: Oxford University Press, 1977), p. 235.
[70] Feinberg, *op. cit.*, p. 93.
[71] Tumin, *op. cit.*, pp. 390–391.
[72] This argument, in principle, is not applicable to those societies where the education is free.
[73] See Anne L. Kallenberg and Larry J. Griffin, 'Class, Occupation and Inequality in Job Rewards', *American Journal of Sociology* 85 (1980), pp. 731–768, esp. p. 740.
[74] This method is described and critically assessed in Pen, *op. cit.*, pp. 303–304.
[75] S. W. Lerner, J. R. Cable and S. Gupta quoted in Brown, *op. cit.*, pp. 128–129.
[76] Pen, *op. cit.*, pp. 39–40.
[77] Brown, *op. cit.*, p. 129.
[78] Homans, *op. cit.*, p. 92.
[79] See also Norman Daniels, 'Meritocracy', in John Arthur and William H. Shaw, eds., *Justice and Economic Distribution* (Englewood Cliffs: Prentice Hall, 1978), pp. 164–178; Michael Walzer, *Spheres of Justice* (New York: Basic Books, 1983), pp. 135–139.
[80] See Section 1, this chapter.
[81] *Ibid.*
[82] John Hospers, *Human Conduct* (New York: Harcourt, Brace & World, 1961), p. 433. Cf. also Eckhoff, *op. cit.*, p. 229; H. J. McCloskey, *Meta-Ethics and Normative Ethics* (The Hague: M. Nijhoff, 1969), pp. 231–232.
[83] Hayek, 'The Principles...', *op. cit.*, p. 614.

CHAPTER 6

[1] Joel Feinberg, *Doing and Deserving* (Princeton: Princeton University Press, 1970), p. 93, emphasis added.
[2] Charles R. Beitz, 'Economic Rights and Distributive Justice in Developing Societies', *World Politics* 33 (1981), p. 344. See also James S. Fishkin on 'subsistence needs': *Tyranny and Legitimacy* (Baltimore: The Johns Hopkins University Press, 1979), pp. 33–43.
[3] Joel Feinberg, *Social Philosophy* (Englewood Cliffs: Prentice Hall, 1973), p. 111.
[4] James P. Sterba, 'Justice as Desert', *Social Theory and Practice* 3 (1974), p. 109. See also William A. Galston on natural absolute needs: *Justice and the Human Good* (Chicago: The University of Chicago Press, 1980), pp. 163–168.
[5] Rodney Peffer, "A Defense of Rights to Well-Being", *Philosophy and Public Affairs* 8 (1978), p. 80.
[6] S. I. Benn and R. S. Peters, *Social Principles and the Democratic State* (London: George Allen and Unwin, 1959), pp. 145–146.
[7] *Ibid.*, p. 145.
[8] See Graciela Chichilnisky, 'Development Patterns and the International Order', *Journal of International Affairs* 31 (1977), pp. 275–304.
[9] See Scott Gordon, *Welfare, Justice and Freedom* (New York: Columbia University Press, 1980), p. 112–113.
[10] Note, 'Developments in the Law: Equal Protection', *Harvard Law Review* 82 (1969), p. 1169.
[11] Frank I. Michelman, 'In Pursuit of Constitutional Welfare Rights: One View of Rawls' Theory of Justice', *Univ. of Pennsylvania Law Rev.* 121 (1973), p. 980, n. 57.
[12] Charles Frankel, 'Equality of Opportunity', *Ethics* 81 (1971), p. 198.
[13] Robert Nozick, *Anarchy, State, and Utopia* (New York: Basic Books, 1974), p. 234.
[14] See, in particular, Michael Walzer, *Spheres of Justice* (New York: Basic Books, 1983), pp. 86–91. See also Guido Calabresi and Philip Bobbit, *Tragic Choices* (New York: W. W. Norton, 1978), pp. 89–92.
[15] See Thorstein Eckhoff, *Justice* (Rotterdam: Rotterdam University Press, 1974), p. 220.
[16] Kai Nielsen, 'True Needs, Rationality and Emancipation', in Ross Fitzgerald, ed., *Human Needs and Politics* (Sydney: Pergamon Press, 1977), pp. 144–145. On similar problems raised by a Marxist theory of needs, see Wojciech Sadurski, 'To Each According to His (Genuine?) Needs', *Political Theory* 11 (1983), pp. 419–431.
[17] Eckhoff, *op. cit.*, p. 220.
[18] Christian Bay, 'Human Needs and Political Education', in Fitzgerald, *op. cit.*, p. 2.
[19] Nielsen, *op. cit.*, p. 143.
[20] Friedrich A. Hayek, *The Constitution of Liberty* (Chicago: University of Chicago Press, 1960), p. 298.
[21] *Ibid.*, p. 299.
[22] A. H. Maslow, 'A Theory of Human Motivation', *Psychological Review* 50 (1943), p. 394.
[23] Ross Fitzgerald, 'Abraham Maslow's Hierarchy of Needs: An Exposition and Evaluation', in Fitzgerald, *op. cit.*, p. 38.

NOTES   297

24 *Ibid.*, pp. 44–45.
25 See T. D. Campbell, 'Humanity Before Justice', *British Journal of Political Science* 4 (1974), esp. pp. 13–14.
26 Nozick, *op. cit.*, p. 238, footnote omitted.
27 *Ibid.*, p. 238.
28 Ronald Dworkin, *Taking Rights Seriously* (London: Duckworth, 1978), p. 269.
29 *Ibid.*, p. 194. See also L. P. Francis and J. G. Francis, 'Nozick's Theory of Rights: A Critical Assessment', *Western Political Quarterly* 29 (1976), pp. 634–644.
30 Judith Jarvis Thomson, 'Some Ruminations on Rights', *Arizona Law Review* 19 (1977), pp. 45–60.
31 *Ibid.*, p. 48.
32 See Neil MacCormick, *Legal Right and Social Democracy* (Oxford: Clarendon Press, 1982), pp. 212–213.
33 Nozick, *op. cit.*, p. ix.
34 See Les Holborow, 'Human Rights and the Role of the State', in F. C. Hutley, E. Kamenka, A. E.-S. Tay, eds., *Law and the Future of Society* (Wiesbaden: Franz Steiner Verlag, 1979), p. 158. See also H. L. A. Hart, 'Between Utility and Rights', *Columbia Law Review* 79 (1979), pp. 828–846, esp. p. 835.
35 See Charles Fried, *Right and Wrong* (Cambridge, Mass.: Harvard University Press, 1978), p. 111.
36 *Ibid.*, pp. 110–114.
37 See also Henry Shue, *Basic Rights* (Princeton: Princeton University Press, 1980), pp. 38–39.
38 *Ibid.*, pp. 41–46.
39 *Ibid.*, p. 40.
40 See Nozick, *op. cit.*, pp. 28–35.
41 *Ibid.*, pp. 33–34.
42 See Maurice Cranston, *What Are Human Rights?* (London: The Bodley Head, 1973), pp. 66–67.
43 See Julius Stone, 'Approaches to the Notion of International Justice', in Richard Falk, Cyril E. Black, eds., *The Future of the International Legal Order* (Princeton: Princeton University Press, 1969), Vol. 1, esp. pp. 430–460. See also Julius Stone, *Social Dimensions of Law and Justice* (Sydney: Maitland Publications, 1966), pp. 116–117, 796–797; Douglas W. Rae, 'A Principle of Simple Justice', in P. Laslett and J. Fishkin, eds., *Philosophy, Politics and Society*, Fifth Series (New Haven: Yale University Press, 1979), pp. 135–136.
44 Myres McDougal, Harold Lasswell, and W. Michael Reisman, 'The World Constitutive Process of Authoritative Decision', in Falk and Black, *op. cit.*, pp. 73–75.
45 Quincy Wright, 'Law and Politics in the World Community', in George A. Lipsky, ed., *Law and Politics in the World Community* (Berkeley: University of California Press, 1953), p. 6.
46 Richard Falk, 'The Interplay of Westphalia and Charter Conceptions of International Legal Order', in Falk and Black, *op. cit.*, p. 62.
47 McDougal, Lasswell, Reisman, *op. cit.*, p. 73.
48 Stone, 'Approaches . . . ', *op. cit.*, p. 452.
49 Ian Brownlie, *Principles of Public International Law* (Oxford: Clarendon Press, 1973, Second Ed.), p. 253.

⁵⁰ UN General Assembly Resolution 3281 (XXIX) of 12 December 1974, reproduced in *International Legal Materials* 14 (1975), 251.
⁵¹ See Note, 'World Hunger and International Trade: An Analysis and a Proposal for Action', *Yale Law Journal* 84 (1975), pp. 1046–1077. See also Wassily Leontief, 'Natural Resources, Environmental Disruption, and the Future World Economy', *Journal of International Affairs* 31 (1977), pp. 267–274.
⁵² George Modelski, 'World Parties and World Order', in Falk and Black, *op. cit.*, p. 190.
⁵³ Carl P. Wellman, 'Taking Economic Rights Seriously', in *Filosofia del derecho y filosofia economica. Memoria del X Congreso Mundial ordinario de filosofia del derecho y filosofia social* (Mexico: Universidad Nacional Autonoma de Mexico, 1981), Vol. 1, p. 77.
⁵⁴ See e.g. Feinberg, *Social Philosophy, op. cit.*, p. 95.

CHAPTER 7

¹ John Rawls, *A Theory of Justice* (Oxford: Clarendon Press, 1972), p. 351; see also pp. 8–9, 245.
² See Henry Phelps Brown, *The Inequality of Pay* (Oxford: Oxford University Press, 1977), p. 235, table 7.9. For similar conclusions regarding socialist countries, see W. Wesolowski, *Classes, Strata and Power* (London: Routledge & Kegan Paul, 1979), p. 132.
³ See Joseph R. Fiszman, 'Education and Equality of Opportunity in Eastern Europe, with Special Focus on Poland', *Politics and Society* 7 (1977), pp. 297–329. See also note 74, below.
⁴ 'Discrimination for Aborigines – report', *Australian*, 4 Nov. 1981, p. 15.
⁵ See, e.g. W. D. Adams, 'Special Admission Aboriginal Students at the University of New South Wales', *Australian Journal of Education* 24 (1980), pp. 325–326.
⁶ See David Partlett, 'Benign Racial Discrimination: Equality and Aborigines', *Federal Law Review* 10 (1979), p. 268.
⁷ See, for example, Donald Rothchild, 'Kenya's Africanization Program: Priorities of Development and Equity', *American Political Science Review* 64 (1970), pp. 737–753.
⁸ See Samuel M. Witten, ' "Compensatory Discrimination" in India: Affirmative Action as a Means of Combatting Class Inequality', *Columbia Journal of International Law* 21 (1983), pp. 353–388.
⁹ Louis Katzner, 'Is the Favoring of Women and Blacks in Employment and Educational Opportunities Justified?', in Joel Feinberg and Hyman Gross, eds., *Philosophy of Law* (Encino, Calif.: Dickenson, 1975), p. 291.
¹⁰ See Chapter 3.
¹¹ For a description of an 'orientation year' for prospective Aboriginal undergraduates at the Monash University in Melbourne, see 'Aboriginals' tertiary boost', *Australian*, 4 August 1982, p. 10.
¹² For example, the special admissions program in the Medical School of the University of California at Davis, see *Regents of the University of California v. Bakke*, 438 U.S. 265 (1978).
¹³ For example, Harvard College Admissions Program, see *ibid.*, pp. 321–324.

[14] For a discussion, see Vincent Blasi, '*Bakke* as Precedent: Does Mr. Justice Powell Have a Theory?', *California Law Review* 67 (1979), pp. 21–68, esp. p. 66.

[15] For example, Kaiser-Steelworkers training program, see *United Steelworkers v. Weber*, 443 U.S. 193 (1979).

[16] An example of a '*ceteris paribus*' scheme: employment preference for Indians in the Bureau of Indian Affairs, see *Morton v. Mancari*, 417 U.S. 535 (1974).

[17] 438 U.S. 265, 315–319.

[18] *Ibid.*, p. 378.

[19] For a useful discussion of this distinction, see George Sher, 'Reverse Discrimination, the Future and the Past', *Ethics* 90 (1979), pp. 81–87.

[20] Ronald Dworkin, *Taking Rights Seriously* (London: Duckworth, 1978), pp. 232–239.

[21] See, for example, Graham Hughes, *The Conscience of the Courts* (Garden City: Anchor Press, 1975), p. 273; *Califano v. Webster*, 430 U.S. 313, 316–321 (1977).

[22] See D. D. Raphael, *Justice and Liberty* (London: The Athlone Press, 1980), p. 150.

[23] Alan H. Goldman, *Justice and Reverse Discrimination* (Princeton: Princeton University Press, 1979), p. 143.

[24] *Ibid.*, p. 143.

[25] Richard A. Posner, *The Economics of Justice* (Cambridge, Mass.: Harvard University Press, 1981), pp. 368–369.

[26] *Bakke v. Regents of the University of California*, 18 Cal. 3d 34, 62–63 (1976).

[27] See pp. 84–85.

[28] See Nathan Glazer, 'Individual rights against group rights', in Eugene Kamenka and Alice Erh-Soon Tay, eds., *Human Rights* (Melbourne: Edward Arnold, 1978), p. 97.

[29] Goldman, *op. cit.*, p. 144.

[30] *DeFunis v. Odegaard*, 416 U.S. 312, 343 (1974) (Douglas, J., dissenting).

[31] Goldman, *op. cit.*, p. 144.

[32] Martin H. Redish, 'Preferential Law School Admissions and the Equal Protection Clause: An Analysis of the Competing Arguments', *U.C.L.A. Law Review* 22 (1974), p. 368.

[33] Erving Goffman, *Stigma* (Harmondsworth: Penguin Books, 1968), p. 14.

[34] *Ibid.*, p. 15, footnote omitted.

[35] *Ibid.*, p. 149.

[36] James R. Kluegel, Eliot R. Smith, 'Whites' Beliefs about Blacks' Opportunity', *American Sociological Review* 47 (1982), pp. 518–531.

[37] Note, 'Developments in the Law: Equal Protection', *Harvard Law Review* 82 (1969), p. 1113.

[38] See, for example, Thomas Sowell, '*Weber* and *Bakke*, and the Presuppositions of "Affirmative Action"', *Wayne Law Review* 26 (1980), pp. 1309–1336.

[39] Derrick A. Bell, Jr., '*Bakke*, Minority Admissions, and the Usual Price of Racial Remedies', *California Law Review* 67 (1979), p. 18.

[40] Hardy Jones, 'Fairness, Meritocracy, and Reverse Discrimination', *Social Theory and Practice* 4 (1977), p. 224.

[41] Irving Thalberg, 'Themes in the Reverse-Discrimination Debate', *Ethics* 91 (1980), p. 140.

[42] Powell, J., in 438 U.S. at p. 317.

[43] R. Kent Greenawalt, 'The Unresolved Problems of Reverse Discrimination', *California Law Review* 67 (1979), p. 124.

44 See, for example, Lino A. Graglia, 'Special Admission of the "Culturally Deprived" to Law School', *University of Pennsylvania Law Review* 119 (1970), p. 353.
45 Blackmun, J., in 438 U.S. at p. 403.
46 See Bell, *op. cit.*, p. 8; Myrl L. Duncan, 'The Future of Affirmative Action: A Jurisprudential/Legal Critique', *Harvard Civil Rights – Civil Liberties Law Review* 17 (1982), p. 531.
47 *Sweatt v. Painter*, 339 U.S. 629, 634 (1950) (Vinson, C. J.). On the importance of diverse student body, see in particular Powell, J. in 438 U.S. at pp. 311–315; Terrance Sandalow, 'Racial Preferences in Higher Education: Political Responsibility and the Judicial Role', *University of Chicago Law Review* 42 (1975), pp. 653–703, esp. at pp. 686–688.
48 Goldman, *op. cit.*, p. 147.
49 Dworkin, *op. cit.*, p. 227.
50 *Ibid.*, p. 227.
51 Bernard A. O. Williams, 'The Idea of Equality', in Peter Laslett and W. G. Runciman, eds., *Philosophy, Politics and Society*, Second Series (Oxford: Basil Blackwell, 1962), pp. 125–126.
52 *Ibid.*, p. 126. See also a discussion of this example by Judge Mathew in the case before the Supreme Court of India *Kerala v. Thomas*, 1976 A.I.R. (S.C.) 490, 513–515.
53 See, *inter alia*, Tord Höivik, 'Social Inequality – the Main Issues', *Journal of Peace Research* 8 (1971), pp. 119–142, esp. p. 127.
54 This view is widely accepted in American judicial practice. See, *inter alia*, *State of Alabama v. United States*, 304 F. 2d 583, 586 (5th Cir. 1962); *Carter v. Gallagher*, 452 F. 2d 315, 323 (8th Cir. 1971); *Parham v. Southwestern Bell Tel. Co.*, 433 F. 2d 421, 424–426 (8th Cir. 1971).
55 Richard A. Posner, 'The *Bakke* Case and the Future of "Affirmative Action"', *California Law Review* 67 (1979), p. 186.
56 Sowell, *op. cit.*, pp. 1314–1317.
57 *Ibid.*, pp. 1317–1318.
58 438 U.S., at pp. 395–396 (Marshall, J.).
59 See Davis K. Cohen, 'Does IQ Matter?', in Lewis A. Coser and Irving Howe, eds., *The New Conservatives* (New York: Quadrangle, 1973), pp. 212–213.
60 Rawls, *op. cit.*, pp. 100–101.
61 Felix E. Oppenheim, 'Egalitarian Rules of Distribution', *Ethics* 90 (1980), pp. 178–179.
62 Goldman, *op. cit.*, p. 88.
63 *Ibid.*, pp. 76–77.
64 *Kerala v. Thomas*, 1976 A.I.R. (S.C.) 490, 531 (Iyer J.).
65 George Sher, 'Groups and Justice', *Ethics* 87 (1977), p. 176.
66 See Gertrude Ezorsky, 'On "Groups and Justice"', *Ethics* 87 (1977), pp. 182–185.
67 Michael D. Bayles, 'Reparations to Wronged Groups', *Analysis* 33 (1973), p. 184.
68 See Paul W. Taylor, 'Reverse Discrimination and Compensatory Justice', *Analysis* 33 (1973), pp. 172–182; Richard Lichtman, 'The Ethics of Compensatory Justice', *Law in Transition Quarterly* 1 (1964), p. 96.
69 438 U.S. 400 (Marshall, J.).
70 Goldman, *op. cit.*, p. 17.

NOTES 301

[71] James W. Nickel, 'Should Reparations Be to Individuals or to Groups?', *Analysis* **34** (1974), p. 155.
[72] See note 52.
[73] *Griggs v. Duke Power Co.*, 401 U.S. 424 (1971).
[74] *Ibid.*, at p. 432.
[75] *Price v. Civil Service Commission* (1977) 1 W.L.R. 1419.
[76] See, *Inter alia*, Sex Discrimination Act (1975) of South Australia, s.16(3); Race Relations Act (1976) of United Kingdom, s.1(1) (b).
[77] Partlett, *op. cit.*, p. 250.
[78] Posner, *Economics* ... , *op. cit.*, p. 371. See also William T. Blackstone, 'Reverse Discrimination and Compensatory Justice', *Social Theory and Practice* **3** (1975), p. 268.
[79] Jones, *op. cit.*, p. 218.
[80] See Wanda Hajnicz, Krystyna Lubomirska, 'Pod górkę do szkoły', *Polityka* (Warsaw) 28 Feb. 1981.
[81] See Witten, *op. cit.*, pp. 375–380.
[82] 1963 A.I.R. (S.C.) 649.
[83] Goldman, *op. cit.*, p. 6.
[84] See 416 U.S. 312.
[85] See 438 U.S. 265.
[86] Katzner, *op. cit.*, p. 292.
[87] See, for example, Robert Amdur, 'Compensatory Justice: The Question of Costs', *Political Theory* **7** (1979), pp. 229–244; Robert K. Fullinwinder, *The Reverse Discrimination Controversy* (Totowa, N.Y.: Rowman and Littlefield, 1980), p. 66.
[88] Goldman, *op. cit.*, p. 231.
[89] J. A. Passmore, 'Civil justice and its rivals', in Eugene Kamenka, Alice Erh-Soon Tay, eds., *Justice* (London: Edward Arnold, 1979), p. 42.
[90] Daniel P. Moynihan, quoted in Burton M. Leiser, *Liberty, Justice, and Morals* (New York: Macmillan, 1979), p. 337.
[91] Passmore, *op. cit.*, p. 42.
[92] See, for example, Robert L. Simon, 'Individual Rights and "Benign" Discrimination', *Ethics* **90** (1979), pp. 88–97.
[93] See Dworkin, *op. cit.*, p. 225.
[94] See Thomas Nagel, 'Equal Treatment and Compensatory Discrimination', *Philosophy and Public Affairs* **2** (1973), pp. 348–363, esp. p. 361; Richard A. Wasserstrom, 'Racism, Sexism, and Preferential Treatment: An Approach to the Topics', *U.C.L.A. Law Review* **24** (1977), p. 618.
[95] Passmore, *op. cit.*, p. 43.
[96] 438 U.S. 412 (Stevens, J.). See also Leiser, *op. cit.*, p. 335.
[97] 438 U.S. 403 (Blackmun, J.).

CHAPTER 8

[1] John Rawls, *A Theory of Justice* (Oxford: Clarendon Press, 1972), pp. 314–315.
[2] *Ibid.*, p. 314.
[3] For the opposite view, see Michael D. Bayles, 'Character, Purpose, and Criminal Responsibility', *Law and Philosophy* **1** (1982), pp. 5–20. Bayles argues that blame and punishment are not directly for acts but for character traits.

⁴ Brian Barry, 'Reflections on "Justice as Fairness"', in Hugo A. Bedau, ed., *Justice and Equality* (Englewood Cliffs: Prentice-Hall, 1971), p. 110.
⁵ For the findings of a survey which support this assertion, see *ibid.*, pp. 112–113.
⁶ Rawls, *op. cit.*, p. 100, my emphasis, footnote omitted.
⁷ See Sidney Hook, 'In Defense of "Justice"', in E. Kiefer and M. K. Munitz, *Ethics and Social Justice* (Albany: State University of New York Press, 1968), pp. 75–84; for an opposite view, see Walter Kaufmann, 'Doubts about Justice', *ibid.*, pp. 66–73; Edward N. Cahn, *The Sense of Injustice* (New York: New York University Press, 1946), in particular p. 13.
⁸ Rawls, *op. cit.*, pp. 310–315.
⁹ *Ibid.*, p. 101.
¹⁰ *Ibid.*, p. 102.
¹¹ *Ibid.*, p. 311.
¹² For a similar theory of punishment, see in particular Herbert Morris, 'Persons and Punishment', in J. Feinberg and H. Gross, eds. *Philosophy of Law* (Encino: Dickenson, 1975), pp. 572–585, reprinted from *Monist* 52 (1968); Alan Gewirth, *Reason and Morality* (Chicago: University of Chicago Press, 1978), pp. 294–299. See also Kurt Baier, *The Moral Point of View* (Ithaca: Cornell University Press, 1958), pp. 205–206; Jeffrie G. Murphy, *Retribution, Justice and Therapy* (Dordrecht D. Reidel, 1979), p. 77; John Finnis, *Natural Law and Natural Rights* (Oxford: Clarendon Press, 1980), pp. 263–264.
¹³ Richard A. Wasserstrom, 'Punishment', in *Philosophy and Social Issues* (Notre Dame: University of Notre Dame Press, 1980), pp. 143–144.
¹⁴ George P. Fletcher, *Rethinking Criminal Law* (Boston: Little, Brown and Co., 1978), pp. 417–418.
¹⁵ See Alan H. Goldman, 'The Paradox of Punishment', *Philosophy and Public Affairs* 9 (1979), p. 44.
¹⁶ See Wasserstrom, *Punishment, op. cit.*, p. 145.
¹⁷ Goldman, *op. cit.*, p. 44.
¹⁸ For this argument, see Lisa H. Perkins, 'Suggestions for a Justification of a Punishment', *Ethics* 81 (1976), pp. 55–61.
¹⁹ Elaine Walster, G. William Walster, Ellen Berscheid, *Equity: Theory and Research* (Boston: Allyn and Bacon, 1978), p. 65.
²⁰ See Nigel Walker, *Punishment, danger and stigma* (Oxford: Basil Blackwell, 1980), pp. 130–131.
²¹ See Walster, *op. cit.*, pp. 79–81.
²² Alan H. Goldman, 'Toward a New Theory of Punishment', *Law and Philosophy* 1 (1982), p. 61; see also Hugo Adam Bedau, 'Retribution and the Theory of Punishment', *The Journal of Philosophy* 75 (1978), p. 617.
²³ See Gewirth, *op. cit.*, p. 297.
²⁴ See Andrew von Hirsch, *Doing Justice* (New York: Hill and Wang, 1976), pp. 144–145.
²⁵ S. I. Benn, R. S. Peters, *Social Principles and the Democratic State* (London: Allen and Unwin, 1959), p. 175.
²⁶ *Ibid.*, p. 176. See also S. I. Benn, 'Punishment', in *The Encyclopedia of Philosophy*, ed. by Paul Edwards (New York: Macmillan, 1967), vol. 7, p. 30.
²⁷ See pp. 11–14 above.

[28] Anthony M. Quinton, 'On Punishment', in H. B. Acton, ed., *The Philosophy of Punishment* (London: Macmillan, 1973), pp. 58–59.
[29] See, in particular, essays published in Acton, *op. cit.*
[30] Antony Flew, 'The Justification of Punishment', in Acton, *op. cit.*, p. 93.
[31] K. E. Baier, 'Is Punishment Retributive?', in Acton, *op. cit.*, p. 133.
[32] K. G. Armstrong, 'The Retributivist Hits Back', in Acton, *op. cit.*, p. 153. Another version of the same question: "Is it ever justified to make an innocent person suffer in the manner usually prescribed for legal offenders . . . ?", see Sidney Gendin, 'A Plausible Theory of Retribution', *Journal of Value Inquiry* 5 (1970), pp. 9–10.
[33] See H. L. A. Hart, *Punishment . . .*, *op. cit.*, p. 6.
[34] John Kleinig, *Punishment and Desert* (The Hague: Martinus Nijhoff, 1973), p. 13.
[35] Henry Weihofen, 'Retribution Is Obsolete', in C. J. Friedrich, ed., *Responsibility: Nomos III* (New York: Liberal Arts Press, 1960), p. 118.
[36] Walter Kaufmann, *Without Guilt and Justice* (New York: Peter H. Wyden, 1973), p. 57.
[37] *Ibid.*, p. 57.
[38] Gerald Gardiner, 'The Purposes of Criminal Punishment', *Modern Law Review* 21 (1958), pp. 120–121.
[39] See Chapter 1, Section 1.
[40] Weihofen, *op. cit.*, p. 119. But see Graeme R. Newman, *Comparative Deviance* (New York: Elsevier, 1976) about the significant cross-cultural consensus as to the wrongness of particular offences. For similar findings, see also Joseph E. Scott and Fahad Al-Thakeb, 'Perceptions of Deviance Cross-Culturally', in G. R. Newman, ed., *Crime and Deviance: A Comparative Perspective* (Beverly Hills: Sage Publications, 1980).
[41] Weihofen, *op. cit.*, p. 119.
[42] For evidence of such a consensus, see V. Lee Hamilton and Steve Rytina, 'Social Consensus on Norms of Justice: Should the Punishment Fit the Crime?', *American Journal of Sociology* 85 (1980), pp. 1117–1144; R. M. Figlio, 'The Seriousness of Offenses: an Evaluation by Offenders and Non-Offenders', *Journal of Criminal Law, Criminology and Police Science* 58 (1967), pp. 330–337.
[43] Weihofen, *op. cit.*, p. 120.
[44] John P. Conrad, 'Where There's Hope There's Life', in David Fogel, Joe Hudson, eds., *Justice as Fairness: Perspectives on the Justice Model* (Anderson Publishing Co., 1981), pp. 4–5. See also Philip Bean, *Punishment: A Philosophical and Criminological Inquiry* (Oxford: Martin Robertson, 1981), p. 28.
[45] J. R. Lucas, *On Justice* (Oxford: Clarendon Press, 1980), p. 148; A. C. Ewing, *The Morality of Punishment* (Montclair: Patterson Smith, 1970, 1st ed. 1929), p. 30.
[46] See Alwynne Smart, 'Mercy', in Acton, *op. cit.*, pp. 212–228.
[47] See pp. 230–231 above.
[48] See note 54, below.
[49] *Cundy v. Le Cocq* (1884) 13 Q.B.D. 207.
[50] *United States v. Balint*, 258 U.S. 250 (1922).
[51] *Laird v. Dobell* (1906) 1 K.B. 131.
[52] See, for example, H. M. Hart, Jr., 'The Aims of the Criminal Law', *Law and Contemporary Problems* 23 (1958), pp. 422–425; Jerome Hall, *General Principles of Criminal Law* (Indianapolis: Bobbs-Merrill, 1960, 2nd ed.), ch. 10; Glanville Williams, *Criminal Law: The General Part* (London: Stevens, 1961, 2nd ed.), pp. 258–261.

53 This argument is made *implicite* by Benjamin M. Quigg, Comment, *Michigan Law Review* 42 (1944), p. 1106.
54 See Richard Wasserstrom, 'Strict Liability in the Criminal Law', *Stanford Law Review* 12 (1960), pp. 734–740; see also Note, *Law Quarterly Review* 74 (1958), pp. 342–343.
55 George Whitecross Paton, *A Textbook of Jurisprudence* (Oxford: Oxford University Press, 1972, 4th ed.), p. 386. It should be noted, however, that this judgment is made by Paton with reference to minor offences only.
56 *Shevlin-Carpenter Co. v. Minn.*, 218 U.S. 57, 70 (1910).
57 For a similar argument, see Joel Feinberg, *Doing and Deserving* (Princeton: Princeton University Press, 1970), pp. 223–225; Hyman Gross, *A Theory of Criminal Justice* (New York: Oxford University Press, 1979), pp. 358–359; see also *United States v. Dotterweich*, 320 U.S. 277, 281 (1943) (Frankfurter, J.).
58 See Wasserstrom, *Strict Liability . . . op. cit.*, p. 744.
59 *Grannis v. Ordean*, 234 U.S. 385, 394 (1913). See also Gross, *op. cit.*, pp. 357–358.
60 Perhaps the leading exponent of views along these lines is Randy Barnett; see 'Restitution: A New Paradigm of Criminal Justice', *Ethics* 87 (1977), pp. 279–301 and 'The Justice of Restitution', *American Journal of Jurisprudence* 25 (1980), pp. 117–132.
61 James F. Doyle, 'Justice and Legal Punishment', in Acton, *op. cit.*, p. 164.
62 Morris, *op. cit.*, p. 573.
63 *Ibid.*, p. 577.
64 *Ibid.*, p. 579.
65 Quinton, *op. cit.*, p. 57.
66 Gardner argues that in the American criminal law there are instances of waiver of 'the right to be punished'; for example, an offender may accept an executive pardon (see Martin R. Gardner, 'The Right to be Punished – A Suggested Constitutional Theory', *Rutgers Law Review* 33 (1981), pp. 852–853). However, it should be noted that in this situation it is not up to the offender to exercise this waiver. Rather, the availability of the waiver depends on whether or not he is offered this option.
67 Ronald Dworkin, *Taking Rights Seriously* (London: Duckworth, 1978), pp. 92 and 191–192.
68 *Ibid.*, p. 139.
69 Immanuel Kant, *The Philosophy of Law*, trans. by W. Hastie (Edinburgh: T. Clark, 1887), p. 196.
70 Morris, *op. cit.*, p. 574.
71 See also Goldman, *The Paradox . . . , op. cit.*, pp. 54–55.
72 Lord Denning quoted by H. L. A. Hart, *Law, Liberty and Morality* (Oxford: Oxford University Press, 1963), p. 65.
73 H. M. Hart, *The Aims . . . , op. cit.*, p. 405.
74 Neil MacCormick, *H.L.A. Hart* (London: Edward Arnold, 1981), p. 141.
75 For such a definitional suggestion, see in particular Feinberg, *op. cit.*, ch. 5; H. M. Hart, *The Aims . . . , op. cit.*, pp. 404–405; MacCormick, *Legal Right . . . , op. cit.*, pp. 30–31.
76 See MacCormick, *Legal Right . . . , op. cit.*, p. 32.
77 Feinberg, *op. cit.*, p. 114. See also Sir Walter Moberly, *The Ethics of Punishment* (Hamden: Anchor Books), pp. 217–225.
78 See Hart, *Law . . . , op. cit.*, pp. 65–66; Walker, *op. cit.*, pp. 32–33.

79 MacCormick, *Legal Right* . . . , *op. cit.*, pp. 242–243.
80 See Feinberg, *op. cit.*, p. 98; H. M. Hart, *The Aims* . . . , *op. cit.*, p. 405.
81 H. J. McCloskey, 'A Non-Utilitarian Approach to Punishment', in Gertrude Ezorsky, ed., *Philosophical Perspectives on Punishment* (New York: State University of New York Press, 1972), p. 122.
82 Johannes Andenaes, *Punishment and Deterrence* (Ann Arbor: The University of Michigan Press, 1974), pp. 7–8.
83 McCloskey, *op. cit.*, p. 124. See also Igor Primorac, 'Utilitarianism and punishment of the innocent', *Rivista Internazionale di Filosofia del Diritto* 57 (1980), pp. 582–625.
84 See J. J. C. Smart, 'Utilitarianism and Criminal Justice', *Bulletin of the Australian Society of Legal Philosophy*, Special Issue (1981), pp. 16–17. See also T. L. Sprigge, 'A Utilitarian Reply to Dr. McCloskey', *Inquiry* 8 (1965), pp. 272–279.
85 McCloskey, *op. cit.*, p. 125. See also Michael Lesnoff, 'The Justifications of Punishment', *Philosophical Quarterly* 21 (1971), p. 142.
86 Ewing, *op. cit.*, p. 80.
87 See von Hirsch, *op. cit.*, pp. 11–16. See also Abraham S. Blumberg, *Criminal Justice: Issues and Ironies* (New York: New Viewpoints, 1979, 2nd ed.), pp. 327–331.
88 See, in particular, Morris, *op. cit.*
89 Weihofen, *op. cit.*, p. 120.
90 *Ibid.*, p. 120.
91 Evgenii Pashukanis, *Selected Writings on Marxism and Law*, ed. by P. Beirne and R. Sharlet (London: Academic Press, 1980), p. 121.
92 See Herbert L. Packer, *The Limits of the Criminal Sanction* (Stanford: Stanford University Press, 1968), p. 67; D. J. Galligan, 'The return to retribution in penal theory', in C. F. H. Tapper, ed., *Crime, Proof and Punishment* (London: Butterworths, 1981), pp. 158–163.
93 John Rawls, 'Two Concepts of Rules', in Acton, *op. cit.*, pp. 107–108. See also Benn and Peters, *op. cit.*, p. 175; H. L. A. Hart, *Punishment* . . . , *op. cit.*, pp. 1–13.

CHAPTER 9

1 John Rawls, *A Theory of Justice* (Oxford: Clarendon Press, 1972), p. 302.
2 See, *inter alia*, J. J. C. Smart, 'Distributive Justice and Utilitarianism', in John Arthur and William H. Shaw, eds., *Justice and Economic Distribution* (Englewood Cliffs: Prentice-Hall, 1978), esp. pp. 106–107.
3 Rawls, *op. cit.*, p. 244.
4 *Ibid.*, p. 9.
5 *Ibid.*, p. 244, see also pp. 203–204.
6 Gerald C. MacCallum, Jr., 'Negative and Positive Freedom', *Philosophical Review* 76 (1967), pp. 312–324.
7 See Norman Daniels, 'Equal Liberty and Unequal Worth of Liberty', in Norman Daniels, ed., *Reading Rawls* (Oxford: Basil Blackwell, 1975), p. 261.
8 See, in particular Isaiah Berlin, 'Two Concepts of Liberty', in his *Four Essays on Liberty* (Oxford: Oxford University Press, 1969); Joel Feinberg, 'The Idea of a Free Man', in his *Rights, Justice, and the Bounds of Liberty* (Princeton: Princeton University Press, 1980), pp. 3–9; Neil MacCormick, *Legal Right and Social Democracy* (Oxford: Clarendon Press, 1982), pp. 9–12, 38–43.

[9] For a thoughful criticism of this distinction, see Daniels, *op. cit.*; see also Kai Nielsen, 'Radical Egalitarian Justice: Justice as Equality', *Social Theory and Practice* 5 (1979), p. 216.
[10] Rawls, *op. cit.*, p. 204.
[11] Brian Barry, *Political Argument* (London: Routledge and Kegan Paul, 1963), pp. 43–44.
[12] See Chapter 5 above.
[13] John Stuart Mill, 'Utilitarianism', in *Utilitarianism, On Liberty, Essay on Bentham*, ed. by Mary Warnock (London: Collins, 1962), p. 320.
[14] *Ibid.*, p. 314.
[15] *Ibid.*, p. 315.
[16] *Ibid.*, p. 315.
[17] Smart, *op. cit.*, p. 104, footnote omitted.
[18] *Ibid.*, p. 105, footnote omitted.
[19] Lauchlan Chipman, 'Equality Before (and After) the Law', *Quadrant*, March 1980, p. 48.
[20] Alan H. Goldman, *Justice and Reverse Discrimination* (Princeton: Princeton University Press, 1979), p. 42.
[21] See John Kleinig, *Punishment and Desert* (The Hague: Martinus A. Nijhoff, 1973), pp. 86–87, who tries to defend 'practicality' as an element of justice in law.
[22] See Thomas Hobbes, *Leviathan*, ed. by C. B. Macpherson (Harmondsworth: Penguin, 1981, 1st ed. 1651), p. 388.
[23] *Hirabayashi v. United States*, 320 U.S. 81 (1943).
[24] *Korematsu v. United States*, 323 U.S. 214 (1944).
[25] 320 U.S. 81, 107 (Douglas, J., concurring).
[26] 323 U.S. 214, 216 (Black, J., delivering the opinion of the Court).
[27] *Ibid.*, p. 223.
[28] *Ibid.*, p. 244 (Jackson, J., concurring).
[29] *Ibid.*, p. 244.
[30] *Ibid.*, p. 246.
[31] Melvin J. Lerner, *The Belief in a Just World* (New York and London: Plenum Press, 1980).
[32] See Jennifer L. Hochschild, *What's Fair? American Beliefs about Distributive Justice* (Cambridge, Mass.: Harvard University Press, 1981). One of her respondents, 'Bruce', believes that "the pay structure in the ideal society would 'be very concerned about skill, contribution, risk and effort.' Nurses should earn more than performers. Boring jobs should have high pay and short hours; perhaps 'the more interesting, exciting the job is, the less you ought to be paid.'" (p. 41).
[33] Michael Walzer, 'Philosophy and Democracy', *Political Theory* 9 (1981), p. 393. From this description it does not follow that Walzer advocates this view.
[34] John Rawls, 'Kantian Constructivism in Moral Theory', *Journal of Philosophy* 77 (1980), p. 518.
[35] W. D. Ross, *The Right and the Good* (Oxford: Clarendon Press, 1930), p. 156.
[36] See Rawls, *A Theory ..., op. cit.*, pp. 42–43.
[37] See Scott Gordon, *Welfare, Justice, and Freedom* (New York: Columbia University Press, 1980), pp. 153–189.

[38] Isaiah Berlin, *Four Essays on Liberty* (London: Oxford University Press, 1969), p. 171.
[39] *Ibid.*, pp. 167–172.
[40] James S. Fishkin, *Justice, Equal Opportunity, and the Family* (New Haven: Yale University Press, 1983), p. 193.
[41] *Ibid.*
[42] Rawls, *A Theory . . . , op. cit.*, pp. 126–128.
[43] David Hume, *A Treatise of Human Nature*, ed. by P. S. Ardall (London: Fontana, 1972), Bk III, Part II, Section II, esp. p. 224.
[44] William A. Galston, *Justice and the Human Good* (Chicago: The University of Chicago Press, 1980), p. 6, see also pp. 116–120.
[45] What we are interested in, is not whether the hypothesis of abundance is realistic but whether abundance cancels the relevance of justice talk.
[46] *The Mahavamsa or the Great Chronicle of Ceylon*, trans. by Wilhelm Geiger (London: Oxford University Press, 1934), p. 199. I am grateful to Prof. C. G. Weeramantry for directing my attention to this text.

SELECTED BIBLIOGRAPHY

Ackerman, B. A.: 1980, *Social Justice in the Liberal State*, Yale University Press, New Haven.
Acton, H. B. (ed.): 1973, *The Philosophy of Punishment*, Macmillan, London.
Ake, C.: 1975, 'Justice as Equality', *Philosophy and Public Affairs* 5, pp. 69–90.
Alves, W. M. and P. H. Rossi: 1978, 'Who Should Get What? Fairness Judgments of the Distribution of Earnings', *American Journal of Sociology* 84, pp. 541–564.
Amdur, R.: 1979, 'Compensatory Justice: The Question of Costs', *Political Theory* 7, pp. 229–244.
Andenaes, J.: 1974, *Punishment and Deterrence*, The University of Michigan Press, Ann Arbor.
Armstrong, K. G.: 1973, 'The Retributivist Hits Back', in H. B. Acton (ed.), *The Philosophy of Punishment*, Macmillan, London, pp. 138–158.
Arthur, J. and W. H. Shaw (eds.): 1978, *Justice and Economic Distribution*, Prentice-Hall, Englewood Cliffs.
Baier, K.: 1958, *The Moral Point of View*, Cornell University Press, Ithaca.
Baier, K. E.: 1973, 'Is Punishment Retributive?', in H. B. Acton (ed.), *The Philosophy of Punishment*, Macmillan, London, pp. 130–137.
Barnett, R. A.: 1980, 'The Justice of Restitution', *American Journal of Jurisprudence* 25, pp. 117–132.
Barnett, R. A.: 1977, 'Restitution: A New Paradigm of Criminal Justice', *Ethics* 87, pp. 279–301.
Barry, B.: 1965, *Political Argument*, Routledge and Kegan Paul, London.
Barry B.: 1967, 'Justice and the Common Good', in A. Quinton (ed.), *Political Philosophy*, Oxford University Press, Oxford, pp. 189–193.
Barry B.: 1971, 'Reflections on "Justice as Fairness"', in H. A. Bedau (ed.), *Justice and Equality*, Prentice-Hall, Englewood Cliffs, pp. 103–115.
Barry B.: 1973, *The Liberal Theory of Justice*, Clarendon Press, Oxford.
Bayles, M. D.: 1973, 'Reparations to Wronged Groups', *Analysis* 33, pp. 182–184.
Beans, P.: 1981, *Punishment: A Philosophical and Criminological Inquiry*, Martin Robertson, Oxford.
Beauchamp, T. L.: 1980, 'Distributive Justice and the Difference Principle', in H. G. Blocker and E. H. Smith (eds.), *John Rawls' Theory of Social Justice*, Ohio University Press, Athens, pp. 132–161.
Bedau, H. A. (ed.): 1971, *Justice and Equality*, Prentice-Hall, Englewood Cliffs.
Bedau, H. A.: 1978, 'Retribution and the Theory of Punishment', *Journal of Philosophy* 75, pp. 601–620.
Beitz, C. R.: 1975, 'Justice and International Relations', *Philosophy and Public Affairs* 4, pp. 360–389.
Beitz, C. R.: 1981, 'Economic Rights and Distributive Justice in Developing Societies', *World Politics* 33, pp. 321–346.

Benn, S. I. and R. S. Peters: 1959, *Social Principles and the Democratic State*, George Allen and Unwin, London.
Benn, S. I.: 1967, 'Egalitarianism and the Equal Consideration of Interests', in J. R. Pennock and J. W. Chapman (eds.), *Equality: Nomos IX*, Atherton Press, New York, pp. 61–78.
Berlin, I.: 1969, *Four Essays on Liberty*, Oxford University Press, London.
Blackstone, W. T.: 1975, 'Reverse Discrimination and Compensatory Justice', *Social Theory and Practice* 3, pp. 253–288.
Blocker, H. G. and E. H. Smith (eds.): 1980, *John Rawls' Theory of Social Justice*, Ohio University Press, Athens.
Boudon, R.: 1973, *L'inégalité des chances*, Librairie Armand Colin, Paris.
Brandt, R. B.: 1959, *Ethical Theory*, Prentice-Hall, Englewood Cliffs.
Brandt, R. B. (ed.): 1962, *Social Justice*, Prentice-Hall, Englewood Cliffs.
Brecht, A.: 1970, *Political Theory*, Princeton University Press, Princeton.
Brown, H. P.: 1977, *The Inequality of Pay*, Oxford University Press, Oxford.
Buchanan, J. M.: 1975, *The Limits of Liberty*, The University of Chicago Press, Chicago.
Cahn, E. N.: 1949, *The Sense of Injustice*, New York University Press, New York.
Calabresi, G. and P. Bobbit: 1978, *Tragic Choices*, W. W. Norton, New York.
Campbell, T. D.: 1974, 'Humanity before Justice', *British Journal of Political Science* 4, pp. 1–16.
Cederblom, J. B. and W. L. Blizek (eds.): 1977, *Justice and Punishment*, Ballinger, Cambridge.
Chipman, L.: 1980, 'Equality Before (and After) the Law', *Quadrant*, March, pp. 46–51.
Cottingham, J.: 1979, 'Varieties of Retribution', *Philosophical Quarterly* 29, pp. 238–246.
Cranston, M.: 1973, *What Are Human Rights?*, The Bodley Head, London.
Daniels, N. (ed.): 1975, *Reading Rawls*, Basil Blackwell, Oxford.
Daniels, N.: 1978, 'Meritocracy', in J. Arthur and W. H. Shaw (eds.), *Justice and Economic Distribution*, Prentice-Hall, Englewood Cliffs, pp. 164–178.
D'Arcy, E.: 1963, *Human Acts*, Clarendon Press, Oxford.
Dick, J. C.: 1975, 'How to Justify a Distribution of Earnings', *Philosophy and Public Affairs* 4, pp. 248–272.
Doyle, J. F.: 1973, 'Justice and Legal Punishment', in H. B. Acton (ed.), *The Philosophy of Punishment*, Macmillan, London, pp. 159–171.
Duncan, M. L.: 1982, 'The Future of Affirmative Action: A Jurisprudential/Legal Critique', *Harvard Civil Rights – Civil Liberties Law Review* 17, pp. 503–553.
Dupréel, E.: 1967, *Traité de morale*, Vol. 2, Presses Universitaire de Bruxelles, Bruxelles.
Dworkin, R.: 1975, 'The Original Position', in N. Daniels (ed.), *Reading Rawls*, Basil Blackwell, Oxford, pp. 16–53.
Dworkin, R.: 1978, *Taking Rights Seriously*, Duckworth, London, 2nd ed.
Dworkin, R.: 1981, 'What Is Equality?', *Philosophy and Public Affairs* 10, pp. 185–246, 283–345.
Dworkin, R.: 1982, ' "Natural" Law Revisited', *University of Florida Law Review* 34, pp. 165–188.
Eckhoff, T.: 1974, *Justice. Its Determinants in Social Interaction*, Rotterdam University Press, Rotterdam.

SELECTED BIBLIOGRAPHY

Ellinghaus, M. P.: 1969, 'In Defense of Unconscionability', *Yale Law Journal* **78**, pp. 757–815.
Epstein, R. E.: 1975, 'Unconscionability: A Critical Reappraisal', *Journal of Law and Economics* **18**, pp. 293–315.
Ericsson, L. O.: 1976, *Justice in the Distribution of Economic Resources*, Almqvist and Wiksell International, Stockholm.
Ewing, A. C.: 1970, *The Morality of Punishment*, Patterson Smith, Montclair, 2nd ed.
Ezorsky, G. (ed.): 1972, *Philosophical Perspectives on Punishment*, State University of New York Press, New York.
Ezorsky, G.: 1977, 'On "Groups and Justice"', *Ethics* **87**, pp. 182–185.
Falk, R. and C. Black (eds.): 1969, *The Future of the International Legal Order*, Vol. 1, Princeton University Press, Princeton.
Feinberg, J.: 1970, *Doing and Deserving*, Princeton University Press, Princeton.
Feinberg, J.: 1973, *Social Philosophy*, Prentice-Hall, Englewood Cliffs.
Feinberg, J.: 1980, *Rights, Justice, and the Bounds of Liberty*, Princeton University Press, Princeton.
Finnis, J.: 1980, *Natural Law and Natural Rights*, Clarendon Press, Oxford.
Firth, R.: 1952, 'Ethical Absolutism and the Ideal Observer', *Philosophy and Phenomenological Research* **12**, pp. 317–345.
Fishkin, J. S.: 1979, *Tyranny and Legitimacy*, The Johns Hopkins University Press, Baltimore.
Fishkin, J. S.: 1983, *Justice, Equal Opportunity, and the Family*, Yale University Press, New Haven.
Fitzgerald, R. (ed.): 1977, *Human Needs and Politics*, Pergamon Press, Sydney.
Flathman, R. E.: 1967, 'Equality and Generalization: A Formal Analysis', in J. R. Pennock and J. W. Chapman (eds.), *Equality: Nomos IX*, Atherton Press, New York, pp. 38–60.
Fletcher, G. P.: 1978, *Rethinking Criminal Law*, Little, Brown and Company, Boston.
Flew, A.: 1973, 'The Justification of Punishment', in H. B. Acton (ed.), *The Philosophy of Punishment*, Macmillan, London, pp. 83–104.
Francis, L. P. and J. G. Francis: 1976, 'Nozick's Theory of Rights: A Critical Assessment', *Western Political Quarterly* **29**, pp. 634–644.
Frankel, C.: 1971, 'Equality of Opportunity', *Ethics* **81**, pp. 191–211.
Frankena, W. K.: 1962, 'The Concept of Social Justice', in R. B. Brandt (ed.), *Social Justice*, Prentice-Hall, Englewood Cliffs, pp. 1–29.
Frankena, W. K.: 1963, *Ethics*, Prentice-Hall, Englewood Cliffs.
Fried, C.: 1978, *Right and Wrong*, Harvard University Press, Cambridge.
Friedman, M.: 1979, *Free to Choose*, Penguin Books, Harmondsworth.
Friedrich, C. J. and J. W. Chapman (eds.): 1963, *Justice: Nomos VI*, Atherton Press, New York.
Friedrich, C. J.: 1963, 'Justice: The Just Political Act', in C. J. Friedrich and J. W. Chapman (eds.), *Justice: Nomos VI*, Atherton Press, New York, pp. 24–43.
Fuller, L. L.: 1972, *The Morality of Law*, Yale University Press, New Haven, 2nd ed.
Fullinwinder, R. K.: 1980, *The Reverse Discrimination Controversy*, Rowman and Littlefield, Totowa.
Gahringer, R. A.: 1979, 'Race and Class: The Basic Issue of the Bakke Case', *Ethics* **90**, pp. 97–114.

Galligan, D. J.: 1981, 'The return to retribution in penal theory', in C. F. H. Tapper (ed.), *Crime, Proof and Punishment*, Butterworths, London, pp. 144–171.
Galston, W. A.: 1980, *Justice and the Human Good*, The University of Chicago Press, Chicago.
Gardner, M. R.: 1981, 'The Right to Be Punished – A Suggested Constitutional Theory', *Rutgers Law Review* 33, pp. 838–864.
Gewirth, A.: 1978, *Reason and Morality*, The University of Chicago Press, Chicago.
Glazer, N.: 1978, 'Individual Rights against Group Rights', in E. Kamenka and A. Tay (eds.), *Human Rights*, Edward Arnold, Melbourne, pp. 87–103.
Goffman, E.: 1968, *Stigma*, Penguin Books, Harmondsworth.
Goldman, A. I. and J. Kim (eds.): 1978, *Values and Morals*, D. Reidel, Dordrecht.
Goldman, A. H.: 1979, *Justice and Reverse Discrimination*, Princeton University Press, Princeton.
Goldman, A. H.: 1979, 'The Paradox of Punishment', *Philosophy and Public Affairs* 9, pp. 42–58.
Goldman, A. H.: 1982, 'Toward a New Theory of Punishment', *Law and Philosophy* 1, pp. 57–76.
Gordley, J.: 1981, 'Equality in Exchange', *California Law Review* 69, pp. 1587–1656.
Gordon, S.: 1980, *Welfare, Justice, and Freedom*, Columbia University Press, New York.
Greenawalt, R. K.: 1979, 'The Unresolved Problems of Reverse Discrimination', *California Law Review* 67, pp. 87–130.
Grey, T. C.: 1976, 'Property and Need: The Welfare State and Theories of Distributive Justice', *Stanford Law Review* 28, pp. 877–902.
Gross, H.: 1979, *A Theory of Criminal Justice*, Oxford University Press, New York.
Hamilton, V. L. and S. Rytina: 1980, 'Social Consensus on Norms of Justice: Should the Punishment Fit the Crime?', *American Journal of Sociology* 85, pp. 1117–1144.
Hare, R. M.: 1975, 'Rawls' Theory of Justice', in N. Daniels (ed.), *Reading Rawls*, Basil Blackwell, Oxford, pp. 81–107.
Harrison, J.: 1971, *Our Knowledge of Right and Wrong*, George Allen and Unwin, London.
Hart, H. L. A.: 1961, *The Concept of Law*, Clarendon Press, Oxford.
Hart, H. L. A.: 1968, *Punishment and Responsibility*, Clarendon Press, Oxford.
Hart, H. L. A.: 1975, 'Rawls on Liberty and Its Priority', in N. Daniels (ed.), *Reading Rawls*, Basil Blackwell, Oxford, pp. 230–253.
Hart, H. L. A.: 1979, 'Between Utility and Rights', *Columbia Law Review* 79, pp. 828–846.
Hayek, F. A.: 1960, *The Constitution of Liberty*, The University of Chicago Press, Chicago.
Hayek, F. A.: 1966, 'The Principles of a Liberal Social Order', *Politico* 31, pp. 601–617.
Hayek, F. A.: 1976, *Law, Legislation and Liberty*, Vol. 2, Routledge and Kegan Paul, London.
Hayek, F. A.: 1978, *New Studies in Philosophy, Politics, Economics and the History of Ideas*, Routledge and Kegan Paul, London.
Hochschild, J. L.: 1981, *What's Fair? American Beliefs about Distributive Justice*, Harvard University Press, Cambridge.
Homans, G. C.: 1962, *Sentiments and Activities*, Free Press of Glencoe, New York.

Honoré, A. M.: 1962, 'Social Justice', *McGill Law Journal* **8**, pp. 77–105.
Hook, S.: 1968, 'In Defense of "Justice" ', in H. E. Kiefer and M. K. Munitz (eds.), *Ethics and Social Justice*, State University of New York Press, Albany, pp. 75–84.
Hospers, J.: 1961, *Human Conduct*, Harcourt, Brace and World, New York.
Hughes, G.: 1975, *The Conscience of the Courts*, Anchor Press, Garden City.
Jaggar, A.: 1977, 'Relaxing the Limits on Preferential Treatment', *Social Theory and Practice* **4**, pp. 227–235.
Jasso, G. and P. H. Rossi: 1977, 'Distributive Justice and Earned Income', *American Sociological Review* **42**, pp. 639–651.
Jenkins, I.: 1963, 'Justice as Ideal and Ideology', in C. J. Friedrich and J. W. Chapman (eds.), *Justice: Nomos VI*, Atherton Press, New York, pp. 191–228.
Jenkins, I.: 1980, *Social Order and the Limits of Law*, Princeton University Press, Princeton.
Jones, H.: 1977, 'Fairness, Meritocracy, and Reverse Discrimination', *Social Theory and Practice* **4**, pp. 211–226.
Kallenberg, A. L. and L. J. Griffin: 1980, 'Class, Occupation and Inequality in Job Rewards', *American Journal of Sociology* **85**, pp. 731–768.
Kamenka, E. and Tay, A. (eds.): 1979, *Justice*, Edward Arnold, London.
Karniol, R. and D. T. Miller: 1981, 'Morality and the Development of Conceptions of Justice', in M. J. Lerner and S. C. Lerner (eds.), *The Justice Motive in Social Behavior*, Plenum Press, New York, pp. 73–90.
Katzner, L.: 1975, 'Is the Favoring of Women and Blacks in Employment and Educational Opportunities Justified?', in J. Feinberg and H. Gross (eds.), *Philosophy of Law*, Dickenson, Encino, pp. 291–296.
Kaufmann, W.: 1968, 'Doubts about Justice', in E. Kiefer and M. K. Munitz (eds.), *Ethics and Social Justice*, State University of New York Press, Albany, pp. 66–73.
Kaufmann, W.: 1973, *Without Guilt and Justice*, Peter H. Wyden, New York.
Kelsen, H.: 1971, *What Is Justice?*, University of California Press, Berkeley.
Kiefer, H. E. and M. K. Munitz (eds.): 1968, *Ethics and Social Justice*, State University of New York Press, Albany.
Kleinig, J.: 1973, *Punishment and Desert*, Martinus Nijhoff, The Hague.
Kleinig, J.: 1976, 'Good Samaritanism', *Philosophy and Public Affairs* **5**, pp. 382–407.
Kronman, A. T.: 1980, 'Contract Law and Distributive Justice', *Yale Law Journal* **89**, pp. 472–511.
Kronman, A. T.: 1981, 'Talent Pooling', in J. R. Pennock and J. W. Chapman (eds.), *Human Rights: Nomos XXIII*, New York University Press, New York, pp. 58–79.
Leff, A. A.: 1970, 'Unconscionability and the Crowd — Consumers and the Common Law Tradition', *University of Pittsburgh Law Review* **31**, pp. 349–358.
Leiser, B. M.: 1979, *Liberty, Justice, and Morals*, Macmillan, New York.
Lerner, M. J.: 1980, *The Belief in a Just World*, Plenum Press, New York.
Lerner, M. J. and S. C. Lerner (eds.): 1981, *The Justice Motive in Human Behavior*, Plenum Press, New York.
Lesnoff, M.: 1971, 'Two Justifications of Punishment', *Philosophical Quarterly* **21**, pp. 141–148.
Lichtmann, R.: 1964, 'The Ethics of Compensatory Justice', *Law in Transition Quarterly* **1**, pp. 76–103.
Lucas, J. R.: 1980, *On Justice*, Clarendon Press, Oxford.

MacCallum, G. C. Jr.: 1967, 'Negative and Positive Freedom', *Philosophical Review* **76**, pp. 312–324.
McCloskey, H. J.: 1969, *Meta-Ethics and Normative Ethics*, Martinus Nijhoff, The Hague.
McCloskey, H. J.: 1972, 'A Non-Utilitarian Approach to Punishment', in G. Ezorsky (ed.), *Philosophical Perspectives on Punishment*, State University of New York Press, New York, pp. 119–134.
MacCormick, N.: 1981, *H. L. A. Hart*, Edward Arnold, London.
MacCormick, N.: 1982, *Legal Rights and Social Democracy*, Clarendon Press, Oxford.
Marshall, G.: 1967, 'Notes on the Rule of Equal Law', in J. R. Pennock and J. W. Chapman (eds.), *Equality: Nomos IX*, Atherton Press, New York, pp. 261–276.
Michelman, F. I.: 1973, 'In Pursuit of Constitutional Welfare Rights: One View of Rawls' Theory of Justice', *University of Pennsylvania Law Review* **121**, pp. 962–1019.
Miller, D.: 1976, *Social Justice*, Clarendon Press, Oxford.
Montague, P.: 1980, 'Comparative and Non-Comparative Justice', *Philosophical Quarterly* **30**, pp. 131–140.
Morris, C.: 1963, 'Law, Justice and the Public's Aspirations', in C. J. Friedrich and J. W. Chapman (eds.), *Justice: Nomos VI*, Atherton Press, New York, pp. 170–191.
Morris, H.: 1975, 'Persons and Punishment', in J. Feinberg and H. Gross (eds.), *Philosophy of Law*, Dickenson, Encino, pp. 572–584.
Murphy, J. G.: 1979, *Retribution, Justice, and Therapy*, D. Reidel, Dordrecht.
Murray, J. E.: 1969, 'Unconscionability: Unconscionability', *University of Pittsburgh Law Review* **31**, pp. 1–80.
Nagel, T.: 1973, 'Equal Treatment and Compensatory Discrimination', *Philosophy and Public Affairs* **2**, pp. 340–363.
Nelson, W. M.: 1974, 'Special Rights, General Rights, and Social Justice', *Philosophy and Public Affairs* **3**, pp. 410–430.
Nelson, W.: 1980, 'The Very Idea of Pure Procedural Justice', *Ethics* **90**, pp. 502–511.
Nicholson, P. P.: 1974, 'The Internal Morality of Law: Fuller and His Critics', *Ethics* **84**, pp. 307–326.
Nickel, J. W.: 1972, 'Discrimination and Morally Relevant Characteristics', *Analysis* **32**, pp. 113–114.
Nickel, J. W.: 1974, 'Should Reparations Be to Individuals or to Groups?', *Analysis* **34**, pp. 154–160.
Nielsen, K.: 1979, 'Radical Egalitarian Justice: Justice as Equality', *Social Theory and Practice* **5**, pp. 209–226.
Note: 1969, 'Developments in the Law: Equal Protection', *Harvard Law Review* **82**, pp. 1065–1192.
Nozick, R.: 1974, *Anarchy, State, and Utopia*, Basic Books, New York.
Oppenheim, F. E.: 1980, 'Egalitarian Rules of Distribution', *Ethics* **90**, pp. 164–179.
Packer, H. L.: 1968, *The Limits of the Criminal Sanction*, Stanford University Press, Stanford.
Partlett, D.: 1979, 'Benign Racial Discrimination: Equality and Aborigines', *Federal Law Review* **10**, pp. 238–286.
Passmore, J. A.: 1979, 'Civil Justice and Its Rivals', in E. Kamenka and A. Tay (eds.), *Justice*, Edward Arnold, London, pp. 25–49.

Peffer, R.: 1978, 'A Defense of Rights to Well-Being', *Philosophy and Public Affairs* 8, pp. 65–87.
Pen, J.: 1971, *Income Distribution*, Allen Lane, London.
Pennock, J. R. and J. W. Chapman (eds.): 1967, *Equality: Nomos IX*, Atherton Press, New York.
Pennock, J. R. and J. W. Chapman (eds.): 1981, *Human Rights: Nomos XXIII*, New York University Press, New York.
Pennock, J. R. and J. W. Chapman (eds.): 1982, *Ethics, Economics, and the Law: Nomos XXIV*, New York University Press, New York.
Perelman, C.: 1963, *The Idea of Justice and the Problem of Argument*, Routledge and Kegan Paul, London.
Perkins, L. H.: 1976, 'Suggestions for a Justification of a Punishment', *Ethics* 81, pp. 55–61.
Pettit, P.: 1980, *Judging Justice*, Routledge and Kegan Paul, London.
Phillips, D. L.: 1979, *Equality, Justice, and Rectification*, Academic Press, London.
Pincoffs, E. L.: 1977, 'Are Questions of Desert Decidable?', in J. B. Cederblom and W. L. Blizek (eds.), *Justice and Punishment*, Ballinger, Cambridge, pp. 75–88.
Posner, R. A.: 1972, *Economic Analysis of Law*, Little, Brown and Company, Boston.
Posner, R. A.: 1981, *The Economics of Justice*, Harvard University Press, Cambridge.
Primorac, I.: 1980, 'Utilitarianism and Punishment of the Innocent', *Rivista Internazionale di Filosofia del Diritto* 57, pp. 582–625.
Quinton, A. M.: 1973, 'On Punishment', in H. B. Acton (ed.), *The Philosophy of Punishment*, Macmillan, London, pp. 55–64.
Rachels, J.: 1978, 'What People Deserve', in J. Arthur and W. H. Shaw (eds.), *Justice and Economic Distribution*, Prentice-Hall, Englewood Cliffs, pp. 150–163.
Rae, D. W.: 1979, 'A Principle of Simple Justice', in P. Laslett and J. Fishkin (eds.), *Philosophy, Politics and Society*, Fifth Series, Basil Blackwell, Oxford, pp. 134–154.
Raphael, D. D.: 1946, 'Equality and Equity', *Philosophy* 21, pp. 118–132.
Raphael, D. D.: 1980, *Justice and Liberty*, The Athlone Press, London.
Rawls, J.: 1972, *A Theory of Justice*, Clarendon Press, Oxford.
Rawls, J.: 1973, 'Two Concepts of Rules', in H. B. Acton (ed.), *The Philosophy of Punishment*, Macmillan, London, pp. 105–114.
Rawls, J.: 1978, 'The Basic Structure as Subject', in A. I. Goldman and J. Kim (eds.), *Values and Morals*, D. Reidel, Dordrecht, pp. 47–71.
Rawls, J.: 1980, 'Kantian Constructivism in Moral Theory', *Journal of Philosophy* 77, pp. 515–571.
Redish, M. H.: 1974, 'Preferential Law School Admissions and the Equal Protection Clause: An Analysis of the Competing Arguments', *University of California Law Review* 22, pp. 343–400.
Rescher, N.: 1966, *Distributive Justice*, Bobbs-Merril, Indianapolis.
Resnick, D.: 1977, 'Due Process and Procedural Justice', in J. R. Pennock and J. W. Chapman (eds.), *Due Process: Nomos XVIII*, New York University Press, New York, pp. 206–228.
Richards, D. A. J.: 1982, 'International Distributive Justice', in J. R. Pennock and J. W. Chapman (eds.), *Ethics, Economics, and the Law: Nomos XXIV*, New York University Press, New York, pp. 275–302.
Ross, A.: 1958, *On Law and Justice*, Stevens and Sons, London.

Ross, W. D.: 1930, *The Right and the Good*, Clarendon Press, Oxford.
Runciman, W. G.: 1966, *Relative Deprivation and Social Justice*, Routledge and Kegan Paul, London.
Runciman, W. G.: 1970, *Sociology in Its Place*, Cambridge University Press, Cambridge.
Runciman, W. G.: 1978, 'Processes, End-States and Social Justice', *Philosophical Quarterly* 28, pp. 37–45.
Sadurski, W.: 1983, 'Non-Comparative Justice Revisited', *Archiv für Rechts- und Sozialphilosophie* 69, pp. 504–514.
Sadurski, W.: 1983, 'To Each According to His (Genuine?) Needs', *Political Theory* 11, pp. 419–432.
Sandalow, T.: 1975, 'Racial Preferences in Higher Education: Political Responsibility and the Judicial Role', *University of Chicago Law Review* 42, pp. 653–703.
Sandel, M. J.: 1982, *Liberalism and the Limits of Justice*, Cambridge University Press, Cambridge.
Sher, G.: 1977, 'Groups and Justice', *Ethics* 87, pp. 174–181.
Sher, G.: 1979, 'Effort, Ability, and Personal Desert', *Philosophy and Public Affairs* 8, pp. 361–376.
Sher, G.: 1979, 'Reverse Discrimination, the Future, and the Past', *Ethics* 90, pp. 81–87.
Shue, H.: 1980, *Basic Rights*, Princeton University Press, Princeton.
Simon, R. L.: 1979, 'Individual Rights and "Benign" Discrimination', *Ethics* 90, pp. 88–97.
Simpson, E.: 1982, 'The Priority of Needs Over Wants', *Social Theory and Practice* 8, pp. 95–112.
Singer, P.: 1972, 'Famine, Affluence, and Morality', *Philosophy and Public Affairs* 1, pp. 229–243.
Singer, P.: 1974, 'Sidgwick and Reflective Equilibrium', *Monist* 58, pp. 490–517.
Slote, M. A.: 1973, 'Desert, Consent, and Justice', *Philosophy and Public Affairs* 2, pp. 323–347.
Smart, A.: 1973, 'Mercy', in H. B. Acton (ed.), *The Philosophy of Punishment*, Macmillan, London, pp. 212–227.
Smart, J. J. C.: 1970, 'Free Will, Praise and Blame', in G. Dworkin (ed.), *Determinism, Free Will, and Moral Responsibility*, Prentice-Hall, Englewood Cliffs, pp. 196–213.
Smart, J. J. C.: 1978, 'Distributive Justice and Utilitarianism', in J. Arthur and W. H. Shaw (eds.), *Justice and Economic Distribution*, Prentice-Hall, Englewood Cliffs, pp. 103–115.
Smart, J. J. C.: 1981, 'Utilitarianism and Criminal Justice', *Bulletin of the Australian Society of Legal Philosophy*, Special Issue, pp. 1–20.
Smith, J. C.: 1976, *Legal Obligation*, Athlone Press, London.
Sowell, T.: 1980, ' "Weber" and "Bakke", and the Presuppositions of "Affirmative Action" ', *Wayne Law Review* 26, pp. 1309–1336.
Spiegelberg, H.: 1944, 'A Defense of Human Equality', *Philosophical Review* 53, pp. 101–124.
Sterba, J. P.: 1974, 'Justice as Desert', *Social Theory and Practice* 3, pp. 101–116.
Sterba, J. P.: 1980, *The Demands of Justice*, University of Notre Dame Press, Notre Dame.
Stone, J.: 1965, *Human Law and Human Justice*, Maitland, Sydney.

Stone, J.: 1966, *Social Dimensions of Law and Justice*, Maitland, Sydney.
Stone, J.: 1968, *Legal System and Lawyers' Reasoning*, Maitland, Sydney.
Stone, J.: 1969, 'Approaches to the Notion of International Justice', in R. Falk and C. E. Black (eds.), *The Future of the International Legal Order*, Vol. 1, Princeton University Press, Princeton, pp. 372–460.
Stone, J.: 1979, 'Justice not Equality', in E. Kamenka and A. Tay (eds.), *Justice*, Edward Arnold, London, pp. 97–115.
Swanton, C.: 'Is the Difference Principle a Principle of Justice?', *Mind* 90, pp. 415–421.
Taylor, P. W.: 1973, 'Reverse Discrimination and Compensatory Justice', *Analysis* 33, pp. 177–182.
Thalberg, I.: 1980, 'Themes in the Reverse-Discrimination Debate', *Ethics* 91, pp. 138–150.
Thomson, J. J.: 1977, 'Some Ruminations on Rights', *Arizona Law Review* 19, pp. 45–60.
Tinbergen, J.: 1975, *Income Differences*, North-Holland Publishing Co., Amsterdam.
Tumin, M. M.: 1953, 'Some Principles of Stratification: A Critical Analysis', *American Sociological Review* 18, pp. 387–394.
Tussman, J. and J. tenBroek: 1949, 'The Equal Protection of the Laws', *California Law Review* 37, pp. 341–381.
Unger, R. M.: 1975, *Knowledge and Politics*, Free Press, New York.
Van Dyke, V.: 1975, 'Justice as Fairness: For Groups?', *American Political Science Review* 69, pp. 607–614.
Vierdag, E. W.: 1971, 'Non-Discrimination and Justice', *Archiv für Rechts- und Sozialphilosophie* 57, pp. 187–202.
Von Hirsch, A.: 1976, *Doing Justice*, Hill and Wang, New York.
Waddams, S. M.: 1976, 'Unconscionability in Contracts', *Modern Law Review* 39, pp. 369–393.
Walker, N.: 1980, *Punishment, Danger and Stigma*, Basil Blackwell, Oxford.
Walster, E., G. W. Walster and E. Berscheid: 1978, *Equity: Theory and Research*, Allyn and Bacon, Boston.
Walzer, M.: 1981, 'Philosophy and Democracy', *Political Theory* 9, pp. 379–399.
Walzer, M.: 1983, *Spheres of Justice*, Basic Books, New York.
Ward, M. D.: 1978, *The Political Economy of Distribution*, Elsevier, New York.
Wasserstrom, R. A.: 1960, 'Strict Liability in the Criminal Law', *Stanford Law Review* 12, pp. 731–745.
Wasserstrom, R. A.: 1977, 'Racism, Sexism, and Preferential Treatment: An Approach to the Topics', *U.C.L.A. Law Review* 24, pp. 581–622.
Wasserstrom, R. A.: 1980, *Philosophy and Social Issues*, University of Notre Dame Press, Notre Dame.
Weale, A.: 1978, *Equality and Social Policy*, Routledge and Kegan Paul, London.
Weihofen, H.: 1960, 'Retribution Is Obsolete', in C. J. Friedrich (ed.), *Responsibility: Nomos III*, Liberal Arts Press, New York.
Wellman, C. P.: 1981, 'Taking Economic Rights Seriously', in *Filosofia del derecho y filosofia economica. Memoria del X Congresso Mundial ordinario de filosofia del derecho y filosofia social*, Vol. 1, Universidad Autonoma de Mexico, Mexico, pp. 73–85.

Wesolowski, W.: 1979, *Classes, Strata and Power*, Routledge and Kegan Paul, London.
Williams, B. A. O.: 1962, 'The Idea of Equality', in P. Laslett and W. G. Runciman (eds.), *Philosophy, Politics and Society*, Second Series, Basil Blackwell, Oxford, pp. 110–131.
Witten, S. M.: 1983, ' "Compensatory Discrimination" in India: Affirmative Action as a Means of Combatting Class Inequality', *Columbia Journal of International Law* **21**, pp. 353–388.
Wolff, R. P.: 1977, *Understanding Rawls*, Princeton University Press, Princeton.
Zaitchik, A.: 1977, 'On Deserving to Deserve', *Philosophy and Public Affairs* **6**, pp. 370–388.

INDEX

Abbott, Lord 287
Abilities. *See* Natural assets
Aborigines, Australian 185–187, 210
Abundance 282–283
Ackerman, Bruce A. 102–103, 105
Adams, Stuart 148
Affirmative action. *See* Preferential treatment
Ake, Christopher 108, 138, 292
Alves, Wayne M. 140
Amdur, Robert 301
Amnesty 247
Andenaes, Johannes 305
Aristotle 11, 12, 25–27, 33
Armstrong, K. G. 236
Assets, natural. *See* Natural assets
Austin, John 37–38

Backwardness, criteria of 211
Baier, Kurt 107, 235, 302
Bakke v. Regents of the University of California 191. *See also Regents of the University of California v. Bakke*
Balaji v. Mysore 211
Balance of benefits and burdens. *See* Equilibrium of benefits and burdens
Barnett, Randy 304
Barry, Brian 16, 267, 285, 302
Barry, Norman P. 288
Bay, Christian 166
Bayles, Michael D. 300, 301
Bean, Philip 303
Beauchamp, Tom L. 293
Bedau, Hugo Adam 302
Beitz, Charles R. 296
Belief in a just world 275
Bell, Derrick A. 194, 300
Benefits and burdens
 distribution of, as subject of justice 14, 19, 36, 113
 measures of 108, 278
 See also Equilibrium of benefits and burdens
Benn, Stanley I. 160, 233, 305
Benoit-Smullyan, Emile 295
Berlin, Isaiah 281, 305
Berscheid, Ellen 302
Bickel, Alexander 90
Black, Hugo L. 306
Blackmun, Harry A. 220, 300
Blackstone, William T. 301
Blame 133–134, 173, 301
Blasi, Vincent 299
Bloom, Allan 289
Blumberg, Abraham S. 305
Bobbitt, Philip 296
Bolling v. Sharpe 291
Brandt, Richard 289
Brecht, Arnold 57
Broek, Jacobus ten 291
Brown, Henry Phelps 295, 298
Brownlie, Ian 297
Buchanan, James M. 62–63
Burdeau, Georges 28

Cable, J. R. 295
Cahn, Edward N. 302
Calabresi, Guido 296
Califano v. Webster 299
Campbell, T. D. 297
Campbell Soup Co. v. Wentz 31
Capability tax 128–130
Carter v. Gallagher 300
Categories of indeterminate reference 43
Causation
 and desert 132–133
 distributive justice and 24–25
Character traits, responsibility for 122–123, 221–222

319

Charity 35, 125
Chichilnisky, Graciela 296
Child labour 82
Chipman, Lauchlan 271
Civil Law 32, 37, 258
Civil Rights Act 1964 (U.S.) 208
Classification
 criteria of, in law 80–94
 non-discriminatory 83–93
 purpose of 85, 87, 90–92
 racial. *See* Discrimination, racial
 and sex. *See* Women, discrimination against
 suspect 89–91
Clifford Davis Management Ltd. v. W.E.A. Records Ltd.
Code Civil (French) 32
Common Law 37, 43, 258
Commonwealth v. Daniels 291
Compensation
 costs of 214, 216
 and equilibrium of benefits and burdens 105–106, 114, 116, 130–131, 227
 role of, in reflective equilibrium 102–103
 for undeserved burdens 123, 126, 130, 275
 for unpleasant job 80, 101–103, 268
 See also Desert, compensation and; Needs, compensation and; Preferential treatment, compensatory justification of
Compensatory justice
 distribution of jobs and 153–156
 and equilibrium of benefits and burdens 102, 107, 144
 preferential treatment and 184, 186, 189
 status inconsistency and 148–150
Conrad, John P. 240
Consensus
 impossibility of moral 76, 277
 about principles of justice 64
 about scale of desert 139–140
 about scale of punishments 239
Constitution
 India 211

 United States 46, 89–90
Consumer Credit Act 1974 (U.K.) 286
Contract
 freedom to 28, 31
 law of 28–32
 unconscionable 28–32
Contracts Review Act 1980 (N.S.W.) 29
Cozens-Hardy, Lord 29
Craig v. Boren 291
Cramer v. Virginia Commonwealth University 291
Cranston, Maurice 297
Criminal trial 51–55
Cross, Rupert 53
Cruelty 12, 20–21
Cundy v. Le Cocq 303

Daniels, Norman 292, 295, 305, 306
D'Arcy, Eric 294
Definition 9–11, 41, 236
DeFunis v. Odegaard 213, 299
Democracy
 justice and 55–56
 moral judgments and 84, 192, 279
Denning, Lord 286, 304
Desert
 beneficial effects of action and 116, 137–138
 compensation and 144–146
 based on contribution 116, 134–138
 distribution of jobs and 153–155
 effort as basis of 116, 127, 134–135, 154, 156–157, 222–223, 275
 and equilibrium of benefits and burdens 106–107, 109, 130–131, 137, 154–155
 freedom and 157, 223
 fundamental and derivative notions of 224–225
 intention and 137–138
 measurement of 138–143
 moral worth and 222, 225
 natural abilities and 122–131, 223
 notion of 116–122, 144–145, 155, 224
 Rawls's theory of justice and 223–225

INDEX 321

role of, in theory of justice 156–157, 169, 223–225, 275
See also Entitlement(s); Free will; Merit; Needs
Determinism 131–134
Deterrence 242, 250–253, 255, 282
Difference Principle 13, 68, 109–112, 127–128, 222, 223–225
Differentiation, in legal rules 86, 88, 93–94, 209
See also Classification
Diplock, Lord 30
Discrimination
compensation for effects of 87, 89, 184, 204, 206, 212, 216–217
defined 187
against Japanese-Americans 272–275
positive 186, 187
by proxy 208–209
racial 87, 89–92, 185, 193, 207–210
reverse 187, 190, 205, 212, 217
(*See also* Preferential treatment)
statistical evidence of 202–203
See also Classification; Rectification, for past discrimination; Women, discrimination against
Distribution
maximization and 13, 267, 270–271
natural 23–24, 62–63, 124, 126
retribution and 14, 221–225
See also Benefits and burdens; Desert, distribution of jobs and; Redistribution
Distributive justice
allocative justice and 113
commutative justice and 25–36
entitlement theory of 120
liberty and 129–130, 266
market society and 22
measures of desert and 141–143
natural facts and 23–25
non-distributive justice compared with 14, 16
procedural justice and 112
See also Desert; Distribution; Justice; Social justice
Douglas, William O. 273

Doyle, James F. 304
Due process of law 51–52, 246, 288
Duncan, Myrl L. 300
Dupréel, Eugène 22, 286–287
Duress 35, 230
Duty to obey law 41
Dworkin, Ronald 9, 37, 45–48, 58, 87, 172, 190, 199, 246–247, 285, 288, 292, 301

Eckhoff, Thorstein 166, 295–296
Education
as investment 150–151
and self-realization 219
See also University admissions
Educational opportunity 85, 110, 185, 191, 201–202, 209–210
Edwards v. California 291
Efficiency
economic equality and 110
equality of opportunity and 199–201
justice and 111–112, 155, 225, 267
status inconsistency and 149
See also Utility
Effort
abilities and 122, 127–128, 141, 144–145, 156
contribution contrasted with, as bases of desert 134–138
and equilibrium of benefits and burdens 105–106, 144, 151
measurement of 141, 151, 278–279
See also Desert
Egalitarianism 110, 115, 190, 268
Ellinghaus, M. P. 286
Employment Appeal Tribunal (U.K.) 209
Endowments, natural. *See* Natural asserts
Entitlement(s)
desert contrasted with 118–121, 142, 145, 155, 156
legal justice and 42
power and 35
procedural justice and 50
over things 135–136, 171
See also Rules, valid, as grounds of entitlements
Epstein, Richard E. 287

Equal Employment Opportunities Act 1972 (U.S.) 94
Equal treatment 18–22, 48, 78–81, 95–96
Equality
 Aristotelian concept of justice and 25
 and equilibrium of benefits and burdens 114–115
 presumption in favour of 115
 social, and status inconsistency 149
 value of 13, 83, 190
Equality before the law 77–79 *passim*
Equality of opportunity
 compensation and 204
 concept of 198–202
 efficiency and 199–201
 genuine 204
 right to 171, 216
 See also Preferential treatment
Equilibrium (balance) of benefits and burdens, principle of, described 101–108
 Difference Principle compared with 108–115
 and hiring 155
 moral equilibrium compared with 107
 See also Compensation; Desert; Effort; Equality; Needs, basic; Punishment
Equity 28–29, 43, 106, 186
Equivalence 25–27, 102, 105
Ericsson, Lars O. 292
Evidence, in criminal trial, inadmissible 52–54
Ewing, A. C. 303, 305
Exchange
 distribution and 26–28, 32, 266
 equivalent 25–27
 unfair 11–32
 See also Contract, unconscionable
Exclusion
 differentiation and 93–97
 equality of opportunity and 200, 202
Ezorsky, Gertrude 300

Falk, Richard 297
Feinberg, Joel 14–21 *passim*, 101–103, 117, 120, 158, 248, 287, 295, 296, 298, 304–305

Figlio, R. M. 303
Finnis, John 38, 302
Fishkin, James S. 281, 296
Fiszman, Joseph R. 298
Fitzgerald, Ross 296
Flatham, Richard E. 79, 290–291
Fletcher, George P. 302
Flew, Antony 235, 303
Francis, J. G. 297
Francis, L. P. 297
Frankel, Charles 161–162
Frankfurter, Felix 30, 43–44, 287, 304
Fraud 28–30
Free will
 contract and 31
 desert and 131–134
 responsibility and 245
Freedom. *See* Liberty
Fried, Charles 128–130, 297
Friedman, Milton 121–122, 127, 293
Friedrich, Carl J. 55
Frontiero v. Richardson 291
Frostifresh Corp. v. Reynoso 31
Fry v. Lane 286
Fuller, Lon L. 38–42
Fullinwinder, Robert K. 301

Galligan, D. J. 305
Galston, William A. 296, 307
Galtung, Johan 295
Gardiner, Gerald 303
Gardner, Martin R. 304
Gendin, Sidney 303
Generosity 34–35, 141, 213
Gewirth, Alan 302
Ginsburg, Ruth Bader 291
Glazer, Nathan 299
Goffman, Erving 193
Goldman, Alan H. 125, 135–136, 191, 197, 204–205, 207, 229, 231, 271, 299, 300–302, 304
Goldring, John 286
Good, theory of the 113, 278–280
Good Samaritanism 24–25
Gordley, James 286
Gordon, Scott 296, 306
Graglia, Lino A. 300
Grannis v. Ordean 304

Greenawalt, R. Kent 195, 299
Griffin, Larry J. 295
Griggs v. Duke Power Co. 301
Gross, Hyman 304
Gunther, Gerald 291
Gupta, S. 295

Hajnicz, Wanda 301
Hall, Jerome 303
Hamilton, V. Lee 303
Hard cases 45–48
Hare, R. M. 74
Harkins, M. J. 290
Harlan, John H. 291
Harm, mutual abstention from 104–106
Harrison, Jonathan 289
Hart, H. L. A. 41, 297, 303–305
Hart, H. M. Jr. 303–305
Hawkins v. United States 288
Hayek, Friedrich A. 1, 22–24, 83–85, 111, 126, 138–139, 167–168, 289, 295
Hirabayashi v. United States 272–273
Hobbes, Thomas 32, 37, 60–61, 272
Hochschild, Jennifer L. 306
Höivik, Tord 300
Holborow, Les 297
Holmes, O. W. 287
Homans, George Caspar 153
Honoré, A. M. 287
Hook, Sidney 302
Horwood v. Millar's Timber and Trading Co. Ltd. 286
Hospers John 117, 289, 295
Hughes, Graham 299
Humanitarianism 53–55
Hume, David 307

Ideal theory, distinguished from nonideal 184
Incentives, inequalities and 110, 112, 115
Income
 distribution 140, 149, 154–155
 job satisfaction and 152
 right to 120, 126, 137
 See also Wage(s)
Incrimination 53

India, preferential programs in 186, 211–212
Indian Reorganization Act 1934 (U.S.) 94
Inequality
 of bargaining power 28, 31
 economic 109–111
 functions of, distinguished from grounds of 112
 See also Incentives
Injustice
 comparative and non-comparative 18–21
 distributive 25, 35
 judgmental 21
 sense of 84–85
Inner morality of law 38–42 *passim*
Insanity 230, 245, 254
Interests
 justice and 113–114
 moral judgments and 63, 75
 needs and 165–167
 rights based on 172, 176
Intuition
 moral reasoning and 64, 67, 69–76
 principle of equilibrium and 103–104, 108, 275
Intuitionism 72–76

Jackson, Robert H. 79, 96, 274–275, 291
Jasso, Guillermina 294
Jenkins, Iredell 13
Johnston, John D., Jr. 291
Johnston v. Hodges 291
Jones, Hardy 194, 210, 299
Judge-made law 36–37, 45–49, 258
Judicial error 234
Justice
 absolute/comparative, distinction 16
 allocative/distributive, distinction 113–114
 circumstances of 282–283
 comparative/non-comparative, distinction 14–22, 36, 42
 concept of 9, 12–14
 conception of, distinguished from concept of 9–10

conservative 42
criminal 225, 227, 231–232, 243
First Principle of, in Rawls 67, 261–263, 266
formal 22, 36, 39, 54
global/particular, distinction 11–15 *passim*
legal/social, distinction 34–49 *passim*, 261
natural 51–52, 242, 246
political 56
prosthetic 42
reformative 42
retributive, compared with distributive 14, 108, 221–225
Second Principle of, in Rawls 13, 67, 262
(*See also* Difference Principle)
subject of 13–14, 22–24
theory of, and law 48–49, 76, 277
See also Compensatory justice; Desert; Distributive justice; Entitlement(s); Interests, justice and; Liberty, justice and; Needs; Procedural justice; Punishment; Social justice
Justice constituency 16, 178–181

Kallenberg, Anne L. 295
Kant, Immanuel 247
Karniol, Rachel 285
Katzner, Louis 298, 301
Kaufmann, Walter 141–143, 238, 302
Kelsen, Hans 38, 44, 79, 287
Kerala v. Thomas 300
Kleinig, John 286, 293, 303, 306
Kluegel, James R. 299
Korematsu v. United States 272–274
Krishna Iyer, V. R. 205
Kronman, Anthony T. 128, 286

Laesio enormis 32
Laird v. Dobell 303
Lasswell, Harold 179, 297
Leff, Arthur Allen 287
Legislative purpose 81, 85, 91–92
Leiser, Burton M. 301
Leontief, Wassily 298

Lerner, Melvin J. 276
Lerner, S. W. 295
Lesnoff, Michael 305
Lex talionis 26, 237
Lexicographical order 280–281
Liability,
 moral 24
 strict criminal 241–242
Liberty (freedom)
 as benefit 226–230
 capability tax and 128–130
 desert and 157
 extensiveness and equality of 262–266
 justice and 13, 22, 261–267, 281
 positive/negative, distinction 263–264
 priority of, in Rawls 67–68, 262
 worth of, and existence of 264–265
Lichtman, Richard 300
Lloyds Bank Ltd. v. Bundy 286
Locke, John 60–61, 135
Love 125
Loving v. Virginia 291
Lubomirska, Krystyna 301
Lucas, J. R. 303
Luck 23, 116, 275, 290

MacCallum, Gerald C., Jr. 264
McCloskey, H. J. 251–252, 289, 295
MacCormick, Neil 249, 288, 297, 304, 305
McDonald v. Board of Election Commissioners 291
McDougal, Myres S. 179, 297
McLaughlin v. Florida 291
Majority rule 55–56, 84, 139
Market
 distribution 22, 139–140
 economy 225
 society 22–24, 139–140
Marshall, Geoffrey 82
Marshall, Thurgood 81, 203, 207
Maslow, Abraham 168–169
Mathew, K. K. 300
Matrix of variables 281
Medical protection 111, 162–163, 167–168, 173
Mercy 240, 247, 251

Merit 25–26, 33, 107, 140, 205–206
  distinguished from desert 145
  grading 15, 17–18, 21
  university admissions and 83, 194–196
Michelman, Frank I. 161
Military service 81, 88, 91
Mill, John Stuart 12, 25, 78–79, 147, 268–269
Miller, Dale T. 285
Miller, David 117, 144–145, 293
Moberly, Walter 304
Modelski, George 298
Moneylenders Act 1900 (U.K.) 29
Montague, Phillip 285
Moral judgments,
  in reflective equilibrium 69–71, 76, 103–104
  truth and 72–75
  See also Democracy, moral judgments and
Moral principles
  judicial decision and 45, 48
  justification of 65
  plurality of 74, 281
  in reflective equilibrium 69–71, 103–104
Morris, Clarence 55
Morris, Herbert 244–245, 247, 302, 305
Morton v. Mancari 292, 299
Moynihan, Daniel P. 301
Murphy, Jeffrie P. 302
Murray, John E. 286

Nagel, Thomas 301
Natural assets (abilities, endowments)
  arbitrariness of distribution of 124–127
  common pool of 127–128, 224
  nullification of effects of 126–127, 131, 223–224
  as undeserved 117, 122–123, 130–131, 145, 150, 224
Needs
  basic
    concept of 159–162
    desert and 162–164, 169–170
  equilibrium of benefits and burdens and 106–107, 158, 169, 275
  hierarchy of 168–169
  principles of justice and 158–159, 162–167
  relativity of 159–162, 181–182
  rights to satisfaction of 170–185 *passim*
  compensation and 131, 158–159
  desert and, compared 117, 130–131, 156, 158–159, 165–166
  true and false 165–167
  wants and 164–167
Negligence 242–243, 247
Nelson, William 288
Newman, Graeme 303
Nicholson, Peter P. 287
Nickel, James W. 208, 291
Nielsen, Kai 165–166, 306
Northington, Lord 30
Nowak, Stefan 294
Nozick, Robert 120–122, 124, 127–128, 135–137, 162–163, 171, 173, 285, 293, 297

Oppenheim, Felix E. 204
Original position, in Rawls 58–72

Packer, Herbert L. 305
Pareto's principle 112
Parham v. Southwestern Bell Tel. Co. 300
Parole 247
Partlett, David 298, 301
Pashukanis, Evgenii 255, 305
Passmore, J. A. 119, 215, 301
Paternalism 50, 166
Paton, George Whitecross 304
Peffer, Rodney 159
Pen, Jan 140, 152, 295
Penalty-fixing 26, 237, 250, 253
Perelman, Chaim 287, 290
Perkins, Lisa H. 302
Person, as an end 177
Peters, R. S. 160, 233, 305
Pincoffs, Edmund L. 294
Pitney, M. 291

Plessy v. Ferguson 291
Poland
  preferential programs in 185, 211, 219
  principles of community life in 44
Political obligation 59–61
Political philosophy
  aim of 276–277
  external approach to 276
  internal approach to 276–278
Posner, Richard A. 110, 191, 202, 300–301
Poverty
  and discrimination 201–202, 208
  as involuntary feature 87
  liberty and 266
Powell, Lewis, F. 188, 291, 299, 300
Powers, Kathryn, L. 290
Praise, moral 97, 134, 138, 156, 280
Pratt, Joan L. 286
Preferential treatment
  affirmative action and 187–188
  compensatory justification of 184, 189, 204–205, 212
  distributive and collective approaches to 206–208
  diversity of student body as aim of 197–198
  divisiveness of 191–192
  equality before the law and 81, 86, 89–94
  and equality of opportunity 198–204
  and equilibrium of benefits and burdens 184, 189
  examples of 185–186
  groups or individuals as beneficiaries of 204–213
  justifying and administrative bases of 208
  as lesser evil 215–216
  over- and under-inclusiveness of 205, 210–212
  principle of 186
  qualifications and 194–196, 218–219
  as removal of unfair advantage 217
  and rights of non-preferred persons 214–216
  stigmatizing effect of 192–194
  utilitarian arguments for 189–198
  victims of 213–218
Prevention of crime 250–252, 254–255, 257–258, 282
Price v. Civil Service Commission 301
Primorac, Igor 305
Privileged communications 53
Procedural justice
  compared with substantive 13, 23, 49–56
  imperfect 51, 56
  perfect 51
  pure 49–51, 68, 113
Protection
  from criminals 251, 256–258
  right to 174–176, 182
Prudence 67
Punishment
  aims of 227, 250–255
  annulment theory of 243–244
  bad character and 221–222
  capital 46–47, 255
  concept of 234–237
  criminal's suffering and 230–231
  equilibrium of benefits and burdens and 106–108, 225–232, 243, 244, 249–250
  expressive theory of 243, 248–250
  free will and 133–134, 245
  guilt and 51–52, 233–238, 241, 251–258 *passim*
  of the innocent 18–20, 234–237, 252–253
  of insane persons 230, 245, 254
  justice and utility of 250–251, 255–256
  natural 231
  proportionality and 20, 26–27, 51, 237–238, 255
  retributive theory of 233–250 *passim*, 251, 255–258
  right to 244–247
  secret 248
  self-imposed 247–248
  severity of, and gravity of crime 229, 238–239, 253

system of, distinguished from acts of 235, 256–258
utilitarian theory of 241, 250–258
See also Responsibility; Restitution

Quigg, Benjamin 304
Quinton, Anthony M. 234, 304

Race Relations Act 1976 (U.K.) 301
Rae, Rouglas W. 297
Railway Express Agency v. New York 290, 292
Raphael, D. D. 287, 299
Ratio legis 47
Rawls, John 2, 4, 12–13, 39–40, 49–51, 56–74, 101, 108–115, 126–128, 184, 204, 222–225, 256–266, 276–277, 282, 285, 292–293, 306–307
Rectification
of effects of natural inequalities 127
of injustice 144, 184, 210, 215–216
of past discrimination 198, 215
Redish, Martin H. 299
Redistribution
and entitlements over things 135–137
international, of resources 180
of rewards, not of abilities 124–127
and sacrifice 177–178
and utility/justice trade-off 271
Redress, principle of 109, 204, 223
Reflective equilibrium 57, 69–71, 76, 101, 103–104, 223
Reform of the criminal 250–251, 253
Regents of the University of California v. Bakke 89, 188, 203, 213, 217–218, 220, 291, 298–301
See also Bakke v. Regents of the University of California
Rehnquist, William H. 81
Reisman, W. Michael 179, 297
Reparation 173, 206
Resnick, David 288
Responsibility
as burden 138, 146, 151
for character traits 122–123
and free will 131–134

for inaction 24–25
and punishment 230, 241, 245
Restitution
commutative justice and 27
punishment and 227–229, 237, 243–244
Restraint of trade 29–30
Retribution. *See* Distribution, retribution and; Justice, retributive, compared with distributive; Punishment, retributive theory of
Rights(s)
capacity to use 182, 226, 266
conflict of 171–173
to fair trial 174–175, 245–247
to free speech 171
to fruits of one's labour 135–136
infringement of, distinguished from violation of 172–174
to non-interference 174
over own body 135
to physical security 174–176
positive/negative distinction 173–178
and practicability of implementation 178–182
property 63, 171, 177
as protected interests 172, 176
of recipience 170–182 *passim*
to satisfaction of basic needs 170–182 *passim*
as side constraints 176–177
as trumps 172, 247
violation of, distinguished from failure to protect 175–176
to vote 174–175
waiver of 246
See also Entitlement(s); Equality of opportunity, right to; Preferential treatment, and rights of non-preferred persons; Punishment, right to
Rightness, theory of 280
Robinson, Richard 285
Ross, Alf 57
Ross, W. D. 280, 306
Rossi, Peter H. 140, 294
Rostker v. Goldberg 290
Rothchild, Donald 298

Rousseau, Jean-Jacques 60–61, 79–80
F. S. Royster Guano Co. v. Virginia 291
Rule(s)
  application of, distinguished from applicability of 94–95
  general, contrasted with *ad hoc* decisions 22, 78, 212
  justice of, distinguished from proper application of 18–20, 28, 36, 42
  social, and legitimate expectations 224
  valid, as grounds of entitlements 119, 155
Runciman, W. G. 292
Ryan, D. E. J. 286
Rytina, Steve 303

Sadurski, Wojciech 286, 296
Salaries. *See* Wage(s)
Sampson, Edward E. 295
Sandalow, Terrance 300
Sandel, Michael J. 293
Scarcity 282–283
Schaefer, D. L. 289
Schlesinger v. Ballard 88
A. Schroeder Music Publishing Co. Ltd. v. Macaulay 286
Scott v. United States 286
Scott, Joseph E. 303
Self-realization 158, 164, 219
Self-restraint 104, 226–229, 232, 239, 255, 278
Sex Discrimination Act 1975 (South Australia) 301
Sher, George 205–206, 299
Shevlin-Carpenter Co. v. Minn 304
Shue, Henry 176, 297
Sidgwick, Henry 14, 287
Simon, Robert L. 301
Slavery 78, 232
Smart, Alwynne 303
Smart, J. J. C. 269–271, 294, 305
Smith, Adam 128, 148, 294
Smith, Eliot R. 299
Smith, J. C. 86
Social contract, 57–72 *passim*
Social justice
  entitlements and 28, 34, 119

equality before the law and 77
and equilibrium of benefits and burdens 101, 103, 108, 221
importance of 12, 261, 282–283
and legal justice 34–49, 261
political justice and 56
procedural justice and 55
See also Distributive justice; Justice
Social psychology 21, 148, 231, 275–276
Sowell, Thomas 203, 299
Sprigge, T. L. 305
Standards of care 242–243
Starvation 16, 25, 161–162, 169–170
State of Alabama v. United States 300
Status inconsistency 148–153, 275
Sterba, James P. 296
Stevens, John Paul 271
Stewart, Potter 290
Stigma 192–194
Stone, Julius 287, 290, 297
Strict liability 241–243
Strict scrutiny test 89–90
Supererogatory actions 35, 125
Swanton, Christine 292
Sweatt v. Painter 300

Tasman Dry Cleaners (Balmain) Pty. Ltd. v. Diamond 286
Taxation 136–137, 268–269
  See also Capability tax
Taylor, Paul W. 291–300
Thakeb, Fahad Al- 303
Thalberg, Irving 299
Thomson, Judith Jarvis 172–173
Tinbergen, Jan 128, 152
Tumin, Melvin 149–151
Tussman, Joseph 291

Unconscionability 28–32
Undue influence 28–29
Unfair Contract Terms Act 1977 (U.K.) 29
Uniform Commercial Code (U.S.) 31
United States v. Balint 303
United States v. Bethlehem Steel Corp. 30, 35

United States v. Dotterweich 304
United Steelworkers v. Weber 299
University admissions 46, 81, 83, 85, 87, 92–93, 185–220 *passim*
Utility
 as an aim of law 272–275
 and causation 133
 compensatory justice and, in hiring 118, 154–155
 distributive justice and 267–272
 Mill's principle of 147, 268–269
 rights and 172, 177, 246–247
 See also Efficiency; Preferential treatment, utilitarian arguments for; Punishment, utilitarian theory of

Victim
 condemnation of 276
 restitution for 227, 229, 243
Vinson, Fred M. 197
Vivian, Frederic 294
Volenti non fit injuria 50
von Hirsch, Andrew 302, 305

Waddams, S. M. 286
Wage(s) (Salaries)
 education and 150–151, 185
 as incentives 151
 job satisfaction and 148, 152
 just 26, 33–35, 112, 267–268
 market forces and 140, 225
 as part of global rewards 148
 and product of work 136
 and scarcity rents 117
 status and 152–153
 See also Income
Wagner, W. J. 287
Walker, Nigel 302, 304
Walster, Elaine 292, 302
Walster, G. William 292, 302
Walzer, Michael 276, 295–296
Ward, Michael Don 292
Wasserstrom, Richard A. 301–302, 304
Wawrzyniak, Jan 85
Weale, Albert 293
Weeramantry, C. G. 307
Weihofen, Henry 237, 239, 303, 305
Wellman, Carl P. 298
Wesolowski, Wlodzimierz 149, 298
White, Byron R. 188
Williams, Bernard A. O. 200–201, 208–209
Williams, Glanville 303
Witten, Samuel M. 298, 301
Wood v. Abrey 286
Women
 discrimination against 85, 88, 90, 91, 209
 military service and 81, 88
 occupational limitation laws and 88
 preferential programs for 186
World community 179–181
Wright, Quincy 297

Zaitchik, Alan 293